Published by

F6, Sector A2, Trans Delhi Signature City,
Ghaziabad- 201102, U.P.

Reprint 2026, 2025, 2011

Published by Atlantic Publishers and Distributors (P) Ltd.

Printed & bound in India

PREFACE

This 'Comprehensive History of Political Thought' provides a detailed study of various thinkers during different periods. The study of their life and thought will prove most useful to the students of today. The students of today are the statesmen and administrators of tomorrow. Therefore, it is imperative for them to be thoroughly conversant with political thought.

I have written this book primarily to meet the requirements of the students preparing for B.A., (Hons), M.A. and competitive examinations. Almost all important points have been discussed. The style is lucid and simple and would easily fall within the grasp of even moderate students. I hope that the book will prove to be more useful to the students than any other book on the subject available in the market.

I wish to pay my sincere thanks to my Publishers — M/S Primemax Books, New Delhi — for their whole-hearted co-operation in the publication of this book.

Suggestions, if any, for the improvement of the book in the next edition will be highly appreciated.

N. Jayapalan

Contents

1

Plato (427 B.C.-347 B.C.)

Introduction

Plato, the "father to the idealists, romanticists, revolutionists and utopians of political philosophy" (C.C. Maxey) was born in 427 B.C. to Ariston in Athens. He was christened as Aristocles; but later because of the breadth of his shoulders and the expanse of his brows he was nicknamed as Plato. He began his career as a soldier. However, his "subtle soul had found a new joy in the 'Dialectic' game of Socrates." (Will Durant — The Story of Philosophy, p. 12). So since he was aware of the Pelapponesian wars together with the rule of the Four Hundred, and their disastrous effect on his nation at the hands of Sparta a state wedded to discipline, he expressed his avowed dislike to democracy and marked "inclination towards sterner discipline of a state like Sparta" in all his works like the Statesman and the Republic.

Plato's ***Republic.*** There is a list of 36 dialogues of Plato. Of these, The Republic is the most important. It is the longest of his works and is certainly the greatest of them. The more you read of it, the more you are struck by the astonishing genius of Plato, his great speculative powers, his wit and the universality of his interests. According to Bhandari, "It is the parent of idealism in philosophy, in politics and in education." The Republic is a 'dramatized philosophy of human life.' "The whole Republic is really an attempt to interpret human nature psychologically, the postulate upon which its method rests is that all the institutions of society, class, organisation, law, religion, art and so on, are ultimately products of the human soul, an inner principle of life which works itself out in these outward shapes." In The

Republic, Plato draws a picture of what the social organisations and institutions must be if an individual is to realise fully his highest capacities. It is the foundation study of the moral and civil life of man. The Republic no doubt, projects an ideal society and is a utopia but it also embodies a bold criticism of actual conditions of society in the days of Plato. For this bold criticism, The Republic has been called an indictment of Greek civilization. It is definitely written with full consciousness of the failure of Athens and of the deterioration of the Greek city-state which was happening in Plato's time. The book is indeed a treatise on social and political reform. It is also the representation of the noblest and the best in life. According to Crossman, "It contains Plato's plan for the building of a perfect state in which every citizen is really happy." According to Sabine, "Few books that claim to be treatises on politics are so clearly reasoned or so well-coordinated as The Republic. None, perhaps, contains a line of thought so bold, so original, or so provocative. It is this quality which has made it a book for all time, from which later ages have drawn the most varied inspiration." The Republic aimed at the representation of human life in a state perfected by justice and governed according to the idea of good. But the idea of good and justice cannot be inculcated unless there is also a sound system of education. This was suggested by Plato in his Republic, Rousseau rightly calls The Republic "the finest treatise on education that ever was written." Plato gave much importance to education because the fundamental political idea in The Republic is the doctrine that the governing authority must be associated with the broadest knowledge and culture. The Republic is Plato's masterpiece the crowning achievement of his art and philosophy. Though the Republic conceived by Plato was a utopia, the fact remains that it contains a philosophy of life the ideals of which still stand as a challenge to human nature and which will continue to guide and inspire as long as man exists. The entire philosophy of The Republic can be summarised in answering two questions: What is a good man? and how is a good man made? To Plato it was clear that a good man must be a member of a state, and can be made good only through membership of a state. From this, the question arises: what is the good state, and how is the good state made? Here moral philosophy moves into political science. Thus, The Republic is a treatise on morality and a treatise on political philosophy.

Plato's Theory of Ideas. Before examining the portrayal of the Ideal State as given in the The Republic, it is desirable to know something about Plato's Doctrine of Ideas — the keystone of his political thought. The entire Greek political thought is nothing but a search for the ultimate reality. If to Thales water was the ultimate reality, it was the Infinite or Boundless for Anaximender, and for Anaximenas air was the ultimate reality of the whole universe. To Pythagoras the abstract principle — the number, was the ultimate reality. To Heraclitus it was change. Still, to some others it was permanence or stability that was the real nature of all things. In the language of Paranindes 'being alone remains unmoved, which is the name for all.' There was the absolute world of the one, unchanging, unified and eternal on one hand and on the other the shifting world of appearance, ceaselessly changing, eternally unreal, the real of non-being. Against this background of speculation Plato developed his Theory of Ideas.

The permanent character of a thing is what Plato calls the "Idea". This Idea of a thing is eternal and final, having an independent and absolute reality. Thus, there are two worlds, the world of Being and the world of Becoming. The first is a world of perfection and the second is dynamic and imperfect. The world of Being is the ideal world and such is the real world. It is a world of universal concepts which are true for all times and places. They are unchangeable, imperishable and eternal. The world of Becoming is always in a state of flux, unreal and imperfect. The World of Being is realised through Reason and that of Becoming through sense perceptions. The Actual is not real as it is always in a constant state of flux undergoing changes social, economic and political. It is only an Ideal State based on universal and eternal principles which can be real. It is in The Republic that Plato portrays the picture of an Ideal State. The object of his Ideal State is the Good life and in his effort to portray the Good, Plato pursues his thought to its utmost limits. Plato tries to achieve his Idea of the Good by the establishment of a state which is free from the evils of all other states because it does not degenerate, or because it does not change. The state which is free from the evil of change and corruption is the best; it is the perfect state. It is the state of the Golden Age. His belief in perfect and unchanging things is usually called his theory or doctrine of forms or Ideas. It constitutes the central doctrine of his philosophy. It is on this theory of the Idea, that the rest of the theories of the Ideal state are based. An Idea in Plato's sense is not part of the world of time and space. It is eternal, final and independent reality. The Idea, of course, cannot exist independent from the object of change, even then it is eternal. The Idea is, therefore, the name of the quality in all things which is the essence of a thing. These Ideas revolve around and are determined by the Idea of the Good. These Ideas are eternal, absolute and a divine order of reality transcendent to human knowledge or earthly existence. These Ideas can be known through the dialectical operations of mine and purified of sensuous experience. They are the forms through which the supreme Idea of the Good manifests itself. They constitute the beauty of any beautiful object. According to Edman, "The Platonic Idea is the original and the origin of the thing, the reason of its existence — the stable, sustaining principle in virtue of which it exists. It is the virtue of the thing, its ideal its perfection."

Thus, Plato's discovery of Idea as the ultimate reality has led to the development of the concept of two worlds — the world of objects and the world of Ideas. The first world is unreal and the world of Ideas is the real world. The first world is only the world of shadow. Of the Ideas, Plato calls the Idea of Good as the final and independent reality existing 'itself by itself'. It is the source of all goodness. It is by virtue of participation in it that men are good. It is only in following after good that man will find respite from their many afflictions.

Plato's Ideal State. Plato's Ideal State was an imagination of the man's best and noblest self and represented the frame within which an individual found his best self. He builds up his Ideal state in true successive stages or waves. In the first he shows that men and women have the same education and should participate in the same public functions. In the second he advocates the abolition of the family on the basis of communism of wives and property among the two upper classes. The third wave is concerned with the idea that the good of society depended on government by philosopher kings. His Ideal state is hierarchical in its composition and functioning.

At the head of his Ideal State is a philosopher ruler who is above passion or prejudice and who represents virtue in action. He is unrestrained by law. But Plato was wise enough not to leave the good of a whole community on the chance existence of a philosopher ruler. There must be a regular supply of philosopher guardians. For this purpose Plato provides a well-regulated system of education under state control. Under this scheme, it would be possible to train and educate guardians of the state and also to shift the capable from the incapable. Plato divides the guardian class into two categories, the perfect-guardians and the auxiliaries or administrators. Plato divides the entire community into three classes. The lowest is the producing class consisting of artisans, farmers, etc. To this class, Plato assigns no higher status. The members of this class are producers of consumable goods only. The members of this class have no leisure and so are unfit for the contemplation of the good. Above the producing class are the two higher classes of guardians or rulers. From the class of ordinary guardians or auxiliaries are to be selected the perfect guardians who represent the highest class. This is to be done through his system of education. For the guardian class, Plato proposed the system of communism of family and property in order to enable them to give their best to the state. He also demanded emancipation and equal education and opportunities for public service to women. The Ideal State of Plato is absolute and totalitarian. There is hardly any sphere of life which it cannot touch and regulate. There is no freedom of thought and association. But this state is Ideal and is ruled by supreme wisdom.

The Ideal state of Plato as depicted in The Republic is open to many objections. In his organistic conception and construction of the state, Plato finds too much analogy between the individual and the state. His classification of human nature into three elements, viz., Reason, Spirit and Appetite, and his subsequent division of society into three classes; guardians, auxiliaries and the producing class, is rather illogical and false. Plato fails to distinguish Ethics from Politics. He tries to build a city in which the city and the citizen become one. In his state, which is collectivist, there is very little scope for full freedom and all-round development of the various faculties of man. His stress on functional specialisation and his idea of justice are likely to dwarf the personality of an individual. It condemns an individual to a single function in life. There is need for development of man as a whole and not as a part. In his Ideal state, the majority of the people who constitute the producing class are reduced to the position of serfs, and they are ignored altogether as if they are soulless. He neither advocates nor makes any provision for their emancipation. In the guise of discovering justice he assigns the possession of knowledge to the privileged a few only. He equates, the state with the ruling class. His men of brass and iron are doomed to remain brass and iron because his educational scheme is meant only for the guardian class. In his Ideal state, we find nowhere any condemnation of the situation of slavery which was so rampant in his days. The scheme of communism of wives and property is most intolerable. It violates even human nature. His system of temporary marriages is most unworkable. The rule of philosophy and of philosopher kings is unrealisable. To make the philosopher king above law is to make him most absolute and authoritarian. It is nothing but espousing the cause of the worst type of dictatorship. In his portrait of the Ideal state, Plato has ignored the most important needs of the community, such as rules and regulations for the appointment of officials, rules regarding instituting of courts, etc. Plato's principle that the state is everything and that it can and should control absolutely the entire lives of citizens is assured. The fact is Plato's polity is 'intolerant, absolute and impracticable.' Aristotle was most critical of Plato's Ideal state.

Plato's Conception of Justice. The primary issue of The Republic is the discovery of the nature and habit of justice. The Republic, therefore, is called a treatise on justice. Dr. Barker has rightly said: "Justice is the hinge of his thought, and the text of his discourse." Incompetence and factionalism, unrighteousness and injustice and ignorance reigned supreme in his days. So, Plato was keen to find out a solution to all these evils and in justice he found the remedy for curing these evils. Before reaching his conclusions and giving his own view of justice, Plato reviews various traditional theories of justice and rejects one by one. The traditional theory of justice was propounded by Cephalus and Plemarchus. According to this theory justice meant being true in word and action and paying one's debts to gods and men. Thus, justice meant giving due, that is to say, doing good to friends and harm to enemies. This theory is rejected by Plato on the ground that there may be many cases in which to adhere to the letter of this formula may involve the violation of the spirit of right, and this formula does not admit of being taken as a sound universal principle of life. The conventional theory of justice regulates relations between individuals on individualistic principles and ignores society altogether. Who is in reality a friend or an enemy, is very difficult to find out. Appearances may be deceptive. Then the Radical Theory of justice as propounded by Thrasymachas defines justice as the interest of the stronger. It is identical with the supreme authority in the state. In other words it means that might is right. Plato rejects this theory also. According to him, governing is an art. All art is for the sake of perfection of the material it handles and not for the sake of the artist. The rulers practice the art of government, and should rule not in their own interest but to bring about the improvement of the government in the interest of the governed. True justice is not the interest of the stronger. The rules are for protection of the ruled and exist for the good of the governed. This view gives rise to a very important principle of modern politics i.e., 'Power is a trust'. Then there was the pragmatic theory of Glaucon. This theory regards justice as 'the interest of the weaker'. It is a child of fear. "It is a mean or compromise among the best of all, which is to do injustice and not be punished, and the worst of all, which is to suffer justice without the power of retaliation." The weaker, fearing more injustice than they can inflict, instituted law and government through a sort of social contract. It is through this artificial rule of justice and law that the natural selfishness of man is chained — a dictate of the weaker many, for the interest of the weaker many, as against the natural and superior power of the stronger few. This theory is also rejected by Plato.

According to Plato, justice is not conventional or external. It is the right condition of the human soul and is something internal. It is found both in the state and the individual. It is natural and not artificial. It is not born of fear of the weak of the longing of the human soul to do a duty according to its nature. Thus, Plato after rejecting all previous theories of justice, gives his own.

Having rejected the various theories of justifice Plato propounds his own theory which he regards as true and final. To comprehend Plato's conception of justice it is essential to bear in mind that Plato strikes an analogy between the human organism on the one hand, and social organism on the other. Plato saw in justice the only remedy against the political and social ills of the city-state. Justice, according to Plato, resides in the ideally constituted community and is identifiable with complete virtue which consists of four virtues, i.e., wisdom (philosophers), courage (which includes strength of will), obedience and discipline (soldiers), temperance or self-control, and justice. To Plato "Justice is the virtue which remains in the state when the other virtues of temperance and courage and wisdom are abstracted; and is the ultimate cause and condition of the existence of all of them." The Platonic conception of justice is inseparable from that of the Ideal state. The two blend in one. Justice is the order, that is, the true condition of the state and the ideal state is the visible embodiment of justice. One is the soul and the other is the body. A good and just life is one lived in society and justice demands an organic unity in the state arising out of a harmonious balancing of functions, of the three classes of society; the appetitive, the spirited and the rational. And justice is Plato's language means the will to concentrate on one's own sphere of duty and not to meddle with the sphere of others; and its habitation, therefore, is the heart of every citizen who does his duty in his appointed place. Thus, justice depends and grows with the specialisation of functions. The justice of the state is the citizen's sense of duty. To Plato, justice is an indispensable quality of moral life in the community. It is the ethical code by which Plato's polity lives. Justice of the individual means that each of the three elements — appetite, spirit and reason — keep within their proper limits. Justice of the individual is both a public and a private virtue because it maintains the highest good of both the society and the individual. To Plato, justice for the individual is identifiable with virtue or excellence. It generates the spirit of self-restraint and self-regulation in man and makes him a useful member of the community. Thus, justice is no purely a personal virtue. It is a bond of societies and states. It keeps men together in healthy social relationship by making them good and social. Plato also makes a distinction between legal or particular, and perfect or universal justice. The perfect justice can only be in the ideal state which is based on right education, principle of communism, functional specialisation and perfect wisdom of a philosopher king. In a state which is not idea and which is based on law, there obtains legal or particular justice. Plato's idea of distributive justice is that men should get offices according to their ability and according to their devotion to the state.

Plato's theory of justice is of immense value. It is a kind of thesis against individualism. The conception postulates a view of the individual as not an isolated self, but part of an order, intended not to pursue the pleasure of isolated self, but to fill an appointed place in that order. Plato's justice is universal in character, and is another name for the whole duty of man. According to Dunning, the Platonic conception of justice "on the political side proper brings out in highest relief, first the necessity of an organic unity in social life; second, the importance of systematic education, as contrasted with the haphazard legislation in regulating the commit interest; and third, the optional basis of aristocracy in government". Plato's theory bestows upon the state a personality and independent existence of its own. There is no doubt that the theory is a revolt against political selfishness and ignorance. Justice in Plato is a part of human virtue and also a bond of state at the same time. It is that bond which joins men together in society. It makes man both good and social. "This identification is the first and the fundamental principle of Plato's political philosophy." This conception also gave birth to the organic theory at the state. In a way it also resolves the problem of individual liberty and the Leviathan state. It brings the final identification between the individual and the society to which he is born. The conception is of importance also due to the fact that it brings into prominence two important principles of division of labour and specialization of function for efficiency and harmony in the state. The significance of Plato's theory lies in the fact that it is the forerunner of the psychological explanation of the state. States do not come out of a rock, they grow from the characters of men.

Criticism. In spite of the great value of theory of justice, there has been a lot of criticism of it. It is, in no sense, a justice definition of justice. Self-control and devotional self-abnegation in the interest of society, which lie at the base of Plato's justice, are moral principles having no sanctions behind them. There is no provision for clash of individual wills and interests. It visualises only a dull uniformity and harmony of social life. The theory is based on the conception of functional specialisation, but it ignores its evils. To condemn a man to one special function is to assume that he is all appetite or all reason, whereas an average man has all the three elements in him. The ideal of 'one man one work' militates against the full development of human personality and deprives the community of a full and rich variety of life. Platonic justice is too subjective hence it is no justice at all. It does not issue forth in a concrete judicial organization. Though his theory of justice the reconciliation Plato attempts to effect between self-interest and public duty is not very satisfactory. It is a system of duties only. Rights are ignored altogether. Platonic justice fails to promote the happiness of all. According to Aristotle, "Plato in the Republic deprives the guardians of happiness, and says that the legislator ought to make the whole state happy. But the whole cannot be happy unless most, or all, or some of its parts enjoy happiness". Plato's justice assigns ruling power in the hands of one class, however well-trained morally and spiritually, is bound to demoralize that class and corrupt the state. The Platonic justice with communism of wives and property ignores the essentials of human psychology and denies satisfaction to the fundamental cravings of the human soul. The whole concept is impracticable and unrealizable. As a matter of fact Plato's philosophy of justice "is the most savage and the most profound attack upon liberal ideas which history can show. It denies every axiom of progressive thought and challenges all its fondest ideals. Equality, freedom, self-government, all the condemned as illusions which can be held by idealists whose sympathies are stronger than their sense", writes Crossman.

Plato on the Rule of Philosophy. "Until philosophers are kings and princes of the world have the spirit and powers of philosophy, cities will never have rest from their evils" (The Republic). In these words Plato sums up his views regarding the government of the Ideal state which must rest with philosophers. Plato was thoroughly disgusted with the evils of Athenian democracy and he found salvation only in the rule of the philosopher-kings. According to him, only by the rule of the philosopher-kings can the state have a government in which the rulers rule in wisdom and in unselfishness for their eyes have seen the truth and they think of their exalted offices not as opportunities for self-aggrandizement but as a sacred burden to be borne for the good of the ruled. According to Crossman, "Plato remained an aristocrat, convinced that the peasant, the craftsman, and the shopkeeper were incapable of political responsibility. Government was the perquisite of the gentry, who did not need to work for a living and could, therefore, devote their lives to the responsibilities of war and politics." There must be a ruling aristocracy and a subject class. Plato conceives of a philosopher as 'the spectator of all time and all existence'. He is a lover of truth and has always a passion for reality. He hates falsehood and possesses self-control. He is free from all sorts of meanness or spitefulness or little-mindedness. He is just and gentle and shows due proportion in all things. He does not fear death. He has a vision of the unity of knowledge. The Platonic philosopher must know the Idea or essence of justice; and of beauty and temperance in order that he may fashion into their likeness the characters of those whom he rules. He must know the purpose of all-being and all-doing and the end of all human existence and human action. The Platonic philosopher, however, is not the devoted seeker for wisdom but its proud possessor; he is a learned man and a sage, by the rule of philosophy. Plato means the rule of learnedness or the rule of the intellect. It is in this rule of intellect that the Socratic doctrine of 'knowledge is virtue' is fully realized in its institutional form. According to Popper, "Plato gives the term philosopher a new meaning of a lover and a seer of the divine world of forms or Ideals." It is this philosopher who becomes the virtuous founder of a virtuous city. By creating the philosopher king-Plato made an attempt to create a friend, a philosopher and a guide at the same time who could, by leading a life of ascetic simplicity and virtue, inspire confidence among his subjects. Plato's philosopher-king is similar to the ancient Indian Rajarishi who is the embodiment of all knowledge, all virtue, all beauty and all divinity.

Plato was convinced that the philosopher rulers, after a thorough education and undergoing vigorous discipline, would become infallible and that the power in their hands would not corrupt. He was all out for their absolute and unlimited government. The philosopher ruler was to be free from the shackles of written laws. His philosopher-ruler is the embodiment of reason, and law is the product of convention and human experiences. Thus it follows that the supremacy of the law before the supremacy of the philosopher-king is meaningless. But Plato was aware of the fact that he was enunciating a very dangerous conception. So, in Laws, he replaced the personal rule of an individual by the personal rule of an institution. The philosophic power which is sovereign and supreme in the state is in fact that trained and scientific intelligence which Plato thinks is the only remedy for the ills of the state. It is only through the rule of knowledge that the real progress of society can be achieved. This fact led Prof. Sabine, to remark, "The true romance of the **Republic** is the romance of free intelligence, unbounded by customs, untramelled by human stupidity and self-will, able to direct the forces even of custom and stupidity themselves along the road to a rational life. The **Republic** is externally the voice of the scholar, the profession of faith of the intellectual, who sees in knowledge and enlightment the forces upon which social progress rely."

Plato's philosopher-king was no doubt above law, all powerful, and an embodiment of complete knowledge but it was not Plato's intention to support an unqualified absolutism. The ruler was not to be free from all restraints. According to him the philosopher-ruler must respect the fundamental articles of the constitution. He must not alter the basic principles on which the state is constituted. The rulers will have to watch against the entry either of poverty or of wealth into the state. They will have to limit the state to the size consistent with unity, neither too large nor too small. They must maintain the rule of justice and ensure that every citizen is occupied in the discharging of his specific function. Lastly, they must ensure that no charge shall ever be made in the system of education. Thus, in this way, Plato aimed to make his philosopher-kings the servants of a fundamental and unchanging social order.

Criticism. In his insistence on the rule of philosophy, Plato seemed to ignore many things and for that reason his doctrine of the rule of philosophy has been subject to severe criticism. By propounding this theory, Plato ignored altogether the Greek conception of the state as being an association of equals, having only the sovereignty of law. His new monarchy was likely to degenerate into an enlightened and beneficial tyranny. The moral value of freedom and civic virtues of self-government are altogether ignored by Plato. Plato's theory ruled out direct as well as representative democracy. What is required in a ruler is not so much knowledge of good as his knowledge of what is good for different individuals, different conditions of society, and different states. It is difficult to make out how Plato's philosophers are to be fitted for their work of government by the study of mathematics and dialectics. We do not come across such philosopher-rulers in history. Then, a philosopher-ruler, is likely to be given too much to contemplation as to find time for quick decision-making which is urgently required under certain circumstances. Excessive philosophic contemplation makes a man concentric and an eccentric man is always misunderstood. So, the rule of an eccentric man will be unpopular, unjust and unbalanced. Plato, on the whole, remains an utopian and his attempt at the creation of philosopher-rulers remains a very difficult task to be achieved. We do not find anywhere in the **Republic** general principles of government. According to Jowett, "The philosopher-ruler is apt to be looking into the distant future or back into the remote past and unable to see action and events of the present."

Plato's Theory of Communism. In his attempt to build an Ideal state in which justice should reign Plato propounds a theory of a new social order, under which the governing class surrenders, in the interests of the state, both family life and private property and lives under a system of communism. Communism was meant to destroy the false conception of self as an isolated unit and replace it by a conception of a self as a useful and integral part of a social whole. It was to serve as a means for achieving spiritual reformation of the ideal community which Plato wanted to bring about. The idea was not a new one. But Plato used it as a means towards spiritual end. Plato believed that "conditions were most favourable for the life of the spirit under a system of communism". But Plato's communism is meant for the guardian class only. It is for the rulers, and soldiers only. The purpose is simply political. The aim is to secure the unity of the state. Property and family stand in the way. Therefore, they must go. To Plato the community as a whole was everything and the individual apart from the community, nothing. A citizen confined to his allotted task must merge himself in the state and render specialized service to the state. In the Ideal state consisting of three classes, the upper two classes, guardians and auxiliaries (including soldiers) must live under a regime of communism if they are to perform their duties well and unselfishly. These two classes represent Reason and Spirit. They must restrict themselves to these elements and must renounce the element of Appetite. They must abnegate the economic side of life which is purely appetitive. Unless the appetite side is absolutely renounced, it may get the better of reason and may lead to personal ambition, selfish acquisition, neglect of duty, etc. Reason without communism, may remain dormant, or inactive or may be impaired by appetite. The two upper classes must be made free from the worries and shares of economic and domestic life. Plato holds "Both the community of property and the community of families, as I am saying, tend to make them more truly guardians: they will not tear the city in pieces by differing about 'mine' and 'not mine'. The guardians are not to be allowed to have their own houses or families lest their minds should get diverted to the preservation and extension of such property."

In the entire theory of communism of both property and wives, the basic assumption is that much can be done to abolish spiritual evils by the removal of material events and temptation. Unity of state demands a state regulated system of education and communism of wives and property for the ruling classes. Plato believed that the highest life for the individual would be as a member of the state family and not of a private family. Plato thought that his communism would not kill individuality; rather, it would raise individuality to the highest spiritual level. Of course, there is slight difference between communism of wives and communism of property. In the case of property, there is common renunciation of property rather than common ownership by the guardians. In the case of wives and children, there is common ownership and not renunciation. Plato wanted communism of property as union of political and economic power in the same hands is proved by universal experience to be fatal to political efficiency. He, therefore, gave monopoly of political power to the guardians and monopoly of economic power to the commercial class. Plato had firm faith that man, entrusted with the exceptional function of ruling, must be exceptionally equipped and must submit to exceptional regulations. The combination of two powers makes one avaricious, greedy and neglectful of his duties. "Plato's communism has a touch of asceticism and medieval monasticism about it. It is aristocratic in conception and demands abnegation from only the best in the community. It is for, and not by, the whole community. It is political and not economic conception."

Plato's scheme of communism embraces both the property and the family. It contemplates the community of wives. He regards family affection, directed towards particular persons, as another obstacle to state unity and state loyalty. So Plato wished the rulers of his state neither to be troubled by distraction from their work, nor by temptations towards self-interest. His aim was to kill the idea of 'mine' or 'yours' in his rulers. Plato wanted the wives of guardians to be common to all of them: the children too were to be considered as common to all of them: To Plato the house was a stumbling block in the way of state unity. So it had to go. According to Barker, "In a word, Plato sees in the family on the one hand a root of selfishness, which may grow into family feuds and civic sedition, and on the other hand a drag on development, which prevents men and women from being what they might be and discharging the function which they might discharge, and therefore, prevents them from being just themselves or making just the state in which they live. The day of its abolition will be the day of the inauguration of unity for the state, of liberty for the individual and of justice for both." However, Plato does not deny the ruling class a normal sexual life and the production of children. Mating will be allowed to produce the best among the best fitted. It was to be managed on festivals. The children born out of this union were to the common property of the state. The state would see to their upbringing provide equals advantage for all and make arrangements for their education by the most skilled and experienced nurses and the most competent teachers. Plato makes the state the family and the family the state. Both are fused together.

Plato's communism of wives serves many purposes. It frees the rulers from the narrowness and worries of family life. It emancipates the best among women and makes them useful for the service of the state. It brings perfect unity among the guardians which is so essential for the unity of the state. It paves the way for a better and healthier stock of children. It brings about the social equality of men and women. Communism of property makes the rulers free from unnecessary distractions and selfishness. For development of reason, private property must be abolished. Then political and economic powers are not to be concentrated in the same hands. It will bring mutual dependence between the ruler and the ruled. The rulers will depend upon the subjects for their necessities and the subjects will depend upon the rulers for their protection and good government.

Plato's communism and modern communism have many similarities and dissimilarities. Plato's communism did not aim at the removal of property as an institution, whereas modern communism aims at the removal of private property as an institution. Plato's communism is rather half-communism. It is not an institution of social whole. It affects only the two upper classes, whereas modern communism affects the whole society and is applicable to all. Plato's communism is not based on the principle of equality, whereas modern communism is based on the principle of equality. Then, Plato's communism means communism of wives also, whereas modern communism does not touch the family. It stands for abolition of property only. Plato's communism is to be attained through the agency of the state, whereas modern communism regards the state as an institution of exploitation in the hands of the capitalisms. It is to be abolished root and branch. For Plato the state is all partnership in science, art, virtue and in all perfection, whereas modern communism is to be attained through the establishment of a classless society. Plato's communism establishes dictatorship of a philosopher-ruler, whereas modern communism advocates the dictatorship of the proletariat. Plato's communism is national in character and is achieved through an appeal to the altruism of the governing classes, whereas modern communism international in character and is achieved through an appeal to the fidelity of the workers. Platonic communism is achieved through education and peaceful means, whereas modern communism believes in revolution and violent means for bringing the communist society into existence. Lastly, Plato's communism is spiritualist whereas modern communism is all materialist. Of course, both are similar in some respects. Both ignore the individuality of the citizen. Both are based on the ignorance of the essentials of human nature and human instincts. Both are impracticable if applied on a very vast scale. Both aim to dominate unregulated economic competition. Both aim to promote political unity and social harmony and to develop a sense of social service among the individuals. Both visualize a social whole in which an individual secures his own interests best by securing the general interest.

Criticism. Plato's system of communism was so much illogical and impracticable that even his most faithful disciple Aristotle could not prevent himself from criticizing this scheme. His grounds for disagreement with the concept of communism if wives were:

(i) that the community of wives would create confusion and disharmony in the social order. In an attempt to attain unity we would be arranging the very destruction of it;

(ii) that children common to all, were bound to be neglected. A thing which belongs to everybody, in fact, belongs to none. Everybody thinks chiefly of his own, hardly at all of the common interest. Everyone's son is nobody's son;

(iii) that extreme unification is not good. It is self-sufficiency which is most desirable;

(iv) that it is absurd to use the analogy of animals in support of the community of wives. Human beings are not animals. Unlike the animals, they have consciousness of self;

(v) that state-controlled mating would be unworkable and would not bring the best males and females together;

(vi) that it would make the guardian class most unhappy.

Aristotle further points out that one female cannot be the wife of all guardians. If so, it will create disharmony, instead of unity, which is the aim of Plato. The family is a natural school of moral conduct and is a preparation for the state. Under Plato's communism unholy acts may be done against near relatives because the relationship is unknown. The private family is a natural institution as also a sound one. It must not be sacrificed for attaining a false notion of unity. Aristotle is also critical of the communism of property. Under this system those who work hard and get little will have a grievance against those who work little and get more. Common ownership is a great source of dispute. Men are more efficient when set to work at that which is their own. Love of self is a feeling implanted by nature. The experience of life is against communism. Property represents and natural and normal instrument and extension of personality, a source of pleasure and an opportunity of good and moral activity. To communism property is to try to get rid of human selfishness by ineffective social legislation. The best cure for selfishness is education and not communism.

In conclusion, we can say that Plato's communism was a heroic remedy for unsurmountable ills pervading the Greek society of those days. Aristotle's criticism is partly valid and partly invalid. Plato was not wholly unjustified. His approach was not totally idealistic. It was logical, practical and even pragmatic.

Plato on Education. No scheme of human life was so important to Plato as education. The Platonic conception of justice depended for its realization on two institutions; a system of common education by the state, and a social order of communism. Common education by the state was meant to give that training for excellence in a special work and that instinct for keeping unselfishly to the performance of which justice demanded. According to Barker, with Plato education is a means of social righteousness and realization of truth and not of social success. As regards the object of education, Plato writes, "The object of education is to turn the eye which the soul already possesses to the light. The whole function of education is not to put knowledge into the soul, but to bring out the best things that are latent in the soul, and to do so by directing it to the right objects. The problem of education, then, is to give it the right surrounding." In his scheme of education, Plato was greatly influenced by the Spartan system of education. The great purpose of education in Sparta was to develop courage through test and trials. But, unlike Sparta, the Platonic system of education aimed at the development of the whole man. It aimed at the all-round development of human personality. Plato borrowed from the Spartan system only the social aspect of education — that it must be controlled by the state with a view to preparing citizens to find their place in society. Plato sees in education the only true way to the permanent stability of the state. It is true to say that the modern idea of education is a never-ending process, embracing adults as well as the young was propounded first by Plato. In Plato's system of education the main objective is simply to bring the soul into a particular surrounding, so nothing is said of direct teaching. The true business of the teacher is to bring out what is best in his pupil. As regards the instruments of education, he found literature the main instrument of education. To it may be added elementary knowledge of some art and the rudiments of the sciences of number and figures. The second instrument was gymnastics which was in common practice. Plato was convinced that the right system should be based on the right understanding of the nature of the soul. The soul is reached at different stages of its growth by different agencies and through different media. In early life, imagination, fancy and feeling play a predominant part. In the second stage, reason beings to develop, while in the third stage is formed love of the beautiful; and in the last stage, comes love of truth. The object of training in the sciences is to make the soul love truth. The function of education is to set the environment in which the active and the 'reminiscent' mind looks on things beautiful and good. The true function of education is to make a man and a woman useful and fit socially, economically, intellectually and politically. His education is meant for both the sexes.

Plato's plan of education represents a state controlled system of compulsory education for both sexes. It is divisible into two parts; elementary education and higher education. In childhood, up to the age of six, the aim is not truth as a matter of principle. The child is to be taught first simple religious truths and then simple moral truth and to learn the lessons of good manners and good taste. A child must learn to properly hate and love things. In early boyhood, till the age of eighteen, education is to be both physical and intellectual. Here is provided music for the soul and gymnastics for the body. Gymnastics includes all that is related to the care of the body. At the stage, Plato recommended music as it was through music, he held, that the soul learnt harmony and rhythm, and a disposition of justice. Music also moulds character and brings refinement of feeling. It preserves and restores, health. It lends grace and health to the soul and body. At this stage there must be a study of the elements of the sciences. The real value of the study of sciences is two-fold. They teach one to think; and in studying the sciences, the mind comes gradually to understand certain principles or forms of being which lead to the understanding of the good. Mathematics trains a mind to think clearly and precisely. Thus, up to eighteen there is to be general education in music, gymnastics and elementary sciences. From eighteen to twenty, there is to be exclusive training in gymnastics, including military exercises, with the aim to develop courage and self-control, character and discipline. At the age of twenty men without good intellectual capacity will be shunted off as a result of a public test. Higher education extends from the age of twenty to thirty-five. It is further divided into two parts — from twenty to thirty and from thirty to thirty-five. In the first part men and women are to be given systematic scientific education. At this stage education is both intellectual and physical. Natural and mathematical sciences are to be taught. Stress is laid on mathematics, including arithmetic, plane and solid geometry, astronomy, logic and the development of dialectic power. There would also be training in public service, particularly military service. At 30, there shall be a second selective test. The less gifted are weeded out as auxiliaries or subordinate officers of the state. The more gifted are given further training in the science of dialectics. They are given positions of authority in the state. This lasts for 15 years. At 50, the selected few approved would study the good itself. They are to govern and organize the state. They will be the supreme council in the state, dividing their time between theoretical study of the good, the practical government. In this system of education of Plato, there is no place for vocational and technical education. The system was essentially one for leadership. Leaders must have knowledge, experience, character, courage, self-control. They must have intelligence knowledge and insight. The Platonic system had a psychological basis and was progressive in character. It meets the demands of the soul. It was an education for all-round development.

Criticism. Plato ignores education for the artisans. The vocational and technical part are altogether absent from the scheme. Sabine writes, "It is extraordinary that Plato never discusses the training of the artisans and does not even make clear how, if at all, they are to be included in the plan of elementary education. This fact illustrates the surprising looseness and generality of his conclusions." The system is unjust arbitrary to the producing class. Plato's education is simply meant for the rules and administrators. It gives too much importance to mathematics and too little to literature. The system will produce an ideal philosopher but not an ideal man of action. The scheme is meant for a very small group. The system condemns the guardians to the life of military monasticism. The scheme is likely to kill initiative in man as it goes on up to 35. Plato fails to realize that education should be relative to the character of the individual. In his theory of education, there is a certain wavering between the ideal of action and that of contemplation. Sometimes the goal is the Idea of the Good, sometimes social service, sometimes perfect self-development, and sometimes social adaptation. His system equates the guardians with the state. The scheme is expensive and impracticable.

Plato on Functional Specialization. The Ideal State of Plato is built on his conception of functional specialization. The idea was taken by Plato from the Socratic view that expert knowledge was necessary for the conduct of public affairs. The Spartans deliberately breed for military efficiency. Plato admired efficiency but he wanted to eliminate the danger of Spartan dullness and uniformity by insisting on functional specialization based on different kinds and degrees of nature, aptitude and intelligence. The theory was based on his conception of the reciprocal needs of human beings and the necessity of division of labour. The wants of individuals are multifarious and everybody by himself, cannot meet all his wants for lack of time and capacity. According to Plato, "all things are produced more plentifully and easily and of a better quality when one man does one thing which is natural to him and does it at the right time and leaves other things." This principle of one man one work according to nature, leads to division of labour, satisfaction of mutual needs and exchange of services. This theory of Plato flowed directly from his conception of justice, according to which an individual performed efficiently that task for the society for which no was best fitted. Society is a system of services in which every member both gives and receives. Taking his stand on the necessity and usefulness of specialization Plato divides his ideal polity into three classes. The guardians, the auxiliaries (administrators and fighters) and artisans and farmers. Each of these classes has its own function in the state and each must perform its function only. Plato believed that functional specialization led to the unification of the state. If each class of professionals kept within its own sphere, there would be no inter-class conflicts, no social and political disorder in the state. Selfishness world disappear and unity pervade the state. It would bring peace, efficiency and unity as there would be no competition. Plato's division of society into three classes was not on economic basis but on that of different types of service rendered.

Then Plato's class-state, with its three classes of rulers, soldiers and producers, is based on the two principles of division of functions and capacity for virtue. Plato's state is a class-state because he identifies authority with virtue. Plato thought that it was to the advantage of the producing class man to summit to the guidance and control of guardians who represented virtue and wisdom. But it was not a caste state as alleged by some. A caste man is born into it and cannot go out of it. In Plato's system a person could be promoted from one class to another on the basis of tests. Career was left open to ability and character. Plato's highest class is philosophers, not priests. The lowest class is not a servile class as in India. Property is confined to the lowest class.

Criticism. It is wrong to presume that specialization promotes unity and efficiency in state. While expounding this theory, Plato did not realize the wholeness of the human being. The personality of man is not capable of rigid divisions into watertight compartments. Most men are endowed with all the three faculties of appetite, courage and reason. If one is confined to one function, one's personality cannot be fully developed. The all-round view of the amateur is sacrificed for the specialized knowledge of the professional. It promotes sectionalism which is dangerous for the unity of the state.

Elements of Individualism in Plato. Though Plato is said to be the first communist and the first totalitarian, there are still some traces of individualism in his theory of the state. Of course, his collectivism was a reaction to the rapid individualism which destroyed the harmony of civic life in Athens. Sophism believed in atomic and extreme type of individualism. Plato believed in social individuality. In his Republic, Plato emphasized the excellence of the individual; yet, the individual per se is not out of his mind. A man must discover the type of work for which nature has endowed him best from the moral, intellectual and physical points of view and must concentrate on it. It would not mean destruction of the individual personality, rather, it would mean enrichment of it. An individual would be master of one trade, and also of himself. Plato's statement that "in a proper state the individual will himself expand, and he will secure the common interest along with his own" shows clearly that Plato was not adverse to individualism. It is only a very small minority of the people whom he makes to merge themselves in the state. It is for the good of the vast majority that Plato makes his guardians to make sacrifices. He demands sacrifice from the ruler and not from the ruled. Plato leaves untouched the individualistic system of production. He is against atomic individualism and not against the individual who is a part and parcel of the whole. One's personality expends only when on functions as a part in a social whole. Though Plato was sure of inequality, he conceded equal opportunities for all as a principle. This is evident in his system of education. The later works of Plato are more individualistic than his Republic. In Laws he gave recognition to the personality of the individual more than what the communism of the Republic allowed. He allows the holding of property to the guardians. After Plato, Greek political theory definitely became more individualistic than before.

Plato on Democracy. Plato came of a family which was highly critical of democracy. He refers to democracy in his Republic as "a charming form of government, full of variety and disorder." Again, he writes that "the laws of democracy remain a dead letter; its freedom is anarchy; its equality the equality of unequals." Democracy is for Plato a state of civic dissolution in which everyone follows his own inclination and pursuit. It is lawless and disorderly. According to Plato, in democracy even horses and asses claim all the rights and dignities of free citizens. Plato's hatred of democracy is due to the fact that he associates political power with trained intellect. Plato forgot one thing, that the rule of the philosopher king or of the aristocracy of the intellect could not last long. He failed to appreciate the many virtues of democracy. He ignored the importance of civic education which could come through active participation of all in governmental authority.

The Hellenic and Universal in Plato. Plato's philosophy was not only for his times, it is of universal validity. "There was much in Plato of the ephemeral and the provincial," writes Maxey, "but the mid rib of his political philosophy was timeless and universal." He is for all times. In fact, Plato, like Shakespeare, is not for an age but for all times. Plato did not develop his philosophy in isolation. There was close relationship between his doctrines and the currents of practical Greek Politics. The influence of Sparta in the Republic is very obvious. It is crystal clear that most of the thoughts of Plato in the Republic are influenced by the political and social ideas of the Spartan people. As in Sparta, so in the Republic, the ruling class was completely preoccupied with political affairs, living a life of austerity, and partook and supervised a strict discipline in order to maintain complete uniformity among its citizens. Like Sparta, Plato also sacrificed the interest of the individual and the family for the cause of the state. Plato's scheme of education, the idea of the improvement of the race, the system of common tables, community of property and wives, participation of women in the political and military life of the community, hatred for the poets and administrative organization are the direct result of Spartan influence. Plato thought and wrote in term of the city-state of ancient Hellas. Plato's state is equipped for war more than for peace and this was in conformity with Hellenic conditions and traditions. His condemnation of trade disallowance of the enslavement of Greeks and absence of denunciation of slavery show Hellenic influence in his ideas. "In general," wrote Dunning, "the political philosophy of Plato involves an interpretation of Greek history and a judgment upon Greek institution. His perception of the principles that underlie these institutions is in many cases keen and sure, but his attempt to suggest practical improvement that shall more faithfully express the principles never take him beyond the bounds of Hellenic experience."

There is a lot of universalism in Plato. He is the originator of much that is best in the institutions of modern civilisation. He was a source of much inspiration in modern political thought, on the rule of intellect, on functional specialization, on the emancipation of women, on their equality with men and his principles of eugenics are features of permanent and universal interest in his political philosophy. Many of the conceptions of the middle ages — the Renaissance, Reformation and the Humanist movements owe much to him, and show the universality of his philosophy. The Nocturnal Council of the Laws points to the modern inquisition, and modern censorship. Modern communism may be different from his but the aims are the same — unity, the solidarity of the state. His enunciation of the principles of constitutional or divided sovereignty and of natural theology are very useful to us who claim to be modern. His grasp of the fundamentals of life and his political radicalism make Plato a helpful guide for all times and places. The 20th century doctrine of fascism borrowed freely from Plato's ideology. For this reason Plato is sometimes called a philosopher of Fascism because of his strong denunciation of democracy and liberalism. Milton, Locke, Rousseau, Goethe and many others owe much to him for their ideas.

2
Aristotle (384 B.C.-322 B.C.)

Introduction

Born in 384 B.C. in the place called Thrace, Aristotle was fortunate enough to be a disciple of Plato in Athens. His attainment of political maturity in the practical side of politics was an attraction to him and as such he was requested to be the tutor of Prince Alexander whose victorious march up to India earned for him a place of honour among the world conquerors as he was, although late, guided by the principle of universal brotherhood which was indoctrinated in him by Aristotle. He died in 322 B.C. His political theories are enshrined in his "Ethics" and "Politics." These are the two complementary works on social philosophy. The part played by him for the development of politics is unique. Earlier than him it is science which embodied poetry, mythology, religion, ethics, philosophy, and politics. It was Aristotle who broke up science into particular sciences to distinguish ethics, philosophy and politics. So says Dunning that Aristotle "gave the politics the character of independence science." It is true that politics is not a unified and finished work; yet it is clear from it that politics meant for explaining the ideal state but also for helping the actual states. Let us study first his concept of the ideal state and then his analysis and remedy of the actual state.

Ideal State

Aristotle, rejecting the ideal state envisaged by Plato in the 'Republic', constructed one on the basis of the one found in his (Plato's) "Laws." So "his absolutely ideal state is only Plato's relatively ideal or second best state but with some modifications." "In framing an ideal state" says Aristotle, "We may assume what we wish but we should avoid impossibilities." This is the crux and cause of his dissent from Platonic idealism. Plato, while constructing his ideal state, looked upon human nature as infinitely plastic and infinitely perfectable while Aristotle regarded it as only plastic and perfectable as far as its limited potentialities would permit. So says Murray that "Plato is as man in an aeroplane, who flies over a new land catching through the clouds its cantours; Aristotle is the engineer who goes there and makes new roads."

Origin of the State

While trying to analyse the origin of the state, Aristotle attempts at tracing it from two angles — historical and psychological.

1. Historical

He first talks of family. To him family is an association of husband, wife, children and slaves which is claimed to have been "established by nature for the supply of men's every day wants." Of course, man and woman are complementary help contributory necessity to each other. They have no doubt a natural desire to continue their race by leaving "behind them on image of themselves" (Children). The man is intended by nature to rule. If he lacks the power of foresight necessary to place himself as a ruler, he is meant to work with his body and so a slave. He of course, needs other's help for self-preservation. This is the position and composition of a family.

The union of several families with the purpose of aiming at something more than the supply of daily needs makes a village. Similarly when several villages come together to the extent of making self-sufficient and continuing its existence for the sake of good life, the state is born.

2. Psychological

Man is a political animal by nature. He has an end to achieve good life — physically, mentally and morally — since he is distinct from other beings by virtue of his rational nature. The natural instinct in man, since he is a rational being, has driven him to live in a society. The family in which men live and the village which has the collection of families are incapable of supplying the material need. So men are compelled by nature to form a state which alone has the power and position to the supply adequately of material needs, together with providing them with facilities for the mental and moral development. It is, thus, that man could develop himself only in the state. Here it is said that he who is incapable of associating with others and is not a member of the state is "either a god or a beast". So it is obvious that the state is natural and essential to well as men like water to fish. The state, therefore, "stands as the highest of all communities and embraces them all."

End of the State

Ordinary life is different from good life. The state exists only to promote a good life. If life alone is the object of the state, brutes and slaves could form a state; but they cannot because they are denied a share in happiness or in a life of free choice. Besides, the state is not intended for preventing mutual crime and exchanging goods alone. The state on the other hand, in addition to what is stated, is intended for the promotion of a perfect and self-sufficing life by which we mean a happy and honourable life. So the end of the state is the good life of its citizens.

What is the good life of the State?

To answer the question Aristotle takes out a synonyms — good life, best life, perfect and self-sufficing life and happy honourable life. The good life of the state according to Aristotle, not the Platonic Justice of the Republic or Self-control of the "Laws" but it is only "the life of virtue led by all its members having at the same time a mean account of eternal goods for the performance of good actions."

A life of virtue is not passive but active only. It accommodates those noble activities which we have got to perform for the sake of the noble activities because of two reasons. They are: (i) man realizes and exercises his human virtues in those activities, and (ii) man is destined for such activities alone. The noble activities include political life demanding practical wisdom such as the performance of all the functions of the government — legislative administration and Judicial decisions and those activities promoting the welfare of the state. Besides, there are activities of public contests in dramatic performances, in religious service and in the services of the conduct of social relations with fellow citizens which call forth the virtues of temperance, generosity, magnanimity and good fellowship in addition to the pursuit of science and philosophy. So the "good life" of the state according to Aristotle consists of or is born of the activities mentioned above in general and the political activity in particular.

The state becomes meaningless and mockery if the individuals are not in existence there. The state should strive for its best life. The best life of the state is the best life of all its members. "The best life is one in which every member can act best and live happily. The best life both for individuals and the state is the life of virtue, having external goods enough for the performance of good actions. The reason is that man by nature is a political animal and cannot perfect himself except as a member of the state." Aristotle, here, as a renowned materialist denounces or unwilling to take cognizance of even God to perfect man as done by the religious propagators, announces the significance of the state which is capable of providing man with "a guide of life, a source of virtuous action and so of happiness." Again "the state exists to make men good husbands, fathers, heads of households, good soldiers, rulers, and subjects and good men of science and philosophers."

The end of the state as envisaged by Aristotle in his 'Ideal State' places him in contrast with the one pronounced by his master, Plato. Ethics to Plato is the fundamental science and politics a branch of it, whereas Aristotle gives the highest place to politics and the inferior position to Ethics. Platonic state is primarily ethical and secondarily political while Aristotle's is primarily political and secondarily ethical.

Ways for the Realization of the End

Aristotle's method is teleological. He, after understanding the end of the state, goes to suggest the ways and means of construction and organizing 'the state' to realize the end.

(a) Constitution of the State

Before commencing to suggest the ways and means to achieve the end, Aristotle wants us to "presuppose many purely imaginary conditions but nothing impossible." Aristotle envisages three classes of people in his state. They are citizens, middle class (resident aliens) and slaves. The citizens own land, enjoy political rights. They are warriors while young, rulers while old and priests after retirement from the political life. The middle class practices industry and commerce and enjoys civil rights. The slaves have neither civil nor political rights; but they cultivate the land of the citizens and the state. The citizens alone are the members of the state while the middle class and slaves are not but only instruments. "A State"? therefore, "is the body of citizens sufficing for the purpose of life. It is not merely a community of living beings but the community of equals aiming at the best life."

(b) Optimum Members of Citizens in the State

Aristotle feels that realization of the best life of the citizens or the state is possible if there is a limit to their number. He emphasizes the point from different angles. "Law is order and good law is good order; but a very great multitude cannot be orderly; only God can introduce order among them." Comparing the ideal state to a ship it is said that "the state like a ship must be of the right size." So if a state is composed of too few it is not self-sufficing at all and if it is too many, though self-sufficing in all mere necessaries it becomes almost incapable of a constitutional government.

He suggests the sort of duties which the citizens are required to perform in relation to election to offices, decisions of law suits etc., should be taken into account to determine the exact limit of the number of citizens which the state should possess. The best and optimum population of the state is, that "number which suffices for the purpose of life." He speaks of the number of citizen in his 'Ethics' as between 10,000 and of 1,00,000. However, in his 'politics' he says that Plato's 5,040 man citizens in the latter's ideal state "require a territory as large as Babylon to support them."

(c) Extent of the Territory

The thus conceived state should have the extent of territory, says Aristotle, sufficient enough "to supply the citizens with the enough of material goods as that they may live temporally and liberally." In other words, the territory should have the enough of landed property to supply the people needed for their quiet life internally and to ward off invasions externally.

(d) Site of the State

The state envisaged should be situated on ideal place in relation to both land and sea. It should well be located near the sea convenient for the protection of the whole country and receiving the products of the soil. Besides, the state should have connection with the sea to enable the citizens to attack or defend or both themselves by land and sea in the event of a war and in times of peace to import from foreign states what they do not produce and export what they produce in excess. In addition, he recommends navy to patrol the coastal regions to avoid and exterminate the entry of foreign national into the state fortification of it by walls.

Organization of the State

The organization of a state is possible when there is order. "Law is order," says Aristotle "and good law is good order." Laws cease to be so when they miss the end of the state viz. realization of the best life of it. So laws are necessary.

Now the question arises whether it is good to have the best laws to rule or the best man capable of ruling not by laws but by his own as Plato expressed in his "Statesman." Aristotle applies the teleological method here also. "Those men whose virtue is so prominent as to eclipse completely the political capacity of all other men and who therefore may be deemed to God among men have to be rulers and for them there is no law — they are themselves law." But such eminent men are not available at all times. Similarly men are not dispassionate while bidding others to follow because "desire is a wild beast and passion perverts the minds of the rulers even when they are the best of men." Here Aristotle is emphatic while pointing out the necessity of law that "man when perfected by law is the best of animals but when separated from law is the worst of all."

Also the Aristotelian state has men with equal power. Everyone should have his turn to rule and be ruled. This, of course, is possible when there is a code of conduct or law. So the rule of law is preferable to the rule of a man, however, he is the best of all. Besides, as Aristotle feels that an individual, however best he is, cannot determine the particulars, all citizens while meeting together are better Judges than the best man. This he concludes by an analogy. It is like a "feast to which many contribute is better than a dinner provided out of a single purse."

Here he warns us not to think that obedience to law is slavery. He, on the other hand, says that "true freedom is obedience to law and obedience to law is moral virtue." So law, to men, is their salvation and thus the final standard of morality. This is how Aristotle expresses his doctrine of political obligation.

However, Aristotle is careful, while speaking of the nature of the laws. They are not infallible and so imperfect as well. Hence it is said that the statesmen must pass regulations on matters or details left untouched or uncovered by the existing laws. Again no law passed is applicable to all time to come. So the laws are to be altered or amended depending on the prevailing conditions. But he warns us the frequent and quick change of laws is an evil. The reason ascribed by him is that "the law has no power to command obedience except that of habit which can only be given by time."

Aristotle is not a revolutionary in the matter of the customary laws. Just as a typical English he gives importance to customary laws existing in a country. He emphasizes the importance of it thus: "A man may be a safer ruler than written law but not safer than the customary law."

Education

The realization of the significance of education is as old as knowledge itself. Aristotle, who realizes that the end of the state is the good life of its citizens, says that the good life can be attained with the help of education as well. So education must be the monopoly of the state. The whole state has only one end. So education, a means to attain the end, should be the same for all. He says that no citizen belongs to himself; but all citizens belong to the state. Each of the citizen, is therefore a part of the state and as such care of each part becomes inseparable.

Says Aristotle that just as training and habitation is a must for the learning and cultivation of art so also training and habitation is a necessity for education. The thus emphasized education is liberal. The subjects recommended by him include reading and writing (which accommodates arithmetic also for he expects his citizen to be experts in money-making management of a household and public life), gymnastic (for health and courage), drawing (to develop the sense of correct judgement) and music which as Plato has enabled us to understand "a powerful agent of the formation of character and which is an intellectual enjoyment of high order in leisure."

Aristotle, no doubt, is aware of the slow process in the training and habitation of the young citizens in moral and intellectual virtue. He says that habit must be formed first before the development of reason in education, just as body is formed before the soul. To him, education must be imparted to children only when they attain the age of seven. But he suggests way to develop a sound body before a citizen's 7th age. So that each citizen can be a good citizen which means a good ruler, a good warrior and a good subject.

He suggests that infants should be administered with plenty of milk. He does not advise to give plenty of wine because he says, "the less wine the better if they would escape disease." Besides, the infants should be trained to enable themselves rather immune to heat and cold. Then up to the age of five the children should learn play. They should be forbidden from listening to improper stories and looking at indecent pictures. Then in the following two years they must be on the look out of "the pursuits which they are hereafter to learn." As the infant stage is so impressionable, he says that the children up to their seventh age are prohibited from leaving their home even to temple in addition to the total ban imposed on them to mix with slaves.

Education, with all such preliminaries, should begin at the age of seven. It has two stages. The first stage ends with the age of puberty and the second stage goes on till the age of twenty-one. The first stage of education comprises the teaching of music to the extent that the pupils become not only critics but also performers of it and mild gymnastic exercises. This will go on until the attainment of boyhood. Then three years should be spent on other studies.

Aristotle's educational system, despite its accommodation of the views of his master Plato, differ from Plato as found in the latter's "Republic" and "Law". He, of course, fails to give a picture of the process of education after the age of twenty-one. He simply tells us that the period after the age of twenty-one "may be devoted to hard exercise (Gymnastics) and strict regiment. Again he, makes us understand that the citizens must be educated to serve the state — as warriors while young, as rulers while old and as ones devoted to the study of speculative philosophy, the highest of human development and finally to be priests living in union with God while very old.

Private Property

Aristotle has a strong defense in favour of private property system. Human nature is, in his opinion, so intimately associated with property for its personality development and so if there is a system of state property system, then the human nature should have to be brought under the state's authoritarianism which, no doubt, produces evil and not good and hence the destruction of the very purpose for which the state is formed. Therefore, Aristotle says that property is an instrument and a necessary instrument to good life. He strongly pleads that the citizens must be owners of property for such a status enables them to develop their personality and good life. To Aristotle labour is inimical to virtue and so a curse. Besides, man is after all happy while kind to and doing service to his friends, guests and others. This he can do so when he has his own property.

Plato defends the abolition of private property and introduction of a system of communism which looks beneficial because the cases such as suits about contracts and flatteries of the rich which are inherent in the private property system may not arise. Can we say that these evils are due to the existence of the private property? In fact it is because of the wickedness of human nature. Communism is advocated for the sake of unity. Unity is must for the state. But if it is carried too far the state can no longer be a state. The state is a plurality of various kinds of men. It should be united and made into a community. This can be achieved by education. Here it is strange to note that Aristotle, who denounces communism of any kind, proposes the regulation of character in the line vogue in Sparta respecting the common meal system, instead of philosophy. The Guardians, proposed by Plato cannot be happy for they are denied the chance of possessing landed property and of doing anything excepting their specialized work. Free man presupposes a certain amount of freedom allowed in his personal choice of the means of realizing his best life. But Platonic free men are permitted to do only the specific work assigned and dependent on others for their subsistence. This, of course, fails them in their endeavour to realize their best selves and discharge satisfactorily the work expected of them.

It is, thus, that we understand the significance of property in making or marring personality "If Guardians are not happy the whole state is not happy."

However, Aristotle advises that each of his citizens should possess property of a mean or optimum size. He says that each citizen should have that much of property which enables him to live temperately as envisaged by Plato in the 'Laws'; and liberally and temperance are the virtues which have to do with property. So Aristotle, while suggesting equalization of property, insist on the equalization of the desires of mankind by education to avoid crimes emanating from poverty and love of honour. "Herein lies" says Chance "the real force of Aristotle's attack on Plato's radicalism. He maintains that the unity of the city depends on its character and not on external uniformity..."

While advocating the equalization of property Aristotle says that each citizen should have two lots — one near the border and the other near the city — which alone in his opinion involves all citizens in wars if they break out.

Aristotle is careful in seeing the continuance of the fixed amount of property for generations. This he wants to achieve it by fixing the number of children lest the law governing the fixed amount of property has got to be broken. To quote Aristotle "the limit must be fixed by calculating the chances of morality in children and of sterility in married persons. The neglect of this limit is a never-failing cause of poverty." No doubt Aristotle is one of the advocates of the birth control which the present day's politicians and economists are bent upon propagating; but unfortunately he fails to think that even if the children are fixed as expected by the philosopher, the two lots as recommended by him would hardly suffice at least after the second generation.

Aristotle likes a good moralist distinguishes between the natural and unnatural acquisition of property. He says that the acquisition of wealth from land-crops or animals — is natural while the wealth by exchange of commodities for profit or interest or usury is unnatural. He, of course, condemns usury for he emphasis that money is "intended to be used in exchange but not to increase at interest." So he maintains that agriculture is the proper and natural function of the citizen.

Despite his preference to the system of private property, Aristotle like his master has a definite leaning in favour of common meal system. He expresses that all citizens — rich and poor — must attend to the common meal except the state whose income, in his opinion, from land is to be sent partly on the common meal and partly on the maintenance of the state religion. He prefers the system because it will enable the citizens to understand each other, thereby fostering unity to a great extent in the state.

Family

Family, which is a moral and natural union fomenting and involving friendship and mutual service between husband and wife deternal care and filial affection between parents and children, is a necessity for Aristotle, to enable the citizens to have a "perfect and self-sufficing life." Every family revolves on the union of a man and a woman. But both sexes are not equal, although they are capable of virtue. They differ in physical powers and moral capacities. Male by nature has the power to command female by nature weak and less self-sufficient than male. So the husband superior to the wife, is born to rule. However, the husband is not a dictator but as a constitutional head must treat the wife as a free partner. Therefore, both are free but with unequal rights.

Similarly, the father exercises his control over his children with affection and regard but the child has no right against the parent for it is a part of the parent. Because the father has duty to the child, he rules the child in the interest of the latter. Such a kind of affection and regard is conspicuously absent in the Platonic family. The children in the Platonic family will be neglected. Each citizen in the Platonic family "will have a few thousand sons who will not be his sons individually; but anybody will be equally the sons of anybody and therefore will be neglected all alike."

In addition, in a state where women and children common, love, capable of binding persons, will be absent. The father can not and will not say 'My son'; or the son 'My father.' So unholy acts like assaults and murders against fathers, mothers, and near relations are most likely to take place if the relationship is unknown.

So Aristotle gives importance and significance to family life for it is the fountain-spring of love and friendship leading the bond of union in the state. It is because of this he remarks sarcastically that "community of wives and children seems better suited to the husbandmen than to the guardians." Since it would weaken the bonds of union among them and make them more obedient than before.

The thus-fostered family is to be controlled by the state. The children born can be prepared for the life of virtue by the state only. It is for this purpose that the state is empowered to take care of the children from the moment of their birth. This can be done meaningfully if the marriage and married life is regulated.

So, says Aristotle that the 18 and 37 should be the marriageable age for women and men respectively. Early marriage is not advisable for the couples from the health point of view. As he is interested in taking care of the children even when they are in wombs he suggests that pregnant women should maintain their body by resorting to physical exercises such as walking and to nourishing diet.

As he is for the optimum size of the family to perpetuate the mean property, he says that the number of children should be fixed taking into account of the probable infant mortality and sterility in married persons. However, he strictly warns that procreation should be avoided when fathers reach the age of 50 or 53 because the children born of old fathers are walkings. He advocates abortion also when couples have children in excess.

The brought up of the children after birth is on the line that we have already discussed under the caption 'Education.'

Classification of Government and the Best Suited Government for the State

Aristotle speaks of three true forms of government. They are: (1) Royalty, (2) Polity or Constitutional government, and (3) Aristocracy. They are in the hands of one, a few and many respectively. They all, of course, promote, in accordance with the principle of justice or equality, the common interest. However, Aristotle prefers only the rule by many to his state. He concedes that the rule by one or some is a perfect form of government if the some or one excel "others in body and in mind in the same degree in which gods and heroes are supposed to excel mankind in general." However, he is aware that such a rule is unattainable and "Kings have no marked superiority over their subjects." It is, therefore, that all citizens should take the chance of governing and being governed.

How will all citizens be governed and will govern in turn? Aristotle answers the question simply thus: When young they will be governed and be warriors as well; but when old they will rule. He does not say anything more than that, and goes on analyzing the existing states. His ideal states, therefore, incomplete. So, says Sabine that Aristotle pictures only the ideals of the ideal state. Nevertheless, we can know the mind of the philosopher on the organization of the government by the citizens of the ideal state.

In fact, he knows that laws are not perfect. There are points and particulars untouched and uncovered by laws. To transact, to deliberate and to determine such points and particulars all the citizens meet in assemblies. They elect Judge and Magistrates. The reason is that "the collective judgement of citizens is better than that of the wisest man," just as a feast contributed by all guests are better than the banquet presented by a single man. Also it is said that many are incorruptible than a few like the greater quantity of water is less easily corruptible than a little quantity of water. However, he asserts that important offices are to be discharged by men elected by vote on merit. Polity is the name assigned by the philosopher for this type of government. It is of course a fusion of the principles of democracy and those of the aristocratical virtue and merit.

Here it should be understood that he supports democracy to the extent that the collective judgement of the citizens could take the place of a monarchy or aristocracy. The democracy which is the government by the people as known ordinarily to any modern mind, is not the one spoken here or supported by him. Besides, modern democrats believe in the government for the people of the people and by the representatives of the people and not by the people themselves; but Aristotle believes in the collective wisdom of the citizens.

International Relations

Aristotle is conscious that his state cannot exist alone; on the other hand, it should co-exist with other states while doing so war is inevitable. However, he says that war is not the end of the state; on the contrary it is only a means of peace and good life of the state. Since he is conscious of the war effects, he says that state can "seek to be masters only over those who deserve to be slaves" (barbarians). Besides, he is sure that property in the state is a factor which either excited the envy of or invasion by other states. So he suggests that his state should have such an amount of property which can enable its citizens to resist the enemy within and without. It is for this purpose that military force is advocated. His aim, therefore, is internal and international peace.

Remedy of the Existing Government

Aristotle is not only dogmatic but also pragmatic as while he is like his master interested in creating an ideal state, he never fails to see the obvious defects in the existing constitutions and working of various states and he suggests ways and means of improving them. He, therefore, says that statesmen and legislators must give a deep thought not only on "what kind of government is best in abstract" but also "on what kind of government is best in concrete," possible and attainable by every state, in addition to finding out remedies for the defects of the existing constitutions. He is not theoretical only but practical as well. So he pictures his ideal state in accordance with his aspiration and presents possible and attainable remedies for the existing constitutions on studying as many as 150 constitutions.

He first of all suggests that remedy follows only after studying what is existing. So he says that we must first know the constitutions existing however different they are.

After studying the constitutions in vogue, Aristotle has found out the general tendency in favour of democracy and oligarchy as the two chief forms of government; the other forms are only their variations. But Aristotle dismisses the tendency and expresses that there are three true forms of government. He emphasizes that government is either in the hands of one or a few or many. Such governments are known as royalty oligarchy and polity respectively. However, if the rulers, instead of dedicating themselves for the common good seek their own interest the three will get perverted and take the name of tyranny, aristocracy and extreme democracy of the needy (mobocracy) respectively.

While using the term 'democracy', Aristotle does not seem to be consistent. However, it is obvious that he, by democracy means a government by many. He differentiates democracy and oligarchy. The difference between democracy and oligarchy lies in poverty and wealth. So "wherever men rule by reason of their wealth — they be a few or many — that is an oligarchy and where the poor rule that is democracy." The difference between the two forms — oligarchy and democracy — is viewed from the points of wealth and freedom. Here, it is worth-mentioning that liberty and equality is the basis and end of democracy. It is liberty because all can rule and be ruled in turn. It is equality because the poor, who are the majority (whose will is supreme) have more power than the rich. It is, therefore, that the form of government while free and ruled by the poor who are the majority, is democracy and while ruled by the rich who are few in number, is known as oligarchy.

While bringing out the feature of these forms of government, he expresses that out of give forms of democracy "the worst is the rule by the mob and demagogues with utter rejection of the sovereign laws." Similarly the rule by hereditary supreme magistrates is the worst of the several kinds of tyranny.

Aristotle is aware and conscious of the fusion the existing forms of government thereby creating a new form enshrining therein the features of the two. Aristocracy, for him is a fusion of democracy and oligarchy. Its leaning towards oligarchy is obvious in the sense that the wealthy are entrusted with the special offices because of their merit. It is, therefore, a fusion of freedom, wealth and virtue. But polity is a fusion of oligarchy and democracy. It is also a fusion of the wealth of the rich and the freedom of the poor.

After discussing the characteristic and formation of the forms of government, Aristotle turns to analyse the best constitution which every state can attain generally. He is sure that the aristocracy, a fusion of wealth, freedom and virtue is beyond the scope of the many states because states in general are average with no exceptional education and exceptional advantage. The best form is, therefore, a peculiar mean between oligarchy and democracy. In other words, it is that form in which the middle class which is majority is entitled to exercise its power. It is no doubt, not similar to polity.

To Aristotle, every state has three classes of citizens — very rich, very poor and those neither very rich nor very poor but in-between. He says that moderation and means are the best in everything. So he prefers moderation in the gift of fortune as well. Reason is very important in the life of men. The very rich and the very poor flout the dictates reason because the former refuses to accept authority and the latter is incapable of holding civil or military offices. Again the sons of the former refuse to be obedient in the school while those of the latter are not given any recognition. Therefore, the rule of the former despotic and the rule of the latter, since they do not know how to command proved confusion. In the light of such an argument he concludes that he prefers that state where middle class is larger than either the very rich class or the very poor class because the middle class does "not covet their neighbour's goods nor plot against others."

The concept of the rule by the middle class emanates purely from the mind of Aristotle; it is of course unknown to the Greeks of his age. Moreover, the middle class in large number was conspicuously absent then. So the Greeks states were either wedded to democracy or oligarchy. If so by what name the form of rule preferred by Aristotle can be called? It is no doubt in no way similar to polity, a balanced fusion of democracy and oligarchy. If so what? Aristotle himself answers the question. He says it "more nearly approximates to democracy (moderate form of democracy accommodating liberty and equality of citizens and sovereignty of law) than to oligarchy and is the safest of the imperfect forms of government."

Revolution and Remedial Measures

Revolution is fomented either to changes the existing constitution or to seize power. It is effected either by force or fraud or by both. Aristotle is not concerned with the revolutions raised to seize power but to change the existing constitutions. His analysis with masterly acuteness "unsurpassed by any subsequent thinker" is, indeed, scientific and so true at all times and to all states.

Universal Causes

The root of the revolution, says Aristotle lies in the very principle of the various forms of government. The democrats for example, feel falsely that all are equal in all respects and so they want to be absolutely equal. The oligarchs feel that those who are unequal in one respect, are unequal in all respects. "All these forms of government have a kind of Justice and when people think that their share in the government does not accord with their preconceived ideas and notions, revolutions take place." Aristotle points out that the inferiors revolt in order that they may be equal and equals that they may be superiors. In addition to the feelings causing revolutions, he says that motives do contribute for revolution. The desire of gain and honour of the fear of dishonour and loss — a cause of revolutions — is attributed to motives.

Particular Causes

(1) Insolence and avarice of the magistrates who are conspiring against one another and also against the constitution for the sake of their personal gains, is a cause of the revolution.

(2) Love of superiority poses a cause of revolution. "When one or more persons" writes Aristotle, "have a power which is too much for the state and the power of government" there arises "a monarchy or a family

oligarchy." In this connection he cites the example of Athens which faced such a danger by its device of Ostracism.

(3) Fear is regarded as a cause of revolution. Men who are afraid of punishment and who commit wrong foment revolutions as a smoke screen conceal their misdeeds, cause revolutions. In addition, it is said that men who expect to suffer wrong or are desirous of anticipating enemies, engineer revolutions.

(4) Disproportionate increase in any part of the state is considered as a cause of revolution. The symmetry of a body is maintained when the parts of the body are grown proportionately. The state like a body has many parts whose symmetry and real form can be maintained if they grow proportionately. If the number of the poor in democracy and the rich in oligarchy grow disproportionately the class which has the disproportionately increased number "will always try to offset the preponderance of each other, thus causing dissensions and revolutions."

(5) Election intrigues, carelessness, neglect about trifles and dissimilarity of elements throw the people into the state of revolution. Aristotle expresses that election contests cause the change of the form of government. He cites, in this connection the example of Haraea. In Haraea the people, bidding good-bye to the traditional method of electing their magistrates, chose them by lot. This was, of course, fittingly objected to by the electors whose resentment caused revolution. Similarly, in support of his statement that careless is a cause of revolution, he quotes the incident at Oreum. Soon after the accession of Heracleodorus to the highest office at Oreum, the conventional oligarchy was overthrown and the democratic and constitutional government was installed. To prove the point that the neglect of trifle is also a cause of the revolution, Aristotle brings out the example of Ambracia. The qualification for office in Ambracia was very low at the beginning; but later it was reduced to nothing. The Ambraciots did not relish the change and caused revolution. Dissimilarity

of elements, a potent cause of revolution, means to Aristotle, "the difference of races which have not acquired a common spirit." In emphasizing the point Aristotle says that the state is neither the growth of a day nor its multitude is brought together by accident. "Hence, the reception of strangers in states either at the time of foundation or afterwards has generally produced revolution." The detection of the new colonists at Byzantium and their subsequent expulsion by force is quoted as an example.

(6) Aristotle, in addition to them, speaks of the particular causes of revolution in particular states. He traces the causes in democracy, oligarchy, polity, aristocracy, monarchy and tyranny. In democracy revolution is caused because of the "intemperance of demagogues" who set the rich and the poor at enmity for their own advantages. Aristotle cites the incident of the overthrow of democracy by the wickedness of demagogues at Cos. Similarly the revolution in oligarchy take place owing to the tyrannical and oppressive rule by the oligarchy or to the personal rivalries among the oligarchs. Revolutions in aristocracy are because of a few persons' share in the honour of the state while a majority of the people believes that they are as good as rulers. So also, monarchy faces revolution in the event of the monarch becoming tyrannical or while the monarch insulting some notable persons.

Remedies

Aristotle, who enumerates various causes of revolutions, now gives a list of remedies either to avoid or to avert revolutions. First of all the statesman should guard against the beginning of change. Secondly, the rulers should avoid scrupulously any attempt to deceive the people because such attempts bear no fruits. Thirdly, the governing class should abstain from maltreating those who are excluded from the government; but it should recognize the leading spirit in them. Fourthly, the rulers should keep up patriotism at a 'fever-pitch' by inventing "terrors, bringing distant dangers near in order that the citizens may be on their guard and like sentinels in a night watch, never relax their attention." Fifthly, dangers emanating from the disproportionate increase of power or honour should be counteracted. The property qualification introduced for a share in the government should invariably be altered — raised or lowered — depending upon the circumstances. It should be seen that no single individual is invested with more honours to the extent of causing inequality of position; nor he should be permitted to have much power derived either from his friends or from money. If anyone has it, by chance, he along with his friends should be expelled from the state. Institution of a magistracy is suggested to have a vigil on the dangerous individuals. Similarly, no class should be allowed to be prosperous. Estates, therefore, should pass by inheritance. But none should have more than an inheritance. Sixthly, the middle class should be permitted to increase its number to balance the rich and the poor. If not, both in democracy and oligarchy all should be given equal share in all except the principal offices of the state. These offices must be reserved only to the ruling class because loyalty to the established constitutions, administrative capacity and prudence are required in the persons occupying such offices. So it is clear that "democracy should not become too democratic and oligarchy too oligarchic but find a salvation in the mean" accommodating rich and poor in the desirable proportion to make it a good government. Seventhly, special honours like magistrates should be extended to the persons of integrity and honesty. Their tenure of office should not exceed a year mainly to enable others to occupy the same offices which, of course, reduce any tension possibly fomenting revolution. Eighthly, "adaptation of education to the form of government" says Aristotle, "contributes to the permanence of constitution"; but he desires "in our own day this principle is universally neglected." So, he suggests that "the young are trained by state and education in the spirit of the constitution if the laws are democratical democratically or oligarchically if the laws are oligarchical." But at the same time he warns us saying "to have been educated in the spirit of the constitution is not to perform the activities in which oligarchs and democrats delight but these by which the existence of a democracy or an oligarchy is made possible."

In addition, he suggests ways to avoid and avert revolution under monarchy and tyranny. The powers of the monarchs should be limited. In the case of tyranny he advises that "the tyrants ought to show himself to his subjects in the light, not of a tyrant, but of the master of a household and of a king." Also to forbid the tyrant to take away anything he likes in his realm, Aristotle suggests that "he should not appropriate what is theirs (the subjects), but should be their guardian; he should be moderate in his way of life and should be the companion of the notables and the hero of the multitudes.... Let his disposition be virtuous or at least half virtuous; and if he must be wicked let him be half wicked only.

Can modern rulers be prudent enough to avoid the much detested revolution by following the remedies suggested by Aristotle?

Slavery

Aristotle, talking of slavery, which has become a cause of the American civil war, justifies it from the point of view of master and slave without minding the heat generating to the extent of exploding a social and constitutional structure. He says that a slave belongs to another, a free man and as such he exists only for the sake of the good of the another. Free men exist for their own sake. While moralizing the existence of slavery as an "institution of nature," he is emphatic in pointing out that there are 'some who are intended by nature to be slaves.'

Each citizen (free man) needs private property and slaves. These two are like instruments necessary to achieve and practice good life. Since manual labour is incompatible with virtue, a must for good life, a citizen, whose end of life is virtue, cannot live a good life of virtue. He, is like a musician who cannot produce an instrumental music without an instrument, cannot produce a good life. Here although property also is an instrument, he gives a stress on the slaves because the slaves are living instruments of action producing goods not wealth getting but for immediate consumption while property is the lifeless instrument of production. So Aristotle justifies the existence and use of slaves by free men for the sake of attaining a good life of virtue. Nevertheless he warns the free man not to convert a slave into a factory slave who, by feature, is instrument of the production of wealth.

While justifying the slavery in the name of nature Aristotle says, "from the hour of birth some men are marked out for subjection and others for rule." By way of explanation he says that men of "capacity, foresight, self-reliance and the life of virtue are intended by nature to work with their mind." Persons lacking such characters are intended by nature to work with the body. He, again, explains it that just as by nature the soul ruling the body, the mind the passionate, and the male, the female so also men working with mind is empowered to rule those who do by body and so masters and slaves respectively. Aristotle does not say that the slaves are machine without having any capacity to employ reason; but he admits that they have capacity to discharge intelligently their own duties only.

Aristotle justifies slavery from the point of a slave also. He becomes a slave because he is born for that. Naturally he should be placed under the control of a master who possesses that which he lacks. Temperance is a quality needed for a good life. The slaves have no temperance but they acquire a derivative temperance by submitting themselves to a temperate master. Since the slaves have derivative temperance, like the moon having the derivative light, the choice for them is not between the inferior and the perfect form of human virtue; but it is between the inferior form and none. It is on this score that Aristotle has a preference for a slave to a mechanical labourer to artisan attains excellence in proportion as he becomes a slave because he is less closely connected with a master whose help for the slaves to develop a close, nay closer, contact enables the slaves to first become more or less a member of the master's family and to attain "self-control of a servant subordinating himself to his superior."

Aristotle defends only the household slavery and not the industrial slavery. His justification of it is the same as Plato's justification of the permanent subjection of the producing class. He does not say that all Greeks are masters and the non-Greeks are slaves. On the other hand, the persons devoid of the capacity needed for the good life of virtue are deemed slaves. However, he insists on the humanitarian treatment to the slaves. But the modern thinkers in unison denounce the theory of slavery as it is a blot on the human civilization. Denouncing the natural superiority of a race over other as Aristotle has pointed out. Montesquieu says that slavery is against nature which has created all as equals and hence condemnable. Nevertheless the existence of slavery either in the form of domestic service or racial discrimination on the basis of the reasons advocated by Aristotle is still a common feature.

3

The Epicurean Philosophy and the Stoic Philosophy

The two schools of thought developed after Plato and Aristotle in Greece were Epicureanism and Stoicism. Their trend of thought was philosophical in nature. Their outlook on life was more individualistic and more cosmopolitan as compared with that of Plato and Aristotle. They wanted individual self-sufficiency independent of society. Individual had to learn living in new form of social union larger than city-state. Both the schools agreed in making individual happiness the aim of life. They differed in defining happiness and in the method by which it might be secured. The Epicureans advocated the temperate satisfaction of every desire, sensual and intellectual; the Stoics taught the suppression of the emotions and the subordination of immoral desires to the demands of reason.

Epicureanism founded by Epicurus (306 B.C.) and expounded by the Roman poet Lucretius, was a development of Cyrenaicism, which was established by Aristippus who claimed to have derived his ideas directly from Socrates. According to it the greatest aim of life was the greatest happiness, which was nothing but absence of pain or worry. Epicurus himself, however, identified happiness with virtue and himself lived on bread and water only. A wise man, to him, would reduce his desires to minimum. Maximum happiness could be achieved by making oneself independent of state and by withdrawing from cares of public life, because active membership of the civil society creates desires and ambitions in a man. Family life, too, should be avoided as much as possible, as it adds to the worries and pain. Being free from these worries one could devote one's energy to self-improvement internally or to the pleasures of the soul rather than of the body.

Epicurean principle that happiness is the aim of life brought deterioration in Greek political thought because the high principles of right, virtue, justice gave place to the low notions of happiness or utility. In this way Epicureanism may be called the basis of utilitarianism. The Epicureans based, the State upon individual self-interest. They believed that men were essentially selfish. The curbing of individual selfishness necessitated a common superior authority. They defined law as an agreement of utility and expediency entered into among individuals in order that they might be secured against violence and injustice. The Social Contract theory of the State was here foreshadowed. They believed that political life is burdensome and that the wise man will take no part in it unless his interest absolutely demand it. The Epicureans taught submission to any government that maintained peace and order and ensured easy social intercourse. Efficient despotism was as good as democracy. However, they preferred monarchy as the strongest and the best form of government. The Epicureans were in live with Hobbes in ascribing the origin of the state to the need of security. They taught submission to any efficient de facto government, a doctrine that suited to the situation after the conquest of Greece by Alexander and by Rome.

Stoic Philosophy

Stoicism was more important than Epicureanism as it exercised greater influence on the development of political theory and Roman jurisprudence in its formative stage. It was responsible for the formulation of the concept of the Law of Nature based on reason and cosmopolitanism or world-citizenship, which became part and parcel of western civilization and culture. It was founded by Zeno about 300 B.C. He was said to be the pupil of Crates who was the leader of the Cynic school. Stoicism influenced first Greece and then the Roman thinkers like Cicero, Seneca, Aurelius, Emperor Marcus etc.

Like Epicureans, for Stoics also the aim of life was to achieve human happiness, but while the former allowed a moderate indulgence in both physical and intellectual desires, the latter declared against physical satisfaction and advised pursuit of intellectual pleasure based on reason and not on feelings. They agreed with the basic ideas of Cynicism, i.e. perfect self-control, independence of circumstances, self-sufficiency and life according to Nature. But they were constructive and positive as against wholly negative and nihilistic doctrines of Cynicism. Stoicism gave shape to the political thought from Cicero till 18th century.

True happiness, for Stoics, lay in virtue, which was nothing that following the law of nature, which was definite, unchangeable and based on reason. Thus, life according to law of nature was, to live according to reason. But an individual was not to follow such individual reason, but the reason as shown by universal approval or judgement. In other words, human reason, as the source of natural law, did not mean the independent judgement of the individual, but the common judgement of mankind. Like as rational beings, are essentially alike. They are subject to the same natural law and have equal rights. Upon this doctrine, a cosmopolitan political theory was created. All men, whether Greek, slave or barbarian, are naturally brothers, follow citizens in a world republic. This city of God is an abstract conception like Plato's ideal city found in the Republic. Subjection to one law by all inevitably leads to the doctrine of natural equality of men as opposed to natural inequality and slavery advocated by Plato and Aristotle. Liberty, equality and fraternity of today represent a modern version of Stoicism. Brotherhood of man depends on the observance of Natural Law, which unites all men into one great community. Universal natural law and universal citizenship were Stoic ideals. The significance of these conceptions in a society based upon slavery is at once evident.

The Stoics conceived of nature as the embodiment of universal law. Reason, as the creative source of law, was the revealer of nature. The law of nature was therefore fixed and immutable. It was the reflection of the process of nature, in harmony with human reason, the divine element in the universe. In this form the idea of natural law was handed down through Roman law and through mediaeval political thought.

The Stoics rejected the crude naturalism of Cynics and substituted an idealist view of life. Nature, according to them was not jumble of events or chaos, but rational system or order ruled by divine reason. They recommended resignation to the course of things and indifference to the events of fortune and values of social life. In their view the life according to Nature mean life according to law. Nature was the manifestation of the single and homogeneous spirit of the world based on reason. The law of Nature is that common, universal divine and good rule of reason, which governs creatures combined in a natural association. Natural law is objective reason. Civil law must be based on Natural law which is sovereign and universal standard of right or wrong.

Stoics considered individual as a unit by himself, self-sufficient and distinct from the society. The Stoic philosophy was the negation of Platonic and Aristotelean philosophy namely, that good life could be lived only within the State. To the Stoics, the good man was different from the good citizen. The controlling or guiding force was Ethics and not Politics. Private life was more important than public life. Participation in politics, therefore, was condemned. But according to Stoics, a wise individual, in spite of his individualism, would recognize society, even though as a necessary evil, and would do all he can to help it. They believed in the general depravity of mankind and thus they justified the existence of the institution of government. This belief foreshadowed the cardinal Christian doctrine of Original Sin.

With the Stoics justice represented a form of universal reason, based on the sense of equality among human beings. Although they did not advocate the abolition of slavery, they pleaded for mercy to be shown to the slaves as freedom of spirit was the true freedom and its lack true slavery. Thus the Stoics gave to the world the notion of equality based on the spirit of freedom and the notion of universal brotherhood based on universality of natural law. They played a tremendous part in moulding human thought after the death of Aristotle till the advent of Christianity. The Stoic philosophy greatly influenced the writings of Cicero, the doctrine of original sin of Christianity and became the characteristic philosophy of the Roman rulers.

Although the Stoics developed their ideals of brotherhood of man and of world-State, which represented an ideal Universal Empire of Reason, from a philosophic and humanitarian point of view, the conditions of the time soon became favourable to their political application. The empire of Alexander broke down the barriers between Greek and barbarian, and diverse people became members of one political system. Universal law and universal citizenship became matter of fact under the Roman Empire and Roman jurists adopted the idea of law of nature and principles of common justice to all men. The conception of human brotherhood was taken over by Christianity and expanded all over the civilised world.

(i) POLYBIUS (204-122 B.C.)

The first of the Roman political philosophers who wrote on Roman government and its constitution was a Greek hostage named Polybius. Rome had, by this time, become a great state and had brought Greece under its control. Polybius admired the Roman policy which had enabled Rome to become a great political power. So he wrote his famous History of Rome to show her greatness and to find out and enunciate the cause of this greatness. He was a promising young thinker whose scholarly greatness was discovered by the Roman rulers. Even Coker writes, "In Italy, the experience and ability of Polybius were recognized and utilized. He was sent to Greece on a mission of mediation between Rome and the Achaeans. Though this mission was fruitless, he became subsequently representative of the Roman government in the reconstruction of Greece. Most of his later life, however, he spent in scholarly leisure, enjoying the friendship and patronage of Roman statesmen — particularly of Scipio Africanus, the younger." He travelled widely in military and diplomatic missions in Europe and Asia. His histories are in forty books, of which the first five are fully preserved and the remaining are found in fragments. Polybius was definitely a great historian. He was the first historian to apply the institutional method to the study of politics and to examine the institutional fabric of a state as the chief determining factor in the formation of national strength. The main purpose of writing the History of Rome was "to enable students to understand why it was that the whole world fell under the power of Rome in the short space of less than fifty-three years." His conclusion was that Rome had achieved that glory and greatness because of her sound and stable system of government. His treatment of history was most scientific. It was really superb. From this great work of his we get a clear glimpse of his political ideas on government and its various aspects.

Polybius on Classification of Government: Like Plato and Aristotle, Polybius also accepts a six-fold classification: monarchy, aristocracy and democracy with their respective perversions as tyranny, oligarchy and extreme democracy or mobocracy. To him, the earliest form of government was monarchy based on force first but later on sanctioned by popular approval. Monarchy degenerated into tyranny. This was overthrown and followed by aristocracy based on virtue and intellect. Aristocracy degenerated into oligarchy, which was followed by democracy. Democracy, then also, degenerated into mobocracy of mob-rule of force and violence. Then, again, mob-rule is taken over by some bold leader with popular support and thus monarchy or one-man rule gets established again. Thus, the cycle of change continues without any interruption. It is evident from this classification that each form of government contains within itself the germs of its decay and ruin.

Polybius on Mixed Form of Government: To Polybius, the best safeguard against political upheavals was the incorporation in the constitution of the best elements of all the three pure forms of government, and this he found in the Republic of Rome; and this was the main cause of the greatness of Rome. In the Roman constitution, the consuls represented the monarchic principle, the senate was essentially aristocratic and the popular assemblies were democratic. Each one of these three elements watched and controlled the other two elements. No one was allowed to function independently without the consent of all. It was an elaborate system of checks and balances. According to Gettell, "Polybius was the first writer to make a clear statement of the advantages of a mixed form of government, and of the principle of checks and balances in constitutional organization. These conceptions were recognized in theory and practice in later periods, and in a slightly changed form, remain valid in modern political thought."

Importance of Polybius: The importance of Polybius in the history of political thought is no doubt great. The general principles of his political reasoning are as valid today as they were in his own days. His influence on Cicero was tremendous and even Marsilius of Padua and Thomas Acquinas are not free from his influence. His writings have contributed to the constitution of the U.S.A. According to Maxey, "Polybius deserves remembrance as the first to state the famous check and balance theory in a full and formal way." Dunning also holds the view that "Polybius conceives of a mixed constitution as expressed in the existence of three organs, embodying in each a distinct principle and acting through-self-interest as restraints upon one another." Though not original, his contribution to political thinking is great.

(ii) TULLIUS CICERO (106 B.C.-43 B.C.)

The death of Aristotle sees the death of an era in the history of Political Philosophy because the life of his great politician-disciple (Alexander) who happens to have died a year before his political guru, marks the birth of a new era in politics. "Man as a political animal, a fraction of polis or self-governing city State had ended with Aristotle; with Alexander begins man as an individual" (Tarn). So man was forced to learn to live alone, as they had never done and as such they were again forced "to learn to live together in a new form of social union much larger than the city state." This situation, in the history of political philosophy has, of course, caused to clear the idea of individual and the idea of universality and to interweave them into a common scheme. Reinterpretation and re-adaptation of the ideas and the scheme which went on hectically, especially during the past Aristotle period, contributed much to the muse of Political Philosophy. Philosophers of the Stoic School were the last of such contributors. Their political ideas served as a basis for the exact and matter-of-fact philosophy which was the creation of the Roman mind. So says Mommsen that the Stoic creed "was really better adapted for Rome than for the land where it first arose." (see History of Rome, Vol. iv, pp.

201-04). In fact, the Stoic ideals of universal law and universal citizenship became practical facts with the Romans for they had already made themselves receive such ideals as their own as philosophy owing to the military and administrative genius of the Romans. Philosophers like Cicero, dedicating themselves to the preaching of the doctrine of the universal brotherhood of man inherited from Greece converted Rome as the chief medium through which the Greek political philosophy was interpreted and spread throughout the world. So Cicero's was almost unoriginal. However, he has, by his magnetic touch, immortalized the inherited hellenistic ideas which, of course their originators failed to do or could not do. It is, in this way, that his two works De Republic and De Legibus owe their form and general subject matter to the Greek philosophers — Plato and Aristotle. It is said that the De Republic is a pale replica of Plato's Republic, although the views of Cicero expressed are totally different from those of Plato. Cicero deals in the work with the origin and nature of the state, the forms of government and the nature of justice and the part played in the forms of government. Cicero has given importance to justice as the main theme in the work and so St. Augustine is forced to say that the work is "a keen and powerful defense of justice as against injustice." His another work De Legibus also resembles with the Laws another Plato's work. He deals with law which of course refers to those found in Rome rather than those of Greece.

Ideal State

Origin

It is in the work De Republic that Cicero brings out his conception of an ideal state as Plato has done in the Republic. He strongly believes that the state is 'not merely an assembly of men brought together in a fashion whatsoever' 'but an assemblage of many, associated by consent to law and by community of interest.' So the essential idea of state is "common wealth." The common wealth here means "the wealth of the people understanding by a people, a multitude united by a common-sense of right and of a community of interest." Cicero expresses that the prime cause of the people coming together is not weakness but rather a sort of mutual affinity for each other. That is why he calls the state as the "republica respopuli" meaning the affairs of the state are the affairs of the people. So it is obvious that the state exists for the enforcement of law, for the common good of the people. As such the state is to be regarded as an ethical community. If the state, therefore, is not a community for ethical purposes and again if the state is not held together by moral ties it would be reduced to be a "highway robbery on a large scale" as St. Augustine has put it. The state, thus, is the corporate body of the people accommodating the moral law to continue in order to make morality possible, even if the state becomes tyrannous and rules with brute force; failing which the state losses its reason for existence and its real character. So it is clear that the state for Cicero is "the association and assembly of human beings united by a common agreement about law and right and by the desire to participate to the advantages of each other."

Plan of the State

The state should be enduring and have a long life; for which Cicero gives us some plan. The distribution of the governmental power is the basis of the plan. Cicero says that the governmental powers may be exercised by 'one person', 'chosen ones' or 'the multitude of people.' According to this the form of government will be kingdom, aristocracy and democracy respectively. He is firm that the forms of government would never undergo a change if the state machinery is directed according to justice or the purpose of administrative is justice. If not the forms of government is likely to degenerate into tyranny, oligarchy and mobocracy. Besides, Cicero is of the view that these forms have serious drawbacks. In kingdom the people, in general, are deprived of their common rights and liberty to participate in counsels. Similarly wider aristocracy the people in general are excluded from all common counsel and power. So also the people are forced to suffer under democracy for it, as a result of a non-recognition of gradation of merit, or a recognition of equality, tends to create evil. So Cicero says that it is that form of government accommodating all the three elements — monarchic, aristocratic and democratic — is the best one to direct the state. "Cicero, therefore, considered a balance combination between kingship, aristocracy and democracy, the best constitution; his belief in the virtues of the mixed construction went back to Aristotle, but it was also a lesson of Roman political history that an astute observer like Cicero could hardly have missed" (W. Ebenstein — Introduction to Political Philosophy, p. 41).

Justice

State, once born, needs "the plan of the state" for its longevity. Similarly the highest justice is a must for its maintenance. Cicero in the De Republic discusses justice which, according to him, consists in acting in accordance with the law of nature which is the dictate of right reason. Reason is found in every man and so every man is equal. Cicero says, while addressing the Romans, "Let the Romans, if they wish to be just, restore what they have seized from other peoples and sink back to the same state of poverty and wretchedness from which their conquests raised them." So it is clear that justice to Cicero means restoring and recognizing the right of everyone, besides providing equality of opportunity to all.

Mistrust and distrust among the people and mutual fear are said to jeopardize the very foundation of justice. Cicero, in this connection affirms that "one man fears another, man against man, order against order and no one dares trust to himself — a kind of pact is joined between the people and it is only from this that arises that thing; a united form of state. Therefore neither nature nor volition is the mother of justice but defencelessness." So it is clear that protection of rights is the very basis of justice.

Cicero clearly draws a distinction between wisdom and justice. He says that 'wisdom prompts us to enlarge our wealth and power' whereas justice commands us to spare others and respect their rights and properties.

Law

Cicero strongly holds that 'true law is the law of nature which means the dictate of right reason. This law is eternal and immutable. It is applicable and applicable to all peoples and for all times. Any legislation, under any circumstances, in contravention to it, is not entitled to be known as law for none has the power to make right what is wrong.' This law is regarded as the basis of the civilized life because in the absence of it existence "for a household, a city, a nation, the human race, physical nature, and the universe itself' becomes impossible.

Dunning expresses, while commenting on Cicero's thinking on Law, "there can be no doubt that in the border region where ethics and jurisprudence and politics meet Cicero performed a work which gives him an important place in the history of political theory. The work was the development and application of the concept of natural law." Since the natural law as developed by Cicero is enforceable through right reason without waiting for any formal authority and compulsion, it "exercised a profound influence on the early fathers of the Church" and "at the beginning of the Middle Ages he was perhaps more widely read and quoted than other ancient political writers."

Equality and Liberty

In the light of their law of nature, which is eternal, Cicero says that all men are equal. Here he does not follow the traditional line of the Plato in explaining the equality of men. On the other hand, he explains that men are not equal in learning nor in the possession of property but in the possession of reason in their underlying psychological make-up and in their general attitude towards what they believe to be honourable or base all men are alike. However Cicero is aware of the inequality existing among men. He says that errors, bad habits and false opinions prevent men from being equal. Cicero writes, "All men are alike rational. No men is like to himself as like to all," though evil habits may bring apparent diversity.

Carlyle, commenting on the concept of equality by Cicero, says that "no change in political theory is so startling in its completeness as the change from Aristotle to a passage such as this" (A History of Medieval Political Theory, Vol. I, p. 8). While appreciating the comment, it is said that Carlyle has done a great service to the thinkers of Political Philosophy, by emphasizing the concept, the Doctrine of Equality as "the dividing line between the ancient and modern political theory."

Cicero is much farther than Aristotle in his stress on liberty. "Liberty has no dwelling place", says Cicero, "in any state except that in which the people's power is the greatest and surely nothing can be sweeter than liberty; but if it is not the same for all it does not deserve the name of liberty." From this, it is clear that his doctrine of liberty embodies two important features: (1) Liberty is a product to be enjoyed by all citizens regardless of their classes or distinctions. (2) Consent of the people is the only source for the legitimate government. Of course the features, embodying in the conception of liberty, have great significance in the struggle for democracy and popular self-government throughout the world.

4

St. Augustine (354-430 A.D.)

Introduction

St. Augustine, called by Foakes-Jackson as "The most important figure in Church History since St. Paul was born in the Roman Province of Numidia (Northern Africa in 354 A.D.). His father was a pagan but his mother was a devout Christian. The boy was a brilliant student in his early days. So his father sacrificed everything to give him the best education. He was specially trained as a rhetorician and he became a great scholar. On finishing his education, he became a teacher of grammar in his home town and about the same time, embraced the Manichaean religion which was just a combination of Zoroastrianism and Christian Ghosticism. But in due course as his scholarly aptitude developed he became increasingly dissatisfied with Manichaeism and with life in his native city. So in 383 he migrated to Rome. Soon he was invited to go to Milan as a teacher of rhetoric whereupon he broke away from Manichaeism altogether and became a skeptic. He got converted to neo-platonism. But soon his stay in Milan brought him into close contact with the great scholar Ambrose, Christian bishop of Milan who had shown the courage to defy the Roman emperor and declare that the emperor had no jurisdiction over a Christian Church, saying that in matters of religion bishops were emperors, not emperors bishops. It was under the influence of Ambrose that Augustine got converted to Christianity. Soon he became a very active and highly enlightened Church man. After spending some time in Rome in literary work he returned to his native Africa and was soon made bishop of Hippo. The remaining part of his life was devoted to the service of the Church. He continued in the post of bishop of Hippo till his death in 430; at that moment the Vandals were laying siege to his city. He was a prolific and celebrated writer. Besides his famous Confessions, he wrote a very large number of treatises on general philosophical questions. It is difficult to name his greatest book but 'The City of God' (De Civitate Dei) may be called the most important of his work. He took more than twelve years to write this book, which is composed of twenty-two books. The first ten books are devoted to the defence of Christianity. They are concerned with rebutting the charge that Rome had perished in the Christian days and due to Christian doctrines. In the other twelve books he gives most comprehensively his conceptions of man and society. He also makes a distinction between the City of God and the city of this world. "The City of God consists of the redeemed in this world and the next. The city of the world is the kingdom of the devil and of those who follow him." According to Maxey, Augustine wrote 'The City of God' because "In 410 A.D. Alaric the Goth captured and sacked the city of Rome. For three days the pillage lasted, and when it was done the world stood aghast at the portentous significance of the event. The Eternal city had fallen; the hub around which civilization had turned for upwards of eight centuries had gone to smash; the once proud mistress of the whole Mediterranean's world had been brought to the nadir of shame and humiliation. Such, the foes of Christianity were promptly heard to say, was the penalty Rome must pay for deserting her ancient gods. Had she shunned the debilitating faith of the Nazarene and remained steadfast in her old ways, she never would have come to such a fate." To refute this sophistry and provide a political credo for Christians, St. Augustine wrote 'The City of God.' This book of philosophy is no doubt a book of lasting interest and importance. According to Coker, the book has exercised "a profound influence over later medieval discussion of questions concerning the origin of political society; the relations of civil government to divine law, natural law, and justice; the qualities of a just ruler and of his opposite — the tyrant; and the Christian attitude towards slavery and private property." According to Prof. Mc Ilwain, "St. Augustine's City of God probably had a greater influence on subsequent medieval political thought than any other book written in the early Middle Ages." The City of God was not a kingdom in the heavens but it was a divine kingdom on earth. It was based on Christian virtues and with the 'saved' as its citizens. It was a Christianized Church state from which non-believers were excluded.

The Philosophy of St. Augustine

According to Prof. Sabine, "His philosophy was only in a slight degree systematic but his mind had encompassed almost all the learning of ancient times, and through him, to a very large extent, it was transmitted to the Middle Ages." While elaborating and illustrating the main themes of the City of God, Augustine blended certain basic ideas of Greek and Roman scholars, particularly Plato and Cicero, with the emerging Christian ideas on the essential nature and functions of a political community. Again, according to Sabine, "His writings were a mine of ideas in which later writers, Catholic and Protestant, have dug. His most characteristic idea is the conception of a Christian commonwealth, together with a philosophy of history which presents such a Commonwealth as the culmination of man's spiritual development. Through his authority, this conception became an ineradicable part of Christian thought, extending not only through the Middle Ages but far down into modern times." In Augustine, we find a tendency to depreciate the forms and functions of political authority, and to exalt the spiritual life of the faithful. According to Dunning, "His most comprehensive work, De Civitate Dei, though covering substantially the whole realm of human history, theology and philosophy, has for its central theme the concept of God's elect as constituting a commonwealth of the redeemed in the world to come — a commonwealth of which the Church is a symbol on earth. In developing this idea, he works consciously on Plato's lines and formulates from the political philosophy of that master and of Cicero a system in which the leading dogmas of the Christian faith assume a controlling part."

Augustine's Conception of Two Cities

In the 'De Civitate Dei,' Augustine developed his conception of two cities — the City of God and the City of the Devil, with the aim to explain the downfall of the Roman Empire. According to him, all earthly states were liable to destruction but there was a city that endured, and that eternal city was the City of God where the latest and most perfect terrestrial manifestation was the Christian Church. Augustine extolled the virtues of the City of God by comparing it with Civitas Terrana — the worldly state. Augustine built up his Civitas Dei by mixing together the conceptions of the state of Plato and Cicero and presenting them in a setting of Christian theology. The City of God is universal in time and space. It was founded on the love of God. Civitas Terrana or the worldly state was based on self-love. The City of God was for the promotion of good, and Civitas Terrana pursued evil. The City of God aimed at justice and the City of the worldly state aimed at power. There is some indefiniteness in Augustine's City of God By Civitas Dei, Augustine not only meant heaven, to which the Christians looked forward as their eternal home, but also its earthly counterpart the body of true believers. The Church was thus the concrete embodiment of Civitas Dei because it was in the Church alone that virtue and goodness prevailed. The state was, however, a weapon of the Church for the promotion of good, and so they were both interdependent. Augustine's conception of a true Civitas Dei was a Christianized Church state from which non-believers were excluded. In it the supreme power lay with the leaders of the Church. It was not a kingdom in heaven but a divine kingdom on earth, based on Christian virtues and with the saved as its citizens.

The City of God is based partly on the conception of the Church of Christ and partly on the conception of the universal brotherhood of man advocated by the Hellenistic schools, and by Cicero. Augustine's City of God is meant for everybody, but, unlike Cicero's universal society, does not include everybody. Men can become members of the City of God by grace, and since all men do not deserve grace, all men are not members of the City of God. The real qualification for membership of the City of God is grace, and not race, state or class. The City of God had its origin in the creation of angels, the other Civitas Terrana commenced with the fall of Satan. One was founded on earth by the pious Abel, the other by the impious Caine. One is founded in the hope of heavenly peace and spiritual salvation, the other is founded on earthly, appetitive and possessive impulses of the lower human nature. According to Augustine, all human history is a dramatic story of the struggle between these two cities and, according to him, the ultimate victory must fall to The City of God. It was in this way that he explained the fall of Rome. According to this interpretation, all earthly empires must pass away because they are mortal. According to Bryce, "St. Augustine had unquestionably drawn a new ideal of the kingdom of God on earth, in which the Empire should take its place within the Church, and the Church, through it, should govern the world."

The City of God realizes two important virtues: justice and peace. Justice to Augustine is conformity to order and respect for duties arising from this order. An individual is just if he fulfils these duties. Justice is that virtue which gives to each his own, and it cannot be predicated of the community which takes man himself away from God and gives him to the demons. He denies to non-Christian earthly states all social virtues. Absolute or universal justice is to be found outside the state, in universal order. For Plato, justice lies in the individual and classes conforming to the order of the state, but for Augustine justice is not bound by time and space and therefore, it represents a more absolute conception of justice. Then, peace, according to Augustine, is not mere absence of conflict. It means a positive relationship in concord. Peace is the aim of the earthly state as well as that of The City of God. But the former aims at peace 'as a concord of man in ordered relations with one another, while the latter looks at peace as the most orderly and concordant partnership in the function of God and of one another in God.' According to Augustine, justice could prevail only in a Christian state.

Augustine on the Church

According to Augustine, for man's entry into the eternal kingdom of heaven — The City of God — there must be some visible agency on earth which may lead him in the right direction. Such an agency is the Church. He regards the Church as a part of the heavenly city that 'sojourns on earth and lives by faith.' It lives like a 'captive and stranger in the earthly city.' The Church is for human salvation. It is through this social union of all true believers that the grace of God works in human history. The history of the Church is the march of God in the world. It is through this that mankind can be united. It gave a position of pre-eminence to the Church.

St. Augustine on the State

St. Augustine found the origin of the state in the gregarious instinct of man, and his sin resulting from the Original Sin. To him the state was the result of sin and also represented a divine remedy for sin. The state, though originating in sin, did not represent sin. It was derived from God Himself. But, in spite of its divine origin, the state represented the kingdom of the Devil whereas his own Civitas Dei was the kingdom of Christian — to whom the state was necessary for his Church — Civitas Dei, because the Church wanted property and buildings, rights to which could only be granted by the state. The state conferred rights and could take them back. The state had a divine sanction and so it must be obeyed. The relationship between the Church and the state should be one of mutual assistance and co-operation as the two are necessary for each other. A Christian king needs the spiritual guidance of the Church and the Church cannot function without the law and order which are provided by the state.

Augustine on Property and Slavery

Augustine was of the view that holding of property was legitimate. The property, as an institution is not natural but conventional. The right to it grew from the state. This view, according to Carlyle, "is the opposite of that of Locke, that private property is an institution of natural law, and arises out of labour." On the question of the use of property, Augustine's views are somewhat like those of Aristotle. Augustine justifies private property in order to avoid the danger of violence and confusion, which arises from common possession. But he insists that the institution of private property cannot override the natural right of man to obtain what he needs from the abundance of that which the earth brings forth. It is justice to give to a man that which is his own, and the needy have a moral right to what they require. Augustine also justified slavery as a punishment for human sin. Consequent on Original Sin, slavery was divinely obtained as retribution for sin. But the argument is untenable.

Augustine's Place in the History of Political Thought

St. Augustine is the greatest thinker of the Christian age. With him a new era begins. The Middle Ages actually began with him. Almost all the typical medieval political ideas and institutions owe their origin to Augustine. The theory of two swords of Gelasius I, was based on the dualism of Augustine. The principle of Parallelism in the Middle Ages is based on his distinction between co-ordinate spiritual and secular authorities, each free in its own sphere. The principle of universalism, the keynote of Medieval thought, is based on Augustine's concept of a single Christian commonwealth — a universal Brotherhood. The concept of Papal Supremacy was based on his view that The City of God was superior to the secular state. His view of justice was taken over by St. Thomas Aquinas and many others. According to Niebuhr, "Augustine was, by general consent, the first great realist in Western history. He deserves this distinction because his picture of social reality in his Civitas Dei gives an adequate account of the social factions, tensions, and competitions which we know to be well-nigh universal on every level of the community." St. Augustine was in reality a great thinker, a great theologian, and a great man.

5

St. Thomas Acquinas (1227-1274 A.D.)

The Middle Ages witnessed problems entirely new to politics which of course was beyond the comprehension of either Aristotle or any philosopher of his time. They, centred round the Church and the state to establish the point of supremacy — either spiritual or temporal. No doubt political writings of the period covering half a millennium between the 11th century and the 17th century were born of the controversy between the spiritual power and the temporal authorities. So it is not wrong if said that the Middle Ages were essentially unpolitical.

The reign of Frederick II witnessed an unremitting battle between the Roman Emperor and the Roman pontiff. The failure of the temporal authority in its battle against spiritual authority tended to produce a lot of literature either supporting or opposing any one of the authorities. Among the books written there are two books — one on either side — have the names of lasting renown. The book "On the Government of Princes" by St. Thomas Acquinas defends ably the papal claims while the "De Monarchia" by Dante upholds the cause of the independence and superiority of the temporal authority.

Background of the Defenders

St. Thomas and Dante lived in a ideally unified and symmetrical society-republic Christiana. The final ruler of the Society was God and His Holy will was the final law of the society. The society was therefore governed by two agents of Him. They were the Pope and the Emperor. The Pope was in-charge of exercising his power and exerting his control over the causes of spiritual and the Emperor over temporal. The Pope was the head of the hierarchy of cardinals — bishops and clergy — while the king had the hierarchy of kings nobles and knights. The only problem disturbed the beautifully well-unit and arranged society was the one regarding the relation between the two powers. Were they independent or inter-dependent or co-ordinate or equal? Was the one superior to the other? While approaching these questions St. Thomas and Dante differ and oppose one another because to St. Thomas the papacy was the highest power while Dante upholds that the Emperor had the traditional claim of superiority over the other.

Scholasticism in the Middle Ages

The period (13th century) in which St. Thomas lived saw a great religious and intellectual movement. It was in this period that scholasticism as a system of thought flourishing. Scholasticism "was a system of thought in which philosophy in the pure sense, was so subordinated to the established theological doctrines that where philosophy and theology trod on common ground the latter was received with absolute norm and criterion of truth" (Dunning). So scholasticism which was the logical interpretation of religious dogmas, was bent upon strengthening the religion life and the Church by the intellectual support of the religious faith. The rational element and the theological element which embody the scholasticism were furnished by the philosophy of the Ancient Greeks and Church fathers respectively that were of course transmitted to the Middle Age through the dark ages.

Synthesis of Aristotle and Christianity

The works of the Greek Philosopher were made known to the West through "Latin translation made by Jews from Arabia commentaries on Greek text" at the earlier stage. But the complete works of Aristotle made their entry towards the later half of the 12th century through Spain where their Latin translations had long been in use in the Moorish Universities. A little later the original texts in Greek were brought from the East by the Crusaders. So by the middle of the 13th century the greatest works, which the human reason had produced were in the midst of the philosophers of the period. The reaction of the Church at the earlier stage for the Aristotelian works was not one of encouragement because they bore for the Church "the stigma of infidelity". However, the Church began to learn them. Aristotle stands for the supremacy of reason while the Christianity for the supremacy of faith. Reason and faith, according to St. Thomas are not contradictory but rather complementary to one another, Aristotle is for scientific inquiry whereas Christianity stands for divine revelation. St. Thomas aims at blending the teaching of divine revelation as found in Christianity on the one hand, and the philosophical and scientific inquiry on the other. So the intellectual virtuality of the medieval Christianity rapidly received Aristotelianism and made it "a cornerstone of the Roman Catholic Philosophy" (Sabine). Thus in so short a period that which had been feared as a source of antichristian and capable of opposing Christianity was turned into a permanent system of Christianized philosophy.

Theory of Knowledge

The essence of St. Thomas's philosophy is 'an universal synthesis on all embracing system; the Keystone of which is harmony and consilience. God has the capacity-enough and opulent-enough to afford for all endless diversity. St. Thomas holds that faith is the fulfilment of reason. He speaks of three types of knowledge which he arranges only in an ascending order. They are: (1) scientific knowledge, (2) philosophy, and (3) Christian theology. He places the scientific knowledge at the bottom of them. It consists of that which can be had from sciences like economics, politics, biology, physics etc. Above it he places philosophy which is, according to him a rational discipline that seeks to formulate the universal principles of all sciences. On top of them Christian theology is placed. It is, according to him, the consummation of the whole system. However, he stresses that theology or revelation is in no way contrary or contradictory to reason, although it is above reason. Besides, it is said that theology completes the system whose beginning has been made by science and philosophy. So it never destroys its continuity. Faith is the fulfilment of reason. All these three together build the temple of knowledge and as such they do not at any place conflict with one another or work at cross purposes. This plan of knowledge is in close conformity with the hierarchy reaching 'from God' at its summit down to the 'lowest being' (Read Sabine, A History of Political Theory, p. 218).

St. Thomas has never failed to incorporate Aristotelianism method and content in his discussion of politics proper. He says that man is essentially political, thereby he admits that man is by nature a social being and that social existence makes a government necessary for the common welfare. Of course to Aristotle city state is the self-sufficing and perfect association; but St. Thomas views that a province or kingdom which consists of a number of city states has a higher degree of self-sufficiency because of greater resources. The Province or kingdom, thus introduced into the system of political philosophy, has been considered and treated by St. Thomas as a 'natural organisation.'

Political Authority

Just as Government is traceable on the Aristotelian line to the nature of man, so also political authority is traced to God. St. Paul says "there is no power but of God." St. Thomas cites numerous other texts of the Bible, in addition to St. Paul's.

St. Thomas, in conformity with Aristotle, says that the origin of the state was due to the nature of man, a social being. "Man is naturally a social being and so in the state of innocence he would have led a social life." It is obvious here that an order or organization is a must for social life. So it is upheld that if some surpass others in knowledge and Justice, the superiority in them need be used for the common good of all. "St. Thomas, thus, bases the need for government of man's social nature and the organization of government on the superior wisdom and morality of the rule for the benefit of the ruled" (W. Ebenstein).

So it is clear that society requires an order or organization. It presupposes a ruling authority. This is explained with the help of soul and body or higher nature and lower nature. In other words just as the soul ruling the body or the higher nature ruling the lower one. So also in the society the higher guides and directs the lower. The common good, which is the end or purpose of the authority, is what determines the rights and duties of the higher, the ruler and the lower, the ruled. The human society presents a sort of hierarchy accommodating different classes with assignments to each class with the explicit purpose of expecting their duties due from than for the realization of common good. Thomas compares "the founding and ruling of states, the planning of cities, the building of castles, the establishment of markets and the fostering of education to the providence whereby God creates and rules the world." The ruler, however, is not an authoritarian or a dictator; but he is only a promoter of the good of the community as a whole. Hence, rulership as an office is a trust for the whole community. The ruler's power, therefore, is a ministry or a service owed to the community of which he is the head because his power is derived from God for the happy ordering of human life. The moral purpose of government is, therefore, paramount. Specifically speaking, the function of the earthly ruler is to lay the foundation for heavenly life by maintaining peace and order. Here St. Thomas is firm that heavenly life is beyond the power of the ruler and is in the keeping of priests. The Church knows what is heavenly life for it has the knowledge of revelation. It is, therefore, "not a Church but the Church since it has one head and arbiter." It is in this way that St. Thomas upholds the universal papacy. In addition, he maintains that the spiritual matter is superior to that of temporal, 'the criminal catching order.'

Forms of and Obedience to Authority

St. Thomas like Aristotle follows the classification based on the distinction between those that aim at the good of a few and of one, the ruler alone, while discussing the forms of political authority. The former alone is just and good. However, St. Thomas is also as fluctuating as Aristotle as between the democratic form and monarchic form but ultimately he is seen leaning towards monarchy as Aristotle is towards democracy. In spite of his definite leaning towards monarchy his dislike of tyranny is obvious for he expresses that tyrants ought to be overthrown and it should not be by a private revolt but by the public authorities who could proceed constitutionally. Here the constitutional authority is the Church because the sacerdotalism to St. Thomas, is a higher kind of authority than the imperium. So it is clear that he prefers only an elective monarchy like the Holy Roman Emperor.

Law and Justice

Dunning observes that St. Thomas' Theory of Law and Justice "is the channel through which the doctrines of Aristotle, the Stoics, Cicero, the Roman Imperial Jurists, and St. Augustine blended into a rounded whole were transmitted into modern times." While discussing the theory of Law as defined by St. Thomas Dunning says that law is "an ordinance of reason for the common good, promulgated by him (the sovereign) who has the care of a community." This definition compels us to conclude that (1) law is the product of reason, (2) the command of the sovereign, and (3) has the common good on its base.

Besides, St. Thomas makes a four-fold classification of law. They are: (1) eternal, (2) natural, (3) human, and (4) divine which of course commands Sabine to say as the most characteristic part of St. Thomas philosophy (Read Ibid., p. 221). "The eternal law is the controlling plan of the universe existing in the mind of God." "Natural law is the participation of man, as a rational creature in the eternal law through which he distinguishes between good and evil and seeks his true end." "Human law is the application, by human reason of the precepts of natural law to particular earthly conditions." The Divine Law is "that through which the limitations and imperfection of human reason are supplemented and man is infallible and directed to supermundane end eternal blessedness; it is the law of Revelation."

The first and the last classes of law embody the characteristic conclusion of Christian theology. The Eternal Law, the first of the classification, is the supreme reason of God while the Divine Law, the last of it is the Will of God as revealed in the Testaments — old and new. Dunning, therefore, expresses that St. Thomas' exposition of Eternal Law and Divine Law has been of high significance in the history of theology and philosophy. In Political theory his treatment of Natural Law and Human Law has had important result.

St. Thomas' definition of Law is, no doubt, a stage in the development of the concept of Law. The Greeks regarded Law as the conclusion of reason and not an expression of the Will whereas the Romans considered that it was either a conclusion of reason or an expression of Will. St. Thomas defines it as "an ordinance of reason for the common good promulgated by him (the sovereign) who has the care of community." In addition, he holds that law is rather a rule and measure of action than a command.

Place of St. Thomas in the History of Political Thought

St. Thomas is regarded as "merely Aristotle is rewarmed" by many. But the stateman is fanciful and fantastic grotesque and misleading. St. Thomas, on the other hand, aims at fusing the two great traditions of human thought. They are: (1) idealist, transcendentalist, dogmatic, static and (2) pluralist, empirical, utilitarian, scientific. The one is the theological doctrines of Jesuits and the other is the rational belief of Aristotle. It is in this way that St. Thomas has caused a fusion between the two. It is perhaps because of such a unique position ascribed to St. Thomas. Forster concludes that St. Thomas sets "a Christian coping upon a Greek sub-structure."

6

Dante Alighieri (1265-1321 A.D.)

Introduction

Dante was born in Florence in 1265 in a distinguished family. Having studied in Dominican Schools in Florence under Albert the Great and Thomas Aquinas he gathered wide knowledge of classical and medieval vernacular languages and also considerable knowledge of theology. Because of his opposition to Pope Boniface VIII he was banished from Florence in 1302 where he remained in exile till his death. He was a versatile genius. As a diplomat, soldier, politician, pamphleteer, philologist, theologian and philosopher, Dante achieved grand success. His contribution to the anti-Papal doctrine was great. He laid stress on world order and on the empire as an instrument of peace. His philosophy was the need of the hour. According to Sabine, "Dante's political philosophy was related both to his exile from Florence as a result of factional political quarrels and to the endless dissension between the Papal and the imperial parties in Italy during his lifetime. In this situation he saw no hope for peace except in the unity of the empire, and under the all-embracing authority of the emperor." It is with this object in view that he wrote his famous work De Monarchia in 1311 A.D. In it he visualized a super-state with a universal emperor having many princes, the Pope and emperor as semi-autonomous members. It would bring all conflicts of the princes, people, the Pope and the emperor to an end.

De Monarchia of Dante: The De Monarchia was a scholarly work which Dante wrote in Latin. It was a plea for a universal empire. "In such an empire," writes Maxey, "there would be no place for a papacy exercising secular power, for the emperor would derive his power directly from God without Papal intervention." According to Dunning, "His Latin work, De Monarchia, is in substance a plea for that secular world empire which had had a basis of reality in the days of the Hohenstaufen, but had since become the shadow of a name." Dante's genius gave to his treatise a form however which makes it logically the most complete and perfect system that we have of imperialistic philosophy. The book, though not original, is a fine defence of imperial independence against papal control. While developing this important doctrine. Dante greatly benefited himself by "the Aristotelian metaphysics and politics, Roman and Jewish history and the civil and canon law, as well as the myths and the texts of scripture which were still on every tongue." This important work consists of three books. The first book deals with the question whether monarchy is essential for the well-being of the world; the second book deals with the question whether the Roman people rightfully acquired the monarchic office; and the third book deals with the question whether the monarchic authority is derived immediately from God, or rather from some servant or vicar of God.

Universal Temporal Monarchy: Dante's De Monarchia represents the 13th century imperial opposition to papal supremacy. Dante's primary aim in writing this work was to secure peace and unity of Italy and this aim led him to find out the best form of government. To him, monarchy was the best form of government because peace, a necessary condition to all other virtues, could be maintained only by a monarch. So he advocated an unlimited monarchy as the best form of government. He, however, went a step further and pleaded for a universal monarchy as necessary for the peace of mankind and help the view that a universal monarch, having neither fear nor any further ambition to satiate must rule justly and wisely. His De Monarchia was a strong plea for the restoration of a secular universal empire and for depriving the Pope of all secular authority and power of interference in secular matters. Dante is all out for a single universal society, governed by two divine authorities — the Emperor and the Pope. Both these powers must have their own well-defined and separate jurisdiction, and must not interfere in the affairs of each other. Dante wrote in De Monarchia "There must be one to guide and govern, and the proper title for this office is Monarch or Emperor. And so it is plain that Monarchy or the Empire is necessary for the welfare of the world." Sabine describes Dante's case for the universal empire thus; "Since the special character of man is reason, the end or function of the race is to realize a rational life, and this is possible only if there is universal peace, which is the best of things for human happiness, and a necessary means to the ultimate end of man. Every co-operative enterprise requires direction, and hence every community must have a ruler. In this way Dante proved that the whole race forms one community under a single ruler. The government of this ruler he compared to the government of God over nature. As the latter is perfect because of its unity, so the former, to be perfect, must embrace all men under a single authority. That which has the most reality has the greatest unity, and that which has the greatest unity is best." According to Dante peace among men is an impossibility unless there is the highest judge who is above greed, passions and partiality, who can adjudicate quarrels between kings and princes. Similarly, Freedom is impossible unless there is in the world a power which is altogether above tyranny and oppression. He holds that complete and full justice can be possible only in a world government which is headed by a monarch. Then Dante considers liberty as the greatest of Gods' gifts to human nature and it is through liberty that men become happy here, and gods elsewhere. According to him this liberty can be realized only in a world monarchy. His universal empire, however, did not mean subjection and slavery of other communities; what he advocated was that the different nations of this world having particular feature of their own culture and law, would be regulated by different systems of law and the universal monarch will simply adjust and co-ordinate their relations. It will be a universal state consisting of autonomous communities, each having its own separate existence. It is with the aim to establish world peace. Ebenstein writes on this issue thus, "with all his enthusiasm for a universal state under a monarchical ruler, Dante does not believe in uniformity for its own sake. He recognizes that although a world state would unify mankind with respect to law and government, many ethnic, cultural and linguistic groups and nations would continue to exist, each with its own traditions and needs dictated by history and external circumstances, such as climate. Trifling matters would therefore not be brought to the attention of the monarch of the world state but would be regulated by municipal and national laws, and authorities. Only matters that affect all mankind require a common rule of law, and a common authority. Dante is thus one of the first writers on the problem of world government to separate the issue of political sovereignty, which must be vested in the central organ of world government, from the issue of cultural autonomy which the individual nations and nationalities will fully preserve in a political world community." Dante's monarch was not different from Plato's Philosopher King. Dante was for an enlightened monarch ruling according to justice and law. To such a government Dante gave a divine sanction and origin. Gettell writes on the universal Emperor thus: "Dante's Emperor was not a universal despot, but a sort of international overseer, whose duty it was to decide contentions among the rulers of the various principalities and cities, and to keep the peace among them. National independence and individual freedom were to be maintained as far as possible within the limits of the universal state. Dante believed that a single monarch, having no rival to dread, and no further ambition to satisfy, could have no motive to rule otherwise than justly. His monarch was Plato's heaven-born statesman transferred from the Greek city to the European empire." Dante's universal monarch exercises an authority that knows no frontiers. He has no feeling of greed. He has feelings of love and justice. Such a monarch will always act in accordance with justice. Such a monarch will be a true monarch and such a monarch will have no enemies. Thus, we reach one conclusion that Dante wanted to see unity in the world of beings and this unity he aimed to bring through a universal emperor.

Dante on Superiority and Nobility of the Roman Character: In the second book of De Monarchia, Dante, as the true patriot he was, tried to prove Roman superiority to other peoples with a view to establishing the claim of the Romans to universal Empire. This claim was largely based on the noble ancestry of the Romans, the pre-eminence of their laws, their selfless guardianship of the world, their private virtues and public spirit. It was further substantiated by the decrees of providence giving Roman victories over their enemies. According to Dante, anarchy having followed the decay of the Roman Empire, establishment of perfect peace required the restoration of the universal empire of the Romans. He further proved the universality of the Roman Empire by pointing out that Christ who represented the entire mankind, was within the jurisdiction of the Roman empire. The Roman people acquired their power and authority by the will of God, and since they were the noblest people, they should be set above all others. They always acted strongly and unselfishly and always in the interests of the community. According to Dante, Romans were ordained that they should be revealers, under God, of law and order and justice to mankind. Dante, of course, was not an Italian nationalist. His conception of world monarchy was entirely medieval though, as a true Italian, he thought of Rome as the natural capital of that world monarchy. It is not right to say that he was an imperialist as he advocated world empire. According to Sabine, "Neither by birth nor by breeding was Dante a partisan of the imperial cause. His imperialism was purely an idealization of universal peace."

Dante on Rule of Law: To Dante, it was not the person but the office that mattered. It was not the world empire and not the world emperor that won his reverence and his allegiance. Again, he held the opinion that the world empire existed not for the sake of the world emperor but for the sake of the ruled. He held the view that the emperor, like the Pope, was a servant of servants (servus servorum). To Dante, the empire was "Law personified, Law throned and crowned, and invested with majesty and honour." Dante's universal monarch was not a universal despot. His monarch belonged to a much higher order, whose authority was the very voice of reason. His empire was based on law and service. He exercised his authority not for his own benefit but for the sake of the ruled. According to Pollock, "Dante's monarch is not a universal despot, but a governor of a higher order, set over the princes and rulers of particular states and keeping the peace between them. He is to have the jurisdiction, in modern language, of an international tribunal." However, it is unfortunate that Dante made no provision for the machinery through which such a jurisdiction was to be exercised. Even according to Ebenstein, "Dante stresses the Aristotelian idea that the rule of law is to be preferred to the personal judgement of men, because such judgement is likely to be perverted by personal interests, whereas the monarchical head of a world state would be in the best position to dispense justice in accordance with general rules of law."

Dante on Imperial vs. Papal Authority: In the third book of De Monarchia, Dante tried to prove that the Imperial Roman authority was derived not from the Pope of the Church, but directly from God himself. He admitted also that the Pope also derived his authority directly from God. According to Dante a man was, by nature, worldly as well as spiritual and as such he wanted a temporal as well as spiritual authority to guide him. Both these authorities were represented by the emperor and the Pope and both of them had their authority from God directly. Both the authorities had their distinct spheres of work and must not encroach on each other's jurisdiction. The Pope must not meddle in secular affairs. He should be purely a spiritual head of purely spiritual Church. The emperor was as divine as the Pope. Dante says in his De Monarchia "for man needs a double direction to his two-fold end to wit, the supreme pontiff who leads the human race to eternal life by Revelations; and the Emperor who directs the human race to temporal felicity by the counsels of the secular philosophers." There are two ends of human life — the blessedness of earthly life and the blessedness of heavenly paradise. For the realization of the first, we need the emperor who guides mankind to happiness in this world, in accordance with the teachings of philosophy and reason. For the realization of the second end, we need the Pope to lead mankind to eternal life according to the things revealed in the scriptures. In support of the superiority of the secular authority it was also said by Dante that the Roman emperor possessed power and authority even much before the Church existed. So, history was on the side of the temporal authority. The Church could not be its source. Though Dante wants Caesar to observe reverence to Peter, it does not mean that the Pope possesses a position of superiority. His argument "Render unto Caesar the things that are Caesar's and unto God the things that are God's," clearly separated the Church and the state.

Dante's Place in History: Dante was perhaps the first political philosopher of the Middle Ages who advocated the theories of international government. But his idea of universal monarchy is not in keeping with the theories of international politics. According to Maxey, "Some writers have professed to see in Dante's De Monarchia a forerunner of later-day philosophies of international government; but it is well not to impute too much to the vision of the great Florentine. Certain similarities do exist between the De Monarchia and some contemporary doctrines of internationalism but the evidence of kingship is not too convincing." R.G. Gettell writes about the importance of Dante thus: "While the ideals of his secular world empire and his method of reasoning, and of combining classic philosophy, history, civil and canon law, theological dogmas and mythical analogies were distinctly medieval, he revealed traces of the modern idea that the state should exist for the sake of the individual and that the individual should have a share in its management." Henceforth, political literature emphasized the reasonableness of peace. According to Ebenstein "As an artist and thinker, Dante clearly announces the dawn of the Renaissance." According to Gilson "Separation of philosophy from theology in Dante's thought has had even more far-reaching effects in western intellectual history than his affirmation of the independence of political authority in relation to the Church." Doyle is of the opinion that "He produced a curious hybrid of Christian, Roman and Greek conceptions resulting in the postulation of a world state to meet the peculiar needs of fourteenth century Italy." His call for universal peace through the universal state headed by an emperor is the goal of the human race even today. So far it has remained a dream.

7
Marsiglio of Padua (1270-1343 A.D.)

Introduction

Born sometime between 1270 and 1280 of a notary attached to the University of Padua, Marsiglio, after completing his education in the Paris University, worked as a Rector of the University. He and his friend John of Jandun joined the court of the Emperor Louis IV of Bavaria. When he went to Rome on a pilgrimage, he found to his dismay the total degeneration among the clergy and returned as a great supporter of secularism. He, "the worst heretic" as claimed by Clement VI, died in 1343.

Marsiglio is regarded as the greatest thinker, during his age, after Aristotle. He is the most original thinker of 14th century. He, as a true follower of Aristotle, "tries to use common sense and empirical verification rather than abstract speculation and authoritative dogma" (Ebenstein). The Defensor Pads (The Defender of the Peace) is the important work produced by him. The book is divided into three parts. The first part deals with the general principles of a state in addition to the fundamental principles of political philosophy. The second part is devoted entirely to the attack on the papacy. The third part is intended to give a brief summary of what he has discussed in the first two parts.

Theory of the State

It is true that Marsiglio is regarded as the original thinker of his century. But we can see that he has freely borrowed from Aristotle the base and the points while developing his conception of the state — origin, nature and function. He, like Aristotle, holds the view that the state is the greatest institution a self-sufficing community. It promotes the welfare of man in this world and safeguards it for the world to come. It is a living and developing organism born of common needs.

He, like Aristotle, traces its origin from the family. To him the family is incapable of satisfying all common needs. This is responsible for the birth of the association of families. It is, thus, that Marsiglio feels that the increasing necessity of co-operation in social life to achieve a common end has necessitated the birth of the state.

However, he is aware that all men are not alike in their desires. He says that men's desires differ and perhaps conflict with each other because man is after all by nature "selfish, violent and aggressive." This 'nature' of course leads him to think others as his rivals. This 'perverse will,' as it is called, makes the co-operation inefficient and even impossible. So "repression of the perverse will in man" becomes inevitably "primary business" of the state. All is done for the establishment of peace and security, the prime condition for all progress and prosperity, within the community which, in the opinion of Marsiglio, is the final end of the political society. To quote him "Where peace is, intellectual capacities increase and moral activities improve as human kind multiplies generation by generation." He is concerned with perfect peace, for it, perhaps, tends man to achieve perfection in progress and prosperity. Perfect peace is not an impossible venture, but a possible attainment. It "involves", says Marsiglio, "a perfect adjustment of the means to the ends, a perfect co-operation in which there is neither waste nor friction. Government, therefore, is required not only for the repression of perversity but for the organisation of co-operation (as well)."

While discussing the function of the government, Marsiglio says that the business of the government is to allot proper work to each man and to see him discharging it in such a way that "each may subserve the common ends without involving any wastage of time and labour." The end of the state, is, therefore, as pointed out by Hearnshaw, material prosperity and so essentially socialistic in character.

Law

Then Marsiglio begins discussing the organization of the state. Organization requires a constitution. The conception of law is the prime consideration in this regard. Law, to him, "is an imperative expression of the common need formulated by reason promulgated by recognized authority and sanctioned by force." Again he says that it is "a judgment as to what is just and advantageous to the community."

Who is the legislator of such a law? The legislator, to him, is either the whole community or an effective majority. However, he is conscious that the community as a whole is ineffective in the matter of initiation of legislation. So it delegates its power of law-making to others. Nevertheless, he warns that the people as legislator ought not to be forgotten because a universally accepted law alone is perfectly operative. So the community, by obeying law, proves as law-maker. This means that law is the expression of a common need. This, in fact, takes Marsiglio nearer to Rousseau.

Marsiglio discusses among others two kinds of law — Divine Law and Human Law. "Divine Law is a command of God, without human deliberation, about voluntary acts of human beings to be done or avoided in this world but for the sake of attaining the best end, or some condition desirable for man, in the world to come." So Divine Law is not born of the human deliberation but of the command of Him to indicate what a human being should do to attain the best end in the world to come. "Human Law" to him, "is a command of the whole body of citizens, or of its prevailing part, arising directly from the deliberation of those empowered to make law, about voluntary acts of human beings to be done or avoided in this world, for the sake of attaining the best end, or some condition desirable for man, in this world." While talking of "a command" he wants to enforce it "in this world by a penalty or punishment imposed on the transgressor."

So it is obvious that the Divine Law and the Human Law have provision to impose penalty on those who violate the laws; but the penalty of the Divine Law is not earthly for God is empowered to give punishment on violators in future life whereas the Human Law enshrines earthly punishment on such law-breakers.

Machinery of Government

Marsiglio believes that the legislative and the executive are the important organs of a governmental machinery. The power of legislation vests in the community as a whole. So the whole community is the legislator here. The source of political authority lies either with the whole community or a part of it. The King, to Marsiglio, represents the executive part of the government. He is elected by a community and so a mere instrument of the community. He is expected to "regulate the political and civil acts of man." Marsiglio is, no doubt, aware that the person carrying out such a function is obliged to become despotic and tyrannical for the abuse of the authority is more often a reality. So he imposes some check on the king. He says that the king, in the event of himself abusing the authority conferred on him, should be corrected and if need be, punished by the community or the legislator. Besides, the legislator or the community is empowered even to remove the king by direct action or through its appointed agency. However, Marsiglio cautions that punishment ought not to be too far; it should, on the other hand, be in proportion to the gravity of offence committed. It should be strictly in accordance with law of the land if in existence; if not, it may be at the discretion of the community or the legislator.

So the king is after all a servant and creative of the people (McIlwain), although he is entrusted with enormous power but handicapped with limitation. His provision of imposing limitations on the power of the king commands us to say that he is "almost the first writer who has clearly in mind...a modern limited monarch...." (McIlwain).

Here, it is worth mentioning the clear separation of legislative and executive functions in his state. This of course makes the king, a mere administrator, and the community the supreme legislative body. He has done that not whimsically but having the welfare of the society in mind. Promotion of the welfare of the society is the object of the government. Education in his opinion is the most important agency promoting such a welfare. So while pleading for an elaborate and effective system of education, he advises that education ought to be a main concern of the government. In addition, the government should regulate the economic life of the people and see to it that no great disparity in the wealth of the people need exist, because it is this disparity which will generate jealousy which will, in turn, no doubt, destroy the very harmony of the community and disturb the peaceful order of the society.

Church

Marsiglio who got dismayed over the behaviour of the clergy at Rome, became a secularist to the extent that he was dubbed as a "heretic." But he is not irreligious; but a secularist. He wants the principle of popular sovereignty and representative system to be adopted in the organization of the Church. The Church, to him, is "the body of the faithful believing in and calling upon the name of Christ." Again, he says that Church is the Christian Commonwealth. The body of the citizens is the source of authority in the Commonwealth. He speaks of the constitution of the General Council of the Church consisting of the secular and ecclesiastical delegates. Following the principle of the popular sovereignty, he says that the Council should be the final authority. The Pope is to be elected by the Council and as such he is to be held responsible to the Council. So he says that the Council and not the Pope is the final authority. Since the Pope is elected and assigned to power by the Council, he contends that the authority of the Pope is derivative and human, but not divine as popularly believed. The Church governed by the Council is, thus, a corporate body empowered to depose the Pope in the event of his misbehaviour. The Council in his opinion, has the right to interpret the scriptures, ex-communicate the offenders, and such other things connected with the Church, in addition to controlling the Church officials from the Pope downwards. Thus, says Sabine, Marsiglio "transfers to the Church an element of his political theory, assuming that the whole body of Christian believers, like the whole body of the citizens in a state, is a corporation and that the General Council like the political executive, is its delegate."

Although the General Council consisting of the secular and ecclesiastical delegates from the territorial division of

Christendom, shall have the right to interpret the scriptures and to impose its decision on all in general and on the priests in particular, he contends that the General Council shall be the dependent on secular government because it needs the help of the state to enforce its decisions.

Marsiglio condemns the world-mindedness of the Pope. Since he feels that the possession of property leads to worldly pleasures he says that the Church, the spiritual body should be forbidden to own property. The Church, on the other hand, should be wedded to the life of primitive penury and poverty. The concept of 'Daridara Narayana' spoken by the Mahatma is worth remembering here.

Again he says that the Pope should be confined to the performance of the spiritual functions such as teaching of the scriptures and administration of the sacraments. Nevertheless, he desires the exclusive right to be given to the secular authorities in the matter of the enforcement of the punishment and admonition.

At the same time, he says that no punishment should be inflicted on any for the offence against the Law of God by any authority on earth. Here he brings out an argument which runs as follows: the priest is the "healer of souls." He, like a physician, diagnosing the ill of the body, finds out the ills of the souls. If such a physician declares a man a leper, it does not mean that the physician can expel the ailing man from the community. Similarly he cannot compel the ailing man to observe the health rules; but simply he can warn him of disease and death if he fails to observe the rules. So also, the priests the "physician of souls" can warn the individuals of the punishment in the world to come while the latter practising those things affecting "the eternal health of the soul." The priest is forbidden to expel any from the Christian community; "but it is the work of the body of the citizens or their deputy." The methodical argument by Marsiglio to make every agency in the world to do its work without meddling with the Divine Law and its enforcement is convincing and as such it places the Church as dependent organ of the state or department.

On Secularism

Marsiglio lived during the time that the authority of the Pope was unquestionable and unchallengeable. The argument in vogue, in support of the supremacy of the Church, could not so easily be combated in the battlefield of reason. However, the wide knowledge he had gained stood by the philosopher to establish his secularistic ideas as against conventional ideas and practices in defence of the papal supremacy. His arguments, therefore, constitute as a source of medieval secularism blossoming against the papal authorities when the people realised the atrocities perpetrated by the clergy — all in the name of religion and God. He says that the Church could never be an independent organ subordinated to the state only. He even advocates that the civil government alone is to be empowered "to regulate the number of Churches and temples, priests and ministers." He is of the view that the bishops either collectively or individually should be forbidden to grant licence to any for the public teaching or practice of any art and discipline because it is the right of civil government only. In this connection, he brings out the practice of Christ and says that Christ himself did have "no ambition for secular rule." He is very particular that the clergy should not be permitted to be above secular laws. But they all should be treated only as ordinary citizens for anything contrary would cause a division.

His interest in favour of the state-dependent Church is such that he goes to the extent of calling the Bishop of Rome called "Pope," as the disturber of the peace of Christendom. He is vehement in saying that the power of the Pope is not born of divine sanction but only conferred on him by man. So it may be and should be destroyed by man and until it is destroyed there can be no peace (McIlwain).

Conclusion

Although Marsiglio was born in the medieval period yet his thinking is all applicable to the modern period and so he is a modern thinker in many respects. His contribution to the modern world among other things is the concept of secularism by his methodical argument to separate Church from state and to make the former a dependent of the latter. He is an advocate of the representative government and the sovereignty of the people which of course are in line with many modern thinkers. His strong advocacy of the removal of economic inequality and the regulation of the several walks of the life of the community by the state paved the way for the birth of the recent theories of welfare state. Though he has drawn inspiration from the philosopher of the ancient period, yet his contribution to political thought and philosophy is no doubt modern and applicable to the modern period.

8
William Ockham

William of Ockham is the last secularist in the Medieval period, who fought against papal supremacy. He was an English Franciscan and a colleague of Marsiglio of Padua in the University of Paris. Along with Marsiglio, he was also ex-communicated by the Pope for his attack on the papal authorities, for his support of secular independence, and his defence of the doctrine of apostolic poverty. He also took refuge in the court of the German Emperor Lewis. He was more conservative and moderate in his attitude towards the papacy than Marsiglio. Unlike Marsiglio he exercised a considerable influence over his own generation. He was a scholastic theologian, influenced greatly by Aristotelian philosophy. He always presented both sides of a case in the true scholastic fashion and then gave his own suggestion instead of making dogmatic statements. He did not oppose reason and faith in his profuse writings as Marsiglio had done.

His political ideas bear a great similarity to that of Marsiglio. He was more of a dialectician than a philosopher. Hence, there is nothing of systematic political philosophy in his writings. But he developed certain ideas which became the centre of violent controversy for the years to come in the political as well as ecclesiastical spheres. According to Ockham, the state and the Church were useful institutions in their respective fields. He gave a little higher position to Church, which was, to him, like the soul and the state was like the body. The central point in his thought was that every kind of authority, secular or ecclesiastical, must be limited to the purpose for which it has been created and it should be used for the common welfare based on reason. If any wielder of authority outstripped its limit, it could be justifiably deposed. Marsiglio had placed final authority in the hands of the citizens in the state and the general body of Christians in the Church. But Ockham did not think that general people had the ability to control the Emperor and the Pope in their respective spheres. He, therefore, suggested that both the Pope and the Emperor must be bound by the law of nature. He believed that a universal empire in secular and ecclesiastical side was an impossibility.

William of Ockham was greatly disturbed by the exaggerated claims and aggressive intrusion of Pope John XXII in secular affairs. He emphatically declared that the Pope had no right to interfere in secular matters, but his authority was confined to spiritual affairs. In his own words, the Pope could have only those powers, which "could safely and prudently be committed to one man for the sake of the common utility, in regard to all things necessary to the governing of the community in relation to good morals and the spiritual needs of believers." He did not give any coercive power to the Pope and the priests. He believed that all human institutions, including the Pope and the priests were fallible. Therefore, he saw no reason in universal supremacy of the Pope. The whole body of Christians was superior to the Pope. So he could not exceed what was necessary for attaining the end, viz., the common welfare of Christians. Christ had not delegated absolute power in spiritual and temporal affairs to Peter as the head of the faithful. The limits imposed by Christ on the powers of the Pope were that the latter could not deprive men and princes of their goods, rights and liberties. Moreover, the Pope could not command against the Gospel. Hence, resistance was quite justified if he try to exceed his powers.

Ockham would not give to the Pope even the right to interpretation of the Gospel, which was to be exercised by the wisest men known for their piety and integrity in the service of the Church. Thus, he placed great limitations on the power of the Pope, although he considered him the monarchical head of the Church, who could secure the eternal salvation of human souls. According to him, the papal jurisdiction was one of service and not of power. The whole power of the Church vested in the General Council of the Church organized on the federal basis. He suggested that the Christians living in a parish should choose their representatives of the electoral college of the kingdom, who in turn would elect the members of the General Council. It would contain the representatives of both the clergy and the laity, and even the women. He considered such a body to be most truly representative of the whole body of Christians. Ockham would not give to the Pope even the power of convening and presiding over this council. This General Council would have the power of interpreting the scripture, passing a sentence of ex-communication, settling matters of dispute and deposing a Pope who acts in a tyrannical manner.

William of Ockham hated the clerical greed for wealth. He believed that the temporal possessions of the Church made her secular-minded. Therefore, he suggested that the property of Church should be treated at par with any other secular property by the state. It should not be exempted from the taxation and appropriation by the state. Similarly, he advocated that the clergy should be punished like the laity for the violation of the secular laws. He said that both the state and the Church should respect each other's rights.

Ockham did not only plead for the independence of the secular authorities from the control of the Pope, but he placed similar limitations on the powers of the Emperor also, as he had advocated for the Pope. He said that the Emperor should make his rule just and useful to the people and conform to the revealed will of God, natural reason and equity and to the international law. The authority of the Emperor was to be exercised within the framework of law. He opposed the arbitrary power of the Emperor in the same way as he had detested that of the Pope. Whatever the sphere, the transgression of limits imposed by the end or purpose for the sake of which power was entrusted to man galled him and therefore be wanted to place checks upon both the papal and imperial authority alike. Like Marsiglio, he would vest the ultimate power in the hands of the people.

By the time of Ockham, the controversy between the Church and the state came to an end, but the new problem of constitutional versus despotic rule within the Church cropped up. The Conciliar Movement was an attempt to solve this problem. This movement found the source of inspiration in the writings of Marsiglio and William of Ockham.

9
Conciliar Movement

Introduction

The controversy over the absolute power of the papacy was already in the air and the questioning of claims to absolute power by the Pope had become the subject of a vast and popular debate. In this connection, before we take up the study of the nature, causes and failure of the Conciliar Movement, it will not be out of place to know something about the contribution of Wycliff and John Huss in this connection.

Wycliff was one of the best representatives of the political movement of the later Middle Ages. Wycliff, a popular religious teacher and a reformer, was one of the last important writers who denounced papal claim to supremacy.

He wrote a number of essays to refute those who held that the Pope was overlord of England. His best known essays are De Dominio, De Civile Dominio and De Officio Regis. His most important idea is his theory of 'Dominion of Grace.'

According to it, all dominion is founded upon the will of God, and Dominion means power or lordship. It is of three kinds: Divine, Natural and Civil or Political. God is the creator and master of the whole world and therefore all power belongs to Him. God delegates power to the righteous men, who are under his Grace. Those who hold power, must be righteous, otherwise they would not get their salvation. Those who seek salvation must exercise their power in the service of others. For power and service were indissolubly connected with each other. This doctrine is built on the omnipotence of God. God is not only our absolute but our immediate Lord too. He exercises His Lordship directly. The Church had, therefore no mediating power between God and man. A man can find his salvation only by his direct relationship with God. The priests and other men were, therefore, at the same level. All men were equal in the eyes of God.

According to the doctrine of Grace, a man retained his dominion or power only so long as he retained his grace with God. Natural dominion was one exercised by men before the fall. All men exercised this dominion. It was a joint dominion of all overall and everything. Human sin made civil or political dominion or overlordship necessary. God, as the creator of the Earth, gave His Lordship of the Earth to righteous men and the righteous men are lords and possessors of all men and things. It is only the righteous and not sinner who can exercise lordship and hold property. Power is granted by Him not to one person, the Pope, but to all. The king is as truly God's vicar as the Pope. The secular power is as sacred as the ecclesiastical and as complete over secular things as that of the Church over spiritual things. Thus, we find this doctrine pleading for individualism.

By establishing a direct relationship between God and man, this doctrine made superfluous any meditating priesthood, on which conception the medieval Church was built. Then Wycliff embarked upon a series of Church reforms. Their temporalities came to be subjected to the crown and he wanted the Church to go back to its original poverty. He advised the Pope to surrender all temporal authority to the civil power. He agreed that both the power were supreme in their own fields. He denied papal supremacy as both the powers had divine sanction. He declared the Bible to be the sole standard of religious belief. The papal assumption of secular power was sinful. A bad Pope must not be obeyed and had priests also must not be obeyed. Wycliff gave definitely a position of superiority to the state. For him, the welfare of the individual both in the Church and the state, was of primary importance.

Wycliff had communistic ideas on property. The man who was in the state of Grace owned everything. As everything worked for his good. This precludes any private ownership of property. A sinner had no right to property. All good Christians had equal right to it. His ideas on property influenced the English peasantry and were responsible indirectly for the peasant's revolt. The Church must have no property as all evils flowed from the possession of wealth. He favoured an aristocratic form of government consisting of a body of wise men in a state of Grace with God. His second practical choice was monarchy. It was the most beneficial of all forms of government, he felt and was strong to check evil doers. According to him, theocracy was the worst form of government.

On the continent of Europe, John Huss, Rector of the University of Prague in Bohemia was greatly influenced by the ideas of Wycliff. Huss was also anti-Papalist. The Hussite Movement in Bohemia was an attempt to pull down the already collapsing barriers between the seculars and the ecclesiastics. He also held the view that the Church must be deprived of its property as it was not necessary for it. It could be deprived of it by the secular authority if it abused it.

Like Wycliff, Huss also believed that the real Church was the whole body of believers. He even said that papacy was not essential for the Church and it had no divine sanction. Huss also exalted the state at the expense of the Church. In central Europe, the Hussite Movement was very successful. His teachings, along with teachings of Wycliff, made the Reformation possible by insisting on the purification of the Church, accepting no other authority excepting the scriptures to decide religious questions, and translating the Bible from Latin into native dialects. On the political side, they exalted the state and brought down the papacy by asserting that the kings had the right to deprive the Church of its property and the papacy had no right to interfere in political affairs. Their efforts were responsible for bringing about the Conciliar Movement and did service to democracy by insisting on the sovereignty of God and equality of man.

The Conciliar Movement

Its Meaning and Nature. The history of political thought during the period of the Conciliar Movement i.e., in the first half of the 15th century, represents its last important medieval phase. The audacious claims of the Pope for absolute power were being questioned.

According to Sabine, "The luxury of the Papal court and the venality of Papal government became the ground of bitter criticism, as they continued to be down to the Reformation. The Great Schism, which lasted from 1378 to 1417, made matters worse; it would be hard to exaggerate its effects on popular thought everywhere in Europe. The spectacle of two, and sometimes three, rival Popes, often no more than appendages to dynastic and national ambitions, using all the arts of theological invective and political chicanery against each other, must have gone far to destroy the respect in which the Papal office had traditionally been held. Moreover, the whole ecclesiastical organization became infected with corruptions and abuses, partly the result of the Schism itself, which tended to bring the clergy generally into disrepute." The discrediting of the papacy, aided powerfully by the writings of the secularists, particularly Wycliff and Huss, resulted in a universal demand for the purification of the Church by means of the General Church Council.

According to McIlwain, "The essential point in the contention of the reformers was their assertion of the competence of a universal council of the Church to adjudicate a disputed claim to papal authority, with its important corollary that the jurisdiction of this council is higher than that of any Pope."

The Conciliar Movement was mainly the creation of a group of scholars connected with the University of Paris. It was a sort of revolt against the papal absolutism in the Church. Prof. Doyle described it "as a reaction against the riches, desire for high office, simony and personal laxity which debauched the morals of the clergy. It represented a struggle between two opposite systems of government, constitutionalism versus autocracy."

The immediate cause of the Conciliar Movement was the 'Babylonian Captivity.' From 1309 to 1376 the Popes lived at Avignon in France under the influence of the French monarchs. This captivity came to an end in 1376 when Pope Gregory XI returned from Avignon to Rome. The French party in the college of cardinals withdrew from Rome and elected a French Pope who took the name of Clement VII. On this move, "devout men were now shocked by the unseemly conflict which followed between two men, each claiming to be the vicar of Christ and rightful head of the universal Church, while the adhesion of the European states to one or the other of them was dictated by motives purely political and worldly, and wholly selfish and the spiritual mission of the Church seemed to be utterly ignored."

Neither of the two Popes was prepared to give up his claim. So, in 1409, a council was convened at Pisa by the cardinals of the Church to decide the dispute. The council deposed both the Popes and elected Alexander V as the new Pope. So now there came to be three Popes, each claiming exclusive jurisdiction over all of the Christian world for which he was accountable to God alone. This led to the great Schism in the Church leading to the lowering of the power and prestige of the papacy. Writings of Wycliff and Huss further discredited the Church. As a result, there grew a great demand for the purification of the Church by means of the General Church Council. It was a kind of revolt and this revolt has been given the name of the Conciliar Movement.

The Aims and Objectives. The main aims and objectives of the Conciliar Movement were the purification of Church of all the evils which had crept into it, and the creation and establishment of a new form of government in the Church in place of the absolute and autocratic government of the Pope. For the achievement of these aims, a number of meetings of the General Council of the Church were held. The Council of Pisa met in 1409, the Councils of Constance met in 1414, the Council of Pavia met in 1423 and finally, the Council of Basel met in 1431. The Councils of Constance and basic were, however, very important. The Council of Constance decreed in 1415 that "A General Councils constituting and representing the Catholic Church has authority immediately from Christ which everyone in existence of whatever in status or dignity, even papal, is bound to obey in those things which pertain to the faith, the extirpation of the said Schism and the reform of the Church in head and in members." This decree of the Council was, indeed, a very revolutionary decree in the history of the Church. In 1417, the Council passed another important decree whose provisions included the summoning of General Church Councils at regular intervals of the ten years to follow up and to guarantee the independence of those councils, from papal control. In 1439, these decrees were reaffirmed by the

Council of Basle. Anyhow, according to Sabine, "the effort of the Council of Constance and Basel to draw up a workable plan of constitutional government failed completely and from the point of view of practical politics, the movement seems, at least after the event, to somewhat academic. The Conciliarists could pass resolutions but they could not make a government. After the bridging of the Schism the project of reforming the Church by a General Council, though it could still be talked about even as late as the sixteenth and seventeenth centuries, was definitely not within the region of practical politics. The importance of the Conciliar Movement in political thought lay in the fact that it was the first great debate of constitutionalism against absolutism, and it prepared and spread ideas which were used in later struggles." The main principles of the Conciliarists had already been stated by the opponents of the papacy from time to time, beginning from John of Paris to William Ockham. It was that the Church, being a complete and self-sufficing society, must have all the powers needed to insure its continuance, its orderly government and the removal of abuses as they occur from time to time. As result of it, it becomes imperative that the spiritual power with which it is endowed must be vested in the Church itself, in the whole body of the faithful as a corporate body, and the clergy, including the Pope, are simply the ministers or organs by which the society acts. Prof. Sabine quotes Zabarella on this question as thus: "Therefore, when it is said that the Pope has sovereign power, this should be understood not of the Pope by himself but as he is in the whole body, so that the power is in the whole body as its foundation, and in the Pope as its chief minister, by whom the power is exercised." Thus, it is the whole body which speaks and acts through its organs. The right of a council or other representative body depends upon the fact that it stands in the place of the community and speaks for it.

Leaders of the Conciliar Movement: The noteworthy leaders of the Movement were John Gerson (1363-1429), Cardinal Nicholas of Cusa and Aeneas Sylvius.

(a) John Gerson (1363-1429): John Gerson was one of the most important personalities in the intellectual and religious life of the later Middle Ages. He was born in a peasant family in the French village of Gerson. He received his education in the University of Paris and also studied theology under Pierre d'Ailly. Siding with his tutor he became an active figure of the Conciliar Movement. His writings exercised tremendous influence in eliciting general European support for the movement.

In the Council of Constance he held an eminent position. In this thinking he was greatly influenced by the teachings of Marsiglio of Padua; in his writings he developed the idea of communal sovereignty. Gerson advocated a mixed form of government containing monarchic, aristocratic and democratic elements, both for the Church and the state.

As regards the papacy as a Church government, his attitude was one of the cautions. On the one hand, he totally rejected the extreme claims of papal supremacy, on the other, he repudiated Marsiglio's theory that held that sovereignty in the Church lay in the whole body of believers. He was opposed to both papal absolutism as well as extreme democracy in the Church. He held the Church as the hierarchy of the clergy and assigned sovereignty in the Church to a general Church Council. For him, the Pope was merely an administrative agent of the Church whose authority might be defied in the general interest of the Church.

According to him, the Church as a body was superior to the Pope and it could even depose him acting through its representative body, the General Church Council. The Pope was merely the administrator and not the maker of the law, and as such could not amend or suspend it.

Similarly, he held that the authority of the king might be defied in the general interest of the state. Gerson even went to the extent of allowing a temporal ruler to convene a General Church Council to sit in judgment upon a Pope and depose him if he had disobeyed natural or divine laws. Thus, we find that the utilitarian doctrine of necessity influenced his theory to a very large extent and he justified resistance to Pope and the king when general welfare demanded it. His ideas, put forth in the decrees of the Council of Constance, were helpful in spreading the doctrine of constitutional government throughout Europe and paved the way for later reformers.

According to Gettell, "he aimed to preserve the rights of the Pope and King, within definite limits, and at the same time secure the liberties of the people." He was in favour of a limited monarchy as the best form of government for the state as well as the Church. His ideas of communal sovereignty and representative government paved the way later on for the adoption of representative government both in the Church and the state.

(b) Nicholas of Cusa: Nicholas was another important personality of the Conciliar Movement. His most important work, De Concordantla Catholica, which was presented to the Council of Basel in 1433 was the greatest of the 15th century political writings, and one of the most interesting.

According to Dr. Figgis, "It is almost the last book which treats Christendom as a single organic system, in which a complete theory of politics, whole and parts, is set forth."

The work is known mainly for two of his theories, the theory of harmony or unity, and the theory of popular consent, as the basis of government. His work gives the best exposition of the Conciliar Movement. We take up his theory in detail here.

"The keynote of the work" writes Sabine "is harmony, rather than authority, and it leaves the question in doubt whether ultimate power is vested in the Pope or in the Council."

To Nicholas and his other contemporaries, peace and unity in the Church were the crying need of the day. In his theory of harmony, Nicholas explains the substantial unity of all phenomena material and spiritual. According to him, the universe is conceived as an organism in which every element has its vital role to play. As in God's universe so in human affairs each element of the scheme of providence works in harmony for the perfect end of the whole. The Church and the empire are the two great institutions in which human affairs are organized, and each of these embodies a series of parts whose relations to the whole are one and the same. For maintaining perfect unity and harmony in the scheme of human affairs, it is essential that both the state and the Church should perform their respective functions. So, Nicholas tries to find out some principle of harmony which may unite the secular with the spiritual authority. He does so by asserting that power comes from God ultimately but it comes from the people immediately. This is how he entered the element of consent in medieval politics.

Nicholas regards consent of the Christian community as the source of all papal authority. The Church was regarded by Nicholas as greater than any individual, including the Pope. According to him, Christ was the real head of the Church and He manifested himself through the Council. As such the council was superior to the Pope. The Pope was simply an agent of Christ and he, as agent, did not possess all the powers of his master. The Pope, as man, was capable of sin and hence he was fallible.

According to Nicholas, 'the judgment of a single fallible man was likely to contain less of truth than that of a General Council which reflected the whole wisdom of the Church.' The Pope was simply the executive head of the Church and was subject to the control of the General Council of the Church which could even depose him for abusing his authority. It was only the General Council which could speak on matters of faith.

Nicholas advocated the decentralisation of authority in the Church. He stood for delegation of papal authority to the provincial councils according to a 'new grouping coinciding with national boundaries. Nicholas was of the opinion that reform of the moral world can be better accomplished by the local authorities than by a central authority which might bring a rigid type of uniformity. He called upon secular rulers to summon national councils of lay and clerical representatives to consider the question of reforms. However, he was against interference on the part of secular rulers in purely religious matters. Then, Nicholas applied this system of representative government to the empire also. His aim was to see representative government in every form of society. He proposed the division of the empire into twelve circles for the proper administration of justice. The emperor must consult a permanent council. He advocated grant of considerable authority to the emperor in relation to the Church, for the Emperor must maintain order and defined the faith against the encroachments of external and internal heresies. The emperor was of course, not to interfere in the internal affairs of the Church. The Church and the state were to function as separate organizations. The net conclusion of Nicholas' teaching is that he gave to the representative council the most important position both in the Church and the state. He assigned sovereignty in community.

The officers of the Church and the state were mere agents of the people. The ruling authority in the state, or in the Church, was there merely by the consent of the people and was bound by the people as much as by the laws.

According to him man himself came from God and so human laws based on popular consent were divine. Gettell summarizes the views of Nicholas beautifully thus: "He conceived the universe as an organism or harmony of closely inter-related parts."

Similarly, the Church and the state were composed of various organs each having definite functions; and the same principles could be applied to both the ecclesiastical and political organizations. He considered a representative council to be the central organ in both the Church and the state, and he found the source of its authority in the consent of the whole body. Holding that all men are by nature free and equal he found the source of law and of authority in the people. Kings and bishops were chosen as administrators of popular rule, and they, with the people formed the natural organization or corporation of society. Nicholas taught that rulers hold their position by the choice of their subjects, and that they, like their subjects, are bound by law. Law, based upon the consent of all, is ultimately divine, since man himself comes originally from God.

(c) Aeneas Sylvius (1405-64): Sylvius expounded doctrines which were more or less like those of Nicholas. According to him, men were originally free and equal, living in an isolated state of nature. But realizing the benefits of social life man began to form social and political organizations. For getting out of anarchy men came together and appointed the strongest and best of them as their ruler. Thus arose monarchy. The king was the creature of the people and he could be deposed by them.

Similar arguments were put forward by Sylvius in the case of the Pope too who could also be deposed by the believers, or by their representative council. Thus, we find in the writings of Nicholas and Sylvius the concepts of the state of nature of natural rights and of social contract that became familiar in the revolutionary theory of the 17th and 18th centuries.

Causes of the Failure of the Movement. There were a number of causes responsible for the failure of the movement.

It failed either to reform the Church fully or change its form of government.

The leaders of the movement were trying to do an impossible task. They were trying to lay down a constitution for a Church which would embrace the whole of Europe. It was impossible to draw up such a constitution in the absence of international amity and goodwill.

The meetings of the councils were marked by national feelings.

According to Sabine, "the effort of the Councils of Constance and Basel to draw up a workable plan of constitutional government failed completely and from the point of view of practical politics, the movement seems, at least after the event, to be somewhat academic. The Conciliarists could pass resolutions but they could not make a government. After the bridging of the Schism the project of reforming the Church by the General Council, though it could still be talked about even as late as the sixteenth and seventeenth centuries, was definitely not within the region of practical politics.

The immediate task which the Movement wanted to achieve was the removal of the Schism in the Church. After its removal, the leaders of the Movement could not put forth any inspiring ideal before the people. As such, the leaders of the Movement could not go further than merely passing resolutions.

Moreover, England and France the two main participants in the Movement, became busy in finding solutions to their various national problems.

Added to this was the fact that the medieval mind was essentially conservative, dominated by faith, orthodoxy, fanaticism and other worldliness.

To such a mind, the Conciliar Movement could not make an appeal. The Movement remained confined to the universities.

The Movement also lacked eminent personalities as its adherents.

It was followed by strong papal reaction which resulted ultimately in the triumph of absolutism, both in the Church and the state over constitutionalism.

Significance of the Movement. According to Prof. Doyle, "The Conciliar experiment destroyed for some centuries the belief in the power of the people to control effectively their own political institutions. The ideal of democracy as formulated by Cusanus was discredited. The only alternative was absolute monarchy." He further stated "the failure of the Conciliar Movement left Europe disintegrated into a congeries of separate independent states with only a nominal leader and ready to embark inevitably on the conflict of their several sovereignties, characteristic of modern international politics."

According to Sabine, "the importance of the Conciliar Movement in political thought lay in the fact that it was the first great debate of constitutionalism against absolutism, and it prepared and spread ideas which were used in the later struggles."

He further writes that "the controversy in the Church first drew the lines upon which the issue between absolute and constitutional government was drawn, and it spread the type of political philosophy by which, in the main, absolutism was to be contested. Both the divine right of the sovereign, and the sovereign power of the community were transferred to the field of secular government."

The Conciliar period brought out the idea that political and social institutions originated historically in the deliberate and rationally planned action of men.

In general, it contained ideas if sovereignty, the popular basis of government natural law and rights and the social contract which, under the impulse of changed conditions in objective life, was to characterize the modern age.

The movement resulted in the development of national Churches.

It helped in the growth of national feelings.

The Movement was democratic, federal and national in spirit.

It gave the idea of power as a trust which must not be misused.

It also held that the consent of the governed was the essence of government. This is no insignificant contribution.

10
Niccolo Machiavelli (1469-1527 A.D.)

Introduction

Niccolo Machiavelli, a political philosopher of the Renaissance was born in 1469 of a Florentine lawyer of a mediocre economic status. When he in the prime of his youth, Florence was in the hands of Savonarola. The sudden and miserable end of Savonarola owing to lack of military prowess, caused a great impress on him. He could not but recollect the achievements of "armed prophets" like Cyrus, Theseus, Romulus etc., while thinking of an "unarmed one" like Savonarola, his interest in politics earned for him a place of importance when he was appointed as Diccidella Guerra — a Council of Ten for War — at his 29th age. When Florence was suppressed by the armies of the Holy League in 1512 at the command of Julius II on the score of Florence's refusal to join in expelling the French from Italy, Machiavelli lost the post and was soon exiled from Florence. His stay in the country-side enabled him to produce his most important works. His famous work 'The Prince' was written by him in 1513. It devotes only to practical side. 'The Discourses' which he completed in the same period advocates republics and liberalism. So it is clear that the study of the two works is a must to get a complete picture of Machiavelli.

Condition of Italian Society at the Time of Machiavelli

Although religious preachers were preaching the Christian ethics to be followed, yet self-interest was the policy practised by the religious preacher. It is true that the Italian Society then was a byword for intellectual attainment; but political corruption and moral aggrandizement were eroding the society. Injustice and faithlessness, truthlessness and selfishness, debauchery and cruelty were the ordinary things of the day and as such men in the society proved that they all were "the worst of all animals." The blossoming of the Renaissance and the Reformation, the twin events of Europe of the time paved the way for the ascendancy of the temporal power over the spiritual heads and as such the medieval institutions were obliged to accommodate the spirit of the period and forced to undergo a change in accordance with the same spirit. A definite swing in favour of absolute monarchy even at the expense of the 'Sacerdotum' was seen all over Europe except Italy, which in the opinion of Machiavelli was divided into the states of Venice, Florence, Naples, Milan and the Papal states and fought with one another in utter disregard to the need of the time. So Machiavelli thought of uniting Italy under the strong power of an absolute monarch.

Machiavelli on Forms of Government. Machiavelli's classification of the forms of government is rather unsystematic in a thinker of his calibre. His classification of the forms of government follows the same old Aristotelian classification of governments into monarchy, aristocracy and constitutional democracy with their perversions tyranny, oligarchy and democracy. He agrees with Polybius and Cicero that a mixed type of constitution with proper checks and balances is the best and most suitable constitution for a state. But he has not discussed it in details. He has mainly dwelt on the characteristics and relative advantages of monarchies and republics. But the balance he thought of was economic or social, but not political. He believed in economic determinism and observed a close connection between wealth and political power. Behind all struggle for political liberty, there was always an economic interest. By inclination he was more republican than a monarchist. To him a republican form of government was not only the most suitable but the only form of government for a political community where there was a general economic equality. A republic can maintain its institutions and adapt itself to changing environment and circumstances better than a sentimental prince. It is more enduring and admits more liberty than a monarchical form. A republican system led to more uniform and universal material prosperity and ensured greater equality of opportunity than other forms of government. People collectively show better qualities of prudence and judgment and can select offices of a better type than a prince who is subject to court influences. An aristocracy, particularly a landed aristocracy, led to quarrels and civil disorder. He, however, was not totally for either the republican form or for a monarchy. His chief concern was for efficiency in the state. He recognised that different forms of government suited different times and places. Though by conviction he was a republican, he knew that in the Italy of his day an elective monarchy was the one best suited. The need of the hour then was deliverance from the foreigners — German, French and Spanish — and for this purpose a wise and strong prince was better suited than a republic. He was not very particular on the form of government. He believed in the cyclical character of the forms of government. Dunning sums up Machiavelli's preference for the republican form thus: "A high degree of appreciation for the Commonwealth based on the mass of equal citizens, is a distinguishing feature of Machiavelli's philosophy. But he fully recognizes that circumstances require different forms of organization at different times and in different places."

The Prince and The Discourses of Machiavelli. The two works of principal importance for political theory are The Discourses on the first decade of Titus Livius, and The Prince. The Discourses are a free commentary upon the history of the Roman Republic in which Machiavelli draws lessons and lays down maxims for the guidance of his own time. The Discourses in which he praises the Swiss and German institutions makes out a remarkable case for the republican form of government as the best. The expansion of the republic is the theme of The Discourses. In this work he devotes a full chapter to expose the hollowness of the common saying that money forms the sinews of war. According to him it is not money but good soldiers who are in reality the essence of strength. Money will not always procure good soldiers, but good soldiers will always procure money. The Discourses are a fine appreciation of a republican form of government. In this work he gives a guideline for maintaining and preserving a republic.

But, in the circumstances and conditions then prevailing, he advocated an elected monarchy as the only form of government which could bring unity and prosperity to Italy. The case for this form of government was well-presented by him in The Prince.

The Prince "was a product of personal and national tragedy created, however, in a spirit of hope." The language of the book is not as modern as many of its sentiments. According to Bull, "It was written by a man of strong will and complex passions and the writing faithfully mirrors the exciting thoughts of an imaginative intelligence." The Prince consists of twenty-six chapters which lend themselves to three divisions. Division I presents a general introduction and discusses various forms of absolute government. Division II denounces the then existing system of mercenary troops and pleads for the establishment of a national army. Division III contains the substance of his philosophy. It gives a number of rules for the guidance of the prince, especially the new prince. This work is not an academic treatise and a book on political science. It is 'real-politik.' It is a kind of grammar of the art of government and of political success prepared by the ex-secretary of Florence. In it Machiavelli deals with the mechanics of government. It is pragmatic in character and gives the technique of successful rulership. The whole argument in the book is based on two premises, one, that the state is the highest form of human association and the most important instrument for the promotion of human welfare. It holds that it is by merging himself in the state that an individual maintains the state and finds his fulfilment. The second premise is that the material self is the most potent of forces in individual and public action. The art of government, therefore, lies in the intelligent pursuit by the ruler of his self-interest regardless of ethical considerations. These premises lead to the conclusion that it was Caesar personifying the State, and not God, which was the deity to be worshipped. Things which brought power were the only virtues that mattered. To him what mattered were success and power only. Cunning, deceit, ruthlessness, energy, boldness, shrewdness and strong will were required for achieving the objective. The book is a thorough guide for acquisition, maintenance and preservation of dominions. Like a good physician Machiavelli made a good diagnosis of the ills of his country and suggested the medicine — short range and long range — for getting rid of those ills. This grammar of government can be compared with the Arthashastra of Kautilya. Critics of Machiavelli have dubbed this book as something inspired by the Devil. The book was received with indifference in the beginning but it made its way slowly. According to Maxey, in the book, "A more brutally frank, direct, and simple discussion of the problems of managing a state could not be imagined. The dumbest head that ever wore a crown could readily grasp every word of it. No fine spun theories, no obtuse speculations, no complex doctrines find room in its twenty-six brief chapters, but only tried and practical rules derived from experience, rules amply tested in the laboratory of everyday affairs." Machiavelli's Prince was thus a practical guide to statecraft rather than a general theory of politics and many rulers beginning from his days to our own have followed its precepts. According to Ebenstein, "His Prince is destined to remain one of the half-dozen political writings that have entered the general body of world literature." It is a book "which still arouses men's passions and around which controversy still rages. Its meaning, its purpose, even the date of its composition and whether it was first composed without its traditional dedication and last chapter, are still matters, on which no final, unchallenged judgment has been given."

End justifies means — Politics an end itself

Machiavelli does not confine his thoughts to political theory. He, like Kautilya, is concerned with the mechanics of government, the means to enable the state strong and expand in power and the possible mistakes leading to the decay and destructions of the state. While discussing them he appears to have been concerned with the contemporary Italy and Italy only as he does not seem to have taken pains to think whether or not the possible means, as advocated by him, to attain the position of a strong power were in order. But he is more concerned than anything else with the ways to enable a person to realize, somehow, his will in the state and with the maintenance of what the person has achieved. So he is dominated by the political needs and the means to attain political supremacy even at the cost of moral religious and social bindings. It is such a consideration which compels Machiavelli to assert that "right and wrong have nothing to do with government." Here again he says that his Prince should be capable of using "both the beast and the man" to his advantage and as such he advocates success as the sole aim of the Prince for the same success alone ensures "power, unity and stability" to him. So to him end justifies means. He explains this maxim thus: "A Prince... who desires to maintain himself must learn to be not always good, but to be so or not as necessity may arise.... For all things considered, it will be found that some things that seem like virtue will lead you to ruin if you follow them; whilst others that apparently are vices, result in your safety and well-being." While giving room for even wrong deeds of utterances if necessary, he advises his "prince who wishes to hold his own to know to do wrong and to make use of it or not according to necessity." So it is clear that Machiavelli wants his Prince to be shrewd, systematic, diplomatic; no matter he is good or bad but he should have an eye on his success only not minding the moral religious or ethical sanction attached to his whatever actions. The prince's action is measured in terms of his success in obtaining, preserving and increasing his power. It is thus that he makes it clear that politics is an end itself.

From this it is easy to draw a conclusion that the Prince need not keep up faith for the sake of faith; but he should if it pays him. Besides, Machiavelli advises his Prince to be merciful, faithful, humane, religious and upright; but at the same time he warns his Prince to be so balanced to the extent that he should know how to change himself and his behaviour if contrary to those qualities prove to be advantageous to him. So the Prince is always ready to change his mind and attitude towards men and matters in accordance with the exigence of time so that he can always remain in power. However, he warns his Prince not to make anyone understand that he is against any one of the qualities mentioned even while he behaves in opposition to them. So the Prince must be 'a vulpine beneath veneer.'

His advocacy of end justifies means divorces politics from ethics and religion. This is of course a sacrilege; any encouragement of which no doubt produces unprincipled and immoral persons of high order whose affluent existence indeed will end the state of orders essential for the maintenance and continuance of state. So Machiavelli wrote the 'Discourses' perhaps during the same time when 'The Prince' was written. Before criticising Machiavelli it should well be understood the circumstances in which his country was. The most disorderly condition rampant there warranted a strong power capable of controlling and suppressing the disturbing elements and forces. Besides, he has drawn such a conclusion on the premises that the human nature is selfish. He frequently expresses that "men are in general bad and that the wiser ruler will construct his policies on this assumptions." In defence of this view it is said that the social scientists and psychologists maintain that "certain instincts, urges and passions in man" are not possible to eradicate at any time; and so they say that human nature remains the same for the last two thousand years. This view in turn, is brought under criticism on two grounds: (1) It is totally baseless to assume that human nature is fixed and immutable. The view is repugnant to "rational approach to the problems of the social, economic and political reconstruction," (2) It is impossible to bring out to light clearly the nature that goads an individual to be a power-monger and the nature that keeps an individual under domination, selfishness, envy, rage etc. But as spiritualists claim that when once an individual is aware of such a nature as attributed by Machiavelli to human nature, he will endeavour to "transmute and sublimate it into something good."

Machiavelli — Irreligious

Can we say that Machiavelli is immoral and irreligious when he gives room only for political virtues in the place of moral and religious virtues? To answer this question we must go through his 'Discourses' also. He gives importance to religion by discussing it under a separate title in his 'Discourses.' The title speaks of the necessity of religion for the continuance of a state and of the ruin of Italy when it "failed in this respect through the conduct of the Church of Rome." He remarks, while discussing the part played by religion for the continuance of a state, that the "Princes and republics," interested in maintaining "themselves free from corruption" should "preserve the purity of all religious observances...for there is no greater indication of ruin of a country than to see religion condemned." He is aware of the danger for the state if the people are guided only by the fear of the temporal punishments alone. But at the same time he is against the evil effects of Christianity as practised. Since it gives much attention to heaven and it makes men feeble "by preaching the famine virtues." So it is clear that although Machiavelli accepts the Christian theology, yet he denounces its moral codes such as non-resistance, love of peace and denunciation of war. It is because of this that Machiavelli advocates to adopt whatever course — justice or injustice, mercy or cruelty, praise or ignominy — that "will save the nations existence and liberty." Again it is because of this that Machiavelli exonerates Alexander VI when he indulged in cheating and Romulus when he killed his brother. Such a cheating and such a murder are "honourable frauds" and "glorious crimes" to Machiavelli.

Politics devoid of religion is deathtrap to persons like Gandhiji; but Machiavelli is emphatic in saying that morality and religion are simply rather the handmaid of politics. This view might look defective for moralists and religious personalities. But ordinary persons cannot but uphold the view for they are mindful of the unity, stability and continuance of their governments and they are interested in the enjoyment of worldly pleasures like fame, glory, position etc., Machiavelli is an ordinary person mindful of the worldly gains in relation to his own country. Italy was unfortunately politically divided and as such it had lost its original glory. So his main aim was to place his country on the highest pedestrian of glory and fame even, if need be, at the cost of morality and religion. Nevertheless he does not like to throw away religion into; he, in fact, recognizes the significance of it and at the same time he never hesitates to advocate to throw away ethics or religion if it stands on the way of the state becoming strong and stronger than before.

He is, therefore, concerned with power — political power. He deplores the attitude of moralists saying "right will prevail," or "the triumph of evil is short-lived," for it does a great harm to a state tending to become politically powerful. He is aware that power depends upon opinion which in turn relies on propaganda. Greater the propaganda greater the virtue. It is perhaps because of this that success goes "to the side which has the most of what the general public considers to be virtue." A careful analysis of events taking place in the medieval and modern period in all parts of the world, of course, supports Machiavelli in this regard. So Machiavelli is not immoral; nor is he irreligious; but he is moral and secularly religious.

Machiavelli – a Believer of Republic and Supporter of Princedom

Because Machiavelli talks of the subordination of everything including religion and ethics to politics, can we say that he is an ardent believer and supporter of princedom? We can get an answer for it from his "Discourses." To him princedom is an unfree state whereas republic is a free state and he says that republic is superior to princedom because of its inherent nature and advantages. The people are by far superior in electing their magistrates than princes. The people can hardly be influenced to elect a man of corrupt character and habit for the post of dignity whereas a prince can succumb to such an influence. Similarly the people are bestowed with the quality of making laws, forming civil institutions, maintaining the institutions established better than a prince. Besides, he says that the people are less guilty and as such their errors are less important than those of the prince. His glorification of the people is understood from his expression that "the voice of the people is the voice of God."

While discussing the necessity of princedom he brings out a comparison of a living organic body with the state. A state is composed of a certain structure of organization just as an organic body is composed of organism "by a similar structure of among its parts." The structure of the state, in turn, consists of class and institutions intended to govern the people. Here the philosopher brings out a difference in the nature of laws in a free state and an unfree state.

The people in a free state spontaneously adhere to the laws of the state whereas coercion will have to be used to compel people to follow laws in an unfree state. He compares the unfree state to an unhealthy body which needs the compulsion of a doctor to its functioning. Similarly the free state is like a healthy body which is proper in functioning without subjecting to medical care. Nevertheless he prefers princedom because he feels that people are corrupt and selfish and have scarcely the respect for laws of the land. Under such a circumstance a superior power "with a royal hand and with full and absolute powers" is needed to curb and correct the corrupt and selfish people. If people in general are good and live for the fulfilment of virtue than he says that "a republic (free state) is definitely far superior to an unfree state." So it is clear that he believes in republics but advocates princedom because of the inherent weakness of the people in general.

Machiavelli's Place in the History of Political Thought. Machiavelli's influence on modern political thought has been tremendous. His greatest contribution was that he brought political theory into line with political practice. He is a political scientist concerned with the means and not ends or ideals. He followed the empirical method of observation and experience and his political philosophy was realistic, mirroring the conditions of the moment. His doctrine of aggrandizement speaks of realism. He is the first exponent of power politics and the first modern totalitarian thinker. He was the first to make a distinction between standards of public and private morality. For him, security of the state and its unity and prosperity were everything and they had to be protected by the prince even at the expense of his soul.

Machiavelli was an excellent epitome of his time. About his place in history, Jones writes "In his cool, calculating cynicism, his frank and undisguised naturalism, his extreme individualism, his pragmatism, his devotion to classical antiquity, in his rejection of religion and of supernatural sanctions in favour of 'here and now' philosophy, and a hedonistic morality — in all these things he is characteristic of the Renaissance and, to a very considerable extent, of the modern mind...Machiavelli more than any other individual, and despite the fact that he is hardly a political theorist, is the father of modern political theory. He makes the first decisive break with the thought of the Catholic

Middle Ages on political problems. For Machiavelli, the state is a natural entity. It rises out of, and exists in the midst of, a play of natural forces, which the ruler must understand and make use of if he and his state are to survive in the ruthless competition which is living. Here, Machiavelli lays the foundation for Marx and those later theorists who reduce politics to the study of power-conflicts and their control." His conviction that the state can be understood only in terms of human lusts and appetites and his recognition that the successful ruler must learn to control these forces, mark an epoch in political thinking and form the basis for the development of modern thought. It is he who laid down the foundations of the nation-state, with an all powerful central authority, which is supreme over all institutions and individuals. According to Catlin, "The role and importance which he ascribed to the new prince, the insistence on a national militia and on the military aspect of government, the whole science which he developed for the preservation and increase of the reputation of the prince, really represented in him a great practical wisdom." He was definitely a sincere and ardent patriot and one of the fore-bearers of modern nationalism. It is not wrong to say that nationalism had its birth in him. He saved political thought from the scholastic obscurantism of the Middle Ages. For him ends such as justice, law, good life and freedom had no meaning. He was indeed the first, if not the noblest, of the great pragmatists. The only end sought was attainment of political power and its expansion. He separated power from morality, ethics, religion and metaphysics. For him, religious institutions were simply the instruments in the hands of politicians for giving sentimental support in order to maintain the stability and authority of the state. He was the first exponent of power-politics. Economic determinism was a most important feature of his thought. He laid stress on the idea of economic interest as a crucial factor in the power process. According to Maxey, "At the back of all struggles for liberty, self-government and the rights of men, there always lurks, in his opinion, some sort of economic interest in the outcome." His philosophy had enchanted Jones so much that he declared "We may not like the world as it is; but we cannot improve it by closing our eyes to its deficiencies. Neville Chamberlain, for instance, would have learned a great deal about Hitler (and hence about how to deal with him) by studying Machiavelli; and if President Wilson had pondered The Prince, the disaster of Versailles might never had occurred." His concept of the state as a sovereign, unitary, secular national, and an isolated state provided life-blood to the present-day concept of sovereignty as internally supreme and externally independent. He was one of those rare beings who can view human behaviour as objectively as the zoologist does the behaviour of animals. He may be called the apostle of modern nationalism.

Criticism of Machiavelli: There is no dearth of writers who have condemned Machiavelli and his philosophy. Because of his being anti-clerical and anti-religion he has been given the name of devil incarnate. Dr. Murray calls him clear-sighted but not far-sighted. For stating 'what is morally wrong can never be politically right' has condemned the entire range of political ideas of Machiavelli. Prof. Jaszi describes him as the propounder of an immoral and untrue doctrine. He writes, "By the passionate and enthusiastic glorification of political crime he must bear the responsibility of having made from the diffused crimes of isolated princely criminals, a compact of philosophical doctrine which corrupted public opinion in many parts of the world and which envenomed still more an unscrupulous political practice." The greatest weakness of his political philosophy is his total acceptance of absolute realism. He ignores the force of ideas and ideals which can move earth and heaven. The practice of his philosophy has not always met with success. Prof. Sabine calls him "an utter cynic, an impassioned patriot, an ardent nationalist, a political Jesuit, a convinced democrat and unscrupulous seeker after the favour of despots." His philosophy was both narrowly local and narrowly dated. The truth is that he misrepresented completely the state of European thought at the beginning of the sixteenth century. While seeing human nature, he saw only half of it. Man is neither all good nor all evil. The modern conception of a state has long made it a moral person, capable of right and wrong, just as are the individuals composing it. His philosophy is superficial and his writings are a type of diplomatic literature. His theory that ends justify the means is not a correct or sound theory. Political crime can never lead to anything but counter-offence, still graver crimes and ultimate disaster. His theory is actually immoral. According to Allen, "His judgment of human nature was, surely, profoundly at fault. May it not be said that he lacked understanding of just what he most of all needed to know." He was not a logical thinker. He exaggerated the role of the ruler or the law-giver in moulding the moral, religious and economic factors in such a way that they are invariably to the advantage of the state. His view that force alone could hold society together was absolutely wrong. It is the gregarious instinct that keeps society together.

Man is after all a creature of circumstances. So Machiavelli, a man who lived in the troublesome and decadent days of Italy and who lived to see only the ruins of Italy which was once a seat of learning, art, architecture and other activities connected with human civilization. So he was pained to see the sorry state of affairs. Hence, his recommendation to a strong power. Besides, he lived in that society which was replete with corruption and nepotism, bribery and knavery at all levels — political, social and religious. Hence, his pessimism with regard to the nature of human beings. It is this pessimism which compelled him to say like Hobbes that the people are selfish, corrupt and immoral although they are expected to be selfless, corruptless and moral. It is this thought that goaded him to place the responsibility of ruling the people in the hands of a superior power-king. However, he does not want his Prince-king to be reckless and power-mongering alone. He says that his prince should stand for national unity and welfare, in addition to encouraging all that are needed for the prosperity of the people. So he is not against morality, nor is he opposed to religion. Machiavelli is best understood not when a nation is in peace but only in troubles. So it is not wrong if we say that Machiavelli is a true friend of such nations whose stability is disturbed, whose unity is blown out and whose prosperity is marred.

11
Political Theory of the Reformation

The Reformation marks the beginning of a new period in the history of political thought in Europe during the 16th century.

Politically, Reformation represents the modern version of the medieval quarrel between the empire and the papacy. Political theory in the 16th century was greatly influenced by the Reformation. Though primarily clerical the movement also had ethical and political significance. The opposition of the reformers to the sale of indulgence brought about a reunion of morality and theology. While opposing the supremacy of papal authority, the reformers found the princes as their great allies as they were anxious to save themselves from papal exploitation.

The movement naturally increased the power and position of the princes. The reformers also helped the princes against the disorderly elements within the state by preaching the gospel of passive obedience. They joined hands with the princes against dangerous sects like the Baptists, or against dangerous feudal movements like the knights' war or the peasants' war. This type of alliance led to the growth of absolute monarchy. The union between religion and politics which had been broken by Machiavelli, was restored once again. The Reformation was also marked by the reunion of religion and ethics.

The Reformation, called as Protestant Reformation, was a purely religious movement started by Luther for ecclesiastical reforms and theological interpretations. It may be regarded as a continuation the Conciliar Movement. The Movement was of great political significance. It resulted in the transference to the state of a good ideal of jurisdiction and authority which in the Middle Ages belonged to, and were exercised by the Church.

1. Martin Luther (1483-1546). "It was natural" writes Gettell, "that the Reformation which was a revolt against clerical usurpation in favour of a more inward and spiritual worship, should begin in Germany, where the Teutonic love of personal independence and a contemplative and mystical attitude of mind were most pronounced. While most of Europe was interested in the new geographical discoveries, and in the quest for wealth and empire, a German monk started a theological controversy which followed out relentlessly the logic of the Humanists, applied successfully the methods attempted by Wycliff and Huss, and finally split Europe into rival religious camps, with far-reaching results on political and international issues." This German monk was Martin Luther who was born in 1483 at Thuringia. He was endowed with a deeply religious temperament and was never one to compromise with evil. In 1507, he was ordained a priest and was appointed Professor of Theology at the University of Wittenburg. He was sent to Rome in 1511.

Luther's visit to Rome was the turning point in his life; he got convinced that the papacy was the incarnation of anti-Christ, was morally undesirable, and must, therefore, be reformed. A little later he witnessed something which shocked him.

Tetzel came to Wittenburg and preached the gospel that the sins of an individual could be absolved and washed off, and his entry into heaven assured on payment of certain sums of money to the Church. At this, Luther was very much perturbed. After making thorough study of the history of the Church, he reached the conclusion that there was no historical foundation for the claim of the Roman Pope and started preaching with vehemence against the dogma of papal supremacy. His theories and theses represented a challenge to Rome. The Church refused to reform itself and also refused to answer Luther who appealed to the holy Roman empire. The empire because of political necessity, stood by the papacy. Luther, on the other hand, appealed to the German nobility and princes whose leader, John Frederick of Saxony befriended him.

His political ideas are found chiefly in Liberty of a Christian Man, Letter to the German Nobility of Secular Authority, How far is Obedience Due It, and his Table Talk.

According to Gettell, "The chief contributions of Martin Luther to political thought were the clear distinction he made between political and spiritual authority; the emphasis he laid upon the secular as against the ecclesiastical power, and the importance he placed upon passive obedience to the established order in state and society."

He made three important contributions. First, he created a definite and clear distinction between spiritual and secular authority; second, he exalted the national territorial state as against any extra-territorial organization, lay or clerical, the holy Roman empire or the papacy; third, he inculcated the Christian duty of passive obedience to be established social and political order.

His stress on the equality of all Christians as Christians was the revolutionary nature, and his doctrine of the priesthood of all Christians contained immense possibilities that were fully exploited later in England, Scotland, Holland, Switzerland and North America. Luther's protest was an exaltation of the individual.

On this, Doyle writes thus: "His protest implied that the neglect of those in authority might be remedied by the action of individuals. He suggested that the individual had the right, if not the duty, to inquire why those in authority were failing in their duty, that he had the power to decide what the Church ought or ought not to do, that he could, by the light of his own conscience discriminate between what was the law of God and what was not. The individual was bound to obey what he perceived unaided to be God's law, despite threats of persecutions from the Church."

According to Maxey, "only two doctrines of any political importance appear in his voluminous writings. One is his unequivocal insistence upon the genetic differentiation of secular and spiritual occupations and authorities, and the other is his equally positive demand that all good Christians submit to the established system of government."

A detailed study of Luther's political ideas follows:

(i) Luther's Erastrianism: In his letter to the Christian nobility of the German nation, Luther appealed passionately to the

German national sentiment against the papacy for its illegitimate assumption of power and universal interference. His suggested twenty-seven points for reform include the abolition of nearly all jurisdiction and revenue of the Pope outside the Roman Church. According to Luther whatever affects 'money, estate or any material interest' is within the exclusive jurisdiction of the secular authorities. He held that the Pope and the clerical hierarchy are mere officers of the Church and so they are not entitled to any special privileges at the hands of the secular authorities. Thus, in a way, Luther destroyed to a considerable extent the power and prestige of the papacy which, in the absence of any rival clerical organization, were appropriated by the state. To be brief, it can be said that Lutherism led to Erastrianism. Because of his anti-papacy views he was ex-communicated by the Church, and he finally broke away from it.

(ii) Lutherism Leading to Royal Absolutism: The influence of Luther was definitely on the side of the lay authorities of the territorial state. Luther not only weakened the papacy, he also defied and demoralized the Holy Roman Empire. Lutherism went against the spirit of federalism. One of the effects of the teachings of Luther was the consolidation of the state within, and denial of any authority without the state. This naturally led to the development of the theory of the Divine Right of Kings. The state did not exist by the grace of the Church, but had an inherent right to exist. It was as divine in origin as the Church and was responsible to God alone. The doctrine of the Divine Right of Kings was in origin directed towards the independence of the state from powers of the prince as against his own subjects. Luther's exaltation of the state strengthened the absolutist tendency, which was the main feature of the 16th and 17th centuries. The civil power to Luther was essentially holy.

According to Figgis, "Luther is as much the spiritual ancestor of the high theory of the state, as the Jesuits and their allies are of the narrower, utilitarian theory."

The feudal idea of a community of communities was replaced by the modern conception of centralized sovereign states.

Gettell writes, "He viewed the state as sacred. Its ruler was responsible to God alone. By applying these doctrine in practical politics the reformation substituted once for all in men's minds the authority of the state for the authority of the Church. The supremacy of the law of the land over every one within its borders, including the clergy, now triumphed universally. By transferring the idea of non-resistance from the imperial to the royal and princely authorities, and from the ecclesiastical to the political systems, Luther gave to the doctrine of the Divine Right of Kings enduring prevalence. To Luther, the state was essentially holy. Accordingly, he paved the way for the exalted theory of the state held by Hegel and by recent German theorists."

According to Luther, secular authority was sanctioned by God. So all Christians must obey it as it was ordained by Him. Non-Christians must also obey because they have not the guidance of the Holy Spirit and need the iron hand of authority to keep them in peace and order. It was however, the excesses committed by the fanatical sects and a lot of bloodshed by the various revolts which made him support the secular authority in putting down heresies with a strong hand and thus pave the way for absolutism.

(iii) Luther's Theory of Passive Obedience to the Godly Prince: Luther preached the doctrine of passive obedience to the godly prince. In his Of Secular Authority: How far is obedience Due to it, Luther held that secular power was sanctioned by God and was necessary because a great majority of men were non-Christian and were outside the sphere of the Holy Spirit and must, therefore, be guided by the secular sword. Christians also must submit to the secular government with the aim of setting an inspiring example to non-Christians. Luther was against any right of overt resistance to the state for both the divine and civic laws were against such a resistance. But passive obedience was not due in case of tyranny. Of course he wanted the civil authorities to set limits of religious toleration and allowed them to use force when that limit was crossed by those who held religious beliefs subversive of civil order. Luther had no respect for persona; his respect was for the office. He had no confidence in the masses. He stated, "The princes of this world are gods, the common people are Satan, through whom God sometimes does what, at other times he does directly through Satan, that is, makes rebellion as a punishment for the people's sins. I would rather suffer a prince doing wrong than a people doing right." His assertion of the need for passive obedience was very strong. He said "It is in no wise proper for anyone who would be a Christian to set himself up against his government whether it acts justly or unjustly. There are no better works than to obey and serve all those who are set over us as superiors. For this reason also disobedience is greater sin than murder, unchastity, theft, and dishonesty, and all that these may include." But, in this respect, Luther was not very consistent. His political opinions were shaped largely by circumstances. Resistance to civil authority in all circumstances was considered by him morally wrong. As a result of this doctrine, religion gained in spirituality but the state gained in power.

(iv) Luther's Inconsistency: Luther is one of the most inconsistent and vague thinkers in the whole series of political thinkers. On the one hand, he is against interference on the part of princes in ecclesiastical matters, on the other he allows them to set a limit to religious toleration and punish those who hold subversive religious doctrines. On the one side, he stands for the extension of the doctrine of freedom of conscience, on the other, he virtually allows the princes to determine the religious principles of their subjects. His advocacy of freedom of conscience and subordination of the individual to the prince cannot be reconciled. His attitude towards peasants' revolts was quite contrary to his political principles. As he relied on the support of the princes he had to prove to them that there was nothing in his doctrines which were subversive of existing social and political order. Luther had no faith in the essential equality of men. He stood for civil inequality.

2. Philip Melanchthon (1497-1560). According to Maxey, "The political philosopher of reformation, in so far as any one deserves that title, was a scholarly professor of Greek in the University of Wittenburg. Philip Melanchthon, a faithful disciple of Luther, he was intellectually both his superior and, in many aspects, his opposite. Melanchthon was a deep student of the classics especially of Aristotle, and in his hands the intellectual case of the reformation takes on a more pleasing and a more rational aspect." This great scholar was born in 1497 and died in the year 1560. He was deeply imbued with the humanistic spirit.

Unlike Luther, he admired the ethics and politics of Aristotle in spite of the fact that Aristotle was the philosopher of medieval theologists too. He tried to construct a general system of moral political philosophy of universal validity and for this he, like Luther, took his stand on the scriptures.

According to Gettell, "he represented the influence of the liberal, humanistic spirit, and was interested in classical learning. His chief contribution to be political thought of the period was the emphasis he laid upon the law of nature, thus giving to the Protestant world the same criterion for judging government and law that had been applied by earlier pagan and Catholic writers."

As regards Melanchthon's political ideas, he held that the political system is based on the concepts of natural law and natural right. According to him, natural law included certain principles implanted in the human mind as direct revelations of God's will, and certain principles resulting from the nature of man himself. So, whatever institutions and laws could be deduced from either of these sources were considered natural and right. The state was justified as representing God's will, revealed in scriptural texts and, as a result of man's social nature. So, the state was considered by him divine in nature and was given large powers. He believed that it was the duty of the state to promote true religion, prohibit false worship and put down heresies. He justified the confiscation of Church property saying that the state had the right to take property that was misused by its owner. He supported slavery and had no sympathy with the peasant revolt. Like Luther, he was also opposed to the monastic ideal as being incompatible with the unity and equality of believers in a Christian Commonwealth.

He denied all coercive authority to ecclesiastical rule, arguing that the power to make laws did not belong to the spiritual sword. According to him, true communal life was that of the state, and he made the Church distinctly subordinate to the political power. He rejected the theory of universal empire and said that the world should be organized into separate independent states.

Like Luther, Melanchthon also did not bother much about the form of government. Any form of government that did not go against the law of nature, was good. But he rejected the idea of universal rule of the Pope and the Holy Roman Emperor. He claimed a divine origin for kingship and put forward the doctrine that the subjects of divinely established monarchs, must show full passive obedience to their rulers. Even impious or tyrannical rulers were not to be resisted. Thus, in the beginning he was all out for the monarchical form of government, later on he became an admirer of the aristocratic governmental organizations operating in the free imperial cities of his day. He denied any kind of coercive authority to the Church and made it totally subordinate to the state.

He was for total loyalty of the subjects to the state. All other loyalties had to give way. This idea of total loyalty finds support in the Roman law which lays down that without the will of the state no corporation has any right to exist. Thus, both spiritual and secular matters became the concern of the civil government. The Church was reduced to the position of an agency of the state under its supervision and control. Dunning is right when he described the functions of the secular authorities as laid down by Melanchthon thus, "The functions of the secular authorities include the protection of property, safeguarding of liberty, the maintenance of order, punishment of criminal offenders, and the promotion and preservation of true morality and religion among the people." But neither property nor liberty, are however, absolute rights. Property may be confiscated if the owner misuses it and liberty may be abridged in order to preserve the status quo.

3. Zwingli. This Swiss reformer made no special contribution to political philosophy. His importance is more in his methods than in his doctrines. He exercised a good deal of influence on the secular policy of his canton. Zurich, where he succeeded in introducing his reformed religion through the agency of the established secular machinery.

According to Dunning, "at the outset he does not seem to have contemplated the assumption of ecclesiastical functions by the state, his theory as to the distinction in kind between spiritual and secular institutions and authority was not essentially different from that of Luther."

He regarded the Church as the invisible communion of the saints. But regulations necessary for the proper institution of worship and discipline were the main functions of the secular authorities. The state to him was an external agency to regulate spiritual life. Zwinglism, "blended state and Church in a single organization. The community (gemtinde) determined for itself, through its constituted authorities, the form and manner of its spiritual life as well as the rules which should control its mere physical existence." Zwingli was neither a good theologian nor a scholarly philosopher. He was essentially a politician who was greatly influenced by the democratic tendency in Switzerland of his day. A democratic state imbued with the social spirit of primitive Christianity was his political ideal.

4. John Calvin (1509-1564). John Calvin was born in 1509 in a Catholic family of Picardy in France, and died in 1564. He got converted to Protestantism in 1533 as a consequence of which he had to leave his country. After wandering over many places he came ultimately to Geneva where he lived till his death, excepting a break for a brief period. A gifted administrator as he was, he grew steadily in importance and, in later years of his life, became a virtual dictator of the city of Geneva. From Calvin came the most dynamic political thought of the Reformation.

According to Catlin, "if Luther is the Danton of the Reformation, Calvin is its Robestpierre. He represents Augustinianism in theology carried to its final and crucial limit. The logic of this Frenchman, was adopted Geneva as his home, had a clarity such as the German Luther never attained."

It was Calvin who gave form and coherence to the Lutheran doctrines.

Dunning writes, "While Luther was the theologian, Melanchthon the philosopher, and Zwingli the politician, Calvin was distinctly the law-giver of the Reformation."

Gettell calls him the greatest of the reformers from the point of view of his contribution to political thought.

According to Gettell, "he aimed to give a complete and harmonious exposition of the Christian faith based upon a legal conception of order and authority. He tried to bring thought and will, his own life and the lives of other, Church and state, in subjection to law. The Mosaic code exerted a strong influence on Calvin's conception of a well-ordered Commonwealth, both in its general theocratic character and in the details of its provisions."

In his institutes of the Christian religion, he tried to give complete guidance to what was necessary to live a good Christian life according to the injunctions of the Bible. He dreaded revolutionary social doctrines and individual interpretations of the scriptures. His interpretation of the scriptures was based on the sound principles of order and authority. He tried to bring in subordination of thought, action, Church and the state to law. There is no doubt that Calvin was the most important leader of the Reformation from the point of view of political philosophy. His book was written to justify Protestantism and really the French Protestants around it, in reply to an attack on Protestantism by Francis I in 1535. In this book, Calvin asserted very clearly that the Church and the state were two entirely different organizations. The Church should have a system of government and discipline suited to itself and distinct from that of the secular state. The Church organization must have a body or assembly of elders to prescribe rules of proper conduct. It must have the power to ex-communicate the unbeliever, but no severer penalty. It must have the power to exclude the state from clerical affairs and to exclude from its own organization everything of a mere secular character. This book, according to Maxey, "was designed as a complete guide to the soul that sought to live according to God's word; and it furnished, indeed, a much safer resort, in many respects, that the Bible itself."

(i) Origin and Functions of Civil Government: Calvin's conception of the state is based on two fundamental ideas: the Sovereignty of God and the Fall of Man. According to him men are evil, nine out of ten being damned. A secular government is, therefore, necessary for preserving order. It is as essential as the Church or other necessities of life. Calvin held that "the authority of a magistrate is the most sacred and honourable of all things pertaining to mere moral life." The Civil government has two main functions to perform, to preserve order and protect life, liberty and property, and to guard truth and exclude idolatry and blasphemy from society. Every Christian had the moral duty to help the state in the performance of these functions. As regards the form of government, Calvin had no special preference. All are good at their own times. However, Calvin gave some preference to the rule of the aristocracy. Then the primary duty of the secular ruler is the care of the religion because religion represents the soul of the state.

When the Church makes a recommendation it is for the state to carry it out, for Church cannot go beyond ex-communication. Like Luther, Calvin also held the view that it is the duty of a subject to show passive obedience to the ruler in general. Even a bad or cruel ruler must be given due obedience and honour. But in certain cases Calvin justified resistance to tyranny. He gave the representatives of the three estates the right of restraining the absolutism of a tyrant. Calvin also held the view that an individual had the right of resisting his ruler if the latter's orders contravened any Command of God. This view of Calvin gave an easy handle to the Calvinists to rise in the name of God against their rulers in Holland, Scotland and France.

(ii) The Theology of Calvin: Calvin insisted that spiritual authority should be exercised by the elders of the Church. According to him, the government ought not to compel conscience in matters which have been set free by Christ, or force it to deviate from the only law of liberty which it must obey if it is to remain in a state of grace.

Calvin was willing to obey the secular authority as long as it obeyed the theocracy, but where the government was hostile, Calvin developed an attack on the secular authority.

(iii) Calvin and Passive Resistance: In this respect he was a follower of Luther. According to him, since the secular government is an external agency to ensure salvation, the position of the magistrate is very honourable. He is the lieutenant of God on earth and therefore resistance to him is resistance to God. According to him, even a bad ruler, who is a visitation on the people for their sins, deserves the unconditional submission of his subjects no less than the good, for submission is due not to the person but to the office, and the office has inviolable majesty. But it is also true, as pointed out by Sabine that "Calvin, like practically all sixteenth century advocates of the divine right of kings, expressed strong views on the duty of rulers to their subjects. The immutable law of God is binding on kings as well as on subjects, and the evil ruler is guilty of sedition against God. Like Locke later, he held that civil law merely fixes a penalty for what is intrinsically wrong. But the punishment of a derelict magistrate belongs to God and not to his subjects."

(iv) Calvin on the Law of Nature: Calvin had faith in a law of nature. To him the moral law represented human knowledge of the natural. He held the view that the divine purpose for mankind was to bring some men to the supreme happiness of salvation. This happiness was found in the Bible. This was natural law. The end of all human activity was to obey this law, the penalty for disobedience was eternal damnation. This law was divided into rules for conduct towards God, and rules of conduct towards man. Conforming to natural law, there was natural right. Attached to natural right, there were natural duties also. The natural rights are inalienable; they are: right to law, right to liberty, and right to freedom of worship. Non-performance of duty was considered to be a sin. As government was instituted to carry the divine law into effect, obedience to the government was considered a religious duty of the highest order. Any disobedience was considered a great sin.

Conclusion

Finally, we can say that "Calvin introduced, in an acceptable form through the fiction of the authority of the Bible, the most powerful conceptions of the Middle Ages in relation to the nature of law and political obedience." According to Sabine, "In its main aspects Calvin's political theory was a somewhat unstable structure, not precisely because it was illogical but because it could readily become the prey of circumstances. On the one hand, it stressed the wickedness of all resistance to constituted authority, but on the other, its fundamental principle was the right of the Church to declare pure doctrine and to exercise universal censorship with the support of secular power."

5. Political Influence of Reformation. Almost all the leaders of the Reformation Movement held the same opinion that moral law was superior to secular law, and that it was the duty of the political sovereign to be guided by the higher law.

It counteracted the rationalizing, non-moral and non-religious spirit of Machiavelli. In spite of the influence of the Renaissance, the leaders' ethical and political theories were, to some extent, medieval. "To the reformers the relationship of the Church to the state and the moral basis of the latter constituted practically the whole of political theory." In this they followed and developed the medieval doctrines. They rejected the great medieval idea of a universal empire and a universal Church. The reformers greatly enhanced the dignity and power of the princes. The conception of excellence bestowed by God on the elect was really remarkable. It resulted in strengthening absolutism in the political sovereign. But passive obedience was given well-defined limits and the ruler and subject alike were to be under the control of a higher law. It was John Knox who made a change in Calvin's idea of passive obedience by justifying rebellion as part of the duty to sustain religious reform. Finally, it may be said that Reformation was a movement of reform with far-reaching political consequences.

6. John Knox. Knox's writings mark a stage by which Calvinism worked to its logical conclusion and linked up with the idea of natural law. Knox of course abandoned Calvin's belief that resistance is always wrong; he also defended resistance as part of the duty to sustain religious reform. According to Sabine, "His stand was taken upon the ground of religious duty, not of popular rights; but it put one great wing of the Calvinist Churches in opposition to royalist power and boldly justified the use of rebellion."

In his 'Appellation' he asserted that the "duty of every man in his station is to see that true religion is taught and that those are punished with death who deprive the people of the food of their souls, I mean God's lively word." Excepting the question of resistance. Knox did not depart from Calvin's principles. He accepted the truth of Calvin's version of Christian doctrine and also the duty of the Church to force its discipline on all who did not willingly accept it. He rejected Calvin's doctrine of passive obedience and asserted that it was their duty to correct and repress whenever a king acts contrary to the word of God, his honour and glory.

In his Appellation Knox writes, "For now the common song of all men is: we must obey our kings, be they good or bad for God had so commanded. But it is blasphemy to say that God had commanded kings to be obeyed when they command impiety. The punishment of such crimes as are idolatry, blasphemy and other that touch the majesty of God, doth not appertain to kings and chief rulers only, but also to the whole body of that people and to every member of the same, according to the vocation, which God doth minister to revenge the injury done against his glory, what time that impiety is manifestly known." This anti-monarchical Calvinism as given in Knox's revolutionary doctrine reached its fullest development in the writings of Hubert Languet whose work 'A Defence of Liberty against Tyrants' forms one of the landmarks of revolutionary literature.

12

The Political Theory of the Counter-Reformation

Introduction

As a result of the great shock caused by the Reformation Movement, the Roman Catholic Church tried to reform itself. The process of purification of the papacy began under the leadership of a series of great Popes. The General Council of the Church was revamped and reorganized. Old religious orders were revised. New ones were founded. The most important of the new orders was the Society of Jesus. A General Council of the Church was summoned at Trent to decide the issue whether the Pope or the council was supreme in the Church, and how the spiritual and secular authorities should be limited. Ultimately, the supremacy of the Pope was established over the Church Council mainly through the help of the Jesuits. The Jesuits were the main supporters of the Counter-Reformation and they enriched the literature on political science considerably. Their writings had anti-monarchic bias. The Jesuits were known for their brilliant methods rather than ideas. Their political ideas were chiefly borrowed from the general canons of medieval theory. They were thus not original in their political ideas but they capture the minds of the people with the help of a brilliant system of education. The Society of Jesus produced three important thinkers in the persons of Bellarmine, Parsons and Mariana. Besides these, there were many other brilliant scholars who were clever enough to attract the minds of common men.

The Political Theory of the Jesuits

The Jesuits make a clear distinction between the lay and the clerical society. According to them secular society originates in the needs of men; its existence is for securing peace and liberty. This aim is achieved only if society retains power in its own hands. Thus, the basis of political society is the sovereignty of the people. It is the people who possess supreme political power. This doctrine of popular sovereignty, though not an original one, was first brought into limelight by the Jesuits. They regarded the civil state as a corporate personality. It had no divine origin. It was concerned with the peace and protection of property. The king rules because of the power and sovereignty really belong to the people, the king being only an instrument of its expression. The people who gave political power to the king, could get it back also if the king misused it.

According to the Jesuits, the civil state had no connection with religion. The people who were sovereign, by whom political power was delegated to the ruler, had the right to reshape the political society if it was thought necessary to do so.

The Jesuits were opposed to the theory of Divine Right of Kings and they allowed the people the right of deposing their rulers who they held were actually servants of the people. This revolutionary doctrine of the Jesuits was fully made use of by Locke and Rousseau later on.

As regards the relationship between the Church and the state, the Jesuits gave up the medieval doctrine of a single and indivisible Republica Christiana and reverted to the view of the New Testament, the Early Fathers and St. Augustine that there are two separate and distinct societies — a Civitas Dei, and a Civitas Terrana; the first Civitas Dei or the Catholic Church was divine in origin and organization, and inherently the higher of the two; the other, Civitas Terrana national state was human in origin, the mere creature of a contract and deriving its authority from the sanction of sinful men.

The Jesuits not only separated religion from politics but also placed it in a position of divorce between ethics and politics. To the Jesuits, the end justified the means. They regarded law not as a mere command but the reflection of a universal sanction of what was right. The law recognized a right, it did not create it.

The Jesuits, however, supported the superior power of the papacy over secular affairs indirectly. According to them, the Pope was different from other sovereigns as he was in-charge of the life eternal. He represented the reserve power of the society. The sovereignty of the papacy must be exercised in order to protect the subjects from the undue encroachments of the secular power. To achieve this end, the Pope could even declare war. This war was different from ordinary war. It simply meant that the Pope could ask the devoted Roman Catholic kings to declare war against the heretic sovereign as for example, the Pope calling upon Philip II of Spain to declare war against Queen Elizabeth of England. On this indirect power of the papacy over secular states, Grotius built up his theory of international law. Besides, the Jesuits also developed the doctrine of universal right and corporate personality.

After Westphalia, the age of religious rivalry gave place to an age of dynastic rivalry. It goes to the credit of the Jesuits that they provided the secular theory of state after separating religion from politics. The Jesuits, like the Calvinists were opposed to a too powerful national monarchy. But unlike the Calvinists, they utilized their theory to support a revised form of the old doctrine of papal supremacy in moral and religious questions.

Robert Bellarmine (1542-1621): Robert Bellarmine, a Jesuit cardinal, one of the ablest of Catholic writers of the Counter-Reformation Movement. In his Disputations, he touches on almost all the important questions of the day, political and ecclesiastical. In this book he discusses the merits and demerits of various forms of governments in order to find out which would suit the Church best.

According to him of the simple forms of government, the most excellent is monarchy, and constitutional monarchy is better than simple absolute monarchy. Theoretically, simple monarchy is better than a mixed form of government. After discussing all forms of government, Bellarmine concludes that in the interest of the Church the monarchical form of government is the best form of government. The Church could find divine sanction for papal monarchy in the establishment of Petrine authority. Like a good Jesuit, Bellarmine justifies the ecclesiastical sovereignty of the Pope. Though he is of the opinion that ordinary secular affairs are of no direct concern of the Pope, the Pope has the right to interfere in secular affairs when the salvation of souls is in question.

But later on, in his second book On the Power of the Pope in Temporal Affairs he made a compromise with the Pope by refusing to draw any distinction between the secular and ecclesiastical power of the Pope and holding that the Pope had temporal authority also.

According to Gettell, Bellarmine, "Believed that absolute monarchy was the ideal form of government, but that because of the corruption of nature, it was desirable to limit the power of the civil ruler by organs representing the estates of the people. Final political authority resided by natural right in the people, and was delegated by them to their rulers."

Sabine gives the theory of Bellarmine thus: "The Jesuit theory of the papacy was given definite form by Robert Bellarmine conceding that the Pope has no authority in secular matters. Bellarmine argued that the Pope is nevertheless the spiritual head of the Church and, as such, has an indirect power over temporal matters, exclusively for spiritual ends. The power of secular rulers does not come directly from God, as the royalists asserted, nor from the Pope, as the extreme papalists had held. It arises from the community itself for the sake of its own secular ends. The king's power is secular in kind and in origin; only the Pope among human rulers has his power directly from God."

As a result of this theory, the fact become clear that the state is a national society purely secular in origin and purpose, while the Church is world-wide in scope and is of divine origin. Thus, the Church becomes one social body and the state another, membership in one being independent of membership in the other. The conclusion is that political power inheres in the people. It is derived from them by contract and it may be revoked if the ruler becomes tyrant.

Juan de Mariana: His theory was found in De Regeet regis institution in 1599. It was chiefly governed by constitutional considerations. He had great admiration for medieval institutions, especially those represented by the Estates of Aragon.

According to him, the estates were the guardians of the law of the land and the king was fully subject to them, the power of the king was derived from the people through a contract. The people were represented by the estates and to them the power to change the law was reserved. As a consequence of this the king could be removed by the estates for violating the fundamental law.

According to Sabine, "This constitutional theory Mariana built upon on account of the origin of civil society from a state of nature preceding government, in which men live a kind of animal existence, lacking both the virtues and the vices of civilized life." Like Rousseau later, he regarded the origin of private property as the crucial step toward law and government.

The most important feature of Mariana's theory was that he treated the origin and evolution of government as a natural process taking place under the impulsion of human needs. On this ground he based the contention that a community must always be able to control or depose the rulers whom its needs have created. He came much closer than the author of the Vindiciae Contra Tyrannos to a non-theological view of civil society and its functions.

Francisco Suarez: The most important representative of Jesuit political theory was the Spanish scholastic philosopher and jurist, Francisco Suarez. This great scholar was born at Grenada in 1548 A.D. He joined the Jesuit Society in 1564. He took up the teaching of philosophy and theology.

In 1612 was published his treatise on Law and God–the Legislator, and in 1616 appeared his Defence of the Catholic and Apostolic Church against the errors of the Anglican sect. These books were written at the instance of Pope Paul V with the aim of refuting the Apology of James I.

His writings are marked by a scientific detachment from the controversies of the day. His treatise on law contains his political philosophy.

In it the author maintains the medieval notions about the inter-relationship of ethics, theology and politics. He was a keen follower of St. Acquinas.

According to Sabine, "Suarez's political theory was incidental to his jurisprudence. His purpose was to present an encyclopaedic philosophy of law in all its divisions, and, as was usual in his writings, he presented a summary and systematization of all phases of medieval legal philosophy. In Suarez and the other members of what is sometimes called the Spanish School of Jurisprudence, the legal philosophy of the Middle Ages was digested and arranged, and was thus passed on to the seventeenth century."

Political Philosophy of Suarez: According to Suarez all moral beings endowed with reason and free will are determined in all their relations by law. He defines law, "as a just and permanent precept, applying to a community and sufficiently promulgated." A law presupposes an act of goodwill and the dictate of right reason. He classifies law as Acquinas did, as eternal, divine, natural and human. Human law originates from human will and it consists of both ecclesiastical and civil law. The purpose of civil law is to make men good and aim at the true and natural happiness of the political society.

Human law is inferior to the law of nature and must always conform to the latter. Again, "Natural law is that law implanted in the human soul through which right is distinguished from wrong. Its source is God the creator, and its end is the good of the creature." It represents not only a judgment of human reason, but also a command of God. Natural law is therefore, divine law as it has a divine mandate and cannot be dispensed with by any earthly authority. It is just like a code of conduct consisting of many principles and precepts which are applicable to all times, places and men. It is immutable.

According to Suarez, the Jus naturale and jus gentium are distinguishable from each other, for jus gentium, unlike jus naturale is a product of human need and human will, its principles owing origin to social interest and requirements. The distinction between jus naturale and jus gentium is primarily that between jus naturale and jus gentium is primarily that between what is morally necessary and what is socially expedient. The former must always be obeyed, and the latter is obeyed when it becomes a part of civil law.

He also makes a distinction between jus gentium and the civil law. "The jus gentium embodies the sense of customary right, not of one nation or province, but of all." It evolves as an unwritten usage. Its precepts are the common judgements of all, or nearly all people, and so Suarez assigns it a position nearer to **jus naturale** than to **jus civile**. According to him private property and slavery represent **jus gentium**.

As regards the origin of the state, Suarez's conception is more modern than his general scholasticism would otherwise, warrant. According to him man is by nature a free animal. But man is also a social being. Life in society is natural to him and political society is a necessary expression and result of man's social nature. It comes into existence through the deliberate and voluntary sacrifice by its members of their 'individual liberty.' This view of Suarez reminds us of the theory of social contract as given by Rousseau. Social life requires some regulative power which must be in human hands as men cannot be governed directly by God. According to him, a government is not only a coercive agency but also a regulative power, arbitrating between the various social classes. So, naturally governmental power belongs to the whole community and not to an individual. Thus, he propounds the theory of popular sovereignty. The sovereign people can alienate their sovereignty and this alienation is irrevocable save in the case of injustice or tyranny. Thus, the sovereign power is not of divine origin but of human origin, being the gift of the people. Suarez allows the Pope the power to intervene to save souls but he does not allow him direct ordinary power is secular affairs.

As to the forms of government Suarez holds that a political society may be a monarchy, aristocracy or democracy of a mixed type. He however regards monarchy as the best form of government. Like Bodin, he held that the sovereign alone can create law and that a sovereign himself is subject to the law of God and the law of nature. He also holds the view that constitutional laws of a state are superior to the positive laws. He rejects Machiavelli's view that the end of law is preservation and aggrandizement of the state, irrespective of the moral quality of law. Thus, he does not divorce ethics from jurisprudence.

As regards his attitude towards tyrants he holds the view that a ruler who constantly violates common rights is a tyrant and he ought to be deposed. The whole people have the right even to execute him. A tyrant may be a usurper or a legitimate ruler. A usurper may be put to death by private citizens even, but a legitimate ruler can be deprived of his sovereignty only by the whole people acting through its representatives. He may even be killed if public necessity needs it.

His political philosophy has been well-summarized thus by Sabine, "Suarez conceived of the Pope as the spiritual leader of a family of Christian nations and consequently as spokesman of the moral unity of humanity. The Church is a universal and divine institution; the state is national and particular."

On this ground he defended the indirect power of the Pope to regulate secular rulers for spiritual ends. The state is specifically a human institution, depending upon human needs, and originating in a voluntary union of the heads of families. By this voluntary act each assumes the obligation of doing whatever the general good requires while the civil society thus formed has a natural and necessary power to control its members for the general good, and to do whatever its life and needs require. In this way he established the principle that the power of society to rule itself and its members is an inherent property of a social group. It has no dependence on the will of God except as everything in the world depends on His will, but is purely a natural phenomenon, belonging to the physical world and having to do with man's social needs. Aside from the indirect power of the Pope, Suarez's view of society was in no special sense theological. From the view that political power is an inherent property of the community, he concluded, as might be expected that no form of political obligation is absolute, political arrangements are in a sense superficial, a state may be ruled by a king or in some other way, the government's power is derived from the community; it exists for the welfare of the community; and, when it does not work well, it can be changed.

The intent of this theory was no doubt to exalt the divine right of the Pope above the merely secular and human power of the king, but the effect was really to set politics more completely apart from theology. Suarez's political theory was incidental to his jurisprudence.

Suarez's importance as political theorist lies in his enunciation of the doctrine of natural law in very clear terms. He also put forward the modern theory of popular sovereignty. The political community delegates its sovereign power to the law and to its judgment the temporary trustee of its sovereign power is always in the last resort responsible. Then, on the basis of right and reason, he asserted the independence of the secular state from interference by the Church authorities, the Pope to interfere only when religion was at stake.

Thomas Campanella (1568-1639). Thomas Campanella was a Dominican friar of southern Italy; his contribution to political thought is unique. According to Gettell, "His ideas were a peculiar combination of humanistic paganism, Machiavellian materialism, and a narrow Christian theology. Campanella combined platonic and monkish ideals of social organization. He believed that the phenomena of nature and history could be explained by the three principles of power, intelligence, and love; and he viewed the papal autocracy as the Ideal form of political organization."

He tried to bring about a synthesis of philosophy and theology. His political philosophy is best given in his The City of Sol, a utopian work. His is an indissoluble union of secular and ecclesiastical functions. He does not recognize the institutions of family and private property.

The form of government that he pictured in his utopian work has been described by Gettell thus, "In his utopian work, he described, in the form of a dialogue, an unknown Commonwealth, discovered by a Genuese sailor. It was ruled by an absolute monarch. Sol, chosen, like the Pope, by a college of magistrates. Political and religious functions were combined. The chief ministers of Sol were Potentia, in charge of war and diplomacy; Prudentia, in charge of education, art, the public work; and Amor, in charge of the perpetuation and physical improvement of the population. Two assemblies, one composed of the priest magistrates, and another including all the people were provided. Citizens, divided into three classes, lived in common, possessed no private property or individual family life, and were under strict state supervision.

Companella's work is supposed to have inspired the Jesuits to undertake their communistic experiments in Paraguay.

13
English Political Philosophy during the 17th Century

(i) HARRINGTON

James Harrington was born in England in 1611 and died in the year 1677. In the history of political philosophy, he occupies an important place. He wrote 'The Commonwealth of Oceana,' which is his greatest contribution to political philosophy. In fact, he was the first modern political philosopher who put forward a systematic and suggestive plan of government to replace monarchy. Gettell speaking of Harrington says, "The most systematic and suggestive plan of government to replace the monarchy that had been destroyed in England was put forward in a form of a political romance."

Harrington made a thorough study of several books on political philosophy. He made extensive reading in history and followed the method of observations. On the basis of these, he wrote his famous book 'The Commonwealth of Oceana.' Gettell remarks, "He prefaced his plan of a model Commonwealth by a sketch of seven principal republican constitution of history."

The influence of prevailing conditions of England on Harrington was no less. He observed the contemporary events in Europe. He lived for sometime in Venice and studied the working of the government there and derived several of his political ideas from this study.

'The Commonwealth of Oceana' was written in the form of Ethiopia. It was dedicated to Cromwell because Harrington hoped that Cromwell would 'put principles into effect.'

'The Commonwealth of Oceana' was an earnest to his countrymen. No doubt, the book was warmly received but the enthusiasm of English people was short-lived. They preferred to return their earlier institutions. The restoration of monarchy brought Harrington's vogue to an end.

It may, however, be noted that his book had more influence in America. It influenced the writings of some of the American masters of political thought. According to G.P. Gooch, "The constitutions of Carolina, New Jersey and Pennsylvania reflected his thought and a century later his authority was fully quoted in the discussions which preceded and followed the elaboration of the American constitution. His works formed the political Bible of Otis and John Adams, and Jefferson's copy is preserved in the library of congress. Translated into French during the Revolution they supplied sieges with many of his ideas. Thus Harrington's name arrests us in the three great revolutions of the modern world."

Before we conclude, it may be worthwhile to mention that Harrington was a great admirer of Aristotle and Machiavelli. It is possible that Aristotle's Vs. Machiavelli's political thoughts may have influenced him in shaping his own political philosophy.

(ii) SIR THOMAS MORE

In England, during the Tudor Period, people paid more attention for material prosperity coming from strong government than for spiritual or political enlightment. This period was not good for the development of political speculation. People were required to obey without any resistance in Tudor despots. The theory of Divine Rights of the King was the keynote of political life of England of those days.

Sir Thomas More and Richard Hooker were the two writers on political philosophy of this period. Sir More wrote his 'Utopia' during the reign of Henry VIII.

'Utopia' was a satire on the existing society as also on government. More held that institution of private property is the root cause of all social evils. To get rid of these evils and to improve this society, More advocates communism.

In fact, More's 'Utopia' has not contributed anything real to the political philosophy except that it represents a return to Platonic.

The disparagement of war and military glory and a remarkable theory of religious toleration are other important features of 'Utopia.'

(iii) RICHARD HOOKER

Richard Hooker was the most noteworthy philosopher of the Puritan Revolutionary period in England was primarily a theologician and aimed to rebut the attacks of the Presbytarians on the polity of the Anglican Church. Hooker maintains the same principles applied to both secular and ecclesiastical governments. His work exercised an important influence on later political thought. He made an examination of the origin, nature and obligation of law in general.

It was Hooker's belief that men originally lived in a state of nature in which there was no organised authority. Though the condition was full of contention and violence, man, however, was social and accordingly, by formal consent, established organized political authority.

His doctrine of government based on popular consent proved to be very useful to future theorist who had leaning towards democracy.

Hooker also expressed his views on the law of nations. He said if it is good for the individual to avoid anarchy and adopt civil society, it cannot be good for nations to live in anarchy.

Gettell says, "In short his work contained either explicitly or in gem most of the leading ideas of the eighteenth century."

(iv) SIR ROBERT FILMER

Sir Robert Filmer wrote only one book, the 'Patriarcha.' It was published many years after his death. In fact, Filmer does not occupy important place in the political philosophy.

Filmer's political philosophy was greatly influenced by Hobbes and Bodin. Gettell says, 'Though Filmer agreed with Hobbes concerning the absolute nature of royal power yet he attached the social contract basis from which Hobbes derived it.' He pointed out that the state of nature and social compact doctrine was essentially opposed to absolute monarchy, and that if the people originally possessed supreme power and were free to choose their government only a democracy would be lawful.

Filmer's book 'Patriarcha' was important firstly because it was the best statement of a theory of monarchy adopted by many Tories after the Restoration and secondly because it was answered by Sydney and Locke.

Filmer believed in absolute sovereign power. He agreed with Bodin's view that there must be in every state a single, absolute and irresponsible sovereign power. He did not agree with the assumption of originally equality among men. He did not believe the principle that authority should rest upon human consent.

Filmer says, "Government originated in an enlargement of the family, the king being the father and people his children." To Filmer, absolute monarchy was the only government that could preserve true religion. According to him, king was the source of law and Parliament was just an advisory body.

Filmer's conception that the state to natural and organic growth is perhaps the only valuable thing in his theory. He does not accept state as a mechanical organization created by contract. As Lawrence says, "He shifted the main support of the divine right theory from scriptural texts to the teaching of nature. What was according to nature, he held to be divinely ordained. The abandonment of the theological basis of divine right really paved the way for the overthrow of the theory, since it was easier to criticise Filmer's interpretation of history, or to point out that democratic principles are also natural, then it was to meet the theological arguments on their own ground. Besides, the tendency to interpret the principle of the law of nature in anti-monarchic terms was too strong for Filmer, or even the abler thinker, Hobbes, to effectively oppose."

(v) SIR JOHN FORTESQUE (1394-1476)

Sir John analyzed, and eulogized the English system of law and the government. He denied that the will of the Prince was the source of law. "Fortesque conceived of a state of nature," writes Gettell, "existing before the establishment of government, and found the ultimate source of authority in natural law, established by God, and containing the principles of absolute justice. The authority of the King was derived from this natural law, and was conditioned by it." Sir John conceived of the law of nature, "as the universal code of all created things, directed by God and embodying perfect justice." This law of nature governed secular affairs till the rise of customary law. According to him, there was a state of nature prior to the emergence of the political state. Royal power owed its origin to the law of nature which was the source of enactments. To him the English monarchy was the best form of government as it represented a happy mixture of royal and political government. According to him, "the form, at once royal and political, combines an absolute and untrammeled authority of the King at times of crisis with the rule of law in the normal condition of the people." To him, the English law is as good as the English constitution. On the continent, the will of the King brought on the law but in England the royal will was a subordinate element in law, there being the common law and the parliamentary statutes. Fortesque became a source of inspiration to the parliamentary opposition in England in the 17th century. His suggestion that royal power was derived from popular consent found good support in the hands of the opposition in the later revolution, and it was ably put forward by Sir Edward Coke.

(vi) JAMES I

The 17th century in England witnessed both ecclesiastical and constitutional opposition to the Stuart monarchy. On the constitutional side, both the Parliament and the judiciary asserted their independence of the Crown. This opposition was based on legalism rather than in abstract theory. It was Magna Carta and not the doctrine of Natural Rights of Man that was the main weapon in the hands of the opposition against the Stuart kings. The political philosophy of James I was influenced to a very large extent by the bitter experiences of his early life in Scotland. The Scottish Presbyterians belittled the secular power and asserted the right of the subjects to control their rulers. Knox had already said "No oath or promise can bind the people to obey and maintain tyrants against God...justly may they depose and punish them." James, fearing such doctrines, took up cudgels against them. "To the Private Right of Kirk he proposed the

Divine Right of Kings; to the doctrines of popular sovereignty and the right of resistance preached by Knox and Buchanan, he proposed the theory of monarchical sovereignty and the duty of passive obedience." In order to counteract anti-monarchical doctrines, James himself wrote a number of treatises such as Basilican Doron, the True Law of Free Monarchies, etc. In these tracts he upheld the doctrine that kings rule by Divine Right and supported his arguments by appeal to the scriptures, to the law of nature, and to the law of Scotland. He called the kings the breathing images of God on earth. He wrote, "The state of monarchy is the supremest thing upon earth; for kings are not only God's lieutenants upon earth, and sit upon God's throne, but even by God himself they are called Gods." According to James, the king is God's minister. He gets his crown by right of birth and is not subject to any private law of statute. A tyrant feels no responsibility to God, but a true king does. He must be like a true father to his subjects. The kings are responsible to God for their rule but they are not responsible to any earthly power. The king's power cannot be disputed. James wrote "That which concerns the mystery of king's power is not lawful to be disputed; for that is to wade into the weakness of princes, and to take away the mystical reverence that belongs unto them that sit in the throne of God." On this issue, Sabine writes, "James always admitted that he was responsible in the highest degree but responsible to God and not to his subjects. In all ordinary matters he acknowledged that a king ought to give the same respect to the law of the land that he demanded of his subjects, but this is a voluntary submission which cannot be enforced."

James theory clearly held that the king was above the people and the law and was responsible to God alone. "A good king will frame all his actions according to the law; yet he is not bound thereto but of his own goodwill and for good example to his subjects." Kings create laws, not laws the kings. The kings are the authors and makers of the laws, and not the laws of the kings. This view was explained well by Sabine thus: "No considerations of utility can set aside a valid hereditary claim; even an accomplished revolution does not invalidate it; and no law of prescription runs against the legitimate heir. In short, the quality of a king is a supernatural stigma, not to be explained and not to be debated." Even a wicked king should not be opposed. There is no contract of any kind between the king and his subjects. Even the Parliament, to James, is a creation of royal will and is a subordinate legislative body. The subjects' have all duties and no rights. According to James, a king, like God, can create or destroy, make or unmake, give or take life, judge all and is accountable to none. Again James held, "As it is atheism and blasphemy to dispute what God can do, so it is presumption and high contempt in a subject to dispute what a king can do or to say that a king cannot do this or that."

But this claim of James to an inalienable and indefeasible sovereignty did not remain unchallenged totally. "Magna Carta," said Chief Justice Coke, "is such a fellow that he will have no sovereign in the land." But the royal claims of James found allies among the Anglican clergy and the universities. This support however was short-lived. It was out of expediency. Maxey writes, "James believed that his succession to the English throne was a triumph for the principle of legitimacy and hence for that of divine right whereas, for the English, it had been merely an expedient to avoid civil war." By his literary efforts if James became the most important champion of the divine right theory in his day, he also became the chief target of the slowly rising opposition to that theory. The ill-will created by the ill-timed products of the royal pen could not be contained and it engendered more and more opposition to the royal power. This ultimately resulted in the victory of the liberal doctrines of popular sovereignty and democracy.

(vii) FRANCIS BACON

Among the champions of despotism, Bacon was certainly one of the greatest. "Bacon's whole conception of policy," writes Sabine "tended to emphasize royal power, but he thought always in terms of the Tudor Monarchy in which the king was the trusted leader of the nation and of Parliament." The most important of his political doctrines are to be found in his essay entitled "Of the True Greatness of Kingdoms and Estates." It was in thc eighth book of his De Augmentis. The ideal Baconian state is a powerful military state based on a prosperous, well-armed people. A nation must take to arms as its chief occupation, for war is necessary for the greatness of kingdoms. According to him, two main causes of sedition are poverty and discontent. A good ruler must eliminate poverty by improving agriculture, trade and industry. Riches must not be allowed to be concentrated in a few hands.

Bacon's idea of monarchy was of a Tudor type. According to him, the state was an organism in which the king and Parliament had their respective functions. The king was the main motive power in the state and his authority knew no limitation. To him a republican form of government was undesirable as it led to many functions, resulting in danger to national unity. A strong aristocracy ought to buttress an unlimited monarchy. He also held the view that the judges should be like lions under the throne to interpret laws and not to make them. The king is to act as a moderate in every walk of national life. The Church was also to be subordinate to the state. "A generation before Hobbes, Bacon taught the unfettered sovereignty of the state alike over the religion and the politics of its citizens." In Bacon's ideal state a sovereign is irresponsible within the wide and undefined limits of his prerogative. According to him, Parliament was there not for legislative purposes but for registering grievances. To him law was the will of the king. "From his essays it is evident" writes Sabine "that Bacon's political ideas was a strong and war-like people, not overburdened with taxes, with no great concentration of wealth, and with a nobility not too powerful — good Tudor ideals all — led by a king having great resources in crown lands, a strong prerogative, and a vigorous policy of national expansion. In his mind this did not imply absolutism." Thus, we find in the final analysis that Bacon was a supporter of absolute monarchy, though a balanced one.

(viii) JOHN MILTON (1608-1674)

His writings were more moderate in outlook than those of the Levellers. About him, Gettell writes: "The more moderate theory of the Commonwealth was best represented in the writings of John Milton (1608-1674). Milton supported the parliamentary party, advocated complete separation of the Church and state, and, at first favoured the substitution of the Presbyterian for the Episcopal system in Church organization.

Later, he upheld independence and took active part in politics under the Commonwealth and Protectorate. When Parliament issued an ordinance in 1643 for the control of printers and booksellers, Milton defended the right of free expression as a privilege of citizenship and a benefit to the State. He proceeded to defend liberty in general, arguing that it is essential to the dignity of man and to the development of his faculties of reason. He opposed governmental restriction and 'supervision, argued for religious toleration, and was the first Prophet of the belief in individualism that became dominant in the nineteenth century." It was he who held that "he who destroys a book kills reason itself, the image of God." The right of free comment was not only a privilege of free men but was of benefit to the State. Truth was divine and needed no licensing. Thus, he was an ardent supporter of the liberty of the press.

Milton published his Tenure of Kings and Magistrates a few days after the execution of Charles I and approved the establishment of the new republic. He followed the arguments of the anti-monarchists. According to him, men were born free and had the right of self-preservation. To prevent disorder and violence brought about by the original sin, men entered into a social contract, to prevent mutual injury. Commonwealths were founded by mutual contract among men. Kings and magistrates were appointed with administrative powers to execute justice and maintain order, not as masters but as agents or deputies. The kings as deputies of people had only that much power which was delegated to them, and they were subject to laws. As such, the people had the right to depose a ruler who denied rights and law to the people. Milton's radicalism is evident very much when he says, "Then may the people, as often as they shall judge it for the best, either choose him or reject him, retain him or depose him, though no tyrant, merely by the liberty and right of free-born men to be governed as seems them best. The right of choosing, yea of changing their government, is by the grant of God himself to the people."

Milton stood of popular sovereignty as the birth-right of men and nations. His liberty meant an assurance to the individual of a wide sphere of action unrestricted by any government.

Thus, Milton was a great advocate of individualism. For him, an individual was endowed with reason and had to be allowed to work out his own good without much interference from the laws of the country. To him, the best guarantee for individual liberty was a republican form of government. He wrote two pamphlets, Eikonklastes and Defensio Populi Anglicani to refute the arguments of royalists. But he lost faith in the wisdom of the mass of individuals and veered round to the conception of 'aristocratic republicanism.' Hereditary rule, he regarded as contrary to the law of nature. In another pamphlet, Ready and Easy Way to Establish a Free Commonwealth he suggested that a free Commonwealth without first person or House of Lords was the best form of government. He advocated a government consisting of a body of representatives, holding by permanent tenure and choosing from amongst themselves an executive council, which was to be permanent. This suggestion of a permanent council represented a fall from his early views of liberty and democracy. But, "behind Milton's republicationism lay a vague Platonic principle that the real justification of authority is moral and intellectual superiority," writes Sabine. About his importance in the history of politics, Maxey writes thus: "Milton was wholly middle class in derivation and largely so in thought. Though he fully accepted the abstract doctrine that political power and authority belong to the people, he was equally persuaded that the people must act through forms of organization suitable to the time and occasion. Liberty was a fetish with him, but not democracy." He further writes "for what we have of freedom of speech and press and religious worship in the British and American constitutional systems of today, we are immeasurably indebted to the overwhelming eloquence and logic of Milton's political tracts. Milton, the political thinker, deserves our homage no less than Milton, the poet."

14

Jean Bodin (1530-1596 A.D.)

Jean Bodin was born at Angers, France, in the year 1530. At the University of Toulouse, he studied law and later worked there as a lecturer on jurisprudence. But soon after he went to Paris to practice law. In the capital, though he practised law, he, however, devoted his time to learned pursuits also. Soon his literary work attracted attention. He earned the king Heary Ill's favour who appointed him king's Attorney at Laon in 1576, in the same year his great treatise on the state was published. In the year 1596, Jean Bodin died of plague.

His books are:

1. Response,
2. Demonomanie,
3. Hepta-Plomeres,
4. Universal Natural Theatrum,
5. Easy Understanding of History, and
6. 'Six lives dela Republique' or the Six Books of the Commonwealth.

Sovereignty

It is generally agreed that Bodin's doctrine of sovereignty is the most important part of his political philosophy. The presence of sovereign power is taken by him as a mark which distinguishes the state from all the other groupings into which families foil. According to him, citizens are subject to the sovereign and it is his subjection which makes them citizens. The citizens may or may not have common language, religion or customs.

Aristotle in his 'Politics' has also suggested the doctrine of sovercignty but Bodin's concept of sovereignty cannot be identified with that of Aristotle. According to Aristotle, the sovereign power is will in the state had the force of law. But Bodin holds that sovereignty is limited by law which has its source in reason.

In the 16th century, the conditions obtaining in Europe were different than those of the Middle Ages. Pope's supremacy had been reduced and the kings of many states, like England and France had defined a degree of centralization of power. It is a well-known fact that Bodin was greatly favoured by the king of France and it seems, in propounding this theory of sovereignty. Bodin was influenced by this favour.

Bodin has defined sovereignty as follows:

"Sovereignty is the absolute and perpetual power — of a commanding in a state — so far as we have said only that a state is a lawful government of many families and of what is common to them, together with a supreme sovereignty. Now it remains to say exactly what sovereignty as it is — a perpetual power. For if power be held only for a certain time it is not sovereign power and he holds it for that time is not a sovereign prince...."

We may now go on to the other part of our definition, and explain what absolute power is. For the people or the nobles of a state can give the sovereign and perpetual power to any one they choose. This power is given to the prince without any charges or conditions attached, for power given with restrictions is another absolute power, not properly speaking, sovereignty....

Since, there is nothing on earth greater than a sovereign prince, save God alone and since sovereigns are stablished by God as his tenant to rule over men, we must take care that they be always spoken of with honour. For he who is contemptuous of his sovereign prince scorns God himself, of who the prince is earthly image....

I say that the first mark of a sovereign prince is the power of giving law to all the people in general or to each one in particular — without consent of any besides himself. It may be said that custom is as powerful as law — custom acquires its force little by little and after many years by the common consent of all — A law on the other hand, is made in a moment and derives its strength from him who owns the supreme power — the real authority of law and of custom alike rests on the power of the sovereign prince.

The sovereign of course, may give, to certain person the right to make laws, which will then have the same authority as if made by the sovereign himself.

"... Under this power of giving and abrogating laws are included all the other rights and marks of sovereignty."

In the words of Sabine, "The primary attribute of sovereignty is the power to give laws to citizens, collectively and severally, without the consent of a superior, an equal or an inferior."

From Bodin's definition of sovereignty we get the following points:

(a) Within the territorial limits, the power of the sovereign over all the citizens and association is absolute.
(b) The power of the sovereign is perpetual and is not limited by time.
(c) It is indelegated or delegated without limit or condition.
(d) It is not alienable.
(e) The sovereign is the only source of law by which the community is governed and its affairs regulated.
(f) The sovereign is not bound by law. He is supreme and perpetual legal omnipotence. In the words of Pollock, "In every independent community governed by law there must be some authority whether residing in one person, or several whereby the laws are established and from which they proceed, and this power being the source of law, itself be above the law."
(g) Though legally supreme, however, the sovereign is limited in the law of God and nature. "All princes are bound by divine law, by the law of nature, and by that common law of nations which has its source in these."

As head of the state the sovereign also has the power:

(1) To declare war and make peace,
(2) To commission magistrates,
(3) To collect money,
(4) To grant pardons,
(5) To levy taxes, and

(6) To impose punishment.

Sabine says, "In general, sovereignty meant for Bodin a perpetual, humanity, unlimited and unconditional right to make, interpret and execute laws."

It must however, be with that Bodin's definition of the sovereign contains serious confusions which on the one hand, Bodin defines sovereignty 'as supreme power..., unrestricted by law,' on the other hand, this power is not 'so unlimited.' The following limitations have been placed by Bodin:

(a) Though Bodin's sovereign is **legibus soluta**, yet he is not **omnibus soluta**. "All princes are bound by divine law."
(b) The sovereign power is also limited by the law of nature.
(c) The sovereign should not act against the constitutional law of the realm.
(d) The sovereign is also bound by moral duties to observe treaties with other sovereigns.
(e) The sovereign is also morally bound to observe the compact with his own subjects.
(f) The sovereign must not interfere with the private property of individuals without their consent.
(g) The sovereign must exercise his authority with reason.

Criticism

Bodin is the first modern thinker to propound the concept of sovereignty of state. He has thoroughly analysed this theory but his analysis of supreme power contains serious confusions. In order to have a complete picture of Bodin's nature of sovereignty, these confusions must be noted. Sabine says, "that the preceding account of Bodin's theory of sovereign authority takes account of only the parts of his arguments which are clear and out of difficulties. It is entirely, however, the argument is by no mean so simple, but contains serious confusions. In general, to Bodin, sovereignty means a perpetual, humanity unlimited and unconditional right to make, interpret and execute law. The existence of such a right, he believes to be necessary to any well-ordered state. But the exercise of sovereign power which he regulates as justifiable is by no means so unlimited as his definition imply and the result is a series of restrictions that introduce a great amount of confusion into the finished theory."

Bodin holds that the sovereign is bound by the law of God of nature. Though he admits that the law is a sheer act of the will of the sovereign, he, however, never supposed that the sovereign could never right by mere fiat. To him, the law of the nature stands above human law. Though the sovereign cannot be held legally liable for violating the natural law, however, this law imposes some real disabilities on him.

In the words of Sabine, "Bodin never doubts that the sovereign is bound of the law of God and that of nature. Though he defines law as sovereign's will, he never supposes that the sovereign can make right by mere fiat." For him, the law of nature stands above human law, and sets certain inchangeable standards of right, it is the observance of the law that differentiates the true state from mere effective violence. "There is, of course, no way to make the sovereign legally liable for violating the law of nature still natural law does not impose some real disabilities on him. In particular, it requires the keeping of agreement and respect for private property. The sovereign agreement may involve political obligations towards his subjects or towards other sovereign, and in such case Bodin had no doubt he was bound. It was difficult for him to keep these obligations of the sovereign exclusively on a moral plane and so apart from legal and political obligations what, for instance would be the duty of the magistrates of the sovereign were to command something contrary to natural laws. Bodin had no doubt that there might be cases so flagrant that the sovereign ought to be disobeyed. He did all he could to reduce such cases to the narrowest limits but the confusion was none he less there. "Law is at once the will of the sovereign and an expression of external justice yet the two may be in-conflict."

Another confusion in Bodin's theory arose from his fidelity to constitutional law of France. All his natural inclinations are on the side of constitutional government and respect for the ancient usages and practices of the realm. To Bodin, the King of France cannot modify the rule of succession. He admits the existence of a particular clans of laws which are necessarily connected with the exercise of sovereignty itself and which even the sovereign cannot change. Yet he was convinced that the King of France was sovereign in the full sense of the word, in fact was the example 'par excellence' of a sovereign. Sabine says, "the confusion here is manifest; the sovereign is at once the source of law and the subject of certain conditional laws, which he has made and cannot change."

There is a third confusion in Bodin's theory of sovereignty which is more immediately serious than the two already mentioned. This is with regard to his convictions about the unviolability of private property. This right is guaranteed by the law of nature but it constituted for Bodin more than a mere limitation on the power of the sovereign. To Bodin, property is so sacred that the sovereign even cannot touch it without the consent of the owner. Accordingly, he asserted that taxation requires the assent of the estates. But there is nothing whatever about taxation to justify. Bodin in thus setting it apart from other legislation, and he had denied in the most explicit that the estates can act in any but one advisory capacity in the making of law. Indeed the very existence of the estates depended upon the delegation by the sovereign of a qualified authority to a subordinate corporation.

His Views on Monarchy

Like Machiavelli, Bodin also favours monarchy as the best form as also the most desirable form of government. He regarded England, France and Spain as monarchies in the strictest sense. He divides monarchy into three types:

(a) Despotism — In this type, the monarch rules his subject as the 'pater families' rules his slaves.

(b) Royal Monarchy — In this type, the rights and property of the subjects are secure. The monarch respects the laws of God and of nature.

(c) Tyranny — In this type, the monarch abuses his subjects according to his caprice, treats them as slaves and considers their property as his own.

"Of these species, Bodin regards the royal monarchy not only as the ideal type of monarchic state, but also as the best form of state in general."

The following are, according to Bodin, the true qualities of a royal monarchy:

(a) The monarch 'himself is just as obedient to the laws of nature as he desires his subject to be to him,'
(b) The monarch fears God above all,
(c) He is kind towards the afflicted,
(d) He is prudent in business,
(e) He is brave in exploits,
(f) He is modest in prosperity,
(g) He is constant in adversity,
(h) He keeps his promises,
(i) He is wise in council,
(j) He is helpful to his friends,
(k) He is a terror to his enemies,
(l) He is charitable to men of goodwill,
(m) He is dreadful to evil-doers,
(n) He is just to all.

Bodin has also made distinction between a good king and a tyrant. According to him, the following are the parts of difference between these two types of monarchies:

(i) A good king respects the laws of nature while the tyrant does not care for them.
(ii) A good king respects piety, justice and faith while the tyrant 'knows neither God, nor faith, nor law.'
(iii) A good king always thinks and attempts for the well-being of his subjects while the tyrant always attempts for his private profits, for vengeance and for his own pleasure.
(iv) A good king punishes those who do public wrong, while the tyrant punishes those who injure him.
(v) A good king protects the honour of women, while the tyrant triumphs in their shame.
(vi) A good king attempts to maintain peace and unity, while the tyrant sows the seeds of discord.

(vii) A good king seeks to enrich his subject, while the tyrant enriches himself.

His Views on Revolution

Bodin defines revolution as a 'displacement of sovereignty.' Like Aristotle, Bodin also believes in the transformation of states. He holds that transformation of states is inevitable and the effort of man should be directed, not to prevention of change but to the determination of the manner in which it shall take place.

Bodin also distinguishes two types of political changes. One effects any law or institution but the supreme power remains unaffected. The other effects a change in the location of the sovereignty.

On Revolution Bodin says:

"However states be established....whether by the violent act of some strong man or by the consent of all, subjecting themselves freely to a sovereign...and however, long they endure, none lasts forever, so changeable and uncertain are human affairs. Some states rise slowly to great height and then fall all at once of their own weight, they think themselves safest, still others by inferior maladies...by a change of state, I mean a change of seat of sovereignty...whether voluntary or involuntary changes may be either natural or violent...the change of a state may be either slow and gradual that one scarcely notices it...or it may happen all at once, as a consequence of a sudden, violent blow...."

Bodin favours the last type of change, because it is happier and more natural manner.

Causes of Revolution

According to Bodin, the causes that render revolution inevitable are beyond human control. He groups the causes of revolution under three heads:

(a) Divine causes,

(b) Natural causes, and

(c) Human causes.

Divine causes — Divine causes are hidden from man's view and cannot be marked.

Natural causes — "Bodin says, "when I say 'natural causes,' I do not mean the events which immediately precede the effects but rather the more remote celestial causes of these occurrences."

In human causes, Bodin discusses such questions as the appointment of magistrates, differences in religious faith, unlimited freedom of discussion, the right to bear arms, great inequalities in the possession of wealth and frequent changes in the system of laws.

With regard to prevention, of revolution, not as quote Sabine, who says, "His discussion of the prevention of revolutions was a curious execution into the use of astrology for this purpose, while his analysis of the means for preventing them led him to cover every branch of administration and permitted him to display a really great feud of political occurrence and wisdom."

His Place

Bodin was undoubtedly one of the most original and enlightened political philosophers, whose name appears in the chronicles of political thought.

In his 'Political Philosophic' Maxey writes of him in the following words:

Jean Bodin belongs to the immortals. In an age of bigotry and fanaticism he walked by the steady light of reason, in an age of distraction and dissension he exalted unity and order, in an age of irrational creeds he was a believer in none, but an unrebuting foe of intolerance; in an age of intellectual sterility he was an enlightened and independent thinker animated by the true spirit of philosophy.

Bodin belonged to that class of philosophers, who desired the reconstruction of peace and order. Bodin believed that for the success of France 'the suppression of political fictions and religious controversies and the establishment of a strong monarchy' is necessary. He accordingly justified toleration in religion. His works on religion were so broad and tolerant as to draw fire from every quarter.

Bodin was a versatile genius. History, jurisprudence and politics were the fields in which he left his mark. But no less are his essays on money and public finances. Murray says, "He was a scholar, who strove to be a thinker; a lawyer who was interested in the origin of legal rules as the rules in themselves; a man of the world, who brought all the resources of the shrewd common sense to the investigation of political problems; a sociologist who neither dealt in names nor played with words."

His two books — 'A method for the easy understanding of History' published in 1566 and 'Six Books Concerning the State,' published in 1576 brought fame to Bodin as a political philosopher. 'Six Books Concerning the State' is a landmark in the history of western political philosophy. Though the book has some defects, however, its importance is no less. In this respect Murray says, "The book found no lack of appreciation when it first appeared, and instead of diminishing, its significance and importance have increased with the passage of years."

Certainly Bodin occupies an important place in the history of political theories. Though opinions have somewhat various with regard to the precise nature of his position, however there is substantial agreement among historians and critics that Bodin "Brought back political theory to the form and method from which it had gone for astray since Aristotle, and gave to it again the externals, at best of science. Bodin completed the work started by Machiavelli. He supplied from the stores of his systematic philosophy and generalized them as to present comprehensive political science. It is true Aristotelean 'Politics' furnished many, if not most of the categories, which constituted the framework of Bodin's political science, but it is equally true that those concepts on which the French philosopher laid most stress and which gave its peculiar character to his system — sovereignty, the distinction of state from government—the influence of climate — were is the slighted or wholly unknown in the system of the Greek."

Bodin's work exerted considerable influence upon the contemporary thought of England and France. His concept of sovereignty influenced the political thought of his time and it influences the political thought of even our age.

His contributions to political thought may be enumerated as follows:

(1) He expressed the opinion that political theory must be based on historical observation, that political institution must be studied in their development and that political and legal systems of different types and periods must be thoroughly analysed and compared. In the words of Gettell, he "anticipated the analytical method of Hobbes and the historical method of Montesquieu both of whom studied and profited by his work."

Dunning says, "In Machiavelli the method of historical research and contemporary observation was fully appreciated but in its appreciation it became little more than empiricism and produced rather a body of principles for the practical conduct of Government their theory of the state."

(2) Bodin's main contribution to political thought is described by Sabine in the following words:

"Bodin's statement of the principle of sovereignty is generally agreed to be the most important part of his political philosophy."

(3) Bodin makes distinction between legal obligation and moral duty. Thus he made an important contribution to the separation of legal and ethical concepts.

(4) Bodin asserted the theory of human advancement as opposed to the contemporary dogma of human degeneration from a precious golden age.

(5) Bodin condemned slavery and preached religious tolerance. He opposed the communistic theory of equality and recognised the close relations between the distribution of wealth within the state and the source of real political power.

(6) "Bodin's study of the social and political bearings of climate and topography, which be conceived and exalted in a true scientific spirit fairly justifies his claim to originality" (Dunning).

(7) To the concept of citizenship, Bodin gave some modern elements by saying a citizen is a free man who is subject to the sovereign power of another.

(8) Bodin was the first thinker, who paid attention to the necessary elements of the state and propounded a theory of Sovereignty. Murray says, "It was reserved for Bodin to point out that the day of empires, whether Roman or French, had altogether passed away. The day of assent of nationalism had arrived and with its arrival it was high time to devise a theory of sovereignty to this task, Bodin addresses himself in his 'Republique' and it constitutes his most permanent achievement."

15

Hugo Grotius (1583-1645 A.D.)

Hugo Grotius was born in an aristocratic Dutch Van Groot family of Leyden in 1583. As a child he received the maximum care of his parents. He became noted in early childhood as an intellectual prodigy. His Latin verses which he wrote at the age of eight years attracted attention outside of his own family. At the age of eleven, he matriculated and entered the university of Leyden. At the age of twelve, he wrote a Greek ode in honour of the Prince of Orange which was widely applauded. As a university student he was equally shining. At the age of fifteen, he was sent to Paris with a Dutch embassy. After coming back home, he took the degree of doctorate in laws and started practising law. His celebrated work "The Freedom of the Sea" and other studies established his fame as a jurist. At the age of thirty, he was appointed the Magistrate of Rotterdam. He became the chief administrative officer of West Friesland and Holland at the age of thirty-three. In 1925, his greatest work "The Laws of War and Peace" was published which won him a great fame and made him the father of modern International law. He died in the year 1645, at the age of 62.

Law of Nature

Grotius postulated law as a necessary concomitant of social existence. He thus follows Aristotle in holding that man by nature is a social animal. He holds that man and society are so interlinked that cannot exist without the other. He declares that even origands have need of some common regulatory measures. There must — be some noble shift system of law and justice in their common relations. There is a greater need for law and justice in higher types of human society. Human society is the product of reason. Law which is an essential natural corollary of society is also an outgrowth of reason. Therefore, "whenever there is social life there is reason and likewise law-natural law."

Grotius, then conceded there is a body of universal law, the law of nature or right reason, which equally applies to all people and is absolute as supreme reason itself. He believes that, "the law of nature, again, is unchangeable — even in the sense that it cannot be changed by God. Measureless as is the power of God, nevertheless it can be said that there are certain things over which that power does not extend.... Just as even God then, cannot cause that which is intrinsically evil be not evil. Further more something belongs to the law of nature, not through simple relation but as a result of particular combination of circumstances. Thus the use of things in common was in accordance with the law of nature, so long as ownership by individuals was not introduced and right to use force in obtaining own existed before laws were promulgated."

From Grotius view quoted above, it can be well seen that he thought of mankind as being subject to a body of external principles which are part of the very nature of God Himself.

Grotius defines natural law in these words, 'The law of nature is, a dictate of right reason which points out that an act according as it is or is not conformity with rational nature, has in it a quality; of moral baseness or moral necessity and that in consequence such an act is either forbidden or enjoyed by the author of nature, God.'

Grotius says that natural law must be distinguished from voluntary laws. He says, "The distinction between these kinds of law is not to be drawn from the testimonies themselves... but from the character of the matter. For whatever cannot be deducted from certain principles by a sure process of reasoning and yet it is clearly observed everywhere, must have its origin in the free will of man.... The rotational law is based not upon absolute reason but upon mutual consent evinced by unbroken custom and the testimony of those who are skilled in it."

Special attention should be paid to the following facts:

(a) The natural law is the dictate of right reason, agreeing with rational nature and therefore, with God.

(b) Natural law is unchangeable. It is permanent, eternal, universal, authoritative and absolute reason itself.

(c) Its sanction is to be found in its inherently rational nature and not in the fear of God.

Law of Nations

Grotius was the first jurist to produce a comprehensive and systematic treatise on international law and therefore he is regarded as the father of international law. Before Grotius no one had attempted the treatment of the subject in its entirety. Adolphius kept a copy of the law of war and peace with him in his campaigns. Its leading principles were recognised in the Treaty of Westphalia of 1648.

The central theme of Grotius was the totality of relations between states as governed by law. He distinguished just wars from the unjust ones and rejected the idea that states have absolute right to make war. The will of the states was not to be the only source of international law. The bases of international law according to him, is the nature of man which is endowed with goodness, altruism and morality. He rejected the idea of the 'reason of state.'

Grotius also propounded the theory or qualified neutrality by which nations carrying on a just war was to be bound.

The law of nations included those practices which the civilized nations follow in the dealings with one another. Prof. Dunning says, "Its content is what has been accepted as obligatory by the consent of all or of many nations. What is included under it is proved by constant usage and the testimony of the learned. The occasions for such a body of rights is welfare of that aggregate which includes all or many nations just as the occasion for civil law is the welfare of the aggregate which consists of many individuals."

Grotius expressed the view that promises and obligations must be fulfilled in good faith. He also opined that fundamental rights and freedoms of individual should be guaranteed. He was against war and encouraged the settlement of disputes by negotiations. With a view to help the cause of international co-operation, he favoured the extradition of criminals.

As we have already said, Grotius made a distinction between natural law and law of nations. The law of nation is generally based on the consent of the nations. Grotius found that many people of different ages and countries had similar opinion on certain matters. According to him this was due to some general cause. He says, "This cause must be either a just deduction from the principles of natural justice or universal consent. The first discovers of natural law, the second the law of nations. In order to distinguish these two branches of the same science, we must consider not merely the terms which author's have used to define them, but the nature of the subject in question. For if a certain inferred from admitted principles is, nevertheless, found to be everywhere observed, there is reason to conclude that it drives its origin from positive institution."

The main aim of Grotius seems to lay down those rules of justice which would be binding on man and as also to apply those rules, under the name of natural law, to the mutual relations of separate communities. He says, "Natural law is the dictate of right reason, pronouncing that there is in some actions of a moral obligation and in other actions a moral deformity, arising from every respectable suitableness or repugnance to the rational and social nature and that consequently such actions are either forbidden or employed by God, the author of nature. Actions which are the subject of his exertion of reason are in themselves lawful or unlawful and are, therefore, as such necessary commended or prohibited by God."

The view of Grotius was that the rights common to all were derived from natural law "which is the dictate of right reason, indicating that any act from its agreement or disagreement with the rational nature has in it a more turpitude or a moral necessity."

Undoubtedly Grotius had an abiding influence of the history of international law. Starke says, "Grotius had an abiding influence of the history of international law. He was continually relied upon as a work of reference and authority in the decisions of courts and in the textbook of later writers of standing."

Briefly puts his views as follows:

"Few books have won so great a reputation as the 'De Juri Delliac Pacis' but to regard its author as the 'Founder' of international law is to exaggerate its originality and to do less than justice to the writers who preceded him, neither Grotius, nor any other single writer, can properly be said to have 'Founded' the system."

In the words of Sabine, "Grotius, importance in the history of jurisprudence rests not upon a theory of the state or upon anything. That he had to say about constitutional law, but upon his conception of a law regulating the relations between sovereign states....Grotius's contribution to the special subject of international law is beyond the limits of a history of political theory. In respect to the better, his importance lay in the philosophical principles upon which he sought to find his special subject and which he set out especially in the Prolegomena to his great work."

Assessing the importance of Grotius's works, Jackson wrote, "His work has remained a living force. He is no longer read as widely as in past centuries, but the essence of his thought has passed into the conscience of civilized world."

Grotius on Sovereignty

Grotius draws, to a large extent his doctrine of Sovereignty from Bodin and Swarez. However, his doctrine is not as definite and logical as Bodin's. Grotius holds Sovereignty as a 'supreme political power, vested in him whose acts cannot be rendered void by any other human will.'

Grotius is of the opinion that by nature everyone has a right to resist a wrong, but when civil society has been instituted for the preservation of public tranquility this right becomes subject to the prescriptions of the sovereign. Against the sovereign the right of resistance is null, for the reason among others, that those who instituted civil society deliberately willed their rights to the holder of supreme authority.

He further says, "Originally men not by the command of God, but of their own accord after learning by experience that isolated families could not secure themselves against violence, united civil society, out of which act sprang governmental power."

Commenting of Grotius's theory of sovereignty, Dunning says, "Grotius conception of sovereignty falls short, in respect to logical precision and coherence, of that of Bodin is self-evident. An authority that is absolute yet bound by pledges that is at once a unity and divisible, that is complete yet terminable at a fixed time and that inheres equally in protector and protected, in lord and in vassal — is a confusing thing of concept."

16
Thomas Hobbes (1588-1679 A.D.)

Thomas Hobbes was an English man, who lived during the time of Charles II. He was born at Westport in North Wilts in 1588, the year of Spanish Armada. During this time Hobbes said, his mother gave birth to twins-himself and fear. His father was a vicar who later on deserted his wife and three children. When Hobbes was very young, he learned Greek and Latin. He was educated at Malmesbury and then at Oxford. On leaving the Oxford University he became tutor to the heir of William Cavendish later Earl of Devonshire. This association or connection facilitated him to meet many leading figures of his day such as Ben Jonson, Bacon, Clarendon, Harvey and Galileo.

Thomas Hobbes was a man of very studious nature. This enabled him to become a classical scholar. At the age of forty, he turned to philosophy by way of mathematics. As a result, he published his first work of translation of Thucydides. He published his "De Live" in 1642 and the "Elements of Law" in 1650. With the outbreak of the Civil War, he removed to Paris. Here he became tutor to Charles II for sometime. His masterpiece the "Leviathan" was published in 1651 while he was in Paris. The following year he was back in Protectorate England and published "Decorpove Politico" in 1655 and "De Homine" in 1659.

Thomas Hobbes was the first Englishman who wrote comprehensively on Political Philosophy. His most famous work the "Leviathan" was severely and seriously criticised by contemporary writers as expected by Hobbes Whitehall found Leviathan "as full of damnable opinions as a toad is of poison" "a rebels" "catechism" and "good doctrine of a popish cabal." According to Bramhill, it would "put all to fire and flame."

Hobbes was not a political thinker at the beginning for he was only a Tutor for the sons of the nobility after his education at Oxford. The Civil War that broke out in England made him flee away to France and drove him to enter politics for he was much depressed with the circumstances and conditions in the midst of which he was found. He, in his attempt to find solutions to solve the riddle in which he and his contemporaries were kept, wrote two works — De live and De Levithan.

It was during his time that the Rational Political View of the state developed by Greek philosophers like Plato assimilated by the Jesuit writers of the Middle Ages and decorated by Nominalists of the 13th and 14th centuries like Marsiglio of Padua, began to lose its ground in the 17th century when the individualism of the Nominalists reached a full blossom. The growth of scepticism, by the 17th century had undermined man's belief in the Natural Law. Besides, the 17th century Political Philosophers regarded Nature as a machine and natural society and state were considered as mechanism. The conception of state as a machine was maintained by Hobbes, Locke, Bentham and Mill. So the conception of state as a machine, the modern school of the political theory indeed, begins with Hobbes (Pollock). Sabine, therefore, says that the strain of modern thought met and crossed in the political philosophy of Hobbes.

Circumstances Influencing Hobbes

Since he was a Tutor of the son of Charles I, the king, he was perhaps drawn closer to the monarch and so his support for monarchy. Again since he lived during the dreadful civil war that resulted in a large scale murder, he was much depressed by and dreaded of the activities and motives of men. So he was not interested in pleasing either side in the historical dispute going on between the royalists and the parliamentarians; on the other hand, he desired to maintain his thought and philosophy independently in all his writings. So his writings were not acceptable to either side in the Civil War. The royalists thought that Hobbes was aiming at flattering Oliver Cromwell, the pillar of the Civil War, while the parliamentarians thought that Hobbes was the staunch supporter of an absolute monarchy.

Universe and Man

Hobbes is of the view that universe is a machine made of particles moving in accordance with mechanical law. The movement or motion, as he calls it, is the very principle of the universe. Man is a microcosm, an epitome of the great universe. So, he is also a machine. He, likes the universe, is composed of moving particles. So Hobbes, insists that a study of political society should commence with the consideration of nature of man the psychology governing the man. It is because of this approach that Catlin calls Hobbes as "the first observational psychologist" and a "sensationalist who had hypothesis about the fundamental springs of human action."

Man and the State of Nature

Hobbes firmly maintains that man is egoistic by nature. As such, he seeks his reservation of life continuously and the means for it. Man, in the state of nature, acts not by reason but by emotion. Appetite and Aversion, expresses Hobbes are the very first emotion, produced in man's heart by the "vital motion". Appetite seeks the good of man, in addition to it being the parent of all good emotions like joy and hope. But Aversion greets evil and is the parent of all bad emotions. The good sought by Appetite is the preservation of life and the means for it whereas the evil shunned by Aversion is death and the cause of it. Man's desire for self-preservation is, therefore, continuous and limitless.

Hobbes, describing the state of nature in the light of the nature of man as discussed above, turns to speak of the state of nature. Every individual motivated by his personal life and security. Individuals are roughly equal in strength and cunning. Their condition, therefore, is "a war of every man against every other man." In other words it is a condition wherein "homo homni lupus — man is to man a wolf' and everyone is in "the posture of gladiators." As such the life is "a perpetual and restless desire of power after power that ceaseth only in death". Such a kind of condition is in no way consistent with any type of civilization demanding or requiring the establishment of industry, foundation of navigation, cultivation of the soil and development of building and art etc., because the life of man is "solitary, poor, nasty, brutish and short". Similarly in such as state there is neither right nor wrong, justice nor injustice because the rule and order of life is "kill whom you can; take what you can." Thus, Hobbes paints an ugly and black picture of the state of nature with a gloomy background. Murray is, therefore, compelled to express that what Machiavelli has found in diplomacy Hobbes has done in the state of nature. "As there are force and fraud in the state of negotiation, so also there are force and fraud in the state of nature".

Natural Law or Natural Right

It is here Hobbes begins his discussion on the Law of Nature or Natural Right. He says that law of nature has two features. Firstly, it is "the liberty that each man has to use his power as he will himself for the preservation of his own nature that is to say of his own life." Secondly, the individual should have the will to surrender to the extent necessary and be content with as much liberty against other men as he would allow them against him. So it is obvious that the law of nature presents two alternatives. They are: (1) each man could insist upon his own absolute liberty and be content with the state of nature, and (2) each man could contract with every other man to divert himself part of his liberty and set up a common power to conserve the liberty of all. Hobbes here traces these two alternatives to 'Desire' and 'Reason' the two principles in human nature. Desire induces men to take what they want while Reason compels them to fly for a contract.

Social Contract

Men are, therefore, driven to escape from the state of nature by fear of fear and death. They are, of course, driven by Reason which had hitherto been dormant in them. They are, thus, driven to enter into a covenant. All men make a contract with one another to set up a government, an Authority and "surrender to it mutually, absolutely and irrevocably all the natural rights except the right of self-preservation". "I authorize and give up my right of governing myself to this man, to this assembly of men, on this condition that thou give thy right to him and authorize all his actions in the like manner.... This is the generation of the great Levithan or rather of that Moral God to which we owe under the Immortal God our plea and defence". Hence, "the government is only the result of and not a party to the contract. This contract is, at once, political and governmental" because state and government are one and the same for Hobbes.

Sovereignty

Hobbes expresses that state is not at all natural; but it is only an artificial man or body. "The ruler bearing the person of multitude is called sovereign and said to have sovereign power while everybody is his subject." The state ceases its meaning if there is no sovereign. Such a state is known literally as "headless multitude." Hobbes strongly holds that sovereignty is state itself. Men confer all the power and strength needed, on a Man who has the right and duty to bear 'their person.' This is their real unity — all in one and the same person. This act of the multitude so united in one person is called a Commonwealth. "What is state; I am the State" — These words attributed to Louis XIV of France explain and express in clear and unambiguous terms the contention of Hobbes that sovereignty is state itself.

The sovereign of Hobbes, therefore, is absolute and unlimited. He is not subject to any law — human or fundamental. He is the 'public conscience' and as such he possesses the sole power to interpret the natural law, divine law, national law, and international law. So he is the sole and only source of laws.

The sovereign is not a party to the contract; but is the result of it. He, as such, receives from the multitudes an absolute irrevocable surrender of all their rights except self-preservation relates only to life. The sovereign therefore cannot command any to kill himself. This is the only limitation imposed on the Leviathan's powers. The Leviathan is supposed to be all-powerful and capable of protecting its multitudes. If he fails to protect the multitudes then they are forced to go back to the state of nature. The sovereign is indivisible; the sovereign is irrevocable, and the sovereignty is inalienable. Besides civil law is the command of the sovereign. Customs are valid as laws only because of the consent of the sovereign.

Hobbes' sovereign, is "a massive figure of a crowned giant made of tiny human figures", bearing a sword in a hand and a crosier in another the emblem of temporal and spiritual authorities respectively. "Render that which is Caesar's to Caesar and that which is also God to Caesar." — Such is the view of Hobbes. A Church is therefore 'a mere corporation' to Hobbes. It should be remembered here that Hobbes is not an atheist or a confirmed sceptic but a convinced materialist rejecting the super-natural and spiritual power because it is for a materialist like him a mere ghost — a figment of imagination.

Hobbes sovereign, therefore, is God on earth or rather more than God Himself and is omnipotent and omnicompetent despite his only limitation. It is because of this McIver says that Hobbes state is "more slave plantation or collection of wild animals than a society of human beings." His theory of sovereignty as Sabine has contended brings to completion the process of subordinating the Church to the civil power which had its beginning when Marsiglio of Padua by his logical conclusion separated the spiritual and the temporal authorities. However, Hobbes, in his anxiety to fortify the doctrine of sovereignty and to leave no excuse for disputing the authority of the state, gives an elaborate account of the construction of the state by an imaginary covenant Pollock. If we are called upon to comment on what Hobbes has aimed at as contended by a thinker we can well says that Hobbes supports a plain and sound doctrine which he felt and experienced by a needless and untenable fiction.

Hobbes' Place in the History of Political Philosophy

Scholars still differ about the place of Thomas Hobbes in the history of political philosophy. Some support him which others criticise him.

Those who support him:

Dunning declares that Hobbes' work "placed at once in the front rank of political thinkers and his theory became, from the moment of its appearance, the centre of animated controversy and enormous influence throughout Western Europe."

Sabine remarks, "Hobbes is probably the greatest writer on political philosophy that the English speaking people have produced."

Prof. Oakeshott says, " 'The Leviathan' is the greatest, perhaps the sole masterpiece of political philosophy in the English language."

Gettell says, "The first comprehensive work in the political philosophy by an Englishman was that of Thomas Hobbes. Hobbes is interesting not only as a political theorist but also as a person. Indeed his personality played a vital role in shaping his views on the 'comfort' of government."

His critics, however, remark:

Lindsay — "His main virtue, as also his supreme defect, is his realism, if we use that term of capacity of seeing with great charms and honesty everything in human behaviour which one without faith or emotion can see."

Murray — "Hobbes' biographer could only find a solitary supporter, while his assailants were countless. Hobbesism, in fact, stood for atheism, materialism, despotism or indeed for many other 'isms' that the fancy of the age suggested."

Geiser and Jaszi — "That his whole political system is very near to that of Machiavelli; he may be regarded as an ethical materialist who reduces all the aspirations of human nature to a brutal egoism, and for the most part to the satisfaction of animal appetites."

Vaughan — "So far as the vital development of political thought is concerned, Leviathan has remained and deserves to remain without influence and without fruit a fantastic hybrid, incapable of propagating its kind."

Hobbes made the following valuable contribution to the history of political thought:

(a) He was the first political philosopher to set forth a clear doctrine of absolute and unlimited sovereignty of state.

(b) "Hobbes made out a thesis for the state as a machine. Its existence is because of its utility." Though Hobbes propounded the theory of absolutism, he, however, never lost the sight of human welfare.

(c) Hobbes provided a scientific bases for absolutism and secularism. He followed the deductive method.

(d) Hobbes gave a new treatment to 'natural laws.' He is the first philosopher of discipline.

17
Benedict Spinoza (1632-1677)

Benedictus de Spinoza was born to Jewish parents in Amsterdam (Holland) in 1632. During the revolt of the Netherlands against Spain, he came to Holland. His studies had been mainly Jewish, but he was an independent thinker. He acquired sufficient knowledge in his Jewish studies to wean him away from orthodox theology. He followed the main principles of Descarte. "I think therefore I am" the dictum of Descarte greatly influenced him.

Spinoza's contributions are: (1) Ethics Geometrically Demonstrated, (2) On the Improvement of the Intellect, (3) The Principles of Cartesian Philosophy, (4) Theologico-Political Treatise, (5) Political Treatise and (6) Treatise on the Rainbow.

Though Spinoza followed the fundamental ideas of Descarte's Physics, he indicated three distinct features in Cartesian metaphysics. Those three features were unsatisfactory to him. They were: (1) transcendence of God, (2) the substantial dualism of mind, and (3) the ascription of free will as liberilm arbitrium both to God and to human beings. According to him, those doctrines made the world unintelligible. He believes that it is possible to construct a system of metaphysics which would be intelligible. One of the main motives in the construction of Spinoza's system was deep religious feeling.

According to Spinoza, God is a conscious thing; really it is an omniscient being, but without free will and purposes. He acts according to the necessity of His own nature. Some people may be good; some may be bad. It does not mean that God should have special care for those people on the basis of their likes and dislikes. All things in Nature are determined by necessity. He argues that all events and man's actions are determined, by their proper course and are just not accidental or providential.

God and universe are identical things. He too observes certain necessary laws in the matts. From this it is clear that his system is based on universal determinism and not on fatalism. In this connection he describes about the importance of knowledge. He defines that the mental correlate for physical action is called knowledge. There are three types of knowledge according to Spinoza viz. opinion or imagination, reason and intuition.

Another feature of his ethico-political system is the denial of human free will. The will and the understanding are one and the same. Man is free in so far as his emotions are active rather than passive. To attain Freedom reason must regulate passions. According to him, the natural man is strictly pre-social as revealed by Hobbes. Men who are good by reason seek useful things to them and they desire nothing for themselves which they do not desire for the rest of mankind. It is thus crystal clear that his ethics is not based on egoism but on altruistic utilitarianism.

After giving a graphic picture about his ethical foundations of political order, he sets forth his idea of defence of democracy in his monumental works. According to him, the philosopher must study human passions and their modifications exactly as if they were properties of atmosphere. But he must also consider the practical side of politics from the human view point. It is found in the Theologico-Political Treatise rather than in the political treatise. From the above works we know about monarchy, aristocracy and democracy with an emphasis upon positive laws and institutions.

In Spinoza's state of nature men lived in accordance with their natural instinctive self-preservation. Active emotion (Reason) was very essential for man. If this was predominant in man there would be no conflict. Hence, no civil authority or government would be necessary. But majority of men are governed by passive desires leading to conflict for possession and properties. Hence, in the state of nature might was right. In the state of nature the individuals surrender their power to a sovereign authority for the sake of enhancing each man's power of self-preservation. Thus, the civil society comes into existence as the result of a common agreement by those individuals. Here, the might of the whole limits the might of the individual. The sovereign authority is for general welfare. He regulates the interest of the people by means of good laws. Law is the epitome of reason and its objective is enlarge the scope of freedom and happiness, stability and security and peace and order. Philosophy is the ultimate end of the state. For the preservation of piety and public peace "freedom of philosophizing" is necessary. It is seen from his Theologico-Political Treatise. He disregards monarchy and favours democracy since it limits the right of the chief magistrates. According to him, "democracy" does not indicate the number of voters from whom the office holders are chosen, but rather that there are laws which specifically determine who will be eligible to vote. He further says that a viable democratic government is based upon consent and co-operation but is run by the rational men, and governed by just laws towards the end-philosophic freedom.

Spinoza puts great stress on the necessity of religion to obtain the best republic. Religion must be purified for the same. He considered Bible as a compendium of practical and precise social and moral law and as a code of behaviour. His object was to avoid subjecting the state to the diverse judgement and passions of everyone. For that purpose, he remarked that the clergymen should not be given political power because it tends to corrupt them. Naturally, it will affect both the Church and the state. According to him, religious functions must be separated from political functions and sovereign is entitled to decide whether a particular thing is lawful or not.

Hence, Spinoza's political philosophy is very significant. He is the first and foremost man to write about the systematic defence of democracy.

18

John Locke (1632-1704)

John Locke is considered as the greatest figure in the history of English political thought. He was born at Wrington, Somersetshire in 1632 to Puritan parents. In 1642, his father was enlisted in the Parliamentary Army and served as a captain of a company volunteers.

Locke received his early education at home. Later, he was admitted to Westminster school. At the age of 20, he entered Christ Church College, Oxford. In 1658, he became Master of Arts and after that he was appointed as a tutor in Greek, rhetoric and philosophy at Oxford.

But teaching profession did not appeal to him. Science had always beckoned him to be decided to take up the study of medicine. He became an assistant to the eminent physician David Thomas and after a few years of apprenticeship Locke became a doctor.

In 1666 Lord Ashley, who later became Earl of Shaftesbury, came to Oxford to get himself treated by Dr. David. The association of Locke with Lord Ashley was not very long, yet Lord Ashley was impressed by Locke very much and the former invited the latter to London as his personal physician and confidential secretary.

Lord Ashley was a great public man of his time. After the overthrow of Cromwell when Charles II became king, he appointed Lord Ashley as his Lord Chancellor. In 1672, he was made Earl of Shaftesbury. Locke being the confidential secretary and personal physician of Lord Ashley, established contacts with eminent persons. Ashley got him appointed as secretary of presentations and secretary in the Council of Trade and Foreign Plantations.

In 1673, Shaftesbury was removed from his office which naturally effected Locke's position. Both of them left England and lived in France. Later Charles II restored Shaftesbury to his previous position.

In 1681, Shaftesbury was charged with the offence of conspiracy. He was tried but acquitted. However, he was compelled to leave England. Locke left his job and went to Oxford. But he was always in danger of persecution. Hence, he sought asylum in Holland.

In 1688, the Bloodless Revolution took place in England and William Orange was invited to occupy the throne. Since Locke had come into contact with William of Orange in Holland, hence when William returned to England, Locke also came back.

During the period 1663 to 1704 when he died, he wrote the books which made him famous. He wrote in such dissimilar subject as politics, economics, education, theology, natural science, philosophy, biography and horticulture. In politics, education, theology and philosophy his works ranks among the highest achievements of human mind.

John Bowler says, "Locke was physically frail as is apparent from his portraits, but of great intellectual power and tenacity".

In the political field, his principal works are as follows:

(1) Four Letters Concerning Toleration (1690).
(2) A Second Letter on Toleration (1690).
(3) The Two Treatises of Government (1690).
(4) An Essay Concerning Human Understanding, published in 1690.
(5) Some Thoughts Concerning Education (1693).
(6) The Reasonableness of Christianity (1695).
(7) The Fundamental Constitutions of Carolina (1706).

His View of Human Nature

Locke holds that all men are naturally in a state of equality. Men are morally equal if, and as just soon as, reason in them, which makes them persons, is sufficiency developed for them to recognise those natural laws which define their rights and duties.

According to Locke, the object of all human action is to subordinate pleasure for pain. Hobbe's view that men is egoistic, competitive, quarrelsome and aggressive by nature and that the state of nature is the state of war of each against all.

Locke believes in the goodness of man. He says men are decent, orderly and they low society and can rule themselves. According to him, rationality is the pervasive characteristic of man. "Rational beings...are called persons because their very nature points them out as end in themselves, that is something which must not be used merely as means... ."

By 'the spark of divine nature' Locke means man is endowed by nature with the light of reason which enables him to discern and follow the law of nature which is behind all things.

Locke says that in the original state of nature peace and reason prevailed. This state of nature was not lawless because man lived under natural law. He describes the state of nature in the following words:

"Though this be a state of liberty yet it is not a state of licence, though man in that state have an uncontrollable liberty to dispose of his person or possessions, yet he has no liberty to destroy himself or so much as any creature in his possession, but where some nobles use than its bare preservations calls for it. The sate of nature has a law to govern it which obliges everyone and reason, which is that law teaches all mankind, who will but consult it, that being all equal and independent, no one ought to harm another is his life, health liberty or possessions.

And...in the state of nature, one man comes by power over another but yet no absolute or arbitrary power, to use a criminal, when he has got him in his hands according to the passionate hearts or boundless extravagancy of his own will but only to retribute to him, so far as calm, reason and conscience dictate, what is proportionate to his transgression, which is so much as may serve for reparation and restraint...every man in the state of nature has a power to kill a murderer, both to deter others from doing the like injury...and also to secure men from the attempts of criminals who having renounced reason, the common rule and measure God has given to mankind has, by the unjust violence and slaughter he has committed upon one, declared war against all mankind and, therefore, may be destroyed as a lion or tiger, one of those wild savage beasts with whom man can have no society nor security and upon this is grounded that great law of nature, who so sheds man's blood by man shall his blood be shed."

Hobbes description of the state of nature as a war of all against all has been condemned by Locke, who describes the state of nature as a state of goodwill natural assistance and preservation. The only defect of nature is lack of organisation, written law and fixed penalties. Locke deems this theory absurd that the state of nature should be governed by anything but the law of nature.

But this state of nature has some effects. The law of nature, on experience, fails man when he needs it most. He is ready enough to apply its restraining canons to the acts of others, he is not quite so ready to apply them equally to his own. Secondly, if he is willing to do justice to others, he is not sure his judgement is not prejudiced.

Locke, however, observes "God having made man such a creature that in his own judgement it was nor good for him to be alone put him under strong obligation of necessity, convenience and inclination to drive him into society as well as fitted him with understanding and language to continue and enjoy it."

Locke says, it was inner nature of man which constrained him to form a social group. Family was the first such group and the government came into existence afterwards. Individuals were unable to maintain their natural rights against injustice or this led to from a body politic.

The Contract

Locke next proceeds to say that civil society came into existence from the consent of its members. He defines civil power as the "right of making laws with penalties...for the regulating and preserving of property, and of employing the force of the community in the execution of such laws...all this only for the good of the public." It is but natural that such a power can arise only by consent. Man thus, entered into a contract, to get rid of the inconveniences of the state of nature and in this way the state of nature changed into a political state.

According to Locke, "Man being born with a title to perfect freedom and uncontrolled enjoyment of all the rights and privileges of the law of nature equally with any other man or number of men in the world has by nature a power, not only to preserve his property i.e. his life, liberty and property, against the injuries and attempts of other man, but to judge of and punish the breaches of that law in orders. But there and there only is a political society, where every one of the members has quitted this natural power, resigned in up into the hands of the community in all cases that exclude him not from appealing for protection to the law established by it. And thus all private judgement of every particular member excluded, the community comes to be umpire and decides all the differences that may happen between any number of the society concerning any matter of right; and punishes those offences while any member has committed against the society with such penalties as the law has established.

Whenever, therefore, any number of men are so united into one society, as to quit everyone his executive power of the law of nature, and so resign it to the politic, there and there only is a political or civil society. And this is done, wherever any number on a single body politic under one supreme government. For hereby he authorises the society to make laws for him. And this puts men out of a state of nature into that of a Commonwealth, by setting up a judge on earth, with authority to determine all the controversies and redress the injuries that may happen to any member of the Commonwealth."

C.E. Vaughan says, Locke's contract is double though he does not say so explicitly. "The first puts an end to the state of nature and substitutes it by a civil society. Thus done, the people in their corporate capacity enter into another contract the governmental contract. But according to D.R. Bhandari, Locke's contract is not double, it is single, because to Locke, man is by nature social."

Gettell says, "The contract was thus specific and limited, not general as Hobbes had said."

Locke says that the sovereign power thus created by the contract is vested in the community as a whole and not in any one single person. The contract must by unanimous and is irrevocable because after having once made it, the people cannot go back to the original state. The contract however, must respect the natural rights — right to life, liberty and property — of man and also abide by the law of nature.

According to Locke, the reason why men give up the state of nature for civil society is for the preservation of their lives, liberties, and estates which call by the general names of property.

Locke holds that the right to property is most important because all other natural rights are analogous to the right of private property. Even in the state of nature men possessed natural right and for the protection of these rights the state is created.

Dunning observes that the more distinctive contribution of Locke to political theory is the doctrine of natural rights.

Locke says, men possessed the right to property in the state of nature hence the creation of a civil society does not add anything to the contract in this respect. In fact, this right was brought by men from the natural state to the civil state. The state has to protect it and cannot deprive any individual of his property without obtaining his consent.

Locke describes natural rights 'as indefeasible or inviolable claims upon both society and government. It is the solemn duty of the state to preserve and protect the property and property rights of every member of the society up to the point where no harm was done to others.'

Sabine puts it in these words: "The life liberty and estate of one person can be limited only to make effective the quality valid claims of another person to the same rights."

Locke says, "God, who has given the world to men in common, has also given them reason to make use of it to the best advantage of life and convenience. The earth and all that is therein, is given to men for the support and comfort of their being.... And...all the fruits it naturally produces and beasts it feeds, belongs, to mankind in common, as they are produced by the spontaneous hand of nature, and nobody has originally a private dominion, exclusive of the rest of mankind, in any of them, as they are thus in their natural state...whatsoever he removes out of the state that nature has provided and left it, in he has mixed his labour with, and joined to it something that in his own and thereby makes in his own property."

Locke further says, "Though the water running in the fountain be every ones, yet who can doubt, but that in the pitcher is his only who drew it out? His labour has taken it out of the hands of nature where it was common, and belonged equally to all her children and has thereby appropriated to himself." This follows from this statement that originally all things provided by nature were not exclusively the possession of any one person, but were the common possession of all. But whatever man produces by his labour, working upon what nature has provided us, becomes his personal property.

According to Locke, "The great and chief end of man's uniting into Commonwealth and putting themselves under government, is the preservation of their property."

Thus, it can be concluded that the preservation of man's natural rights was the principal aim of instituting a Commonwealth or state.

State — Government

John Locke makes distinction between the state and the government. By the first contract the civil society is formed and after the formation of the civil society, the government is formed by a second contract.

Locke lays emphasis on social contract among the people by which the state is formed. The state is formed to remove certain inconvenience of the state of nature.

While describing the relationship between the community and the government, Locke uses the 'trust' and cautiously avoids the use of the word 'contract'. The reason for doing so is the fact that in the opinion of Locke, the government is subordinate to the community. He maintains that the government exists for the good of the people and if it violates the trust reposed in it, it can legitimately be removed. Vaughan also expresses the same opinion. He says, "by adopting the analogy of a trust, rather than that of contact, Locke makes very fair provision not only for popular control of government but also for a progressive extension of that control, as experience may dictate.

Whatever be the exact form of government established by the community there is always one condition which must be fulfilled, and the condition is that both legislative and executive are bound to act for the benefit of the community from whom their authority is derived.

Describing the functions of government, Locke says, "If man in the state of nature be so free...if he be absolute lord of his own person and possessions, equal to the greatest and subject to nobody, while we will part with his freedom? Why will he give up this empire and subject himself to the dominion and control of any other power? To which it is obvious to answer, that though in the state of nature he has such a right yet the enjoyment of it is very uncertain and constantly exposed to the invasion of others.... This makes him willing to quit this condition. Which however, free, is full of fears and continual dangers, and it is not without reason, that he seeks out and is willing to join the society with others...for preservation of their lives, liberties and estates, which I call by the general name property."

In the opinion of Locke, the government has to perform the following functions:

(a) To establish and make known men the standard of right and wrong and the common measure to decide all controversies between them.

(b) To provide an impartial authority which shall decide all the disputes arising among persons in accordance with the established law.

(c) To safeguard the interest of the community and of its members in relation to other communities and their citizens. This has been described as the most important function of the government.

As regards the forms of government, Locke says, if the legislative power is in the hand of one man, it is monarchy, when this power is vested in the few selected men, then it is obligarchy. But when the power is vested in the whole community and the community appoints few officers to execute

19
Giambattista Vico (1668-1744)

Giambattista Vico was the native of Naples. He was born on June 23, 1668 to a bookseller. Vico attended many schools in his early days. Although, he attended many schools, he was by and large self-educated. He took his law degree in 1694 from the University of Naples. For some time, he served as Professor of rhetoric in the same University. In 1735, he was appointed to the high post of royal historiographer.

Vico, the Italian philosopher is considered as the exponent of a "new science of humanity". He published his first work, "On the Method of the Studies of Our Time" in 1709. In the following year, he published his another book "On the Ancient Wisdom of the Italians". His "Universal Law" was published in 1720-22.

Vico has given a graphic picture about his theory of knowledge in his two books viz. "On the Method of the Studies of Our Time" and "On the Ancient Wisdom of the Italians". According to him, precise knowledge is possible in Mathematics through a process of abstraction and definition. The same method can be applied to the natural order to some extent. Hence, one can attain some knowledge. Since, the natural order is made by Nature or God, it is very difficult to measure the same as stated by Vico. The natural order can be completely known to God only because it was made by Him, whereas the human institutions, the civil world, social and political orders are made by men and so men can have knowledge about these. To vindicate and indicate his theory he says that there are three stages, three elements and three principles in everything. It is seen that men at first feel without observing fear of God, then they observe with terribly troubled mind, and finally, they reflect with a clear mind. These three represent the three stages of human history. These three stages give way for three corresponding forms of government i.e. theocracy, aristocracy and monarchy or republic.

In his "Universal Law" Vico points out clearly about rational civil theology of divine providence, principles of power and authority, evolution and growth of human ideas, natural law of nations and the principles of universal history. By employing his triad he says that history develops through a cycle of three stages i.e., divine, heroic and human. These three represent the three stages of human understanding. Finally, these three stages give way for three forms of government.

According to Vico, the historians will be able to bet the above eternal cycle. Men are historical beings subject to constant changes and evolution. Hence, history and understanding of political institutions must be based on the interpretation of historical date. So far as this point is concerned Vico gave a clear way for Hegel who later on gave his own ideas on the interpretation of history.

20

Montesquieu (1689-1755)

Montesquieu was born on January 18, 1689 near Bordeaux. He was the son of a distinguished French lawyer. He belonged to a noble and aristocratic family.

In the beginning, he studied at home but later in the year 1700 he was sent to school at Juilly, where he studied for 11 years. Thereafter, he studied law and in the year 1714, he was admitted to the grade of counsellor. He got married when he was 25.

Until the age of 27, Montesquieu was known by the name of BARON DE LA BREDE ET DE. When his uncle died and he inherited his uncle's title as well as his judicial office. For 12 years, Montesquieu continued as Chief Magistrate of Bordeaux. But this job did not satisfy him, because he was a great reader of literature and history.

His first book, the 'Persian Letters' was published in 1721. In these 'Letters' he had satirized the political, social and religious institutions of France. This book was a great success and though Montesquieu wrote them anonymously, however it soon became known that he was the writer of the book. Thus, he got established as a literary man.

In 1728, Montesquieu started for an extensive tour and visited Austria, Hungary, Venice, Rome, Switzerland, the Rhine, Holland and England. Wherever he went, he carefully observed the local men and institutions. In England, he stayed for 18 months and came into close contact with leading politicians and scholars. He was deeply impressed by the English conception of liberty and English system of government.

The rest of his life Montesquieu spent at his country estate, where he spent his time in supervising his studies and in literary pursuits. He continued writing as long as he could and in 1755 he left for his heavenly home.

Montesquieu's principal writings were as follows:

(a) The Persian Letters.

(b) Reflections on the Causes of the Greatness and Decline of the Romans.

(c) The Spirit of Laws.

The Spirit of the Laws was Montesquieu's masterpiece and placed him among the immortals.

The English Evening Post wrote the following obituary of him:

"His virtues did honour of human nature, his writings to justice. A friend to mankind, he asserted their undoubtable and inalienable rights with freedom, even in his own country whose prejudices in matters of religion and government he had long lamented and endeavoured not with some success, to remove."

His Views on Laws

Montesquieu does not believe in abstract justice. He, however believes that the basic principal of law and justice exist in nature. But he is of the opinion that the teaching of nature are to be found "not in deduction from assumption based on reason, but in the facts of history of the actual working of political life."

He says, the laws should not be accepted merely as a command of the sovereign or as the dictates of reason. It should be found out as to how they came to be. The cause and effect as their origin and development should be traced.

Montesquieu observes, "Laws, in the wider possible connotation are any necessary relations arising from a things of nature. In this sense all beings have their laws: the Diety His laws, the material world its laws, the intelligence superior to man their laws, the beasts their laws, man his laws." Thus, Montesquieu holds that any relation between one thing and the other is a law.

Like the rest of the nature, men stand in order, necessary relations to one another. But law in human behaviour is much more complicated because men are self-conscious and possessed of will. In the words of Jones, it means, "(1) that they do not always automatically follow the pattern established for human behaviour as plants for example, follow pattern established for plant behaviour. In other words, men are free to modify or altogether reject, behaviour patterns, which in the lower-creatures and in inanimate nature are fixed and necessary. Hence, (2) men require to be ordered by another kind of pattern. They need another kind of restraint and thus, being self-conscious, they are able to give themselves. Putting it differently the behaviour of men is complicated by the presence of law in another, but analogous sense.

They are also subject to 'law' in the sense of rules given by some man or assembly or established by custom which they are to follow, subject to certain penalties in failing to do so."

About natural and positive law, Montesquieu holds, "Then intelligent world is far from being so well-governed as the physical. For though, the former has also its laws which of their own nature are invariable, it does not conform so exactly as does the physical world. This is because particular intelligent beings are limited by their nature requires them to be free agents. Hence, they do not steadily conform to the laws of their nature. Indeed they frequently infringe even those of their own instituting."

He goes further to say, "Animals have natural laws, because they are united by sensation, but they do not have positive laws because they lack knowledge. However, they do not invariably conform to their natural laws.... Man as a physical being is governed by invariable laws. As an intelligent being, he incessantly transgresses the law established by, God, and being, and subject to.... As a sensible creature, he is subject to a thousand impetus passions. Such a being might every instant forget his creator. God has, therefore, reminded him on his duty by the laws of religion. Such a being is liable every moment to forget himself, philosophy has provided against this by the laws of morality. Former to live in society, he might forget his creatures. Legislators have, therefore, by political and civil laws confined him to his duty."

From the above statement, it can by concluded that Montesquieu, holds that man is governed by two different sets of laws. These laws are:

1. Laws established by God or natural laws.
2. Laws made by man or positive laws.

Man's conduct cannot be governed by natural laws only, hence they must be supplemented by man-made laws. According to Montesquieu, man made laws are of the following classes:

(a) International law.
(b) Political law, or
(c) Civil law.

International Law: International law arises out of the relation of one state with other states.

Political Law: According to Montesquieu, law governing the relation between the individuals and the government is called political.

Civil Law: The relations between the citizens of the same state are regulated by civil law.

The most important part of 'The Spirit of Laws' is liberty. Montesquieu makes distinction between political liberty and personal liberty. Liberty is a right to do all that what is permitted by law and if a citizen could do what the laws forbid, he would be no longer possessed of liberty because all his fellow citizens would have the same power. Political liberty needs check on political authority, so that neither an individual can be compelled to do things, to which the laws does not oblige him, nor forced to abstain from things which the law permits.

Montesquieu says, "There is no word that has been given more varied meanings, and has evoked more varied emotions in the human heart than 'liberty'". Some have taken it as a means of deposing him on whom they had conferred a tyrannical, authority, others for the powers of choosing him whom they must obey, still others for the right of bearing arms, and of being able to use violence. Others again have meant by liberty the privilege of being governed by a nature of their own country or by their own laws. A certain people for a long time thought liberty consisted in the privilege of wearing a long bead. Some have annexed this name to one form of government exclusively of others, those who had a republican taste applied it to this species of government, those who liked a monarchial state gave it to monarchy. Thus they have applied the name of liberty to the government most suited to their own customs and inclinations.

Montesquieu was very much influenced by the British sense of liberty. British liberty has been achieved by imposing constitutional restrictions on arbitrary powers. According to Montesquieu, liberty consists in acting not arbitrary, but according to law.

Jones says, "Liberty, in a work is dramatically the opposite of despotism. Despotism is the arbitrary irregular and lawless flat of an individual will. True liberty on the other hand, is not the capacity to do whatever happen to will now, for this would be to make of one an arbitrary despot. It is rather the freedom which has its source in the sure, regular and rational restraint of law."

Montesquieu makes clear distinction between civil liberty and political liberty.

According to Montesquieu, civil liberty comes from manners, customs, received examples and even from particular civil laws. In essence it is the security or sense of security that people have civil liberty is the opposite of slavery and grows out of the relation of man to man. To establish and preserve this liberty it is necessary that criminal justice be so regulated that punishment flows naturally from the nature of the crime and not from the caprice of the authorities.

According to Montesquieu, it is necessary to impose checks on political authority, so that no man shall be compelled to do things to which the law does not oblige him nor forced to abstain from things which the law permits.

He further states, "The political liberty of the subject is a tranquility of mind arising from the opinion each person has of his safety. In order to have the liberty, it is requisite the government to constitution that one man need not be afraid of another."

Separation of Powers

According to Montesquieu, separation of governmental powers into executive, legislative and judicial organs is the best guarantee for liberty. "If the legislative power is united with the executive power in the hands of one person or of one body of officials, there can be no liberty nor can there be any liberty if the power to judge is not separated from the legislative and executive powers. There would be an end of everything, where the same man or the same body, whether of nobles or of the people, to exercise those three powers, that of enacting laws, that of executing the public resolutions, and of trying the causes of individuals."

Montesquieu insisted that each power must be exercised by a separate organ and a system of checks and balances should be established.

Sidgewick remarks, "separation of fundamental powers of government, and balanced distribution of them among different organs differently appointed bodies or individual so that by natural play off whole organization, any tendency to oppression on the part of any organ government may be checked by another."

Montesquieu believed that the best safeguard against tyranny and the surest guarantee of liberty is the separation of powers among different organs of the government. He says,

"In every government there are three sorts of powers, the legislative, executive, in respect to things dependent on the law of nations and the executive in regard to matters that depend upon the civil law...."

"By virtue of the first, the prince or magistrate enacts temporary or perpetual laws, and amends or abrogates those that have already been enacted. By the second, he makes peace or war, sends or receives embassies, establishes the public security, and provide against invasions. By the third, he punishes criminals or determines the disputes that arise between individuals. The latter we shall call the judiciary power and the other simply executive power of the state...."

"The political liberty of the subject is a tranquility of mind arising from the opinion of each person has of his safety. In order to have his liberty, it is requisite that the government be so constituted as one man need not be afraid of other...."

"When the legislative and executive powers are united in the same person and in the same body of magistrates, there can be no liberty, because apprehensions may arise, lest the same monarch or senate enact tyrannical laws, to execute them in tyrannical manner...."

"Again, there is no liberty, if the judiciary power be not separated from the legislative or executive where it is joined with the legislative, the life and liberty of the subject would be exposed to arbitrary control, for the judge would be then the legislator, where it is joined to the executive power, the judge might behave with violence and oppression...."

According to Hearnshaw, "If the legislative power is united with the executive power in the hands of one person or of one body of officials there can be no liberty, nor can there be any liberty if the power to judge is not separated from the legislative and executive powers."

"There would be an end of everything where the same man or the same body, whether of nobles or of the people, to exercise those three powers, that of enacting laws, that of executing the public resolutions, and trying the case of individuals."

Prof. Laski also remarks: "The independence of judiciary from the executive is essential to the freedom. In that sense, the doctrine of separation of powers among the three branches of government ensures liberty by imposing a healthy check on the disposition of the government officials."

Criticism

However, Montesquieu's theory of separation of powers is not free from criticism. It is also said that his reading of the English constitution was not very correct. The following criticism are advanced against Montesquieu's theory:

(1) Though Montesquieu felt that the separation of powers was best realized in the British constitution, however, his reading was not very correct. In Britain, there is no full separation of powers between the different organs of government. The House of Lords is both a legislative and a judicial body. The Lord Chancellor in England partakes of all the three functions of government.

(2) If powers are separated and each branch is made independent of each other, every branch will try

to safeguard its own powers which will cause administrative difficulty.

(3) Perfect separation of power is impossible.

(4) Separation of powers will lead to conflict between the three different branches of government because each branch will be interested in its own powers.

(5) Separation of powers presupposes that all branches of government have equal importance which is not correct. Legislative Branch is more important.

Forms of Government

Montesquieu describes three forms of Government:

(1) Republic

(2) Monarchy

(3) Despotism

But he does not regard any form of government to be essentially good in itself, its value is relative. Montesquieu says, "If it be true that the temper of mind and the passions of the heart are extremely different climates, the laws ought to be in relation both to the variety of those passions and to the variety of those tempers."

Republic: When the supreme power of the state rests in the hands of a body of people, it is called democracy. In democracy, the people are sovereign. Montesquieu says, "A republican government is that, in which the body, or only a part of the people is possessed of the supreme power." The sovereignty in republics is exercised but by the votes of the people.

Monarchy: In a monarchy, one person, the monarch, rules according to fixed and established laws. These mental laws necessarily presuppose intermediate channels through which the sovereign power flow, for if there be only the momentary and capricious will of a single person to govern the state, nothing can be fixed, and hence there is no fundamental law.

The most natural intermediate power, according to Montesquieu, is that of nobility. To some extent it is necessary for monarchy, whose fundamental maxim is no monarch, no nobility; no nobility, no monarch but there may be despotic process.

Despotism: In despotism, a single person rules according to his personal will and caprice. There are no fixed or established laws.

Commenting on Montesquieu's classification of governments, W.T. Jones remarks, "This classification is not very satisfactory. Aristocracy appears as an ambiguous sub-type and he is soon obliged to admit that despotism does not belong in his scheme since it is really not a government at all. Though Montesquieu does not quite see this himself, it becomes apparent that he really has two main types of government, those that are moderate and those that are not. And in moderate governments tend to become despotism just so far as they substitute for the rule of law, rule by arbitrary fact — whether it be that of a single individual or mob."

21

Voltaire (1694-1778)

Voltaire was one of the greatest philosophers of the world. He was a French man. He was born on November 21, 1694. He lost his mother when he was very young. He had no affection towards his father. He was very fond of literature. The religious instructions of the Jesuit Fathers served only to excite his skepticism and mockery. The French military disasters of 1709 and the horrors of religious persecutions distressed him very much. Twice he was confined in the Bastille prison for his verbal battles with the government and the Church. As a result, he decided to uphold the rights of men of letters against the arbitrary power of the king and of the nobles.

Voltaire went over to England in 1726 and spent three years there along with English scholars. Further he admired the English liberal outlook and the Freedom in the discussion of religious and philosophic questions. Returning to France, he decided to show England as a model for his countrymen.

"History of Charles XII" and "Philosophical Letters" were published by him in 1731 and 1734 respectively. In the above letters, he has given his criticisms of Descartes and Pascal, Voltaire says that the purpose of life is not to reach heaven through penitence but to assure happiness to all men by progress in both the sciences and arts a fulfilment for which their nature is destined. Moreover, the above letters embody the philosophy of the 18th century and is a landmark in the history of political thought.

As a result of the publication of these letters he had to run away from the inevitable arrest warrant. He was given refuge by Mme. du. Chatelet. Then fame and friendship earned by him in Belgium, Cirey and Paris paved for his success in life. Once again doom and disaster embraced him after the death of Chatelet. So he took refuge at Geneva.

"The Age of Louis XIV" and "History of Mankind" the two great works are still considered as great contributions to cultural history. After 1758, he was aptly called as the innkeeper of Europe since he lived a crowded life with worldwide fame.

Voltaire's main target of attack was the Roman Catholic Church. He constructed a personal encyclopaedia in 1764, which was later enlarged. He was able to retain the leadership of the philosophic movement by speaking and acting against the injustice done to the people by an intolerant Church. He was given a warm welcome when he returned to Paris in 1778 where he died towards the end of May.

Voltaire condemned organised Christianity for its basic belief in the supernatural and for what he held to be its support of social injustice. Hence, he was of the opinion that the Middle Ages was a period of barbarous misery. He hated the Jews for their begotten Christianity. In his "Treatise on Toleration" he writes that a fanaticism composed of superstition and ignorance has been the sickness of all the centuries.

In his "Philosophical Dictionary" which was published in 1764 he gives clear picture about his anti-clerical thoughts and his doubts about the historicity of biblical characters. He further says that the Church and the state should be separated from one another with a view to make the state free and secular. He shuns metaphysics and holds theology in contempt.

Another interesting aspect of Voltaire's thought is the place he attributed to reason in human nature, "That which our eyes and mathematics demonstrate to us, we must hold to be true. In all the rest we must say only, I do not know."

Voltaire was not a defender of enlightened despotism nor was he a democrat. He had firm belief in historical cycles. He had good hopes of four cultural events like Periclean Athens, Augustan Rome, Renaissance Italy and France under Louis XIV. But he had great devotion to Enlightenment. His famous saying that "If God did not exist, it would be necessary to invent Him", has often been misinterpreted as to stamp him as an atheist. He not only attacked atheism but also orthodoxy in his works.

Voltaire was a radical in religious matters but he was a conservative in the matters of politics. Theoretically, he stands for republic. He considers that men are rarely worthy to govern themselves. According to him, monarchy was the most permanent and fittest form of government. That monarchy would be in absolute power. He was for drastic administrative and legal reforms. He was against arbitrary arrest, secret trials of privileges etc. He demanded equitable justice and a new penal code so that torture and death sentence would be abolished.

Voltaire regarded patriotism and nationalism as sentimental fallacy. On this basis he condemned the American colonies who rebelled against established government. On the other hand, he cherished and nourished the ideal of world citizenship. He further stood for centralisation of powers on the basis of freedom. He condemned Rousseau's call to go back to nature. His writings along with the Rousseau greatly influenced the French people during the French Revolution. Voltaire had better and larger vision than Rousseau. However, Voltaire occupies a great place in the history of Political Thought.

22

David Hume (1711-1776)

David Hume was a great Scottish Philosopher. He was a great scholar and thinker. He was also a great historian, economist and essayist.

He was born in a Scottish family in the year 1711 and was a contemporary of Rousseau. After completing his early education he studied law. He seized very early with a passion for literature, however, he hated this profession.

David Hume tried his luck in business but was not successful. He was a failure in all professions that he followed and disappointed. He finally went to France. He wanted to establish himself as a literary figure. He lived in France for few years and wrote 'The Treatise of Human Nature' when he was nearly 26. When this book was published, few people bought it, few read it and none understood it. But now-a-days it is regarded as Hume's masterpiece. Hume died in 1776 at the age of sixty-five.

Hume wrote the following books:

(1) Treatise of Human Nature.

(2) Essays.

(3) History of England.

(4) Enquiry into the Principles of Morlas.

(5) Political Discourses.

(6) A Natural History of Religion.

(7) The Original Contract.

In the words of Gettell, the critical philosophy of Hume was one of the most powerful dissolvents of the century.

N.K. Smith remarks, "His general philosophy is, of course, beyond our scope, but in essence Hume agreed that natural law or any value system could not claim scientific validity because it could not be demonstrated that values were either true or false."

Hume rejects the theological conception of the state as well as the theory of social contract. In his philosophy he owes much to Thomas Locke and to Hutcheson. He discards the use of history to bolster up divine right and social contract and holds that morality is based on general opinion as to what is expedient and that it cannot be separated from positive law.

Gettell observes, "He foreshadowed both the historical method of Burke, on which modern conservatism is based, and the utilitarian doctrines of Bentham through which radical opinion found a means of exceptance."

Social Contract Theory

Hume has criticized the theory of social contract on the following grounds:

(a) The primitive man was not so intelligent enough as to conceive the idea of voluntary contract.

(b) No example of original contract can be found.

(c) The consent of an original contract cannot be their descendants.

(d) The ideas that political authority is based on consent is generally regarded as absurd.

Hume observes, "Were you to preach in most parts of the world that political connections are founded altogether, on voluntary consent or on a mutual promise the magistrate would soon imprison you as seditious for loosening the ties if obedience, of your friends did not before shut you as delirious for advancing such absurdities."

Hume does not agree that consent can be the reason of obedience. He says, "If the reason be asked of that obedience, which we bound to pay to government, I readily answer, because society could not otherwise subsist, and the answer is clear and intelligible to all mankind. Your answer is, because he should keep our work. But besides this, I say you find yourself embarrassed when it is asked why we are bound to keep our work? None can give any answer, but that would immediately, without any circuit have accounted for our obligation to allegiance."

Hume says, "The existence of the state is in its utility. It exists because it is necessary and people are bound to obey it and if they do not, human society will not exist."

Gettell observes, "Hume was opposed to popular government, his writings contained many acute observations of the political issues of his day. He recognised, with Harrington that governing authority tends to accompany the distribution of property. He realized the growing democracy that was making the House of Commons the real centre of power, and he saw the inevitability of parties and the necessity of the free press in popular government."

Hume's Place

Among the political philosophers of the seventeenth and eighteenth centuries, His book 'The Treatise on Human Nature' is an important contribution to the history of modern philosophy.

Prof. Laski says, "though Hume did not make any original contribution to political theory, yet he gave a new form to political speculation."

Maxey observes, "Hume started a sociological explanation of the theory of social contract by giving a sociological explanation to the duty of obedience to the state."

Sabine, writes, "He made a clean sweep of the whole rationalist philosophy of natural right, of self-evident truths and of the laws of eternal and immutable morality which were supposed to guarantee the harmony of nature and the order of human society. In place of indefeasible rights or natural justice and liberty, there remains merely utility, conceived in terms of either self-interest or social stability, and issuing in certain conventional standards of conduct which on the whole serve human purpose."

Hume's economic ideas were in advance of his age. He discarded the mercantilist theories of a strictly regulated trade. He believed in free communication and exchange.

The fact mentioned above are enough to prove that Hume occupies an important place in the history of political philosophy.

23

Jean Jacques Rousseau (1712-1778)

Coker in his "Readings in Political Philosophy" has given a beautiful account about the early life and works of Rousseau in a lucid manner. Rousseau was born of a poor family in Geneva on June 28, 1712. His ancestors came and settled in Geneva from France in the middle of the 16th century as religious refugees. He lost his mother when he was very young. Later on, he used to say, "I cost my mother her life and my birth was the first of my misfortunes." Since his father was a watchmaker and a dancer he was not able to give proper education to his son. He had no stable or practical training of any sort. He ran away from home when sixteen years of age and thereafter for twenty years he led a wandering life. He saw much of Europe "through the eyes of a penniless and at times hunted, vagabond, who did not always know where his next meal come from and where he would sleep." During these days of great stresses and strain he took some note of the ideas and feelings of the poorer people with whom he came into contact; and in his sojourns he devoted some attention to the study of philosophy. While he was in Paris he came into contact with the Encyclopaedists. Hence, he established himself at Paris and did some miscellaneous writing. Diderot accepted him as contributor to the Encyclopaedia. For "His character, his outlook on life, his scale of values, his instinctive reactive reactions, all differed essentially from what the Enlightenment regarded as admirable." Thus, Sabine describes his condition. It was difficult for him, therefore, to establish lasting human relations, except with Levasseuran uneducated woman, with whom he lived for about twenty years.

Rousseau gained a general literary reputation in 1749. In the same year, the Academy of Dijon announced a prize for his essay entitled, "Has the progress of sciences and arts contributed to corrupt or purify morals." He published the essay in 1751 under the title "A Discourse on the Moral Effects of the Arts and Sciences." According to Rousseau, "Our minds have been corrupted in proportion as the arts and sciences have improved. He further charged that we have physicists, geometricians, chemists, astronomers, poets, musicians and painters in plenty, but we have no longer a citizen among us."

Rousseau published his "Discourse on the origin of Inequality" in 1755. In this work, he distinguishes between natural and moral or political equality in a clear-cut manner. His 'Discourse on Political Economy' was published in Diderot's Encyclopaedia in 1755. The 'Social Contract' the Bible of the French Revolution was published in 1762. Of all his works, the Social Contract is regarded as the most famous work in the history of political thought. It is in the Social Contract that Rousseau's idea of the state is most clearly seen. In 1762, he also published his "Emile" a revolutionary treatise on education. This aroused vigorous opposition from political and ecclesiastical leaders due to its dogmas of revealed religion. Since, there was danger of prosecution he ran away to Switzerland. There he was welcomed for his ideas. In England, too he met the same warm welcome. He was able to return to France in 1767 and spent the last decade of his life in retirement completing his confessions. He died in 1778.

Estimate: According to Bergson, his (Rousseau's) was the most powerful of the influences which the human mind has experienced since Descartes. His influence greatly affected the mind of the world on par with other men. C.L. Wayper says that he left the stamp of his strong and original genius on politics, education, religion, literature, and it is hardly an exaggeration to say with Langson that he is to be found at the entrance to all the paths leading to the present. Yet, there has been no writer about whom it has been more difficult to find agreement than about Rousseau. He has been greatly lauded and more maligned at the same time.

Rousseau is considered as the extreme individualist, the latest and greatest of the individualist political theorists. He is also regarded as the greatest absolutist and at the same time the precursor of the 19th century German idealism. Constant said of him, "He is the most terrible ally of despotism in all its forms." Duguit wrote, "J.J. Rousseau is the father of Jacobin despotism, of Caesarian dictatorship and the inspirer of the absolutist doctrines of Kant and of Hegel." To put it in a nutshell, he is both the extreme individualist and extreme absolutist.

Rousseau revived the classical Aristotelean view that man is a political animal whose nature can be filled only in the state. Plato's emphasis that the state is a matter of ethics rather than of law is also reflected in Rousseau's thought. Both the Aristotle and Plato stood for good government at the expense of self-government. Locke and the liberals pleaded for self-government relegating the problem of good government into the background. Rousseau tried to synthesize both. Hence, he is welcomed by the adherents of both organic theory of state and the liberals.

The Social Contract theory is the most ancient theory. It is the most important of all the theories regarding the origin of the state. It has played a prominent role in modern political theory and practice.

Jean Jacques Rousseau the great French philosopher gave his ideas about this theory elaborately and excellently in the "Social Contract" and "Emile". The Social Contract the Bible of the French Revolution was published in 1762. The main substance of this theory is that the state is the result of an agreement entered into by men who originally had no government organisation.

Rousseau's ideas on the state are clearly found in his "Social Contract". This work opens with the remark "man is born free and everywhere he is in chains. One who believes himself the master of the rest is only more of a slave than they. How does that change about? I do not know what can render it legitimate? That question I think I can answer." Thus, Rousseau seeks to answer the question, "What is the state and why should I obey it?" Hence, he says that authority of man over man can have no rational basis except through agreement and consent.

The cornerstone of Rousseau's 'Social Contract' theory was the state of nature. According to him, man by nature never thinks and he who thinks is a corrupt creature. During the state of nature, the people enjoyed unlimited freedom. They had no private property of their own. They did not know about competition, hatred and jealousy. They did not know whether a particular thing was good or bad, right or wrong and useful or useless. Thus, the people of Rousseau enjoyed innocent life of perfect freedom and equality in the state of nature.

Many years passed on and a drastic change took place in their attitude. It was due to two reasons. One was the increase in population and the other was the dawn of reason. By the process of increasing population, many progressive changes took place in the field of economics. As a result, the people who lived in the state of nature lost their happiness, freedom and simplicity. Every man in the society became selfish; there was rivalry; there was enmity; there was suspicion and hatred. They quarreled themselves. So there were wars and murders everywhere. They wanted to save their life and property from danger. Hence, they sought for the formation of a civil society. This led to a social contract.

Accordingly every individual gave up his rights to the community. The community became all powerful with enormous powers. It became sovereign. The sovereignty of the community is inalienable and indivisible. In this contract the people voluntarily made the contract.

The social contract is not a contract which men made with their future ruler. Government is only their agent. If men are placed under the rule of some individuals or community it would mean slavery. But men have come together to fulfil nature which makes slavery impossible. Hence, they must create a society "in such a way that each when united to his fellows renders obedience to his own will and remains as free as he was before." It should be noted here that the 'sovereign' means in Rousseau not the monarch or the government but the community in its collective and legislative capacity.

Rousseau says that law alone is responsible for the obedience of men. It is to law that men owe justice and liberty. Here the question arises what is the law? Rousseau calls it the universal voice. It is the voice of the General will.

General will: The conception of the "general will" plays a very important part in Rousseau's system. What is the "General will"? It is the will of all the citizens when they are willing not their own private interests but the general good. According to Rousseau, the will of the sovereign which is always right is the "general will". Every individual is allowed to will his own will and the majority will is formed. The general will is for the general welfare. The social contract involves that whoever refuses to obey the general will shall be forced to do so. This means nothing less than that he will be forced to be free. This idea of being forced to be free is very metaphysical in nature.

Rousseau says that the General will is not identical with the will of the majority. He distinguishes between our will for our selfish ends and our will for the general good. For common interest, everybody is allowed to convey his will and thus the majority will is found, when we demand something not for us but for everyone, our will is general.

The general will deals with matters of public interest. At the same time it deals with private interest also. Although, other societies and associations may have a General will in relation to their members, a relation to the state their will is particular. The General will of the state is the most comprehensive of all.

According to Rousseau, the General will is inalienable and indivisible. Hence, it cannot be represented in parliamentary institutions. "As soon as a nation appoints representatives" he says it is no longer free, it no longer exists. He declared that "England was only free during elections, after which it is unsaved and counts for nothing." The General will cannot therefore be represented, because representative assemblies tend to develop particular interests of their own. It cannot be delegated in any way. He stated "the moment there is a master, there is no longer a sovereign." As such, nothing less than all the people together can be trusted to will the general will .... As Rousseau expressed it, it is only "the voice of the people is the voice of God".

The General will must be a will which is general in every sense and which is particular in none. According to the agreement of the contract, the General will must respect the wishes of every citizen since they come under integral part of our group.

The General will of Rousseau cannot be an executive will. The people ought not to be responsible for the details of government. Here he clearly distinguishes the difference between the Government and the sovereign people. The people entrusts its executive power to its agent whereas the government retain some limited right of supervision over it. So long as the General will is sovereign it does not matter if the government is a democracy, an aristocracy, or a monarchy — whichever in the existing circumstances is most suitable will be the best. However, Rousseau prefers democracy since it is too prefect for men. He considers that men are too imperfect for kingship since kings have of becoming tyrants. Similarly, he condemns hereditary aristocracy as the worst type of all forms of government.

According to Rousseau, the General will is infallible. He says that it is always right and tends to the public advantage i.e., men must never forget that they come together for the sake of good life and should do nothing to make that good life impossible.

In spite of his above views on the General will he finds some vagueness in the will perhaps it reflects his belief that it would never be easy for men to will it. The illustration of General will that he gives in 'Emile' is a sufficient proof for the same.

Criticisms: The theory of social contract has been criticised on many grounds:

(1) On the basis of history the theory has been considered as mere fiction. We cannot give even a single example for history to show that the state has been created as a result of voluntary agreement.

(2) Sir Henry Maine has criticised the social contract theory on the ground that it is based on wrong assumptions. He further says that contract is not the beginning but the end of society. In primitive society, the people had not such freedom to enter into a contract.

(3) Since the contract is made by the individuals it can remain as long as there is sweet will and co-operation among them. Otherwise there can be no end to it.

(4) Bluntschli and others point out that theory is dangerous. For example, Rousseau had intimate connection with French Revolution. The advocates of this theory actually encouraged revolution.

(5) The conception of natural rights and natural liberty as is said to have existed in the state of nature is illogical and fallacious.

(6) According to this theory men were equals in the state of nature. This view is not correct because Von Haller the German jurist says that inequality rather than equality is natural.

(7) Critics have pointed out that Rousseau's "General will" is abstract one; it is very narrow. It is also mentioned that the General will is neither general nor will. Usually it can be decided by the majority decision. It will definitely pave a way for the state absolutism. According to T.H. Green will not force is the basis of the state, is clearly seen in democracies.

The Social Contract became the Bible of most of the leaders in the French Revolution, but no doubt as the fate of Bible, it was not carefully read and was still understood by many of its disciples. However, it cannot be denied that the states began to have written constitutions after Locke and Rousseau.

State of Nature

Rousseau began by examining the conception of the state of nature. Many influence induced him. Hobbes and Locke envisaged primitive man either rationally bad or rationally good. But to Rousseau primitive man lived an isolated life, had no obligation and near animal than man. He says, "Primitive man near animal than man; he lived an isolated life having no ties and obligations. He was guided by two sentiments — self-interest and pity and having no moral obligation with other men, he could not be good or bad virtuous or vicious. He was a creative of impulse and instinct in whom the quality of foresight was slow in developing. He had a solitary and non-moral life in the state of nature. Even speech was undeveloped, for speech presupposed communication and some social interplay. So primitive man was devoid of language and wandered about the primeval forests begetting his off-spring by the way, hunting for his food, and concerned with the satisfaction of physical needs. In a word, the natural man was neither happy nor unhappy."

Reason and thinking come afterwards and isolate man from his fellows: whereas compassion unites him with others. Uncivilized man is always "foolishly ready to obey the first promptings of humanity. It is the populace that flocks together at riots and street brawls while the wise man prudently makes off. It is the mob and the market woman who part the combatants and hider gentle folks from one another's throats".

Thus, the natural man was an animal whose behaviour was purely instinctive and thought whatever is 'depraved'. In such a state man had no property, no knowledge, no industry and no society. "Selfishness tastes regard for the opinion of others, the art, war, slavery, vice, conjugal and paternal affection all exist in men only as they are sociable beings who live together in larger or smaller groups."

But a stage came when men changed his previous way of living and began to live in settled groups. Social institutions gradually evolved and family unit came into being. "What a man had been content to look upon as his mere possessions, how that he had interest in a given portion of the earth and a posterity to care for he wished to be regarded as his own inalienable good." Man wished that his possessions should be recognised as his personal property. "The first man who enclosed a plot of ground and he thought himself of saying 'This is mine' and found other foolish enough to believe him was the true founder of civil society."

The institution of private property attended the institution of family. This created a sense of jealously and struggle and this arose evils. Division of labour, and the rise of private property created distinction between rich and poor and led to the formation of society the enactment of laws and setting up of the government.

Rousseau says, "Such was, or may well have been the origin of society or law, which bound new fetters on the poor, and gave new powers to the rich, which irretrievably destroyed natural liberty, eternally fixed the law of property and inequality, converted clever usurpation into unalterable right and for the advantage of a few ambitious individuals, and subjected all mankind so perpetual labour slavery and wretchedness."

Since all these institutions — the family, property, the society — came to stay, some form of association was necessary to defend and protect them. Rousseau says, now "the problem is to find a form of association which will defend and protect with the whole common force the person, and goods of each associate and in which each while uniting himself with all may still obey himself alone and remain as free as before".

The Social Contract

Rousseau says that by the creation of the required association, the fundamental problem was solved. This association was formed on the basis of a social contract and all members asserted to it. This association or political society was to provide freedom of the state of nature and the benefits of civil law and order. Rousseau defines, the terms of contract in the following words:

"Each of us puts his person and all his power in common under the supreme direction of the General will, and, in our corporate capacity we receive each member as an indivisible part of the whole. At once, in place of the individual personality of each contracting party, this act of association creates a moral and collective body composed of as many members as the assembly contains votes, and receiving from this act its unity, its common identity its life and its will. This public persons, so framed by the union of all persons, for merely took the name of city, now takes that of republic, or body politic, it is called by its members state when passive, sovereign when active, and power when compared with others like itself."

By entering into the social contract each member gives his all to the society and the community there became absolute. But in spite of this, individuals still possessed equal rights. However, none was a loser, because each giving himself to all, gives himself to nobody.

Rousseau puts this in these words: "Each giving himself to all gives himself to nobody, and as there is not one associate over whom we do not acquire the same rights which are concede to him over ourselves we gain the equivalent of all that we lose, and more power to preserve what we have."

The material and moral transformation which the individual undergoes as a result of becoming a member of the civil society is described by Rousseau in the following words:

"The passage from the state of nature to the civil state brings about a momentous change in man. In his conduct it replaces instinct by justice, and gives to his acts a moral character which was wanting in them before. The voice of duty takes to place of physical impulse right supplants appetite. Now for the first time, man who hitherto had thought only of himself forced to act on other principles, and to consult his reason before listening to his desire. It is true that in the civil society he deprives himself of many advantages which he holds from nature. But in return he gains advantages so great his faculties are so trained and developed, his ideas so enlarged, his whole soul exalted to such a degree that of the abuses of the new order did not often degrade him below the level of that forum which he had escaped, he ought without ceasing bless the happy moment which lose him forever from the old order and which of a stupted and limited animal made him a reasoning being and a man."

Comparison — Rousseau, Hobbes and Locke

The approach of Hobbes, Locke and Rousseau in respect of Social Contract theory is different from person to person. The approaches to society, government, rights, liberty, property and the place of man in the society made by the three writers showed considerable variations. Hobbes and Rousseau held that the state is the result of a contract entered into by men who originally lived in the state of nature. There was only one contract and in that contract the individuals surrendered all their rights to the sovereign. The sovereign was absolute in character. But Rousseau did not agree with Hobbes that the government was absolute. He made the government dependent upon the people and thereby accepted the conclusions of Locke. According to Rousseau, the individual surrendered his rights not to the ruler but to the community. Further he made a very clear distinction between the state and the government. In the above points, Rousseau was in conformity with Locke rather than Hobbes.

Rousseau advocated the complete surrender of rights to the sovereign; Locke stood for a limited sovereignty; Rousseau stood for popular sovereignty; Hobbes stood for absolute sovereignty. The state of nature of Hobbes was both pre-social and pre-political whereas Locke's was only pre-political.

Rousseau's man in the state of nature was a noble savage. He was primitive by nature. He was independent; self-sufficient, contented, healthy and fearless instinct played a very good role in regulating his life.

Hobbes was for a doctrinaire, sordid, rigid and absolute society. Rousseau was all for a free, unfettered, unchained and unregulated man. He also preferred a type of vagabond life since he himself led the life of a vagabond in his early days. The approach of Rousseau is a balanced approach between these two extremes.

In the case of Rousseau, there is only one contract; but in the case of Locke there are two contracts. The social contract gave a decent burial to the state of Nature and substituted for it a civil society or the state. The contract between the government and the ruler was formed by the government. In the second contract, the government was a party to the contract.

Since, Hobbes stood for absolutism he could be said to be nearer Fascist, Nazist and the totalitarian regimes. Rousseau could be said to be nearer anarchist and the communist conception of things but for the fact that he was a strong protagonist of freedom and lesser and lesser authority of the state on men, the communist state is the opposite of it. Locke can be considered to be a forerunner of all parliamentary and democratic governments.

According to Hobbes, the natural man was selfish in character; he was envious, dejected and quarrelsome. The state of nature was a gloomy state. It was a state of constant welfare. According to Rousseau, the natural man was good; he was pleasant and happy. The state of nature was a state of bliss and happiness. According to Locke, the state of nature was neither too good nor one of constant warfare. It was not convenient and comfortable due to the absence of an authority to enforce the rights of man in the state of nature.

Hobbes remarked that if there was a change in government there would be dissolution in the state; the people would return to the state of nature. Locke had a firm belief that the people had the supreme right to have their own government. They could bring a change in the government if they found it unsatisfactory. To Rousseau the government was merely the agent or the tool to execute the popular will.

From the Social Contract theory of Hobbes we know that law was the command of the sovereign. To Locke law must be the expression of the will of the people and it should be consistent with the law of reason. According to Rousseau law is merely the expression of the General Will.

Locke's people in the social contract had the right of revolution. Hobbes too gave his people the right to transfer their allegiance when the sovereign was not able to protect their lives. In the case of Rousseau, there was no such right for revolt to his people.

Whatever may be the merits of the practicability of Rousseau's writings, political philosophers who came after him found his writings very useful. The Declaration of Independence in America, the Bill of Rights, the Revolution of 1688 (Glorious Revolution) and the American War of Independence all owe their origins to the writings of Rousseau.

24

Immanuel Kant (1724-1804)

Immanuel Kant, the father of idealist philosophy and the great German philosopher was born at Konigsberg on 22nd April 1724. His father was a poor saddler; his mother was an uneducated but intelligent Pettiest. After completing his education, he had to spend nine years as private tutor to qualify himself from the university. In 1770, he was appointed as Professor of Logic and Metaphysics in the same University. He had a very low opinion of women and did not marry. He died as a confirmed bachelor on 12th February, 1804.

Kant's ideas of philosophy are mostly taken from Rousseau and Montesquieu. He borrowed his ideas from others and fitted them into his own philosophy. The period from 1770 to 1790 formed a brightest period in his philosophical works. In his three chief works viz. "Critique of Pure Reason", "Critique of Practical Reason" and "Critique of Judgment", we find his more ideas about morality than of politics. Further his political ideas are to be found in his works like "Metaphysical First Principles of the Theory of Law," "Perpetual Peace", "The Principles of Political Right" and "The Natural Principle of the Political Order".

(i) Respect for Personality: Kant's philosophy was essentially individualistic in character. He gave the highest place for the free will of the individual in his political thought. According to him, every individual was an end in himself and no one was to be considered as a means to an end. Further he had a soft corner for the liberty of the individuals and he was not ready to sacrifice the same for the sake of the state.

(ii) Rights and Duties: According to Kant, the rights and duties of individuals should be respected. At the same time he said, "Liberty consists in the power to do anything which inflicts no injury on one's neighbour." One man's rights should not injure other man's freedom. A right is also a burden and an obligation. According to Kant, duty was self-imposed. Hence, Vaughan remarks, "Right expands into freedom and freedom expands into right."

(iii) The Social Contract: Though, Kant accepted the idea of social contract, he did not find any connection of the same with the origin of the state such a thing was irrelevant and dangerous. He further said that man could be compelled to obey a law which he did not accept of his own accord. Thus, his social contract is a constitutional compact by means of which a form of government is established and that compact binds the government and the people. The same contract does not bring about a change from a state of nature to an organised state.

(iv) Moral Philosophy: In his "Critique of Pure Reason" he gives a clear critical analysis of pure reason. According to him, a reason independent of all sense experience is called pure reason. It is knowledge belonging to the structure of mind. It is superior to knowledge. The absolute truths about the existence could be known only by pure reason. It can be practical i.e. it can itself determine the will independently of anything empirical. He tries to find a universal and necessary ethic; a prior principles of morals which are absolute and certain. According to him, moral sense is innate, and not derived from experience. Man is truly free who is also morally free. He has coined the phrase autonomy of the moral will. Acts are moral only if they are done on principles which should conform certain norms. These norms are known as categorical imperatives. By this one can determine whether a particular act is good or not, moral or not.

There are three imperatives according to Kant: (1) "Act as if the maxim of our action were to become by our will a universal law of nature." (2) "Act as to treat humanity whether in thine own person or in that of another in every case as an end, never only as a means." (3) "Act as if you were through your maxims a law making member of a kingdom of ends." Firstly, we are supposed to avoid behaviour, if adopted by all men would render social life impossible. Secondly, every individual can achieve perfection in himself and happiness in others. Thirdly, all laws should be outcome of agreement among rational beings and not the effect of a mythical law given. Finally, he says that man is free as long as his will is free and his will is free when it is acting according to the categorical imperatives.

(v) Property: The institution of private property was accepted by Kant. But he was not in favour of the individualistic view regarding private property. For the expression of will of man the institution of private property was very essential. According to Kant, the possession of property was a derived right. It was not the gift of nature to man.

(vi) Punishment: Punishments should not be inflicted upon the criminals for the sake of vengeance. They should not be tortured or terrorised by way of punishments. Punishments did not involve any idea of reformation of the individual.

(vii) Concept of Law: According to Kant that law can neither be the command of the sovereign nor be based on custom or tradition or precedent. Generally, a sovereign could not act against pure reason. The laws which are formulated contrary to the pure reason and the laws which are not in conformity with priori principles are immoral and hence null and void. The trespassers of law should be visited by punishment.

(viii) Civil State: Kant's philosophy was based on individualism. He could not give too much power to the state. Man is egoistic by nature. Their love for power, gain and glory and the effect of those glories is "the war of all against all." Moral freedom should be promoted by individuals themselves and not by the state. It is the primary duty of the state to remove all barriers to liberty.

In his treatment of state and government there were three and two forms respectively. The three forms of state were autocracy, aristocracy and democracy. Republican and despotic were the two forms of government. As stated by Kant there are three powers in every state. They are the legislative, executive and the judicial. The first two powers must be separated for the sake of liberty. The two forms of government were republican and despotic "according as there is or is not a separation of the legislative and the executive power." According to Kant, the form of government which was not representative was not rational and the function of the representative may be performed by the king or the nobility or the elected deputies. From this view of Kant we know that he favoured constitutional monarchy and opposed despotism.

Kant was extremely opposed to any kind of violence. That could be expected of him because he was a philosopher. In his opinion, the citizen had no right of revolution. He stood for legal change in constitutional set up of the state.

Creation of the World State

The Law of development or the Law of evolution is one of the most important philosophical thinking's of Kant. His development of law takes its growth from a lower to a higher level. It was concerned with the developments inside the human species and pre-supposed the survival of the best. He attempted to give the historical development of social and political institutions with his law of progress in the past and then predict their further developments.

According to Kant, there was no reason or moral sense in the primitive society. They were dominated by instincts of self-preservation, sexual desires, a desire for glory and ego for dominating other people. At the same time, there was social intercourse; there was friendly co-operation and there was desire for company. Kant calls this as the unsocial sociability of mankind. This paved the way for a warfare in the primitive society. Conflict and competition prevailed in the primitive society. It was due to the two kinds of instincts viz., to associate as well as to dominate. Both good and bad results were the outcome of that warfare. It forced the primitive men to develop his reasoning powers latent in him. The state of nature was so horrible. He willingly sacrificed his own lawless liberty and voluntarily submitted himself to the political state in which all men are subject to uniform laws. Hence, the creation of the political state is considered as a landmark in the history of human progress.

Man developed from the savage condition i.e. from the beastly condition to that of a life dominated by reason and moral law. According to Kant, this is not the apex in the evolution of human progress. The mutual antagonism of man brought into existence the creation of state. The mutual hatred of states will bring about a federation comprising of all states in the world, capable of creating eternal and everlasting peace. There is no safety for each state in the world. One is afraid of the other. The will to subjugate or encroach upon others is always there and preparations of defence which often render peace even more burdensome and destructive of internal warfare than war itself can never slacken. For this purpose international justice is to be founded upon public laws. Every state must submit before this law.

In his Essay on Perpetual Peace, he gave some purposeful suggestions for world peace. But his idea of Balance of Power was somewhat confusing. He denounced both secret diplomacy and secret societies since they would deceive the people and the governments. The first and the best guarantee of perpetual peace is the well-integrated constitutional state such as is found in a republic.

Usually the actions of the government rest upon the will of the people in a republican state. War can be waged with its consent. So also peace can be made with its willingness. If they did not require any more war they can put an end to it. Because no nation will be willing to take upon itself the sufferings of a war. In this connection, Kant pre-supposed popular sovereignty in the federation of all states. If such was not the case, the right of a nation to make its own decisions of place or war might place it in a dangerous situation. So Kant said that there should be world republic. World peace thus depends upon the relations of the citizens of the world states.

According to Kant, international law should be maintained in preventing war and preserving peace. He intended that the civil constitution of very state should be republican and war shall not be declared except by a plebiscite of all the citizens. It has prospects of bringing about perpetual peace.

The ultimate goal of Kant was a free association of free people. In his "Jurisprudence" published in 1797, Kant put forth the suggestion of a permanent congress of states. It should be given arbitrary powers. The same idea was realised to some extent by the United Nations.

Many criticisms have been levelled against the philosophy of Kant by many writers. Firstly, his philosophy is too abstract to be understood by the ordinary people. Secondly, Kant could not make up his mind as to whether he stood for freedom both in the ordinary sense and in the higher sense. Thirdly, Vaughan says that Kant failed because "he hovered between the two entirely different conceptions of the state. He tossed between individualism and idealisms". Fourthly, according to critics his philosophy is without content. His theories and doctrines are too abstract and make empirical approach impossible.

It cannot be denied that "Kant ushered in a new epoch in philosophical thought. His major writings constitute a milestone in the history of philosophy. He is one of those great and profound thinkers who by their works, but also by their lives, exercised a lasting influence upon the intellectual life of their own time and posterity...." F. Hebbel called him "a thinker who moved and shook the world much more forcibly than his contemporary Frederick the Great, with all his Canon." Of all the contributions his ethical theory based on categories imperatives is a major contribution to the democratic ideal. By this contribution he has earned a very good name and fame in the history of political thought. In short, his conception of state and individual is undoubtedly a great contribution in the political field.

25

Edmund Burke (1729-1797)

Introduction: Edmund Burke is one of the most important political philosophers of the world. He is one of the most well-known leading figures in English history. He was a sincere statesman; excellent orator; pre-eminent political thinker. He is rated as one of the world's greatest orators. John Bowk says that "Like Rousseau he was a phrase maker of the first order and more than Rousseau a lord of language in the finest lineage of political thought. Yet by origin and temperament, Burke was profoundly un-English."

Early Life: Edmund Burke was born in the year 1729. His father was a protestant solicitor; his mother was a Catholic lady. They gave him excellent education. He took his education in the Trinity College, Dublin. After completing his education there, he went to London to study Law. Since he had no interest in studying law he discontinued the same. For some time he was in England and France.

His Works: Edmund Burke published many works. They are: (i) "A Vindication of Natural Society", (ii) "A Philosophical Enquiry into the Origin of our Ideas of the Sublime and Beautiful", (iii) "The Annual Register", (iv) "Thought on the Causes of the Present Discontents", (v) "Reflections on the Revolution in France", (vi) "Appeal from the New to the Old Whigs", (vii) "Letters on a Regicide Peace". Regarding America his best known statements were two parliamentary speeches, "On American Taxation" and "On Moving his Resolutions for Conciliation with America." Regarding India his best known speeches were "On Mr. Fox's East India Bill" and "On the Nabob of Arcot's Debts".

Edmund Burke married Jane Nugent in 1757. She was the daughter of an Irish Catholic doctor. His political philosophy is not completely available in his single work as that of the "Spirit of Laws" of Montesquieu, "Leviathan" of Hobbes and "The Prince of Machiavelli". But his philosophy is available from his various contributions in a scattered form. Burke died at Beaconsfield, Buckinghamshire on 9th July 1797.

His Views: Burke's ideas of society and state were in direct antithesis to John Locke. It is stated already that Locke's state was a product of social contract. According to Burke, it was not so i.e. it was not created by any social contract. To Burke civil society was made by man himself; it was a product of man's practical intellect working after a basic pattern established by nature. Man perfects his nature through civil society. By nature he is rational and so the civil society is his natural state. Burke's view is that the state has been created to perfect his work to achieve good and moderate life and to promote the welfare. To the people the state is considered as the means which is ordained by nature. For that purpose the state should be given sovereign power. The people must acknowledge the same. According to Burke, the people are not the masters of the state. In short, there is no distinction and difference between state and society.

According to Locke, the people enjoyed certain rights prior to the existence of the state. He termed those rights as natural rights. To Burke the rights exist only in the state and not outside the state. If there is no state there can be no rights. In addition to this, he claims that civil rights should be extended to all whereas the political rights should be given only to those who are having the capacity to enjoy and ability to exercise those rights.

Burke gave a new theoretical synthesis to suit the political atmosphere of those days of Whig and Tory. The new theoretical synthesis was of Whig principal of freedom and the Tory principle of order. They were the following: (1) religious establishment should respect the conscience of the dissenter, (2) aristocracy should leave some limited room for the upward mobility of new talent, (3) tradition must be adjusted, and (4) an imperial nation can maintain order only by respecting the traditions of its colonies.

The key to national prosperity is individual freedom in the economic field according to Burke. His colonial policy is considered a noteworthy feature of his political philosophy. During the American War of Independence, he gave whole-hearted support for the colonies in the Parliament. One of the most important drastic steps taken by the mother country was the introduction of Stamp Act. It was not only damnable but also dangerous one. In 1776, he spoke for the repeal of the Stamp Act as concession to American feelings. At the same time, he did not hesitate to support the Declaratory Act which gave the constitutional right to his country to tax the colonists. In this connection it is the duty of the students of political thought to mention about his two famous speeches in Parliament. They are best known in the world. They are: (i) "On American Taxation" (1774), and (ii) Moving his Resolutions for Conciliation with America" (1775).

Burke's interest in India also cannot be minimised. He in the 1760s and 1770s opposed the interference of English Government in the affairs of the company as a violation of charter rights.

Burke is rightly considered to be the founder and defender of modern conservatism. He put more stress on tradition. His conservatism was due to his implicit faith in Divine Will. He was a great religious man. He was not a democrat. He favoured aristocracy.

Burke's greatest work "Reflections on the Revolutions in France" was published after his first speech against the revolution in 1790. He condemned it as a catastrophe. It was for the leaders only. The motive of the revolution was not so meaningful. He favoured the real rights of man. He wanted that these rights of man to be made moderate and practical by way of "prescription".

Burke was not a die-hard. He favoured liberalism also. He hated uniformity and opposed equality. Further he opposed universal adult franchise. Political thinkers like Stephen, Thomas Morley and H.J. Laski described Burke as a utilitarian. Burke received inspiration from David Hume. According to Laski, the metaphysics of Burke are largely those of David Hume.

His Conservative ideas: Edmund Burke is one of the most well-known figures in English history. He was a sincere statesman; he was a prominent political thinker; he was a great parliamentary orator. He played an important role in all major political issues for about 30 years after 1765. Hence, he remains as an important figure in the history of political thought.

Burke's conservative ideas are found in his works. He is considered to be the founder and defender of modern conservatism. He realised that the basis of conservatism is not force but tradition, that it can be defended not by repression of the opponent but by the gentle force of persuasion and education. That is why he was called the exponent of conservatism. Sabine writes that, "Burke is rightly regarded as the founder of self-conscious political conservatism."

Though Burke was the defender of modern conservatism, he never failed to realise that the basis of conservatism is not force but tradition. Hence, he laid emphasis on tradition. He had great regard and respect for all old things. "Old is gold" the old saying was keenly observed by him. He thought that these things are valuable because they had existed for a long time and had attained maturity. Added to this he had great respect for the wisdom of established institutions. According to him, these established institutions are not invented by anybody; and they are not made also. As days passed far-reaching developments took place in them. Since they grow they must be approached with reverence. Because of experience, familiarity and respect for them the old institutions work well. They are better and fitter for the people. They are very useful for the smooth functioning of government. From the above views of Burke, it is very clear that he was staunch supporter of conservatism.

Burke was an anti-revolutionary. He opposed revolutions and condemned French Revolution. He thought that French Revolution was a damnable and dangerous one. He considered that the destruction of ancient political, religious, social and economic institutions was due to the wrath against conservatism. Since he belongs to the conservative tradition he profoundly and eloquently expressed in the "Reflections on French Revolution" his deep horror of such revolutionary methods.

Another evident to indicate his conservative policy is his views regarding the origin of the state. According to Locke, the state was the product of social contract, for Burke it is a convention of slow organic growth.

Another example for his conservative policy was his faith in Divine will. He was a great religious-minded man. He was of the opinion that religion is the foundation of State. The same religion is the basis for the creation of civil society. Apart from this it is the sole and whole source of all good and comfort. Hence, he put more stress on religion. According to him, the existence of Church was itself an expression of nationhood as well as its consecration. He further said that every individual was very essential for good citizenship.

Burke had high regard for the British constitution. He had full of praise and high esteem over the constitution. The British constitution was a natural growth. One of the most significant and salient features of the constitution is its principle of checks and balances. It afforded, he thought real protection to the liberty and property because they were not mere hypothesis but established rule of action.

Burke disfavoured the idea of popular sovereignty. He opposed the redistribution of seats and universal suffrage. He also denied equality of political rights to the people. In one of his works his attitude towards the English political institutions was expressed thus, "We fear God — We look with awe to the King; with affection to Parliament, with duty to magistrate, with reverence to priest and with respect to nobility." From his statement it is very obvious that he cherished and nourished the flourished old institutions. The people of England had great regard towards their King. Even now they show their respect to the King (Queen). They have imposed their affection to their Parliament. They are very dutiful towards their magistrates. The priests and nobles are reverenced and respected by the people of England.

Burke was not a democrat. According to him, democratic principles are not useful for the stability of a Government. He was convinced that stability and greatness of a nation depended upon the existence of a strong and powerful aristocracy. It itself

Edmund Burke has been and still continues to be fountain of inspiration and ideas for conservative thinkers. Maine, Freeman, Seely, Sidgewick, Lecky, Godkin, Belloc, Hegel and Nietzsche were greatly influenced by Burke. "The modern assault upon the ideological foundations of democracy comprehends much that Burke did not know, but he remains nevertheless, the most eloquent and forceful of all apostles of aristocracy."

Prof. Laski observes, "It is easy to praise Burke and easier still to miss the greatness of his effort. Perspective apart, he is destined author of some maxims that few statesmen will dare to forget them as a creator of a system which, even its unfinished implications, is hardly less gigantic than that of Hobbes or Bentham. His very defects are lessons in themselves. His unhesitating inability to see how dangerous is the concentration of property is standing proof that men are over prone to judge the rightness of a state by their own wishes. His disregard of popular desire suggests the fatal disease with which we neglect the opinion of those who stand outside in active centre of political conflict."

26

Thomas Paine (1737-1809)

Early Career: Thomas Paine was born on 29th January, 1737 at Thetford in Norfolk. He was a Quaker by birth. Since his parent were very poor, he could not get a systematic education. He spent his early days as a sailor; teacher and exercise man. During his early days, he was confronted with miseries and misfortunes and sorrows and sufferings due to the difficulties and hardships. The death of his wife, his unhappy second marriage and his sufferings in life created in him the sympathy for poor and the downtrodden.

Thomas Paine was influenced by two persons, John Wilkes and Benjamin Franklin who were mainly responsible for his great political career. He joined the Headstrong Club at Lewis in 1768. During this time Paine was very much influenced by Wilke's writings.

On the advice of Benjamin Franklin, the American Agent in London, Paine left for America in 1774. Paine became an editor of the Pennsylvania Magazine in U.S.A; and remained there for eighteen months in this capacity. There he published his first pamphlet "Common Sense" on July 4, 1776. This influenced the colonists to clamour more for their liberation and independent from the Yoke of British imperialism. The "Common Sense" swept through Colonies made its deep impression on the American mind, and drove public opinion toward the final break with Britain.

His Works: Pamphlets like "The Crisis," "The Public Good" and "The Right of Man" are best examples of Paine's constructive philosophy. In 1786, he published his "Dissertations on Government; the Affairs of the Bank; and Paper Money." He attacked Pitt's war policy in his "Prospects on the Rubicon", published in 1780. In 1792, he also published his letter "Addressed to the Addressers on the Late Proclamation", inciting the British people to form a republic. The Rights of Man and Address greatly offended the British Government. Hence, he was outlawed from that country.

In France he attacked the policy of the revolutionaries particularly the execution of Louis XVI. Consequently, he was expelled from France. During this time he published his "The Age of Reason" in France; which started trouble in America. In 1796 he published the "Decline and Fall of the English System of Finance" and "Letter to Washington". He died on 8th June 1809 at the age of seventy-two in New York.

His Views: Paine's constructive political philosophy is chiefly found in his two famous pamphlets "Common Sense" and "The Rights of Man." The fundamental basis of his political doctrine is his idea of Society and State. Man is free and gregarious by nature according to Paine. He satisfies his wants with the help of others. He is not able to achieve anything alone. In the circumstances stated above the man was forced to form the society in the beginning. Due to the anomaly and animosity men failed to live peacefully. It necessitated them to form the government later on by a group of men through a contract. So Paine says, "Society is produced by our wants, and government by our wickedness; the former promoted our happiness positively, by uniting our affections, the later negatively by restraining our vices. The first is a patron the last a punisher" ("Common Sense", p. 1). The above difference between State and Society made by Paine is clearly derived from the philosophy transmitted by Locke.

According to Paine society is a blessing one for every state whereas government is necessary evil. Every man should act according to his conscience. If he did so no law would be necessary. If he did not respect his conscience, a government became necessary to make and enforce laws in the society. Since man did not like to lose all liberty, he agreed to create or form a government by sacrificing some of his liberty. From this we know the basic function of government is to ensure his freedom by giving security. According to him the government must be responsible and limited.

Regarding sovereignty he says that it belongs to the people. He further adds that "every citizen is a member of the sovereignty and as such can acknowledge no personal subjection; and disobedience can be only to the laws." Again he says that "nation is essentially the source of all sovereignty, not can any individual, or anybody of men, be entitled to any authority which is not expressly derived from it." So his sovereignty resembles to that of Rousseau's General will.

From Paine's writings we know the vivid description of various types of government. Out and out he was a republican. He divides the government into four types viz. democracy, aristocracy, monarchy and republic. According to him, monarchy and aristocracy represent the corrupt form. They are based on ignorance. Democracy is inadequate to the affairs of an extensive population. Representative Government is the only logical and adequate system. Paine favours the republican form of government because it is built upon universal suffrage and run by representatives elected by the nation. He condemns the British monarchical system and speaks in high praise of a republic as that of America.

Another feature of his philosophy is the conception of rights. According to him, "all men are of one degree and consequently that all men are born equal and with equal natural rights". These words are seen in his "The Rights of Man" part I. The natural rights of man are liberty, property, security and resistance to oppression. These natural rights are highly responsible for the foundation of civil rights. "The Rights of Man" have been compared to the "Ten Commandments". It is the duty of the government to preserve these rights surrendered by the individual and should not make inroad into these natural rights retained by him. In this way, the rights of man serve as a sort of limitations on the government.

Paine then turns his attention towards the conception of Law. It is also another significant feature of his political philosophy. According to him, "all laws are acts, but all acts are not laws. He points out that by no means all the enactment of a legislature are entitled to the name and character of law.

Lastly, it is also significant to note his views on the form and content of the written constitution. He calls the English political system as defective one. Written constitutions could alone secure the natural rights and popular liberty from being encroached upon by government. R.C. Gupta says that "according to Paine a constitution was not an ideal but a fact. It must be visible. A constitution is antecedent to government. The latter is a creature of the former." The constitution is made by the people and not by the government. If we go through the English constitution, we cannot find the above facts in it. Hence, England has no constitution at all.

Paine's enthusiasm is seen in favouring the American constitution. He says "the American constitutions were to liberty what grammar is to language". He further adds, "They define its parts of speech and practically construct them into syntax." At the same time he could not agree with the American constitutionalists with regard to the theory of separation of powers. According to him, there are only two kinds of power. They are making and executing of laws.

Like Mahatma Gandhi, Paine was a great humanitarian. He regarded all of humanity as his country and thought of himself as a universal man. Since he suffered a lot in his early days he was always sympathetic towards the poor and the downtrodden. According to R.C. Gupta, "he had enrolled under the banner of freedom and remained its loyal and energetic apostle to his last day. In its name he had helped to create one country, the United States, played a large role in the life of another, France had left his deep mark on still a third England". He had won in his life time enduring name and fame without any formal education. He had stirred and stimulated the hearts and awaken and shaken the minds of his contemporaries as few men achieved in their life and earned himself a permanent place in the annals of history.

27

Jeremy Bentham (1748-1832)

Jeremy Bentham was the founder of Utilitarianism. He was born in London on February 15, 1748. He was the son of Jeremiah Bentham, who was a lawyer. His father wanted his son also be a lawyer. He obtained a great reputation for Greek and Latin verse writing when he was at Westminster school. In 1760, he went to Queen's College, Oxford where he acquired a thorough acquaintance with Robert Sanderson's logic. Then he went to Lincoln's Inn in England for legal studies in 1763. His mind was learned towards scientific experiments and hence he could not succeed in the legal side. Since, he found the work dull, gave up the same. From the beginning he was interested more in the defects of the legal system than in mastering its details. He was delicate, nervous and precocious.

Bentham went to Russia in 1785 to see his brother. His brother was an engineer and was employed for the creation of a modern Agricultural and Industrial colony in the Ukraine. In 1792, the National Assembly of France conferred on him the title of a French citizen.

Bentham was the chief promotor of the University College, London, which was founded in 1827. From a small college, it developed into the largest University of Commonwealth.

Bentham was very lucky in having a large number of persons as his collaborators and disciples. His first and foremost disciple was James Mill. Sir Samuel Romilly, a distinguished lawyer, David Ricardo, the great economist, J.S. Mill, a great philosopher, John Austin and George Grote, the prominent figures were some of his friends. Lord Shelbourn the distinguished Whig leader, who was the Prime Minister of England in 1782-83 was a friend of Bentham.

Bentham was a great writer. He published as many as 30 works during his lifetime. Nearly 20 works were published posthumously. We find in his writings law, political economy, education, Church, language, poor law, local government, banking, social service, census, international organisation etc. Among them "Fragment on Government" was his first book published in 1776. It may be said to mark the beginning of philosophic radicalism. His other important works were "Defence of Usury", "Introduction to the Principles of Morals and Legislation", "Emancipate your Colonies", "Essay on Political Tactics", "Principles of International Law", "Manual of Political Economy" and "Church of England". In 1809, he wrote his "A Catechism of Parliamentary Reform". In it, he pleaded for annual elections, equal electoral constituencies, wide suffrage and secret ballot.

Bentham's sole insistence was on the principle of utility by which he meant "the greatest good of the greatest number" was based on the end of the state. There is more truth than exaggeration in the words that Hazlitt wrote of him as late as 1825 — "His name is little known in England, better in Europe and best of all in the plains of Chili and the mines of Mexico. He has offered constitutions for the new world and legislated for future times...."

Bentham lived up to eighty-two. He worked very hard till the end of his life. He himself said that he worked "Codifying like any Dragon." His ambition had been no small one. "J.B. the most ambitious of the ambitious" he wrote. He died happily in the thought that the ambition was well on the way to being realised. According to Leslie Stephen, "he is said to have expressed the wish that he could awaken once in a century to contemplate the prospect of a world gradually adopting his principles and so making steady progress in happiness and wisdom."

J.S. Mill says, "A place, therefore, must be assigned to Bentham among the masters of wisdom, the great teachers and permanent intellectual ornaments of human race ...." The service of Bentham to political thought was enormous and also excellent. In the words of Doyle, "Jeremy Bentham stood out as the dominating philosopher of the radical group". He further says that "he was inductive scientist drawing conclusions from his laboriously collected data." Referring to the death of Bentham in his ripe age of 84 the same writer remarks that he died, "Venerated by a group of disciples as a patriarch, a spiritual leader, almost a God, with James Mill as his Saint Paul."

Bentham, the English utilitarian philosopher was one of the principal influences on the reforming thought of the 19th century. He was primarily a legal reformer. Coleridge once said that "until we understand a man's ignorance we are ignorant of his understanding." Hence, C.L. Wayper says "Bentham was not an outstanding philosopher though paradoxically he occupies an important place in the history of philosophy.... He took his theory of knowledge from Locke and Hume, the pleasure and pain principle from Helvetius, the notion of sympathy and antipathy from Hume, the idea of utility from any of half a score of writers...".

Although Bentham wrote on the various aspects of the political state of his day, his distinctive field was Ethics and Jurisprudence. So the English men are greatly indebted to Jeremy Bentham.

Principle of Utility: The moral and political philosophy of Bentham is based on his doctrine of utility. In the "Fragment, on Government" published in 1776, he preached the principle of the greatest happiness of the greatest number. The whole structure of his utilitarian theory rests on his assumption that "Nature has placed mankind under two sovereign masters pain and pleasure." To seek pleasure and avoid pain is the tendency of the human beings. Everything that brings happiness is good, he tells us and nothing that does not bring happiness is good.

According to Bentham, pleasure and pain supplied the motive force to the activities of man. Every man tried to get pleasure and avoid pain. The doctrine of utility therefore is a hedonistic doctrine. While describing the good and bad consequences of an action, he simply meant the happy or painful consequences of an action. Here he accepted that all ideas are derived from the senses. Pleasures are simply individual sensations. But happiness is not merely the individual sensation; it is a state of mind, a bundle of sensations. Every pleasure he tells is a prima facie good and ought to be pursued. But happiness is not the piling up of all pleasures. It is the net result — i.e., it sometimes entails the rejection of some pleasures indulgence in which would have painful consequences. It is on the basis of pain and pleasure that a man performs any action in his life. He calls this principle of pain and pleasure the principle of utility.

According to Bentham, the pleasure and pain depend upon the actions of the individuals. If their actions are right, they would promote their happiness. If their actions are wrong they would promote their unhappiness. When applied to political science, it refers to measures of government. Those measurers of government are right which further the happiness of the community. It is the duty of the government to further the happiness of the community. Indeed the government should increase the happiness of the individual. At the same time, it is very difficult for any government to promote the happiness of every individual of the community. Hence, the aim of the government should be the promotion of the greatest happiness of the greatest number.

Further Bentham is very particular in mentioning the quantity of the happiness rather than its quality. According to him, pleasure and pain could be measured through these factors like intensity i.e., depth of feeling duration, certainty, propinquity i.e., pleasure which is nearer fecundity i.e., pleasure which is followed by a chance of being accompanied by sensations of the same kind is greater than otherwise purity and extensiveness. The extensiveness is concerned with the number of persons who are affected by them. In this connection, he says that it is the foremost duty of the legislators to classify those pleasures. He himself enumerates fourteen simple pleasures and twelve simple pains. They are sense, wealth, skill, amity, good name, power, piety, benevolence, malevolence, memory, imagination, expectation, association and relief. The pains are privation, sense awkwardness, enmity, ill name, piety, benevolence, malevolence, imagination, expectation, memory and association. These pleasures and pains govern all our ideas and all our actions, whatever they may be. Pleasures and pains are further sub-divided into two parts viz. self-regarding and others regarding. Only benevolence and malevolence were others regarding.

One of the seven factors mentioned above for the measurement of pleasures and pains is extensiveness or the number of persons affected. The value of thing is more or less according to the number of persons taking part in pleasure or pain. Here it depends upon their action as stated above.

According to the doctrine of utility, every person is to be permitted to pursue his own way of happiness. Even though it may be a perverted pleasure the sage feels happiness in asceticism. From this, it is clear that every individual will seek pleasure and avoid pain and that every person is the best judge of his own happiness. On the contrary, the principle of utility presupposes that the moral standard of man's action is to be judged from the quantity of general happiness it can produce.

It goes without saying that the principle of the greatest good of the greatest number immensely affected the legislation not only in the 19th century but also in the present century. It gave the politicians and statesmen a measuring rod by which they could judge the utility or otherwise of particular piece of legislation. Although the Benthamite doctrine is narrow and psychologically false "it has an immense value because it denied the infallibility of the supreme person, who endeavours to foist his own morality or his own type of happiness upon others whom he believes to be the pitiful dupes of ignorance", according to Ivor Brown.

The principle of utility of Bentham has been severely and seriously criticised from many directions. Firstly, his base materialism is denounced by moralists and idealists. Secondly, there is no such thing as a moral or an immoral action as Bentham says. Thirdly, it is very difficult to measure pleasure and pain. It may differ from person to person. The highest aim of the government is to augment the sum total of human happiness and diminish unhappiness.

Bentham applied this principle of utility to state, sovereignty, natural rights, law, punishment and government. In spite of the many criticisms levelled against his abstract theory, Bentham has won a prominent place in the history of democratic thoughts and political theory. Even with his limitations, he has been able to preach a message of humanism.

His views on state: Jeremy Bentham is considered as the greatest exponent of utilitarian philosophy. The utilitarian philosophy occupied a prominent place during the 19th century. The utilitarian explanation of the state is not only an explanation in terms of an unlimited end, but also in terms of the particular character of the state which differentiates it from man's other activities. A theory which maintains that the end of the state is the promotion of utility simply identified the end of the state with the end of human life. Yet clearly the state has a particular part to play in human life. The utilitarians including Bentham tell us in what way the state is peculiar, it is the sole source of law, which is the most certain of the four 'sanctions' or overriding motives which govern the lives of men. These are the physical sanction which operates in the ordinary course of nature; the moral sanction which arises from the general feeling of society; the religious sanction which is applied by the immediate hand of a superior invisible being, either in the present life or in a future and the political sanction which operates through government and the necessity for which is the explanation of the state.

According to Bentham, the state is primarily a law-making body by a group of persons organised for the promotion and maintenance of happiness and acting through law to that end. He argues that the state's supreme power is unlimited and absolute in so far as it does not undermine the value of utility. Within the framework of utility, the state can make and unmake any law and no limits can be set to its authority or power. This supreme power of the state is the source of all laws. These laws are made by the state to promote the happiness of the people.

According to Bentham, law should fulfil five important conditions. They are: (i) it should ensure an efficient government, (ii) it must ensure inexpensive justice without inordinate delay, (iii) it must be comprehensive, (iv) it must be uniform, and (v) it should make justice predictable and it should answer the needs of the people. If the above conditions are fulfilled, the law would be the fittest and suitable instrument to promote human happiness or utility.

Punishment: Bentham gives a fine place for the theory of punishment and prison reforms in his political philosophy. According to him, the chief end of punishment is to prevent crime. It should not be merely vindictive. Exactly it should be suited to the purpose. Again it should be neither more nor less. It should secure the good of the community. If there is any necessity for capital punishment it should be given otherwise not. The welfare of society should be the measuring rod. Moreover, the criminal or the offender should be punished in public so that the others may be frightened.

According to him, certain principles should be followed in fixing the punishment according to offence. They are: (i) The quantity of the punishments should be differed according to offence, (ii) The punishment should be equable neither lead to unnecessary pain nor should it be inefficacious, (iii) All similar offences should be punished alike, (iv) Punishment should create an example and serve as deterrent, (v) Punishment should partake of the nature of the offence, (vi) It should rest on the principle of frugality, (vii) It should be a reformation to the criminal, (viii) It should disable him or prevent him from repeating the crime in future, (ix) It should compel the offender as far as possible to compensative those injured by the offence, (x) Punishment should meet popular approval and should not excite sympathy for the offender, and (xi) The punishment should always be remissible. From the above principles, it is very obvious that Bentham was very sympathetic towards the criminals and he stood for the improvement of the lot of the criminals.

Prison Reform: Bentham believed that a great many criminals and evil doers could be restored to society as useful and self-respecting members. On the belief he advocated many salient reforms for the reformation of the criminal and for the teaching of industries while in confinement. He put forth a plan called "Panopticon" for the regular supervision of the daily life of the convicts. He described Panopticon as a mill grinding rogues, honest and idle men industrious. The building i.e., the model prison was a circular glass roofed tank like structure with cells along the external wall facing toward a central rotunda which made it possible for its officers stationed in the rotunda to keep all the inmates (Convicts) under constant and continuous surveillance. The criminals were to be taught useful trades, elementary education, moral and religious ideas. On their release they were to be given employment. He spent lot of money for the same. But he failed in his attempt. Later on some of his reforms were carried out.

Natural rights, individualism and theory of Government: Bentham criticises the idea of natural rights. Natural Rights says Bentham are "simple nonsense; natural and imprescriptible rights rhetorical nonsense — nonsense upon stills". For him natural law and natural rights are meaningless. He substitutes for them the principle of utility.

Like Paine, Rousseau and Locke he has been considered as an individualist. The primary aim of Bentham is to promote the welfare of the community. To quote him, "The community is a fictitious body composed of the individual persons who are considered as constituting as it were its members. It is vain to talk of the interest of the community without understanding what is the interest of the individual. A thing is said to promote the interest or to be for the interest of an individual when it tends to aid to the sum total of his pleasures or what comes to the something to diminish the sum total of his pains."

Bentham stands for free government on the basis of the principle of utility. He tries to differentiate it from a despotic rule. He is in favour of a unicameral legislature elected every year on the basis of adult franchise. A free government is always responsible and accountable for its conduct and policies to the governed. Free government provides the free press and freedom of association. Bentham regards democracy as the best form of government to promote the greatest happiness of the greatest number. But he says that direct democracy is not possible since its representatives may be kept under constant control by enforcing such constitutional safeguards as universal suffrage, annual parliaments, vote by ballot, election of the Prime Minister by the Parliament, the recruitment of civil service by competitive examinations. All are equal before the eye of law and the equal distribution of wealth are other basic principles for the representative form of government.

Justice: Bentham is considered as a great law reformer. He criticises the legal system of England. He is of the opinion that knowledge of the laws of the country should be within the reach of the people. For that purpose, law must be expressed in plain words and short sentences. Further he finds fault with the drafting and the style of the laws of his country. The system of administration of Justice is also not satisfactory there according to Bentham. He condemns the insuperable difficulties that were placed in the way of the litigants to get justice. So Bentham wrote thus "In this country justice is sold and dearly sold and it is denied to him who cannot disburse the price at which it is purchased."

Education: Bentham is considered a forerunner in the field of educational reforms. He believes that mankind can be improved with the help of education. Bentham says that it is the duty of the state to look after the education of the poor children. For that purpose, he suggests certain reforms in the administration of poor law. It is a matter of common knowledge that his views have been accepted and adopted in every progressive country of the world today.

Church: Bentham criticises the Church of England for its sinecure offices. He regards the clergymen as the enemies of progress. He is sceptical with regard to religion as that hinders intellectual progress by supporting belief apart from experience "it is only safe ground." His conclusion is, that religion is useless and harmful.

Liberty and equality: Bentham's theory of rights is based on three principles i.e., (i) the rights are enforceable, (ii) the rights and duties are inseparable and (iii) rights are not considered as postulates of liberty. Law does not aim at liberty. The aim of the government is happiness and not liberty. Liberty is not an important part of happiness. If the object of the state is security, security leads to equality. To Bentham equality cannot be an absolute one; it runs counter to utility. He is not for absolute equality. But he is of the opinion that men are born equal to be happy.

Reforms: Bentham is styled as a great reformer. The number of practical reforms which he advocated are a legion. The principal among them as given by Davidson are; the reform of corrupt and restricted parliamentary systems; a thorough going municipal reform; the humanitarian of the terribly cruel criminal law of the time; the improvement of prisons and prison management; the abolition of imprisonment for debt; the elimination of usury laws; the repeal of religious test; the reform of the poor laws; the suppression of "sturdy beggars", the utilisation of able-bodied paupers, the training of pauper children, the establishment of a vast scheme of national education; the institution of "frugality banks" (Savings Banks) and friendly societies; the forming of code for merchant shipping; the protection of inventors; the encouragement of local courts; comprehensive system of health legislation; the creation of the public prosecutors and of advocates of the poor; a thorough going revision of hereditary rights; the supervision of scientific and philosophical foundation and the recall of public officials. Many of his reforms have since been incorporated into the laws of various countries. Hence, Sir Henry Maine paid a glowing tribute to Bentham in the following manner, "I do not know a single law reform effected since Bentham's day which cannot be traced to his influence."

His attitude towards History

The utilitarian Bentham regards history as little better than an almanac out of date, registering the follies and crimes of mankind as expressed by Voltaire, Montesquieu has taught us that "laws ought to be closely adapted to the people for which they are made that it is very improbable that laws of nation can ever be suited to the wants of another nation". A constitution, therefore, must reflect the character of the people for whom it is intended. But Bentham has a fundamental assumption that 'all human beings be their race'. In other words, all human beings irrespective of the nation which they live are fundamentally same in their requirements. In fact, Bentham was prepared to give on request codes to Turkey, Russia, Spain and Morocco as did for his own nation England. In his opinion the Russians, the Spaniards, the Moroccans and the English might differ in surface individually; but holds Bentham that they all are fundamentally the same. So according to him, every man is alike fundamentally irrespective of his nation. When a nation is constituted by an aggregate of men every nation is the same fundamentally.

The study of history, however, reveals the constant change in the ideas of men. It is said that in the ancient age civic was the foremost virtue. In the wake of Christianity, the civic virtue is replaced by the contemplative virtues. Similarly on the decline of the ascetic virtues associated with the past, the very different ideal of chivalry was born. So history obviously exhibits not the Benthamic standard of happiness. Besides, the character of the nations varies. To emphasise and establish that the following questions are asked. Why should the English people prefer liberty? Why should the French prefer equality while the Irish standing for land? The answer to these questions is obvious. After all, laws are made only to suit the needs and requirements of the people of a land. Prof. Bentham has refused to know the answer of such questions not to speak of his understanding. So Henry Maine remarks that "no genius of an equally high order so completely divorced themselves from history as Hobbes and Bentham".

28

Johann Goltlieb Fichte (1762-1814)

Early Life: Johann Goltlieb Fichte was a great German philosopher. He expounded the theory of ethical idealism. He gave special attention to socialism and to German nationalism. He was born in Saxony in 1762. His father was a weaver. He studied in the universities of Jena and Leipzig from 1780 to 1784. His special subjects were theology and philosophy. Then he left the university campus and went to Prussia. There he mingled with the people and shared their miseries of the Napoleonic conquest. Later on he became a Professor in the newly-established University of Berlin. This period marked the height of his philosophical development and the publication of his most important technical works. Unfortunately, this period ended in disaster and despair. His philosophy which identified God with the moral order was taken by many to be virtually atheistic. As a result, he resigned the post in 1799. Then he turned his attention towards publishing his popular works.

His Works: J.G. Fichte published "The Vocation of Man" in 1800. In 1806 he published his another work, "The Characteristics of the Present Age." In the same year his another work, "The Way to the Blessed Life" was released for reading. In 1808, he published the "Addresses to the German Nation." His important works are "Theory of State" and "Closed Commercial State." Fichte gave an elaborate theory of state socialism and national state. In his famous address to the German people, he put forth an exalted conception of the character and mission of the Germans. No wonder he advocated the ideal of German only.

His Political Ideas: The philosophy of Fichte was the first of the idealist systems derived from Kant, which made Germany the centre of European philosophical activity in the early 19th century. He was much under the influence of Rousseau. He wrote thus,. "Peace be on Rousseau's ashes and blessings in his memory; for he was kindled fire in many souls". Again "My system from beginning to end is nothing but an analysis of the concept of freedom."

According to Fichte, there was no such thing as a pre-social state of nature in which people enjoyed certain natural rights. "The state itself is man's natural condition" as viewed by him. He gave importance to only one natural right i.e., the absolute right of the person to be in the world of sense only cause and never effect."

Regarding social contract Fichte referred to three kinds of contracts, viz., property contract, protection contract and the union contract. He defined the property contract as rights of free action in the world sense. Property contract fixed the boundary to the property of each. According to this contract, every individual gave up his claim to what lay outside a certain sphere on the condition that all gave up their claims to what lay within that sphere. By the protection contract, every individual agreed to contribute his share of force necessary for the maintenance of the partitions made by the property contract. By the union contract every individual agreed with every other individual to unite into a whole for the effective accomplishment of the ends involved in the previous two contracts. This contract completed the social pact and constituted a sovereign.

As regards the functions of the state, Fichte rejected the idea that the end of the "state was to make happy, rich, healthy, orthodox, virtuous and God willing saved eternally." Nor it was merely to preserve and protect each in his personal rights and his property. The function of the state according to him was "to give to each for the first time in his own, to instal him for the first time in his property and then first to protect him in it." It was the duty of the state to give proper aids to all sections of people. The state was to distribute proportionately the raw materials and finished products of the country. Again it was to fix the prices of various commodities. It was the duty of the state to carry on all the foreign trade. He stood for the economic self-sufficiency of every state. Commercial rivalries were responsible for war. Fichte too like Kant had the ideal of a world league of nations.

According to Fichte, natural boundaries should be preserved. Nature indicated the geographical basis of every state.

Fichte held that a government might be monarchic or aristocratic, elective or hereditary but never democratic. Because the whole people can never take part in the governmental work. Fichte said that the right of final judgement upon the conduct of the government must be with the people as a whole. He suggested an institution known as Ephorate whose duty was to watch any violation of the constitution and to provide the machinery, when necessary for the expression of the sovereign will of the people. If this check on the government failed, the people as a whole had the right of revolution. Dunning remarks thus "such was Fichte's contribution to the solution of the much debated problem, how to keep the government in accord with the constitution without permitting any branch of the government to shape the constitution on its will."

Catlin calls him as one of the fathers of fascism. Reinhold Aris says Fichte was the first thinker in Germany who developed a consistent system of liberalism. According to Catlin, "The German Rousseau, humanised cosmopolitan, anarchist liberal, liberal socialist, collectivist national, national socialist, the agony of Fichte's doubts and changes expresses more clearly than it is expressed in any other writer the crisis in civilisation for this age."

29

George Wilhelm Frederick Hegel (1770-1831 A.D.)

C.L. Wayper writes in his "Political Thought" that "The most outstanding advocate of the organic theory of the State and one of the most important and influential thinkers of modern history was Hegel. He was born at Stuttgart in Wurttemberg in Southern Germany in 1770. His father was a civil servant. In his school days, he was very bright and brilliant and hence, he became a school prize winner. Then he studied theology in the University of Tabingen. He fell under the spell of the French Revolution in his youth and declared it as "a glorious mental dawn." During this time he was very thorough with the writings of Rousseau. He worked as a private tutor for sometime. There he wrote the life of Jesus Christ.

After serving as a private tutor for some years he became lecturer in the University of Jena in 1801. During this time, Kant exercised a tremendous influence over Hegel. But Hegel never was a Kantian. The contract between Kant and Hegel is considerably greater than that between Plato and Aristotle.

In 1806, Jena fell before the victorious armies of Napoleon. As a result of this Hegel had to leave that place. After Jena, Hegel worked as a local editor and also became a school headmaster in Nuremberg. He published his three-volume work on the "Science of Logic." Because of this work, he became the most loudly acclaimed of German philosophers. He became a Professor at Heidelberg University in 1816. He was then 47 years old. Here he wrote his "Encyclopaedia of the Philosophical Sciences", the fullest treatment of his general philosophical system that he ever produced.

Hegel then shifted to Berlin University where he accepted the chair of Philosophy. While at Berlin he acted as the official philosopher of Prussia. In this capacity, he expounded the nature of knowledge, god, universe and the state. Hence, his ideas had tremendous effect both upon theoretical and practical politics. He made world history culminate in Hohenzollern Prussia. At Berlin, Hegel did not consider himself under any obligation to enter into the conflicts of the politicians. He criticised the English Parliamentary Reform movement which was responsible for the passing of the Reform Act of 1832. Hegel died of cholera at the age of 61. He was buried next to Fichte.

The Philosophy of Hegel is to be found in his works "The Phenomenology of Spirit", "Logic", "The Philosophy of Right" and the "Philosophy of History."

Hegel represents the climax of German idealism in political thought. Like Kant and Fichte, Hegel too based his political system of psychology i.e. on the conception of positive and self-determining freedom. He combined the historical sense of Vico and Montesquieu with the philosophic eminence of Kant and Fichte in his writings. The corner-stone of his philosophy is evolution, the evolution of ideas by dialectical process.

According to Prof. Sabine, the significance of the political thought of Hegel centres round two points and those are the dialectic as a method and the idealisation of the nation state. These two points became the source of the two most important stands of later political thought.

The concept of Geist was basic in all the political thinking of Hegel. It appeared in many aspects namely Weltgeist (World Spirit), Volksgeist (National Spirit) and Zeitgeist (Time Spirit). It dominated Hegel's idea of historical evolution.

Vaughan has pointed out to the various contribution made by Hegel in his philosophy. In this connection, it is pointed out that Hegel grasped the connection between morals and politics and handled the same with a far greater insight, than any of his predecessors. During the 19th century, Hegel was hailed not only as the official philosopher of Prussia but also as the philosopher of the age in the same way Aristotle and St. Thomas Aquinas were regarded as the philosophers of their times.

Hegel remarked that the function of philosophy was merely to explain and not to create. According to Prof. Sabine, "The philosophy of Hegel aimed at nothing less than a complete and systematic reconstruction of modern thought......." C.L. Wayper says, "Hegel's great influence on philosophy, on political philosophy, on politics is not then to be denied. Unfortunately, he is as difficult to understand as he is important. Language has frequently been accorded pride of place among the major arts of deception."

The Hegelian theory of the state leads to state absolutism, totalitarianism and nationalism and goes against the modern nations of liberty and democracy. His idolising of the state has led to Fascism. His dialectics modified by the materialism of Marx has resulted in communism. Hegel was wrong in identifying the state with society. There is no doubt that Hegel, in spite of many shortcomings in his philosophy was one of the greatest philosophers of the world. One may be critic of Hegel and Hegelian heritage but one cannot gainsay its universal importance.

His Dialectic Method: According to William Ebenstein, "In the German intellectual tradition, Hegel's system of philosophy towards over the rest in more than one way. Hegel's work enompasses philosophy, metaphysics, religion, art, ethics, history and politics. In its range alone his work is unique in Germany and possibly in the whole world."

According to Hegel, the progress of human civilization has not been in a positive straight-line. It was in a zig-zag sort of movement. The main aim of philosophy was to know nature and the entire world of experience and to comprehend the reason for it. The world is essentially a dynamic and it is not static. The true concept must be an active moving process, of evolution. In the process of evolution, something that is undeveloped gets developed by splitting up, assuming many different and opposing forms. It then unites or combines again in a new concrete objects and becomes a unity in diversity. The higher state in the process of evolution is the realisation of the lower. The lower form is negatived in the higher. It gets carried over or sublimated. The whole process of evolution was given the name of Dialectic by

Hegel. The term 'dialectic' was first used by the Sophists and other Greek thinkers. According to them, it was the method of disputation to show that the statement of a speaker was self-refuting. According to Plato, "the dialectic was a process of thinking by which the dramatic conflict of ideas was determined by definition."

According to Hegel, the dialectic was not merely a process by which logical ideas developed. It was a method or process by which all idea in the world developed. History showed a continuous and orderly development. Hegel in and through his dialectic propounded the belief that reality could only be apprehended by a method of contrasting one thing with its opposite. Thus, goodness was only understood when it was contrasted with badness, heat with cold, want with society. To Hegel, the real was the rational and the rational was the real.

The universe of known experience was in constant flux. It was moving towards a definite point. There was imminent necessity for the ends and purposes of that evolution. The whole process of evolution was governed by definite rational principles of thesis, antithesis and synthesis. According to him, we begin with an abstract universal concept called thesis; the concept gives rise to contradiction called antithesis; the contradictory concepts and reconciled in the third, called synthesis. It is the union of the other two concepts. Thus, in the simple example of the evolution of the life germ in an egg the whole dialectic process could be seen. The egg contains a germ (thesis) which when fertilised gradually consumes (negatives) the contents of the egg. This act of destruction results not in death but in the production of a new form of life completely different in nature from its origin, the germ of its environment the contents. A chick (the synthesis of the two forces) emerges from the shell.

Hegel came forward to demonstrate that the laws of thought were similar to the laws of the universe. The thesis "despotism" will call into being democracy, the antithesis and form the clash between them the synthesis "constitutional monarchy" which contains the best of both results. The thesis, the family produces its antithesis, bourgeois society and from the resultant clash the synthesis the state emerges in which thesis and antithesis are raised to a higher power and reconciled.

Further Hegel distinguished between understanding and reason as did Carlyle. For him, "understanding was the mode of mind which seeks precision above all things and insists upon clear distinctions." Reason gives us a deeper insight into the real nature of things than understanding with its formal ratiocination. Apart from this, he differentiated the creative reason from reflective reason. According to him, creative reason was unconscious reason, reason unaware of itself — e.g., building up of family, society, state. Reflective reason reconstructs thought and by a conscious effort of thought the fabric which blinded by the very force of its creative power, it has ceased to recognise as its own.

Hegel also emphasised the need of history and tradition to solve the political and other problems. History is the process by which the spirit passes from knowing nothing to full knowledge of itself, the increasing revelation of the purposes of the Rational Mind. "The history of the world", therefore, says Hegel "presents us with a rational process." The Spirit on the way to its goal makes many experiments. The Spirit or the Reason does not know anything at the beginning of the world process. It develops slowly throughout the history of the world and ultimately reaches the truth Absolute. Hence, it is said "the rational is the real and the real is the rational."

From the above theory of Hegel, it is seen that the main purpose of Dialectic is to display historical necessity. Hegel used his dialectic theory for giving an explanation of the progress of society and its institutions. But he was not successful in his use of dialectic. In his philosophy of the Spirit, Hegel put forth his idea or notion of art, religion and philosophy in which he viewed the art as thesis, religion as antithesis and philosophy as synthesis. But it is not understandable in what sense religion is the opposite of art. It is not proper to say that both are related as germs and species or religion can be regarded as the differential. The fact is that Hegel's dialectic thrives on ambiguities of terminology.

According to Dr. Mc. Taggart, though the dialectic method is wholly valid, its application in the explanation of various facts is questionable. First of all thesis, antithesis and synthesis cannot be recognised except in relation to one another. Secondly, in religion history, law and philosophy the dialectical process is affected by external influences. Thirdly, the application of this method to the field of natural and social sciences is intricated and not systematised.

(1) State: Hegel's "Philosophy of Law" (Philosophic des Rechts) published in 1821, contains the best statements of his political ideas. In his "Philosophy of History" published posthumously in 1837 (six years after his death) Hegel defines the state as "the realisation of Freedom," the state exists for its own sake. Hegel puts more stress on the state and he regarded it as essentially divine in origin. Hence, it must be looked with awe and reverence. He rejected the theory of social contract as the origin of the state. To Hegel the idea that men in the state of nature were free and equal appeared absurd and ridiculous. In the very beginning men lived as groups rather than as individuals. During the state of nature, there was no equality or real freedom since the state was not originated by the voluntary union. He opined that the state was the product of a long process of evolution. It was not the creation of man at one time and place. Man being a social animal stated by Aristotle lived in groups even in a primitive state. First family came into existence. Out of the family the tribe developed and out of the tribe the state at first in a lower than in a higher form. Thus, the first characteristic of the state of Hegel "Divine in Origin" is clearly indicated.

Another characteristic feature of the Hegelian state is the idea that the individual must be completely subordinated to the state, and the wishes and desires of the individual must be rejected in favour of the will of the state.

Another characteristic feature of the Hegelian state is that it was the embodiment of all reasons. It was the actualisation of freedom. It was rational in conception. The state was the incarnation of General will or the real will. True freedom for the individual consisted in obeying the laws of the state and cultivating "the everyday habit of looking on the Commonwealth as our substantive purpose and the foundation of ourselves."

Hegel's State is absolute, omnipotent and infallible. The State is the march of God on earth. The state is God itself. It represented the last individual will. It has its own will and personality, superior to the wills and personalities of the individuals who formed it. As member of the state he had freedom in the state. The state was the creator of all rights and as such an individual had no rights against the state. It represented the unity of the universal and individual will. It was both the objective and subjective freedom. In this way it was eternal.

The state also is an end in itself. It is not only the highest expression to which the spirit has yet attained, it is "the final embodiment of spirit on earth." There can be no spiritual evolution beyond the state. Similarly, there can be any more physical evolution beyond man.

Another characteristic feature of the state according to Hegel is society that must dominate mankind among the social institutions. It is higher and more important than the family, state is higher and more important than the society. Thus, he believed in the hierarchy of institutions.

(2) Freedom: According to Hegel, the idea of freedom is the essence of man. The object of Hegel's theory of freedom was to remove the mistake of the French Revolution. In this sphere, he was no doubt indebted to Rousseau and Kant. But he thought Kantian freedom was negative, limited and subjective. To him individual freedom was a social phenomenon. It was made possible in the moral life of the community. Freedom consisted in giving total obedience to the state and in the performance of one's duties.

(3) Punishment: On the basis of right and morality he discussed in detail the question of punishment. According to him, if a particular right was violated it was the duty of the state to punish the person who violated it. Punishment is a right both of the society and the criminal. It should be given to the criminals.

(4) Property: Hegel was in favour of private property. With the help of that private property, the individual can thrive himself. Without property there can be no progress in him.

(5) Constitution: To Hegel, the state manifest itself in a constitution. There are three essential powers in the state viz. the legislative, the administrative and the monarchic. Among the three the monarchic power is the most important. It is the

verifying force within the state. The first (legislative branch) is a thesis, the second (Administrative) is antithesis and the third (monarchic) is synthesis. The last one prevents the other two from disrupting the state. All other forms of government are regarded by Hegel as imperfect and useless.

As a philosophical conception sovereignty belongs to the state as a whole. As a result, all are brought under the control of sovereignty. Further Hegel did not believe in revolutionary changes in the constitution. Institutions are not made in one day but grow gradually. Every institution is therefore rational even if it is imperfect. With the result of this they have a place in the dialectical movement.

(6) History: According to Hegel, the course of history is governed by reason. Man plays a significant role in history. World history is the world judgment i.e., victory for one people and defeat for another. The course of history is determined by the process of eternal change. He says that the realisation of freedom is essential. This is the end of the world spirit as it moves toward absolute self-consciousness. "It is the hub around with world history revolves. History is divided by going forward to this point and starting from it."

(7) Hegel's Ideas on War: According to Hegel, the essential principle of the state is self-preservation and perfection. War is not to be regarded as an evil but a virtue. "The state of war," says Hegel, "shows the omnipotence of the state in its individuality." War is to national life what winds are to the sea "preserving mankind from the corruption engendered by immobility." War effectively displays the "irony of the divine idea." War destroys the selfish egoism of the individual. For Hegel, "peace corrupts and everlasting peace corrupts everlastingly." War is the state of affairs which deals in earnest with the vanity of temporal goods and concerns — a vanity at other times a common theme for edifying sermonizing. War has the highest significance that by its agency the ethical health of people is preserved in their indifference to the stabilizing of finite institutions; just as the blowing of the wind preserves the sea from the foulness which would be the result of a prolonged calm, let alone 'perpetual peace'. Successful wars have prevented civil boils and strengthened the internal

power of the state." The various weapons of war were not invented only by chance; they fulfilled an essential purpose. To quote Hegel, "the gun is not a chance invention." The same can be said about gun-powder. "Humanity needed it and it made its appearance forthwith." Guns and gun-powder bear the stamp of civilization. "The rights of uncivilized peoples are a mere formality." "The civilized nation is conscious that the rights of barbarians are the unequal to its own and treats their autonomy as only a formality."

Through war, the world spirit decides for itself which of the warring states is its true embodiment. Success in war is a conclusive proof that the victorious state represents more fully and truly the world spirit. However, Hegel makes a qualification here. No state can urge in justification of a war it has begun that it is acting at the behest of the world spirit, though it can always make that claim in justification of war that it has won. Thus, Hegel assigns a great role to war. The world spirit, according to him, fulfils its aim through war and, therefore, it is a virtuous necessity.

(8) Hegel on International Law: To Hegel, the nation-state was the most rational thing. It was the expression of a higher rationality than could be achieved by the individual, or by any private group or corporation. The state was omnipotent and absolute, supreme and sovereign. Naturally therefore, the state is bound by no principles of International Law. International Law represents only certain usages which were accepted so long as they did not conflict with the supreme performance of the state. The other nations have no right against another state. To quote Hegel, "A state is not a private person, but in itself a completely independent totality. Hence, the relations of state to one another is not merely that of morality and private right. It is often desired that the state should be regarded from the standpoint of private right and morality. But the position of private person is such that they have over them a law court, which realizes what is intrinsically right. A relation between states ought also to be intrinsically right, but in mundane affairs that which is intrinsically right ought to have power. But as against the state there is no power to decide what is intrinsically

right and realize that decision. Hence, we must here remain by absolute command. States in their relations to one another are independent and look upon the stipulations which they make with one another as provisional." Thus the interest of the state is the supreme law. It is not bound by any principles of International Law as such laws come in conflict with its self-preservation. Naturally, a thinker who believes in war and regards it a virtuous activity cannot be expected to believe in any principles of international law.

But it is wrong to presume that Hegel did not look beyond the nation-state. To him, nation-state was only in step, but a necessary step in the evolution of humanity towards a world-state. It is only when the nation has developed to their full maturity that they can march towards the ideas of world-state. But of course, Hegel did not write much on the world-state. The idea of world-state was too abstract for him to speculate about it.

(9) Government: According to Hegel, the state manifests itself in a constitution. The three important powers in the state are legislative, administrative and monarchic. Out of these powers, the monarchic power is the most important. Hegel made this division of powers according to the formula of his dialectic. According to him, the legislative branch, which stands for the universal aspect of the state, is the thesis; the administrative organ representing its particular aspect is the antithesis: and the constitutional monarch who may be regarded as their unity in the individual state is the synthesis. Hegel includes the judicial organ in the administrative branch. The constitutional monarch is the medium through which the legislative and the executive are brought into a harmonious unity. Thus, according to Hegel, the monarch is the symbol and embodiment of the unity and supremacy of the state. The sovereignty of the state resides in him and not in the mass of the people. Being constitutional the monarch can be no autocrat; he is bound to the concrete content of the advice of his councillors, and when the constitution is established, he has often nothing to do but sign his name. His function is simply to say, "I will in the name of the state. But this name is weighty; it is the summit over which nothing can

climb." In accordance with his dialectic, Hegel has tried to show that the completely rational state must not only be a monarchy, but also a constitutional monarchy. True freedom is possible only in a constitutional monarchy. However, Hegel disliked parliamentary institutions of the British type. According to him, what needs representation is not the individuals but interests or functional units of society. He favoured the functional system of representation.

Hegel and Kant

Though Hegel was influenced by the philosophy of Kant but he modified it to suit the conditions of his day and his own genius. Like Kant, he based his system upon a spiritual idea, but his method was different from that of Kant. While Kant followed the deductive method, Hegel's method was historical and evolutionary. According to Vaughan, "Analytic criticism is the dominant idea of Kant: the keynote of Hegel's achievement is evolution." Again, Kant started from the individual consciousness. Hegel from the world of externalized knowledge and of organized institutions. Kant was individualistic from beginning to the end; but Hegel rejected individualism in toto. According to Kant, freedom consisted in obedience to the 'Categorical imperatives of Duty;' white for Hegel it contained in obedience to the will of the state. Hegel defined the national state and rejected the idea of international law. On the other hand, Kant was a firm believer in an international order and world-peace. In short, Kant was more individualistic than Hegel.

Implications of Hegel's Philosophy

If we examine Hegel's philosophy shown of its pretentious logical apparatus we would find that he is saying something both very old and very simple. He reaffirms the Greek view that man rises to his full stature only in the state which completes the training in public spirit supplied at the lower level by the family and civil society. His real aim was to restore national unity of Germany which had suffered humiliation at the hands of France. State's own preservation was the first end to be kept in view before the individuals could claim any freedom for themselves.

Freedom to Hegel was something positive, and not merely a negative absence of restraints.

No one can probably object to this view of philosophy but when he cast his arguments in the rigid mould of dialectic, he opened himself to serious pitfalls. To Hegel, dialectic was a law of logic and indeed an iron law, leaving little or nothing to chance or even to conscious human volition. But the most serious objection against dialectic is that it is extremely vague. The 'contradictions' discovered by Hegel consist of so many sorts of different and opposite things that the dialectic frequently loses its plausibility. Thus, to Hegel, civil society is the antithesis of family. It is difficult to see how it is. As a matter of fact, ambiguous use of terms detracts seriously from the value of any theory and the same is the case with Hegel's dialectic. Hegel has reduced individual wishes and preferences to the level of mere caprice. The actors in human history for him are not men but impersonal forces. The deeds of actual men are what Hegel calls 'moments' in the process by which the idea realizes itself in the state. Other and above he tells that the wishes of men are merely 'subjective' made legitimate only in so far as the 'inner drive' of the dialectic makes them coincide with the "universal" ends of the state. As Lancaster remarks, "While Hegel's emphasis on the 'transcendence' of the individual was a useful corrective to the extreme atomism of the Enlightenment, he carries it to the point where individual values disappear entirely."

The most significant aspect of Hegel's philosophy is his exaltation of the state. He makes the individual not only a member of society but also makes him the subject of a state which being the final embodiment of world spirit is supreme and omnipotent. The moral superiority of the state consists not the fact that it is a means to meet the needs of man but in the fact, that it is an end in itself, representing the supreme achievement of reason in human affairs and being the "absolutely rational," the "actuality of the ethical idea," the march of God on earth. Hegel's state stands so far above the individual that the latter has significance only as material upon which spirit works its will. The individual conscience is not to be trusted; the commands of the state are the spokesmen of infallible morality. To raise the state above all moral criticism was to contribute decisively to a disastrous worship of power.

However, Hegel's teaching is valuable too. It insists on man's dependence on society. Individualism ignores the social character of man. Hegel emphasized on the social aspect of man's nature. He made the idea of liberty richer by showing that man's conception of it largely depends upon the institutions which have trained him his education. He emphasized that the state is not a police state, instead it must be regarded as part of man's moral end. His dialectic became in the hands of Marx; the basis of revolutionary communism. Marx converted the dialectic into a scientific explanation of social evolution, an evolution ending not in the exaltation of the state but in its abolition.

Hegel's philosophy led the English idealists of the last 19th century to revise liberalism and rid it of its abstraction which had viewed the individual as a solitary and pleasure-seeking animal. Hegel's theory gave rise to the sociological theory of politics, because he showed that political power was connected with the economic, social and cultural forces in the State. He gave a new emphasis and importance to the State and greatly enriched modern political philosophy. He grasped the connection. Between morals and politics and handled the same with a far greater insight than any of his predecessors. According to Prof. Sabine, "The philosophy of Hegel aimed at nothing less than a complete and systematic reconstruction of modern thought." He set forth a new intellectual method, the dialectic, which should bridge the gulf between reason, fact and value. In his political theory, he set a value on the national state and its place in history which formed so small part of his influence. The social philosophy of Hegel had a direct and intimate relation to the national history of Germany. According to Maxey, "It will be many years before the full influence of Hegel's political thought can be measured. His contribution to the warring ideologies represented on the one side by Lenin and Stalin and on the other by Mussolini and Hitler, constitutes but one part of his significance, and is no more paradoxical than his influence in other directions. Both his view and his methodology have deeply affected the social science." "Divergent streams of thought have also flowed from Hegel's subordination of the whole of civil society to the state. Liberals, seeking an escape from the nihilistic individualism similar to that of Laissez faire have found in the Hegelian conception of the state a plausible basis for programmes of reform carried on by state action. Conservatives, on the other hand, have found the same concept suitable to the support of their interest in the promotion of economic nationalism.

30
James Mill (1773-1836 A.D.)

James Mill was born on 6th April, 1773 at Northwater Bridge in Forfarshire in Scotland. His father was a shoemaker and his mother was domestic servant of farming stock. He studied in the University of Edinburgh where he distinguished himself as a Greek scholar. He studied divinity and became a preacher in the Church of Scotland. During this period, he showed keen interest in the historical and philosophical studies.

James Mill went to London in 1802. There he devoted himself to journalism. He got temporary success in this field. He had nine children and J.S. Mill was the best of all. He had to work very hard for his livelihood.

James Mill published his first pamphlet on corn trade in 1804. From 1805 onwards he directed his attention towards literature. James Mill wrote many books. The most important of them are "History of India" published in three volumes in 1818. "Analysis of the Phenomena of the Human Mind" published in 1829 and "Fragment of Mckintosh" published in 1835. He wrote enormous articles. His most famous article was article on "Government" which was written by him in 1814. His other two authoritative articles were articles on "Jurisprudence" and "Law of Nations" in the Encyclopaedia Britannica.

James Mill's friendship with Jeremy Bentham exercised a tremendous influence upon him since 1808. Hence, he adopted Bentham's principles in his writings. The friendship between the two continued for the rest of their lives. Their relation was that of student and teacher. They were very near and dear each other from 1814 to 1817. James Mill and his wife lived with Bentham. Even after leaving the residence of Bentham, he continued to have the same intimate relations with his master. He was the chief promoter of those principles. And more than anyone else it w. Mill, who opposed the beginnings of romanticism in the typical Benthamite manner. He made regular contributions to the "Anti-Jacobin Review", "The British Review", "The Eclectic Review" and the "Edinburgh Review". Later on, he wrote in a periodical called the "Philanthropist" with co-operation of William Alien. All his contribution mostly related with education, the freedom of the press and the prison discipline. The University of London was established in 1825. He played a significant role in founding the above university.

James Mill wrote "Liberty of the Press", "Prisons and Prison Discipline", "Colony and Education" etc., in 1814. The publication of "History of British India" brought him immediate immense fame. As a result of this, he was appointed an official in the India House in 1819. He became the head of the Examiner's office in 1830. During this period he wrote the "Elements of Political Economy."

After the death of Bentham, he became the leader of the utilitarian school. James Mill exercised tremendous influence on his contemporaries. Lord Brongham, George Grote, Joseph Hume, Roebuck and Ricardo came under his influence. Among them Ricardo was his best friend.

James Mill showed extraordinary leanings for law and law reforms. According to him, neither monarchy nor aristocracy was suitable for the people. He favoured the representative government for the people. At the same time, the representative must act as a check on the abuses of the legislature. He stood for frequent elections to approve or disapprove of the representatives.

James Mill was not in favour of universal suffrage. According to him, the right to vote should not be given to women. He also did not believe that the right of voting should be given every man. It should be given only to those men who were of the age of 40 and above.

James Mill believed that all men pursued their own pleasure and avoided pain. To protect the rights of man authority is needed. Government provides this authority. His desire was to strengthen the House of Commons to meet the obstacle posed by the King and the House of Lords. Hence, he condemned the

House of Lords. He also put forth certain reforms in the House of Lords with a view to decrease its powers. He anticipated the Parliament Act of 1911 when he said that "Let it be enacted that if a Bill which has been passed by the House of Commons and thrown out by the House of Lords is renewed in the House of Commons in the next session of Parliament and passed but again thrown out by the House of Lords, it shall if passed a third time in the House of Commons, be law, without being again sent to the Lords."

James Mill regarded the middle class as the natural leaders of the people. This class also had the sympathy for the lower classes. It was in good position to guide and lead the people. Hence, he stood for the supremacy of the middle class.

James Mill was not opposed to the king. To him the interests of the king were bound up with the interests of the people. If he acted against the interests of the people, he became a curse.

Like Bentham, James Mill stressed the need for education. All men were by nature equal and the differences among them were due mainly, to education. The end of education was to give happiness to the people as a whole. According to him, education was all powerful. "If education does not perform everything, there is hardly anything which it does not perform." Here he echoed the doctrine of Helvetius that "a prodigious difference is produced by education...."

Like Bentham, Mill advocated many reforms in the field of jurisprudence and international law. According to him, jurisprudence was concerned with rights and not with their creation and distribution. It belonged to the legislature. Jurisprudence is concerned with the protection and security of rights. He stood for international law and the pressure of international public opinion would compete the nations to obey international law and justice. There was a necessity of the codification of international law and the establishment of an international tribunal with a well-defined procedure. He handled in a better and fitter way the subject of war and the rights and obligations of belligerents.

It cannot be denied that Mill's version of utilitarianism was illuminated with historical, economic and psychological analysis which Bentham had been unable to supply.

31

John Austin (1790-1859 A.D.)

Early Life: John Austin was a famous English lawyer. He is considered as the most influential English writer on Jurisprudence. He was the disciple of Bentham. Austin was born on 3rd March, 1790. At the age of sixteen, he joined the army and served as a Lieutenant in Malta and Sicily up to 1812. After resigning the job, he began to study law. He was called to the Bar in 1818. He practised the legal profession for seven years in Lincoln's Inn. But it did not suit his taste. His military experiences had a profound influence upon the development of his doctrine of sovereignty and the theory of law. In 1819, he married Sarah Taylor, a beautiful, talented, brilliant, fascinating and remarkable woman. After their marriage, Austin became neighbours in London of Bentham and the Mills.

Austin was appointed Professor of Jurisprudence in the newly founded University of London in 1826. In the following year he went to Germany along with his wife. There he was greatly influenced by the German ideas of classification and systematic analysis. In 1828, they returned home. His opening lectures in 1828 were attended by John Stuart Mill, George Cornwall Lewis, Romily etc. Later on he failed to attract new students and in 1832 he resigned the professorship in bitter despair and disappointment.

John Austin was appointed in 1833 to the Criminal Law Commission but he resigned that post too after signing its first two reports because of utter frustration. In 1836, he was appointed Commissioner with George Cornwall Lewis to give advice on the legal and constitutional reforms of Malta. He went back to England in 1848 and lived with his wife in Paris until his death in December 1859.

His Works: Austin wrote with extreme difficulty. His best known work "The Province of Jurisprudence Determined." It was published in 1832 in the form of six lectures. The second edition "The Province of Jurisprudence Determined" was published by his widow Sarah Austin in 1861. She also reconstructed from the notes of her husband the main "Lectures on Jurisprudence or the Philosophy of Positive Law." She published them in 1863. The substance of his political philosophy is chiefly to be found in this work, "Lectures on Jurisprudence" as edited by Cambell after the death of Mrs. Austin.

According to Lord Melborne, "Province of Jurisprudence Determined" was the dullest book that he had ever read. John Bowle says that the style of Austin is generally clear, if dry and sometimes achieves a severe eloquence.

His Political Philosophy

(a) State: Austin did not accept the Social Contract Theory. According to him, it is artificial, unrealistic, fictitious, false and superfluous. People obeyed the state not due to any formal consent but due to force of their habit of obedience. The state continues to exist on account of its utility to the people.

(b) Rights and Duties: Austin disfavoured natural rights. In his aspect he resembles Bentham. He held that all rights were created by law and that political restraint as necessary as civil liberty. Further he remarked that all rights were created and regulated by the state. According to him, duty was enforced by the power of the state.

(c) Liberty: According to Austin, the extent of the liberty of the people depended upon what sovereign was prepared to give them. He had no belief in absolute freedom. He realised and recognised that law secured liberty and that without law there can be no liberty. The sovereign was not limited by any law in its power of narrowing or widening the bounds of liberty. According to the principle of utility, the sovereign may be narrowed or widened the bounds of liberty. He enforced the Positive law for the good of the people.

Thus, his concept of liberty was aimed at the welfare of the whole community.

According to him, international law depended only on moral sanctions. There was no hope of general obedience to a supranational law. Sovereign power was superior.

(d) Utility: According to him, God's intention is the promotion of the greatest happiness of all his sentiment. Creatures and so his command is that all his human action be directed towards the achievement of that end. Some actions of man are good, some of them are bad. Hence, God prevents those bad actions which would hinder the promotion of the greatest happiness. Thus, he equates his principle utility with God's command.

(e) Law: According to Austin, Law is the command of the sovereign. It is issued by a person, who is politically superior to those who are politically inferior. Austin calls these commands issued by the sovereign in a state as positive laws or laws proper. Further he differentiates the positive law from law of God i.e., fundamental principle of morality and from positive morality. The science of Jurisprudence is called positive law, whereas positive morality is concerned with science of legislation morals and positive international morality. Political sovereign makes those positive laws. Positive morality is set by persons, who have no political authority e.g. by parents over the children. According to Austin, "every positive law is let by a sovereign person or sovereign body of persons, to a member or members of the independent political society wherein that person or body of persons is sovereign or supreme." Austin developed his theory of sovereignty from this principle.

Theory of Sovereignty

John Austin was a famous English lawyer. He wrote a book on Jurisprudence entitled "Lectures on Jurisprudence". It was published in 1832. His theory is the outcome of the teachings of Bentham and Hobbes. This theory is based on the nature of law. According to Austin, "law is a command given by a superior to an inferior." In the word of Austin, "If a determinate human superior not in the habit of obedience, to a like superior receives habitual obedience from the bulk of a given society, that determinate superior sovereign in that society, and the society (including the sovereign) is a society political and independent." From this definition, we can explain the same in the following manner:

(i) The sovereignty is determinate.
(ii) The sovereignty is indivisible.
(iii) The sovereignty is absolute and unlimited.
(iv) The sovereign is human, i.e., he is not supernatural.
(v) The sovereign is superior, i.e., society includes a chain of inferiors and superiors and the sovereign is the last link of that chain.
(vi) The sovereign receives obedience from the bulk of the society. It means that some members of the society may disobey the laws and hence the obedience is not from the whole society.
(vii) The sovereign does not habitually obey another superior. It means that the sovereign may occasionally submit himself to laws, set by opinions or to commands of determinate parties.

Austin says that the Sovereign is a determinate person or body of persons. He is acting as the final source of power. His authority is unlimited. All citizens, unions, associations and other things are under the control of the sovereign. Directly or indirectly, he is not subject to any control in the state. He is an unquestionable man. So long as the laws emanate or come out from the legal sovereign they are called commands of the Sovereign which must be obeyed. The Sovereign receives habitual obedience from the bulk of the community. The command of the Sovereigns is the essence of law. Law is in the form of "You must do certain things" or "You must not do other things". If a person fails in both the cases he would be punished.

From the above analysis of his theory, we know that the Sovereign has supreme power which is determinate, absolute, illuminable, inalienable, all comprehensive and permanent. There is no rival to him. There is no other supreme power in his territory.

Criticism: The theory of Austin has been criticised by many writers including Sir Henry Maine. He criticises the unlimited power of the sovereign as stated by Austin. From history, Sir Henry Maine has given examples that there is no power on earth which can wield unlimited powers. It cannot be denied that the government is the source of power and authority in the state. But even then it cannot control the morality of the people. Further Maine says that Ranjit Singh actually controlled the people of Punjab. But he could not change the customs of the people, their religious belief and superstition. Hence, it is wrong to say that Sovereign is possessed of unlimited powers.

Prof. Laski has also attacked the theory on the similar point. He says that it is impossible to exercise unlimited powers. Further it is also undesirable to give unlimited powers to anybody. Many examples can be cited from history for this. If unlimited power is given to a king or queen in a particular country, there we cannot see the freedom of the people. They would turn as dictators and suppress the people.

In the federal form of government, there is no place for the unlimited sovereign. In U.S.A., the Congress, the states and the President are enjoying the powers. Amendment to the constitution can be made in the U.S.A., by two-thirds majority of the Congress and three-fourths of the state.

It is already mentioned by Austin that Sovereign is a determinate body. This principle of Austin has also been criticised by modern writers. For this also we can quote the U.S.A., for example. In U.S.A., there is no such determinate body having unlimited powers. There the Congress, the Governors of the states, the President and the Supreme Court have limited powers.

Again the absolute and indivisible character of sovereignty is questioned by the pluralists. If the power of the Sovereign is divided he cannot control the whole society. Hence, the idea of divided sovereignty has to be accepted.

Austin says that law is essentially a command of the Sovereign. Law is universal and uniform for all the people but command is not. Every one must obey the law whereas the man who gives the command himself does not obey it.

Further the Pluralists like Laski challenge the supremacy of the state on the ground that state is one among the many associations found in the society and so it cannot be endowed with any superior power.

Finally, the emergence of international law backed by world opinion expressing through the U.N.O. puts definite limits to the authority of the state. From the above facts, it is difficult to believe that sovereignty is absolute or unlimited.

32

John Stuart Mill (1806-1873 A.D.)

His Life: John Stuart Mill is the most widely known nineteenth century British political writer. He was the last of the utilitarian and the foremost of the individualists. He was the eldest son of James Mill. He was born in London on May 20, 1805. No child of James Mill underwent a more "unusual and remarkable" boyhood than young John Stuart Mill according to R.G. Gupta. This fact has been admitted by J.S. Mill himself in his Autobiography which was written during the last five years of his life (1873).

James Mill had a very good plan to bring him up in the Benthamite lines. He was learning Greek by the age of three. At eight he began to study Latin. He studied Greek and Latin classics which included those of Plato, Herodotus, Xerophen, Thucydides, Homer and Polybius. He also learnt algebra, geometry, the differential calculus etc. He studied political economy particularly Adam Smith and David Ricardo. His father was his teacher and constant companion.

At the age of 23, he left the Debating Society which he himself founded. The reason that he adduced is that "he had enough of Speech making." Before the age of 32 he had already worked as the editor of the London and Westminster Magazine. J.S. Mill was appointed to a clerical post in the East India Company in 1823 and became head of his department in 1856. He continued in that post till 1858 when the East India Company was ended and the Government of India was taken over by the Crown.

J.S. Mill's association with Mrs. Harriet Taylor, a woman of high character and brilliant mind paved the way for a great attachment towards her. He married her in 1851, two years after the death of her husband. It is doubtless true that Mrs. Taylor helped to humanise his revised version of utilitarianism. His view was that she was the originator of most of his ideas. After the ending of the company, he refused to accept an offer of a government post, preferring to retire from the administrative service. At the age of 59, he entered Parliament and sat there from 1865 to 1868. He was defeated in the elections in 1858.

After his retirement, he lived along with his wife till her death in 1858. He spent most of his time in France with his stepdaughter, Helen Taylor, as a companion. He died on 8th May, 1873 at Avignon where he now lies buried in a tomb with his wife.

His Works: Mill's first great literary achievements were in the Westminster Review. By his pen he brought himself into prominence. He was a great writer and he wrote a large number of books, pamphlets and articles. In 1843, he published his System of Logic and achieved immense success. He published the Principle of Political Economy in 1848. It became his immediate and exceptional success. Considerations on Representative Government, Utilitarianism, The Subjection Women were published respectively in 1860, 1861 and 1869. His Autobiography was edited by his daughter Helen Taylor and published in 1873 posthumously. The Three Essays on Religion another posthumous work was published in 1874. Apart from this, his another most famous work On Liberty was published in 1859. As the editor of the London Review, John Mill was a regular contributor to the journal from its start in 1834 until 1840.

Green expressed his respect for him by echoing Gladstone's remark that Mill was a saintly man. He considered Mill to have been an "extraordinarily good man." The above comments are Mill's, true epitaph. According to C.L. Wayper, "In the whole history of Political Philosophy, there are few more appealing characters than his."

His Views: (a) Utilitarianism: J.S. Mill decided to modify some of the basis tenets of utilitarianism to defend the same from that anti-hedonist movement led by Carlyle. He opined that some pleasures are of a higher quality than others. For Bentham and James Mill pleasures differ only in quantity. Bentham has put it as "quantity of pleasure being equal, Pushpin is as good as poetry". Mill offers a singular proof that Bentham is wrong. But Mill truly reflects human experience when he says that it is better to be a human being dissatisfied than a pig satisfied; better to be Socrates dissatisfied than a fool satisfied. And if the fool or the pig is of a different opinion, it is because they only know their own side of their question. The other party to the comparison knows both sides. It is surely non-utilitarian view.

According to Mill, "pleasures cannot be measured in an objective manner. The specific cause is, he said absurd and men have always relied upon the testimony of those most competent to judge." According to C.L. Wayper, "what means are there of determining which is the acutest of two pains or the intensest of two pleasurable sensations except of general suffrage of those who are familiar with both?" This argument clearly indicates the hollowness of utilitarianism.

Mill maintained the further non-utilitarian position by holding the view that not principle of utility but the dignity of man is the final end of life. Here J.S. Mill approved of Humboldt's doctrine of "Self-realisation". He asked that what more or better can be said of any condition of human beings than that it brings human beings themselves near to the best thing they can be. This doctrine of "self-realisation" had already been attached by Bentham and James Mill. Their main aim was the achievement of pleasure and the avoidance of pain. To him state was a moral institution with a moral ends i.e., the promotion of virtue in the individual. Utilitarians have always subordinated liberty to the principle of utility; but to Mill, Liberty is a more fundamental end than utility.

(b) Liberty: J.S. Mill in his most famous essay "On Liberty" has given a very valuable and significant views about individualism and Laissez Faire. He was a powerful defender of individual liberty. There should not be any interference by the government in the affairs of the individual. Every individual was to be allowed to develop himself of his own lines. According to him, liberty is the sovereignty of the individual over himself.

Interference with the individuals' liberty is justified only when it is meant to prevent him from harming others. The sum and substance of the thesis of his essay is; "The sole end for which mankind are warranted individually or collectively in interfering with the liberty of action of any of their member is self-protection. The only purpose for which power can be rightfully exercised over any member of a civilised community, against his will, to prevent harm to others. His own good, either physical or moral is not a sufficient warrant. The only part of the conduct of anyone for which he is annuable to society is that which concerns others. In the part which merely concerns himself his independence is absolute. Over himself, over his own body, and mind individual is sovereign."

Mill divided all actions of the individuals into two categories viz., self-regarding actions and other regarding actions. If an individual was to be allowed to do whatever he was pleased to do as regards those actions in which he alone was concerned are self-regarding actions. If his actions affected others, that actions can be called other regarding actions. In this connection, it is pointed out that all that an individual so as affect others. There is nothing that affects him alone in the state.

Mill gave a classic definition for the appropriate sphere of human liberty. The inward domain of conscience, liberty of thought and expression, absolute freedom of opinion and sentiment of all subjects, scientific, moral, theological, practical or speculative are included in it. Every individual should be given freedom of taste and pursuits. Without doing any harm to others they should have the right of freedom to unite for any purpose.

Mill wanted to promote the development of individual men and women for he was satisfied that all wise and noble things come and must come from individuals. According to him, there can be no self-development without liberty. It is necessary for the happiness of society.

Further Mill defined the term 'liberty' as that "Liberty consists in doing what one desires". Again he added that "Liberty consists in doing what one desires and does not desire to fall into the river." Thus, he emphasised the non-interference in the affairs of the individual.

(c) Democracy: After making a thorough analysis of the defects of democracy, he came to the conclusion that it is not suitable for all people. However, the best form of government is representative government. He stood for proportional representation. The right of vote should be given to all those, who were qualified to vote. He advocated the enfranchisement of woman. Certain qualifications were suggested by him. Public voting and plural voting were advocated by him.

(d) His Views on Women: It cannot be denied that Mill had rendered yeoman service to the cause of women. He did the same not only inside of the Parliament but also outside of the Parliament. According to him sex should not be a disqualification to them. Women were denied jobs on par with men in public offices. They were thrown into the background on account of customs and prejudices. Hence, he stood for speedy and needy action of emancipation. As a result, womenfolk achieved tremendous rights as against men including right to vote. Women all over the world have got the right to vote and they should be grateful to J.S. Mill for his vigorous and rigorous advocacy of their cause. Mrs. Taylor was partly responsible for the same for which they should show their gratitude to her forever.

(e) Property: J.S. Mill advocated the institution of private property. It was necessary for the good and progress of mankind. But he opposed to the view of the communists on the point of the institution of the rich people. However, he disliked the abolition of the law of primogeniture. Later on he was attracted towards socialism.

His Views on Democracy: In his "Liberty" and "Representative Government", Mill shows himself very distrustful of democracy. He is one of the greatest of English writers on democracy. After making a thorough analysis, he came to the conclusion that it is not suitable for all peoples. The first element of a good government is "the promotion of the virtue and intelligence of the people". However, the best form of government is representative government.

J.S. Mill is a democrat because he believes as did Bentham that such is the innate selfishness of men that each individual's rights and interests are best defended by himself. Hence, he says that the ideal type of government has to be representative. "The passion of the majority is needed to conquer the self-interest of the few" according to Mill.

J.S. Mill is a democrat because he believes as also did Bentham that freedom is the means to prosperity. Without prosperity there can be no happiness. Democracy not only makes men happier but also it makes them better.

J.S. Mill identifies two kinds of dangers to representative democracy i.e., low grade intelligence in the representative body, and of class legislation on the part of numerical majority. To remove these two evils there should be restricted suffrage. The minority should be given due representation in a real democracy. He suggests the system of proportional representation for that purpose.

According to J.S. Mill, the pure idea of democracy according to its function is the government of the whole people, by the whole people, equally represented. The right of vote should be given to all those who are qualified to vote. He advocated the enfranchise of women. He says that there should be educational qualification for voters. If there is no such educational qualification, democracy is not possible for all people. But where society is ready for democracy than he is certain that all its adult members women as well as men must participate in it. In addition to the educational qualifications, the voters should also have the property qualifications. People with property should behave in a more responsible manner than the propertyless people.

Mill puts more stress on public voting, even though secret ballot is universally recognised today as the best system of voting. He defends public voting on the ground that "the duty of voting like any other public duty, should be performed under the eye and criticism of the public". Secret voting is bound to encourage selfishness. It is to be noted that Bentham and James Mill were the supporters of vote by secret ballot. But J.S. Mill differed from them on this point.

In his "Representative Government" published in 1861, J.S. Mill advocates the plurality of votes to the highly educated citizens. For that purpose, he has given certain group of persons to whom should be given more than one vote. The basis of his groups were mental, cultural and moral qualities. Mill style this system as "weighted voting".

Mill was the advocate of women's suffrage. He was closely connected with the London Committee of the Society for women's suffrage. Apart from this, he did yeoman service to the cause of women. It was due to his wife Mrs. Taylor. According to him, sex should not be a disqualification for them. His intention and contention was that if differences between the sexes were due wholly and solely to external circumstances. Those differences and demarcations should be removed rigorously. Those had been created by man's long continued use of women in one definite line. The difference were bound to disappear if women were given political and social freedom. Those were the outcome of the law of force and not the law of justice. If the law of justice became supreme, the law of force should be ended ultimately they were bound to disappear.

According to Mill, women should be given equal opportunities on par with men. But during his time there was no such equal opportunities. Birth should not be a barrier or an obstacle to the advancement of a person. He stood for full and speedy emancipation of women. Then only they would be happy in the new environment. Society would benefit by the practical turn of the mental capacities and characteristic of women. The services available to society will be doubled on account of the contribution of women. Hence, he advocated the right of vote to women. Ultimately, he succeeded in this task. Women all over the world have got the right to vote and they should be grateful to J.S. Mill for his strong advocacy of their cause.

Mill showed a difference between true and false democracy. According to him, "Every man to count for one; no man for more than one" is a principle of false democracy. On the contrary, true democracy will give weight and influence to all the different elements of society. It will give plural votes to capable persons as mentioned earlier.

In 1835, De Tocqueville published the first part and in 1840 the second of his "Democracy in America". It is considered the most brilliant and penetrating study of America ever written.

Mill called it "the first analytical inquiry into the influence of Democracy". It exercised a tremendous and stupendous influence upon him. For many years, he maintained a cordial correspondence with him. De Tocqueville regarded democracy an inevitable and it rested with man to make it a good or an evil thing. In America, democracy safeguarded the interests of the majority and greatly developed the facilities of the people. But it resulted in general want of merit in legislative and public functionaries. It produced a tyranny of the majority which according to Mill did not "take the shape of tyrannised laws but that of a dispensing power over all laws".

The question which always revolved in the mind of J.S. Mill is, "How can I make democracy safe for the world, how can I ensure that this inevitable process will be for the good and not the evil of mankind?" The answer to the question is beautifully given by Lord Lothian as, "Democracy is not a gift to be conferred but a habit to be acquired. It cannot succeed unless it produces a race of aristocrats — and an aristocrat I would define as one who puts more into life than he takes out of it".

According to Mill, true democracy will never allow MPs to be paid since thereby "the calling of a demagogue would be formally inaugurated". It will insist that representatives are true representatives and not mere delegates. Englishmen were reluctant to exchange this representation of interests for representation of members. He stood for the abolition of the Reform Bill based on the old view of the constitution. It is due to the distinction between False and True Democracy of Mill. He is regarded as a democrat although by 20th century standards a reluctant democrat.

33
Karl Marx (1818-83 A.D.)

The philosophy of Marxism is of paramount importance in the contemporary world. It is "a dialectical theory of human progress." It purports to provide a theory of social change and a scientific philosophy which help in understanding the laws of social development. It also provides a revolutionary programme for the emancipation of the 'exploited classes' and suggests revolutionary methods for changing the present society. It wants to establish society on a rational basis — a society in which 'man shall not be exploited by man.' It will be a society in which all will live in peace, harmony and comfort; enjoy true freedom and liberty; and will have the full opportunity to develop their potentialities and personality. In fact, this society — the Marxists call it the Communist society — shall be a 'classless' and 'stateless society' — a really ideal society.

The Marxian philosophy came into being as a reaction to the failings of liberal ideology. But over the years, its gospel of revolution has spread like a wildfire and has engulfed many countries in the world. Today, Marxism reigns supreme in many parts of the world and, therefore, its proper understanding is very essential for us. However, before we discuss 'Marxism' in detail, it would be quite in order to give a brief biographical sketch of the father of 'Marxism' i.e., Karl Heinrich Marx.

A Biographical Sketch

Karl Marx, the father of Marxism or modern socialism, was born in Trier (Treves) in the Rhineland province of Prussia (Germany) on May 5, 1818. His father, Herschel Marx was originally a Jew but in 1824, the family embraced Christianity to avoid persecution. At that time, young Marx was unable to understand the significance of this change. But it is likely that later on he realized that religion was being used by fanatics as an instrument for persecution. Whatever may be its truth, the fact remains that Marx became an atheist and an avowed enemy of religion.

An intelligent and perspicacious child, Marx, in 1835, at the age of 17 joined the University of Berlin as a law student. In 1836, he went to the University of Berlin. In 1841, Karl Marx took his degree of Doctor of Philosophy from the University of Jena on the subject "The difference between the Natural Philosophy of Democritus and Epicurus." In 1843, he married a charming woman Jenny, the daughter of Freiherr Ludwig von Westphalen with whose family he had close and intimate relations.

From the very beginning Marx was a great rebel. His radical views made him a suspect in the eyes of authorities and this prevented his employment as a university teacher. Because of his bad handwriting he was denied even a clerical job. He tried his luck in the army too but was declared unfit for it. Finally, he entered the field of journalism and began to edit a paper entitled, Rheinische Zeitung. However, its publication too was stopped by the authorities after a year. He then went to Paris. There he struck up a firm and lasting friendship with Friederich Engels, who became his life-long friend, disciple and collaborator. In 1845, in Brussels (Germany) Karl Marx founded an organization called the German Working Men's Association. In 1847, Marx and Engels founded together the International Communist League, with Engels as its first Secretary. Together they drafted the famous Communist Manifesto in 1848 which to this day is a gospel and the Bible for all Communists. In 1849, he settled down in London and remained there till his death on March 14, 1883. In a speech over his grave in High Gate cemetery, Friedrich Engels declared that, "his name and works will endure through the ages."

Karl Marx was an intellectual giant and a prolific writer. In 1847, with the aid and help of Engels, he prepared the Communist Manifesto. Laski described it as "one of the outstanding political documents of all times." According to Bertrand Russell, the Communist Manifesto is "the best contribution that Karl Marx made to the history of Political Thought." It contains his most lucid, clear and compact statement regarding his conception of the struggle between classes in human history; the conflict between the bourgeoisie and the proletariat in modern times; the inevitable destruction of capitalism; and a programme of action for the working classes to establish a classless and stateless society.

Another important and life-work of Karl Marx is Das Capital. It consists of three volumes. The first volume was published in 1867 during his life time. The second and the third volume of Das Capital were edited by Engels after the death of Karl Marx in 1883. They were published in the years 1885 and 1894 respectively. Regarding Das Capital, it is said: "The appearance of this book was an epoch-making event in the history of International Socialism....It was conceived as a comprehensive treatise on the laws of morphology of the economic organization of modern society seeking to describe the process of production, exchange and distribution as they actually occur, to explain their present state at a particular stage in the development constituted by the movement of the class struggle."

Besides numerous articles and pamphlets, the other important works of Karl Marx are the following:

(1) The Poverty of Philosophy (1847).
(2) A Contribution to the Critique of Political Economy (1859).
(3) Eleventh Thesis on Fuerbach (1845).
(4) The Eighteenth Brummaire of Louis Bonaparte (1894).
(5) Civil War and the Class Struggle in France (1849).
(6) The Critique of the Goetha Programme (1891).
(7) Revolution and Counter Revolution.

Development of Marxism

Karl Marx was a social scientist, a great political philosopher and a revolutionary. He was interested in creating a real socialist society. Prior to him, philosophers had only interpreted the world as they had found it. Marx was interested in a critical analysis of society in order to change and restructure it on new foundations and new human relationship. Thus, Marxism not only shows us a way of understanding the world but also provides us with a scientific philosophy with the help of which it can be changed.

According to Laski, Karl Marx was the first socialist thinker, who fully realised the futility of formulating a utopian constitution of socialist society. He, therefore, wholly devoted his attention to find out a new path which could lead to the establishment of a socialist society. This involved the necessity of a detailed analysis of the working and growth of the capitalist system. "Marx", says Laski, "wrote at once the epitaph of the new capitalism and the prophecy of its ultimate outcome. The first aspect of his work, both by reason of the materials he used and the thesis he deduced from them, put the defenders of economic individualism finally upon the defensive; the second provided an inspiration to his followers which has increased in profundity as the years have gone by."

Marxism is not only a revolt against the capitalist system but also a sound alternative to that system. Earlier, the 'utopian' socialists — Thomas More, Fourier, Robert Owen, Saint Simon, etc., had also vehemently denounced 'capitalism' in their philosophy. But, they could never provide the means of ending capitalism or provide an alternative sound system. It was Karl Marx who with his intellectual treatises and active struggle provided both the means to wipe out capitalism and an alternative system for it. It is his abiding and everlasting contribution to political philosophy.

No philosophy can afford to be static. If it can, it becomes dogmatic and ultimately declines forever. Every philosophy has to be adjusted according to the need of the times and the change in circumstances on account of the passage of time. Today, Marxism has been greatly enriched not only by the rediscovery of the old texts written by Karl Marx and his contemporary Engels, but also by the contributions of other thinkers and revolutionaries of the Marxist mould such as F. Mehring (1846-1919), K. Kautsky (1854-1938), G. Plekhanov (1856-1918), V.I. Lenin (1870-1924), R. Luxemburg (1871-1919), L. Trotsky (1879-1940), N. Bukharin (1888-1938), J.V. Stalin (1871-1953), and Mao-Tse-tung (1896-1976). Besides these, many more writers have helped the development of Marxism. They have interpreted its theory and practice according to the changing circumstances and has made it a living creed and philosophy. In fact, the philosophy of Marxism as a philosophy of social and political change cannot be properly understood without a reference to their writings and works.

Marxism as a Theory of Social and Political Change

The value and worth of Marxism lies in its essence as a theory of social and political change. Though many philosophers had pointed out the evils of capitalism and emphasized the need for an equitable and just socio-economic order, it was left to Marx to enunciate scientifically the principles and revolutionary methods to achieve these ends. The intention of Karl Marx was to produce an empirical work by considering "the development of the economic structure of society as a natural historical process," and by studying the "social antagonisms which arise from the natural laws of capitalist production." Therefore, he laboriously studied the system of the capitalist mode of production; class relations in this system and the struggles generated by that mode of production. On the basis of this study, he formulated his philosophy of scientific socialism (or Marxism) and his views on social and political change in society. Marx's Capital is one of the earliest, one of the best and one of the most valuable works of social history. It is not only a great classic and scientific work but also at the same time a strong moral indictment of capitalism and capitalist society. In form and content, it expresses his practical conception of social science and his views on social and political change in society.

Marx's interest in social sciences and in social philosophy was fundamentally practical. He only wanted to discover the law and method of historical and social change. He knew that the discovery of the law and method of historical and social change would make it quite possible and easy for him to formulate the tactics suited to the revolutionary proletarian theory.

According to Meyer: "Marxism is a dialectical theory of human progress." And, when the method of dialectical materialism is applied to the interpretation of history it is known as "historical materialism," and both these form the basis of

Marxian scientific socialism. The idea of dialectic was not an original contribution of Marx; it was known to the Greeks as a method of arriving at the truth by bringing contradictions through a discussion, debate or exchange of ideas. Plato used dialectical process in his dialogues to expose false beliefs of his time. However, Marx gave the dialectics a materialistic bias which became the basis of all social sciences with post-Marxian era.

Marxism has also been defined as a philosophy of history based on a materialistic conception of human development. Therefore, in order to understand Marx's political philosophy and his theory of social and political change correctly, it is imperative for us to know his doctrines of:

(i) Dialectical Materialism;
(ii) Historical Materialism, and
(iii) Economic Determinism.

(i) Dialectical Materialism

For his philosophical concept Marx is indebted to Hegel, from whom he borrowed the science of dialection. Though, Karl Marx rejected the substance of Hegel's philosophy, he did adopt his dialectical method as the basis of his historical materialism. Therefore, to understand the dialectical materialism of Marx, it is necessary for us to know something of Hegel.

According to Hegel, the essence of history lies in the interaction of ideas. Through dialectic he tried to explain and give a complete account of everything — the development of man, laws, thought and the creation of universe. In this view, history depended upon the gradual unfolding the world spirit or absolute idea and it was accomplished according to a divine plan which was imminent in the universe. No idea of consequence was static and all the things were in a state of becoming.

Every idea (thesis), according to Hegel, is incomplete and there are inherent contradictions in every idea (thesis). The incompleteness or inherent contradictions in every idea (thesis) led naturally to its opposite, which may be called (antithesis). From the struggle between the two, i.e., thesis and antithesis there emerged the truth embraced by both. This truth may be called **synthesis**. This synthesis becomes a new thesis and again there came an antithesis and again there emerged a synthesis, and the process goes on repeating itself in an unending chain.

Thus, dialectics is a mode of argument which believes in the infinite possibility of changes through the dialectical triad process of thesis, antithesis and synthesis. Thesis affirms a proposition, antithesis negates it and synthesis further negates the antithesis.

Karl Marx agreed with Hegel that history unfolded itself according to a dialectical plan. But according to him (Marx) the ideas were the result of material conditions. In **Capital** he says: "To Hegel...the process of thinking, which under the name of '**the idea**', transforms into an independent subject, is the demiurgos (the Creator) of the real world, and the real world is only the external phenomenal form of the idea. With me, on the contrary, the ideal is nothing else than the material world reflected by the human mind, and translated into forms of thought." Materialism for Marx, says Prof. Sabine, meant three things — (i) the real motive forces in history were material conditions; (ii) materialism implied a radical rejection of religion, indeed a militant theism, and (iii) suggestion of a new and far-reaching revolution.

Dialectical materialism believes in the inseparability of matter and motion. From the dialectical point of view, any stage may be taken up as a thesis because it serves as a starting point and a working hypothesis. But a changeover from thesis to antithesis and further from antithesis to synthesis is always through struggle and each stage is an advance over the previous stage. Every advance leads to a higher transformation. Thus, if feudalism is thesis, its antithesis is capitalism which represents a distinct advance over feudalism. Synthesis is more progressive than both the thesis and antithesis as it incorporates the valid points of both. Thus, socialism can be taken as a synthesis of feudalism and capitalism. It incorporates the valid points of even capitalism e.g., technology. Therefore, progress takes place through the dialectical cycle of change. Synthesis too is negated and becomes an improved thesis; to be further negated by another antithesis. There is, thus, an unending spiral of progress which ultimately leads to a point of perfection beyond which no progress is possible. This is the acme of progress which in Marxian terminology is the establishment of a classless and a stateless society. This is the consummation most ardently to be wished for an unending and unfailing human progress achieved through constant struggle and contests. It represents the philosophical foundation of Marxism. It is the doctrinal base on which the entire edifice of Marxism stands.

(ii) Historical Materialism

Marx not only accepted the dialectic as a kind of philosophical gospel, he also endeavoured to show that it has actually operated in history through the medium, of contending classes. He aspired to make his socialism scientific and, therefore, began probing into history to discover its rational kernel. His investigations revealed the important role that economic factors play in human history. The importance which he attached to the material forces in history led to the enunciation of the doctrine called "historical materialism." According to Engels, historical materialism is "that view of the course of history which seeks the ultimate cause and the great moving power of all important historical events in the economic development of society, in the changes, in the modes of production and exchange, in the consequent division of society into distinct classes and in the struggle of these classes against one another." Plekhanov says that historical materialism is simply dialectical materialism applied to the particular field of human relations within society. And, Stalin explains: "Historical materialism is the extension of the principles of dialectical materialism to the study of social life, an application of the principles of dialectical materialism to the phenomena of the study of society and its history."

(iii) Economic Determinism

This theory is also known as the theory of Economic interpretation of history or the Materialistic interpretation of history. This theory stresses the importance of economic factors in the evolution of human history. In the preface of his famous work, A Contribution to the Critique of Political Economy (1859), Marx poses the question: "What is the principle that governs human relations"? He himself replies: "It is the common end which all men pursue that govern human relations. That common end is the production of means to support life and the exchange of things produced." This means that all changes are caused by the changes in the mode of production and exchange. A change in any other sphere, such as social or political sphere, will affect history only marginally; a change in the economic sphere will cause lasting changes in history and affect its future course. Hence, history is determined by economic factors such as modes of production and exchange.

There are two factors which enter into production, i.e., the productive forces (the instruments of production, such as land, labour etc.) and the productive relations between men and men (the relations men enter into with one another while engaged in production). Engels explains the transition from materialist to economic interpretation as under:

> "The materialistic conception of history starts from the principle that production, and with production the exchange of its products, is the basis of every social order; that in every society which has appeared in history the distribution of the products, and with it the division of society into classes is determined by what is produced and how it is produced and how the product is exchanged. According to this conception, the ultimate causes of all social changes and political revolutions are to be sought not in the minds of men, in their increasing insight into eternal truth and justice, but in changes in the mode of production and exchange; they are to be sought not in the philosophy but in the economics of the period concerned."

The productive relations depend upon and vary according to productive forces. If in a certain country, the productive forces are land and the plough, the productive relations will be that of the landowner and the peasant. If one varies the productive forces from land and plough to machines, manufacturing and skilled and non-skilled labour, the productive forces will becomes that of mill-owner and the industrial proletariat. Thus, a change in productive forces will indubitably change productive relations also. In the primitive society, the relations of production were those of co-operation owing to the fact that the worker was also the owner of his tools or the means of production, while under capitalism, these relations become relations of conflict. This is because under capitalism, the means of production are privately owned by the capitalist and the worker has no control over them.

Marx calls the economic system of a country the substructure and the rest consisting of social, political and religious life as coming under the appellation superstructure. The economic system is the base and on it rests the superstructure of social, political, ethical and spiritual relationship. The superstructure is built upon and is determined by the substructure. A change in superstructure will be only superficial, only a change in the substructure can be real and lasting. Since the substructure is controlled by the economically dominant class, the superstructure will be so made as to suit the interests of this class. Laws, institutions, political principles, religious precepts, social code and moral values are carefully framed and shaped to suit the interests of the economically dominant class. And, as all laws, social norms and religious beliefs are based on the economic substructure, genuine social changes will not take place by the emergence of new principles of truth and justice as they belong to the superstructure. Real and purposeful changes will take place only if the control of substructure passes from the capitalist to those of the proletariat. So long the productive forces are controlled by the capitalists, productive relations will always be that of exploitation — and this will only provoke a class war. It will only sharpen the existing class antagonisms.

According to the Marxian theory of economic determinism, the forms of production will vary with the systems of feudalism, capitalism and socialism — each representing the three stages of dialectical evolution, i.e., thesis, antithesis and synthesis. However, two things are of paramount importance. First, from the point of view of production, each stage is an advance over the other. Secondly, the transition from one stage to another is always through struggle. This is because the class which controls the levers of economic and political power will try to maintain the status quo and firmly resist any attempts at changing it. However, the Marxian doctrine of dialectic is optimistic in nature. It believes that every struggle will be successful in the end; in the struggle between the bourgeoise and the proletariat, the bourgeoise will be completely defeated by the revolutionary class-conscious proletariat; capitalism will collapse and ultimately a stateless society will be established. Therefore, in history, economic causes predominate — other factors are only of marginal importance.

Though, we have explained in some details the theory of economic determinism or materialistic interpretation of history, it would be worthwhile to say it in the words of Karl Marx himself. In his Critique of Political Economy, he explains it thus:

> "In the social production which men carry on, they enter into definite relations that are indispensable and independent of their will, these relations of production correspond to a definite stage of development of their material forces of production. The sum-total of these relations of production constitutes the economic structure of society — the real foundation, on which rises a legal and political superstructure and to which correspond definite forms of social consciousness. The mode of production in material life determines the social, political and intellectual life process in general. It is not the consciousness of men that determines their being, but on the contrary, their social being that determines their consciousness. At a certain stage of their development, the material forces of production in society come in conflict with the existing relations of production, or — what is but a legal expression for the same thing — with the property relations within which they have been at work before. From forms of development of the forces of production, these relations turn into their fetters. Then begins an epoch of social revolution. With the change of the economic foundation, the entire immense superstructure is more or less rapidly transformed. In considering such transformations, a distinction should always be made between the material transformation of the economic conditions of production, which can be determined with the precision of natural science, and legal, political, religious, aesthetic or philosophical — in short, ideological forms in which men become conscious

of this conflict and fight it out. Just as our opinion of an individual is not based on what he thinks of himself, so can we not judge of such a period of transformation by its own consciousness; on the contrary, this consciousness must be explained rather from the contradictions of material life, from the existing conflict between the social forces of production and the relations of production. No social order ever disappears before all the productive forces for which there is room in it have been developed, and new higher relations of production never appear before the material conditions of their existence have matured in the womb of the old society itself. Therefore, mankind always sets itself only such tasks as it can solve, since, looking at the matter more closely, we will always find that the task itself arises only when the material condition necessary for its solution alone exists or at least in the process of formation."

It is a rather lengthy quotation. Its main points are as follows:

(i) In production, men enter into definite relations which are independent of their will.

(ii) These relations of production correspond to a definite stage of development of their material forces of production.

(iii) The sum-total of these relations of production constitutes the economic structure of society — the real basis on which a juridical and political superstructure arises.

(iv) It is not the consciousness of men that determines their being but on the contrary, their social being that determines their consciousness.

(v) At a certain stage of their development, the material forces of production in society come in conflict with the existing relations of production or property relations.

(vi) Then an epoch of social revolution opens. With the change in the economic foundation, the whole vast superstructure is more or less rapidly transformed.

From the above discussion it is obvious that according to Marx, economic factors are the true determinants of history.

The Contemporary Marxist Political Theory

The Concept of Class Struggle

The theory of class struggle is an important component of the contemporary political theory. Karl Marx was of the opinion that when the superstructure of any society fails to adjust itself to the rapid changes in the system of production and exchange there comes a crisis which can only be resolved by means of a revolution. Unless the new social order uses force, the old social order does not give place to it. In the Communist Manifesto Marx declared that the only way of changing any social structure was the class struggle. He said: "The history of all hitherto existing society is the history to class struggles."

But, what is a class? Marx does not define a class and only obliquely refers to the existence of various intermediary classes. But Lenin gives a comprehensive definition of classes. He defines them as 'large groups of people who differ from each other by the place they occupy in a historically definite system of social production, by their relations, to the means of production, by their role in the social organization of labour, and consequently by the dimensions and methods of acquiring the share of the social wealth they obtain.' A man's class was, therefore, determined not by his belief, but by the position he occupied within the system of production.

Marx maintains that the various intermediary classes, in the end, group themselves into two broad categories or divisions, i.e., the bourgeoisie and the proletariat. He made it clear that he was not the originator of the idea of class struggle. He says: "No credit is due to me for discovering the existence of classes in modern society, nor yet the struggle between them. Long before me bourgeois historians had described the historical development of this struggle of the classes and bourgeois economists, the economic anatomy of the classes. What I did that was new was to prove:

(1) that the existence of classes is only bound up with particular phases in the development of production;

(2) that the class struggle necessarily leads to the dictatorship of the proletariat and

(3) that this dictatorship itself only constitutes the transition to the abolition of all classes and a classless society." The driving force behind the dialectic of history is not the clash of nations, as Hegel and other historians believed, but the class struggle.

As has been pointed out earlier, in the primitive society, means of production were owned by the workers themselves. In this society, the needs of men were few and everybody used to work to produce the means to support life. Products were exchanged through the barter system and there were no intermediaries in between. Hence, the relations of production were those of co-operation and harmony.

However, with the establishment of capitalism, conditions and relations of production changed drastically. Under capitalism, the means of production are owned privately by the capitalists. A capitalist purchases human labour as any other commodity — raw materials, machinery, etc. The labourer by selling his 'labour' gets mere daily wages which are much less than what he should get for the quantity of his real labour. Thus, in return for the poor wages, the labourer loses the entire control over the product of his labour. As the means of production are already owned by the capitalist, he appropriates the 'surplus value' produced by the labourer. This strains the relations between the workers and the capitalist and now the productive relations get entangled in discord, conflict and enmity. In this manner, under capitalism the polarization of society into two hostile camps becomes complete. Whereas in earlier times the divisions of society was at best only nominal; under capitalism the polarization of classes takes place on a vast scale and results in sharpening the class conflict. Now class differences become genuine, sharp and irreconcilable. They can now only be resolved through a violent revolution, which of course, the Marxists believe, will end in the eventual victory of the proletariat. This whole phenomenon has been lucidly explained by Karl Marx in the Communist Manifesto. He says that the history of all hitherto existing society is the history of class struggles. Freeman and slave, patrician and plebeian, lord and serf, guild-master and journeyman, in a word, oppressor and oppressed, stood in constant opposition to one another carried on an uninterrupted now hidden, now open fight, a fight that each time ended, either in a revolutionary re-constitution of society at large, or in the common ruin of the contending classes.

In the earlier epochs of history, we find almost everywhere a complicated arrangement of society into various orders, a manifold gradation of social rank. In ancient Rome we have patricians, knights, plebeians, slaves; in the Middle Ages, feudal lords, vassals, guild-masters, journeymen, apprentices, serfs. In almost all of these classes, again, subordinate gradations are there.

The modern bourgeois society that has sprouted from the ruins of feudal society, has not done away with class antagonisms. It has but established new classes, new conditions of oppression, new forms of struggle in place of the old ones.

Our epoch, the epoch of the bourgeoisie, possesses, however, this distinctive feature. It has simplified the class antagonisms. Society as a whole is more and more splitting up into great hostile camps, into two great classes directly facing each other: Bourgeoisie and Proletariat.

From the above explanation of the class struggle, Marx establishes that (a) the dialectic has actually operated in history through the medium of these contending classes, and that (b) under capitalism this class struggle sharpens and can only end in the revolutionary victory of the proletariat.

Karl Marx is of the opinion that most of the history was written under the great illusion that states have fought and clashed against one another. In fact, the struggle has always been between economic classes and not the states. All the struggles within state, whether they were for a change of government from monarchy to democracy, or the struggle to gain universal franchise or other political reforms, were in essence the struggles waged by different contending economic classes.

Marx, as we have pointed out earlier, divides the classes into two broad categories, i.e., the bourgeoisie and the proletariat or the rich and the poor classes. The rich being the owners of means of production and, appropriators of the 'surplus value,' live on rent, profits, interests, dividends and unearned income.

The poor, on the other hand, sell their labour in return for fixed wages and are, thereby, deprived of all control over the product of their own labour. Marx explains it thus: "Man's own deed becomes an alien power opposed to him, which enslaves him instead of being controlled by him." In the same vein, Herbert Marcuse says: "An uncontrolled economy legislates over all human relationship."

This causes social disequilibrium, which in turn results in a virulent class war. Economic disparity between the two classes goes on increasing and creating irreconcilable class differences. The gap which exists in bourgeoise society, between the rich and the poor; in what the 'labour produces' and what it gets in return and the plight of the labour is explained by Marx with a telling effect in the following words: "...labour produces for the rich wonderful things but for the worker it produces privation. It produces palaces but for the workers, hovels. It produces beauty but for the workers, deformity. It replaces labour by machines but some of the workers it throws back to a barbarous type of labour, and the other workers in turn into machines. It produces intelligence but for the worker idiocy, criticism." With the realization by the workers of the glaring disparities and their own plight, the existing class antagonisms are further sharpened. This leads to a class war, which in the opinion of Marx, will culminate in the revolutionary victory of the class conscious proletariat. Capitalism, to Marx, is marked for destruction. Its own inner contradictions as well as revolutionary efforts of the proletariat shall completely annihilate Capitalism from the earth.

Therefore, according to Karl Marx, class struggle is a very important factor in the historical evolution from the primitive society to the feudal society and the modern bourgeoisie industrial society. Its germs lie in the centuries old struggle of contending economic classes. The struggle is destined to wipe out capitalism and to lead to the establishment of a classless and stateless society. The class struggle will end in the final victory of the proletariat who will ultimately usher in the communistic society.

Theory of Revolution

Karl Marx was not only a great theoretician but also a great activist and revolutionist. The revolutionary idea was central to his thought and is to be found in all his writings. In fact, the theory of revolution is the direct consequence and a concrete expression of his materialistic interpretation of history. Revolution for Marx was a social, political, legal, economic, technological and ideological phenomenon and a historical necessity. He maintained that class struggle and revolution are the "driving forces of history."

In one of his memorable speeches Engels, while paying tribute to his friend Marx, described him 'as before all else a revolutionist.' He pointed out that revolutionary idea was central to his thought; it was present in all his writings. He added that history while unfolding its inevitable dialectical progress takes us to the proletarian revolution. The transition from epoch to epoch are revolutionary 'for revolutions are locomotives of history.'

The class struggle and the resultant revolution cannot be imposed on the system. They are the logical outcome of any system and the 'driving forces of history.' At any given time, in any given system, the economically dominate class will not give away its economic and political power either voluntarily, or of its own. Therefore, this class has to be dethroned by the oppressed class and this can only be done by means of a revolution. But the revolution will not come of its own. It will only come through the organized revolutionary activities of the oppressed class. A revolution is not a conspiracy. Rather, it is a logical, natural and inevitable phenomenon and a great lever for social progress. It comes through the intensification of class struggle which can in turn be intensified through class consciousness and the militant organization of that class.

The Marxists explain that the revolution will come in two stages. In the first stage, the bourgeoisie will struggle for its rights. Its aspirations and demands will be progressive and, therefore, it will be advantageous for the proletariat to support those demands. The proletariat should not seek power till a proper time comes. The second stage of the revolution will come with the proletariat using their power against the bourgeoisie.

In his Sociology of Revolution, Marx explains as to how the revolutionary proletariat acquires power and crushes the bourgeoisie. He distinguishes between social power (economic power) and political power and points out that whereas social power was acquired by the capitalists in the fifteenth century, it was in the nineteenth century that they acquired political power. And, as the economic supersession of the feudal society was preceded by its political supersession, it created a situation in which the economic base (substructure) and political power (superstructure) were not in harmony with each other. In this situation, the state became an independent parasite on the whole society. However, this situation (the feudal lords having political power, but not economic hegemony) did not last long. It was soon followed by a political revolution which sounded the death-knell of the feudal order. This is the first revolution — the revolution of the capitalists to replace the feudal system in society. In this revolution, the proletarian class helps the capitalists to fight against the common foe of both of them — the feudal order.

In the context of this revolution, the setting up of a capitalistic democratic state is important. As long as this democratic state is not established, the last stage in the revolution will not be inaugurated. The political reforms introduced by the democratic state — the right to vote, the right of association, etc., will be useful for organizing the proletariat — and imparting to them the necessary political education. Also, when capitalism is fully developed it becomes a fetter on production. And, as it cannot grow further, it would be replaced by the revolutionary working class through a violent revolution. This is the second and final revolution — the revolution of the working class against the capitalists. As the bourgeoisie revolution is necessary for the proletarian revolution, in the same manner industrial and capitalistic development is essential for the proletarian revolution.

The difference between the capitalist revolution and the proletarian revolution was that the former emancipated the workers from the hegemony and dominance of one class (feudal class) but brought them under the control of another class (capitalist class) and the latter revolution emancipated the workers once for all and liberated mankind from slavery. With the liquidation of the capitalist class, only one class remains — the proletarian class. And, since there is no class below it on whom it could hold power, it would mean that the liquidation of the capitalist class is automatically accompanied by the dissolution of the proletarian class and with this humanity will be ushered into a real classless society.

The important features of the revolution are that it would be a violent revolution; it would be preceded by a long preparation and carefully fostering class consciousness among the workers; it would not be confined to a single nation and would be international in character.

Revolutionary Method

Karl Marx not only gave a theory of the inevitability of revolution for social and practical change, but he also explained its objectives and the methods to make the revolution a reality. The objective of revolution is to capture political power. The method to be followed is 'to create a class' with the revolutionary consciousness to bring about the revolution. Making it more explicit, he says that a class could be a 'class in itself' or a 'class for itself.' A 'class in itself' involves itself in localized conflicts of an economic nature against exploiters and oppressors without being conscious of its revolutionary destiny. The moment it acquires that consciousness of its class position and interest, it becomes a 'class for itself,' a truly national force. Such a class should convert itself into a political party to wage a determined war against the capitalists for the liberation of the proletariat and capture power. In the Communist Manifesto, Marx explains: "The proletariat, during its contest with the bourgeoisie, is compelled by the force of circumstances, to organize itself as a class...by means of a revolution, it makes itself the ruling class and as such, sweeps away by force the old conditions of production."

One important point in the 'Marxian theory of Revolution' is the actual use of physical force. Marx does not rule out its use in bringing about revolution but makes it abundantly clear that force will be used only wherever it is necessary. Force will not be the basis of revolution, it will be used when the ruling classes resist by arms. After the incident of Paris Commune he declared, "We must make clear to the governments, we know that you are the armed power that is directed against the proletariat; we will proceed against you by peaceful means where that is possible and with arms when it is necessary." In 1872, he expressed the opinion that in the developed liberal democracies like Britain and America, a peaceful transition to socialism was possible because of the increased strength of the working class. However, at a later date, Lenin did not agree with this formulation of Marx. He was not in favour of adopting peaceful means to achieve the objective of destroying capitalism and establishing a classless and stateless society. They openly stand for the use of violent means and believe that only by revolutionary methods the transition from capitalism to communism could be brought about. And, to make the revolution a success, Lenin suggested the formation of an organization of professional revolutionaries — a body of small secret people having a highly centralized and efficient organization. In his book, What Is To Be Done, Lenin asserts that the organization of the proletariat is of utmost importance and that no movement can be durable and successful without a stable organization of leaders to maintain continuity. Further, the more widely the masses are spontaneously drawn into struggle and form the basis of the movement and participate in it, the more necessary is it to have such an organization and more stable must it be. The organization must consist chiefly of persons engaged in revolutionary activities as a profession. Also, the proletariat must not only be organized nationally but also internationally and in the actual fight for its emancipation, the proletariat should act differently according to the stage of political development of the country.

However, in recent times, some Marxists have again emphasised the possibility of a peaceful transition to socialism and this possibility has also been duly accepted by the Communist Party of the Soviet Union at its 20th Congress in 1956. Yet, another equally influential group of Marxists do not agree with this 'possibility' and, therefore, the place of revolution in bringing social and political transformation has become a controversial issue in contemporary Marxist philosophy.

Theory of Alienation

The theory of alienation of Karl Marx is to be found in his Economic and Political Manuscripts (1843), known for its humanist content and written by him when he was in his mid-twenties. This theory involves a view of human relationships not based on the principle of equality but of one man being superior to another; of one man being a master and another slave; of one man being an exploiter and another being exploited. Marx needs the theory of alienation to analyse the problem of man and his humanity in a capitalist system and forcefully condemned capitalism as a 'vulgar system' because it resulted in the shameless process of dehumanizing man.

Like his concept of dialectic, the theory of alienation was borrowed by Marx from Hegel and Feuerbach. According to Hegel, the goal of man was the realization of self or freedom. Therefore, all human actions are directed to achieve this goal. However, two factors, i.e., necessity and alienation, prevent its realization. While necessity refers to natural and physical constraints, alienation is dissociation of the subject from the object. Man wants to be a master of himself. Instead, he becomes a tool in the hands of others. Thus, the failure to realize one's self becomes the main reason of human alienation.

After Hegel, Feuerbach carried the idea of alienation further. He identified religious superstitions as the source of alienation. He suggested a simple remedy to overcome this problem — bring the divine back into man through a religion of self-love. It is not God who creates man but man who creates God. If God is the creation of man there is nothing that could stand in the way of man to do what they will.

Though Marx borrowed the idea of alienation from Hegel yet he gave it an altogether different meaning. According to him, the alienation was neither the result of man's failure to realize himself, nor the outcome of religious superstition. It was to be found in 'man's work,' and 'human activity.' Daniel Bell explains: "In locating man's alienation in work, Marx had taken the revolutionary step of grounding philosophy in concrete human activity." As a result of division of labour man has on the one hand, lost control of the process of work and on the other, lost control over the product of his labour. This has led to de-humanisation and depersonalization, respectively. The manufacturing process or the technology is mainly responsible for changing the relationship between the craftsman and his product. Men thus become 'means for the ends' of others. The product dominates over the producer and machine over the machine owner. A worker cannot buy what he produces and those who can afford possession of products do not work; they are idlers. In his Manuscripts, Marx says: "It should be noted first that everything which appears to the worker as an activity of alienation, appears to the non-worker as a condition of alienation."

Alienation, Marx further explains, is a rotten product of capitalism. In the capitalist society, man becomes a slave — the rich man of his property and the poor man of his needs. "In such a society, the worker is alienated from his labour, from society, from nature and fellow beings and becomes a commodity in the capitalist market. The capitalist system, under the cover of hollow slogans of liberty, equality and rights has, in fact been responsible for direct, naked, shameless and brutal exploitation of man by man." In the Communist Manifesto he says: "The bourgeoisie has stripped of its halo every occupation hitherto honoured and looked up to with reverent awe. It has converted the physician, the lawyer, the priest, the poet, the man of science, into its paid wage labourers. It has torn away from the family its sentimental veil, and has reduced the family relation to a mere money relation...the labourers must sell themselves piecemeal, have been reduced to mere commodity, like every other article of commerce...owing to the extensive use of machinery the worker becomes an appendage of the machine. Not only the workers are the slaves of the bourgeois class, and of the bourgeois state; they are daily and hourly enslaved by the machine, by the individual bourgeois manufacturer himself." Thus, in the capitalist system there is a complete alienation of man. A man is alienated from his fellow man because the basis of their relationship is only money-relationship; he is alienated from nature because he has neither the time nor the inclination to enjoy the beauties of nature; and he is alienated from himself because he has to 'overwork' for his bare subsistence and survival.

According to Marx, the objective of socialism is to overcome alienation. And, alienation would end with the revolution of the proletariat which will abolish capitalism and private property and establish a stateless and classless society.

Theory of Freedom

The conception of freedom of Karl Marx has its origins in French materialism and Hegelian idealism. The French materialists had taught that man is the product of his circumstances and that consequently the essence of unfreedom was the absence not of 'the negative capacity to avoid this or that' but of 'the positive power to assert his true individuality' which results from the failure of society to provide 'social scope for the essential assertion of his vitality.' From Hegel had come the insight that 'freedom is the appreciation of necessity.'

Engels succinctly explains the Marxian view of freedom in the following words:

> Freedom does not consist in the dream of independence of natural laws, but in the knowledge of these laws, and in the possibility this gives of systematically making them work towards definite ends..... Freedom of will, therefore, means nothing but the capacity to make decisions with real knowledge of the subject. Therefore, the freer a man's judgement is in relation to a definite question, with so much the greater necessity is the content of this judgement determined; while the uncertainty, founded in ignorance, which seems to make an arbitrary choice among many different and conflicting possible desires, shows by this precisely that it is not free, that it is controlled by the very object it should itself control.

Freedom for Marx and Engels is not a negative quality of being left alone to one's own devices or a subjecting feeling of not being conscious of restraints, but a matter of fact about the extent to which any society enables its members to develop their capacities to the full as social and individual beings.

Marx explains the freedom of the bourgeoisie society and its social consequences. He points out that the freedom which was demanded by the bourgeoisie was freedom for all to use their labour as they thought fit, freedom to buy and sell on an open market. The social consequences of the realization of economic freedom under capitalism were that the workers were free to determine which master they would allow to appropriate the surplus value produced by their labour when times were good, and free to starve when times were bad. Nor were the consequences of bourgeois freedom quite what that class had expected and desired. Engels says:

> The 'freedom of property' from feudal fetters, now veritably accomplished, turned out to be, for the small capitalists and small proprietors, the freedom to sell their small property, crushed under the over mustering competition of the large capitalist landlords, to these great lords, and thus, so far as the small capitalists and peasant-proprietors were concerned, became 'freedom from property.'

The freedom which capitalism establishes is 'not the freedom of one individual in relation to another, but the freedom of capital to crush the worker.'

Marx further explains that this position cannot be remedied by attempts to improve the conditions of the workers for, even if successful, this would mean nothing more than 'a better slave-salary and would not achieve either for the worker or for labour human significance and dignity.' To raise the worker to the level of an individual requires the abolition of the whole system of private appropriation of socially produced products. 'In bourgeois society, capital is independent and has individuality, while the living person is dependent and has no individuality.' The Communist Manifesto declares that 'the abolition of this state of things is called by the bourgeois abolition of individuality and freedom. And rightly so, 'The abolition of bourgeois individuality, bourgeois independence and bourgeois freedom is undoubtedly aimed at.'

'The reason of freedom,' Marx wrote in Capital, 'only begins, in fact, where that labour which is determined by need and external purposes ceases; it is therefore, by its very nature, outside the sphere of material production proper.' He added:

"Freedom in this field cannot consist of anything else but the fact that socialized mankind, the associated producers, regulate their interchange with Nature rationally, bring it under their common control, instead of being ruled by it as by some blind power, and accomplish their task with the least expenditure of energy and under such conditions as are proper and worthy for human beings. Nevertheless, this always remains a realm of necessity. Beyond it begins that development of human personality for its own sake, the true realm of freedom, which however can only flourish upon that realm of necessity as its basis."

Thus, freedom to all can be available only in a free society, i.e., the communist society.

Here, it may be pointed out, the concepts which we have discussed above under the headings 'Marxism as a Theory of Social and Political Change' and 'The Contemporary Marxist Political Theory,' do not cover the whole canvas of the Marxian philosophy. Besides them his views on the origin and nature of the state; dictatorship of the proletariat and 'withering away of the state' are an integral part of his philosophy. They have been discussed in Topic 10, and we shall not repeat them. Also, his views on the 'Nature of the Capitalist State, Capitalism and the functions of the Contemporary Capitalist State' have already been discussed in Topic 12. The canvas of the Marxian philosophy is very broad and for an understanding of his philosophy we need an integrated view of all his concepts and formulations.

Critical Assessment of Marxism: Criticism of Dialectical Materialism

The contention of Marx that the dialectic furnishes a clue to history is not correct. No one can explain history dialectically. "History," as Karl Federn points out, "proceeds from an unending stream of which no one knows the beginning or the end." The span of history being unlimited, it is difficult to determine the stages of history which correspond to thesis, antithesis or synthesis. The difficulty with this dialectical triad is that their precise location in history is more a matter of hypothesis than any actual occurrence.

If every movement of history is a movement towards progress in terms of dialectical process, then how do we account for 'dissolution and decay'? Can we say that this part of history cannot be subjected to dialectic?

The doctrine of dialectic is also not correct because whereas it is only an 'optimistic doctrine,' the actual history is both a record of rise and fall. History is not merely a record of progress. It also tells the story of downfall and regress. Thus, as a theory of continued and uninterrupted progress, the dialectic stands in sharp contrast to actual history which is as much a narrative of rise and progress as a tale of decay and dissolution.

The term 'dialectic' has not been precisely defined and uniformly used. There is no consistency among the Marxists as regards its true import and connotation. In fact, the use of the term 'contradiction' in relation to the dialectic has often been confused with the words 'negation' or 'antagonism.' This makes the confusion worse confounded and hampers a correct comprehension of the Marxian logic and philosophy.

Criticism of Historical Materialism and Economic Determinism

Under this head, we shall consider the criticism of both the Historical Materialism and Economic Determinism together, as both are inseparably linked together. Both the above doctrines have been criticized as dogmatism, historicism, utopianism, historical fatalism, essentialism, holism, etc. The main points of criticism of historical materialism and economic determinism are as under:

The emphasis put on the economic factor as being the final pacesetter or ultimate determinant of all history is out of all proportion to the actual role played by it. No doubt, the economic factor is an important determinant of changes, but it is neither the sole cause nor the ultimate cause in shaping the events of history. Marxism overemphasizes the materialistic elements, ignoring the fact that many other elements also play an important role in the historical development of society.

Marxism maintains that the basis of historical development of society is changes in the mode of production. Various critics, however, point out that historical developments do not take place on the basis of economic changes or changes in the mode of production alone. There are ideological, psychological, demographic or geographic and other factors which have equally contributed to the historical development of society.

The Marxian theory does not say anything about the role and contribution of great men in making and changing the course of history. Alexander's conquests, Ashoka's peace efforts and Akbar's endeavours to bring about amity among the different religious communities of India cannot be explained in economic terms. The teachings of Prophet Muhammed, Jesus Christ or Lord Buddha cannot be explained in terms of economic urges or economic motives. Nor can the Indian nationalism be explained fully in purely economic terms. And, it would be preposterous to trace or explain Homer's poetry, Plato's philosophy, Newton's science and St. Paul's spirituality in terms of economic forces. The fact is that Marx grievously erred and greatly exaggerated the role and relevance of economic factors in shaping human history.

The theory does not take into account the 'contingent element' or 'chance happenings' of great historical significance. Imagine the course history would have taken if Lenin had not been allowed to return to Russia in 1917, or if Hitler had not committed the mistake of attacking Russia. In that case, the entire course of Russian history would have been different. Thus, 'contingencies' and 'chance happenings' also play a decisive role in history.

The Theory of Economic Determinism, the critics point out, is both ambiguous and 'methodologically deficient.' While Marx considered 'production' as the prime mover of history, neither he, nor his friend Engels has clearly defined the meaning of 'production.' It is difficult to make out whether by production Marx meant 'productive forces' or the 'mode of production' or 'productive relations.' Moreover, his contention that the 'mode of production' is determined by technology only is not correct. The mode of production is surely affected by other factors including 'the state of science generally.' And, once we concede to bring in 'other factors' the relationship of the substructure and the superstructure as visualized by Marx cannot remain the same. Therefore, critics consider his theory of economic determinism rather ambiguous and deficient.

Critics also consider the Marxian contention that the requirements of 'productive forces' determine the advancement of science and technology as untenable. In this regard Hallowell comments: "To say that scientific investigation is conditioned by the environment in which it takes place is one thing; to say, as Marx and Engels do, that it is determined by the economic environment is nonsense."

Marx naively assumed that changes in the economic substructure determine changes in the superstructure of religion, laws, institutions, etc., and the superstructure always remained passive. According to him, all changes were caused by changes in the substructure and the superstructure was fully controlled by the substructure. Here, the question which has not been satisfactorily answered by Marx is what brings about changes is productive forces which constitute the economic substructure? Is the change automatic? or, is it brought about by certain other factors in the superstructure? If so, how can we say that productive forces are fundamental?

Moreover, Marx included science in the superstructure and did not realize that it is not economics that has revolutionized science but science that has changed economics so thoroughly and completely. The modern economic system is largely conditioned by and is dependent upon the latest advances in the techniques of science. Technology today entirely depends on science. This clearly dispels the fallacy that the substructure determines and controls the superstructure. Today it is the science-ridden superstructure which is decisively controlling the economic substructure. Even politically, the superstructure is not always passive and recognizing this fact, Stalin at a later date enunciated his famous theory of active superstructure and tried to remove the Marxist fallacy of substructure always controlling the superstructure.

Criticism of the Theory of Class Struggle

The theory of class struggle has been severely criticized by many thinkers. According to Prof. Lancaster, "As a propaganda, this theory is excellent, if for no other reason than that it puts the worker on the side that it informs him that he is sure to win. As a science, it is considerably less satisfactory, since there are grave difficulties about the term 'class' and therefore about the reality of class struggle. In view of the fundamental importance of the conception of class, it is curious to see how little attention the Marxists give to defining it."

In the opinion of Prof. Carew Hunt, the theory of class struggle as an explanation of history is quite untenable. He says: "Marx's thesis that all conflict among men arises from the class struggle, albeit, is of undoubted tactical value as calculated to convince the masses that their misfortunes are attributed to the capitalist system and will disappear with the victory of the proletariat, is nonetheless fallacious. For the supreme source of conflict in life is the inevitable opposition between the claims of the individual and those of society, a conflict which is not reducible to class struggle and cannot be dialectically resolved as it is a part of the unchanging human situation."

The critics of the theory of class struggle also point out that in explaining the role of social classes in history, Marx committed two great mistakes. First, he identified social classes with economic classes. For him, there was no difference between the two. Secondly, he equated the struggle between classes with the struggle between the capitalist employer and exploiter on the one hand, and the exploited labour or wage earner on the other. He called it the 'class struggle.' It is pointed out that class struggle cannot come into existence unless social classes possess the solidarity and unity of purpose. Popper has aptly remarked: "Indeed, the divergence of interests within the ruling and the ruled classes goes so far that Marx's theory of classes must be considered as a dangerous over-simplification, even if we admit that the issue between the rich and the poor is always of fundamental importance. One of the great themes of medieval history, the fight between Popes and emperors, is an example of dissension within the ruling class. It would be probably false to interpret this quarrel as one between exploiter and exploited."

The other important points of criticism of the theory of class struggle are as follows:

The Marxian theory of class struggle is contrary to historical facts. It is not true to say that class struggle has always existed in society. Moreover, the idea of a long continued class struggle is pessimistic and over-dramatic.

The Marxian concept of classes is static and rigid. As Wayper points out: "Classes are not fixed and rigidly maintained blocks."

Marx's polarization thesis of classes is incorrect. To suggest that under capitalism society is divided into two hostile camps is not true. On the contrary, the rise of the middle class consisting of the petty bourgeoisie, white collar workers, the technocrats, the skilled labourers, etc., gives a complete lie to the polarization theory of Karl Marx.

It is pointed out that class struggle is not fundamental in society. In fact, society develops through the processes of harmony and co-operation and it is possible to reconcile the interests of the working class and capitalists.

According to the theory of class struggle, the proletariat are bound to triumph in the long-run. It is pointed out that this may not always be the case. Capitalism may be succeeded by a Fascist dictatorship and not necessarily the dictatorship of the proletariat. Moreover, it is not necessary that revolutions would result in bringing about an idyllic society which is the dream of the Marxists.

Finally, the modern political thinkers and political scientists are of the opinion that society is one indivisible organism. It is a fallacy of the Marxian theory to bifurcate society into two separate parts. In recent times, it has been found that there is more of fusion and integration among various groups in society than separation or segregation. The present-day social requirements are dependent and conditioned by inter-class harmony and not hostility. Since, the organic unity of society cannot be destroyed, the Marxian theory of class struggle is inadequate and fallacious.

Criticism of the Theory of Revolution

The theory of revolution has generally been criticized on the following grounds:

A revolution is destructive; it involves violence; it throws society into a melting pot and to suggest that a revolution will always end in the establishment of the dictatorship of the proletariat is very difficult to predict. It is just possible that some ambitious army general or party potentate may succeed in establishing his own individual dictatorship instead of the proletarian dictatorship.

There is no certainty that the persons who start the revolution will be spared to see it through and direct it through all the stages. Violence results in savagery and barbarism and it is too much to expect to set up a peaceful and just society on such a basis.

A failure of the revolution cannot be ruled out entirely. It is difficult for the workers to fight against capitalists, who are well-organized and better equipped in weapons and armaments. According to Morley, "The revolutionary leaders tread a path of fire." A failure would invite vengeance and reprisals which would be harmful for the workers and wipe off the remaining vestiges of revolutionary resistance.

The task of fostering revolutionary consciousness is entrusted to trade union leaders which is paradoxical in nature. If these leaders succeed in their mission, by implication it will lessen their revolutionary ardour. If they do not succeed, they run the risk of losing the support of the workers.

Criticism of Other Aspects

Marxism is inimical to liberty, individuality, initiative and freedom. It makes the man a prisoner of society and of the laws of social development. Every member of the community becomes a slave of the community as a whole. Everything is managed by the central authority and the individual becomes merely a cog in the machine.

The Marxian view about the transitional nature of the dictatorship of the proletariat is not accepted by critics. It is pointed out that once in power, people do not want to surrender authority. There is no guarantee that the proletariat will do so either.

The Marxists believe that in the evolution of society, the bigger capitalists eliminate the smaller ones as the big fish eats up the smaller fish. However, this view is not supported by the historical facts. Instead, experience shows that side by side with the big capitalists, the smaller capitalists and the middle classes continue. There does not seem to be anything fundamentally wrong with their co-existence.

The dream of capitalism disintegrating owing to its own internal contradictions seems romantic and unlikely to be realized. In fact, greater production makes the foundations of capitalism stronger to withstand the revolutionary onslaughts.

The assertion that in the last analysis, capitalism hinders production is not borne out by facts. In the U.S.A., U.K., France, West Germany or Japan, production instead of being retarded has increased manifold. An increased production means an increase in profits, which in turn means a rise in wages, bonus and other benefits for workers. So, under capitalism if the rich become richer, the poor also become less poorer and their standard of living often tends to rise.

The Marxian thesis of increasing misery of workers is also contrary to facts. In the advanced industrial capitalist countries, the status of the employed is continuously improving and even the unemployed are looked after by the government. They are given unemployment relief which is an effective check against what Marx calls the conditions of increasing misery of the proletariat. Besides, factory legislation and labour laws have succeeded in eradicating many, if not all, evils of the nineteenth century capitalism. Hence, the theory of increasing misery of workers is an unnecessary pessimistic forecast unrelated to the facts of life.

Marx predicted socialist revolutions for advanced capitalist and industrialized countries like Germany or England. His prediction has not turned out to be true. It broke out with backward Tsarist Russia and the agrarian society of China. Moreover, capitalism is still alive and thriving in many countries without any indication of a revolution. The U.S.A., does not even have a strong socialist party.

According to Marxism, the state is a class organization. It is always used for aggressive purposes. It is based on force. It is a temporary institution. It will 'wither away' after the vested interests have been eliminated from society. Critics point out that the state is not a class organization. It is not based on force. It is based on the will of the people. It is a moral institution whose objective is to develop human personality. The establishment of a 'stateless' and 'classless' society is a proposition of a very doubtful nature. The experience of Soviet Russia shows that it is not possible to do away with the state. The state has not 'withered away.' It is becoming stronger instead of weaker.

The Marxian view that a change in the state can only be brought through class struggle is not acceptable. Professor William Ebenstein in his famous work, Today's Isms, says that Karl Marx could not give a proper weight to the great revolutionary changes brought about by the electoral reforms in England by the Act of 1832, and in the United States by President Jackson. He adds: "If Marx had accorded the political factor due weight, if he had fully grasped the importance of the Reforms Act in England and of the Jacksonian Revolution in the United States, he might have realized that socialism, too, might be accomplished without violence in countries that possessed democratic traditions strong enough to absorb far-reaching social and economic changes without resorting to civil war. A recognition of the cultural and political factors in the equation of social changes would have amounted, however, to a virtual abandonment of the central position of Marx, that history is the history of class-wars and that ruling classes defend their positions to the bitter end."

The Marxists overlook the important fact that man co-operates as well as competes. MacIver rightly says that men can live without competition but they cannot live without co-operation. It is wrong to assume that all important social changes are accomplished by force.

Marxism fails to take into account the forces of nationalism and even racialism. The two world wars have conclusively proved that the working men of the world do not all unite together in putting down wars which are largely capitalistic in character. Instead, they take side of the governments of their own countries and bring about untold hardships on the working classes everywhere.

Marxism is also too abstract and doctrinaire. It is based on broad generalizations rather than hard facts or evidence. It is apocalyptic in nature in that it builds a beautiful vision of the future without taking into account some of the baser elements of human nature.

Max Lerner refers to six errors of emphasis and calculation of the Marxists. They are: (i) an underestimate of the strength of capitalism; (ii) an overestimate of the revolutionary character of the proletariat; (iii) an underestimate of the strength of the middle class and the misreckoning of its direction; (iv) an underestimate of the strength of the nationalist idea; (v) a faulty theory of human nature in politics, and (vi) the misreckoning of proletarian dictatorship.

Finally, critics of Marxism say that "Like all dogmas, Marxism is strong in what it asserts and weak in what it denies." Marx did not have proper understanding of social psychology, religion or ethics. "He was at his best only when he was thundering as a Prophet against the capitalists."

In spite of all the criticism that has been levelled against Marxism, it can neither be dismissed nor ignored. It is an accepted revolutionary philosophy of the toiling masses and Marxism as a philosophy of social and political change has come to stay. It does provide a coherent and consistent account of the history of mankind and its scientific approach reveals a universal phenomenon of society. It brings to the forefront the question of the inadequacy of the present social organization. It is an admirable 'diagnosis of capitalism.' Hallowell writes: "We may reject the programme of Marxism but we cannot ignore the indictment which it makes of capitalism." It is a coherent socialist system with a definite purpose and a clear programme of action. It discloses to the proletariat its historical mission.

It is also a fact that Marxism has profoundly influenced a whole generation of political philosophers, writers and statesman alike. How deeply it has influenced them can be seen from one of the passages of Pt. Jawaharlal Nehru's autobiography in which he writes:

> "The theory and philosophy of Marxism lightened up many a dark corner of my mind. History came to have a new meaning for me. The Marxist interpretation threw a flood of light on it, and it became an unfolding drama with some order and purpose, however unconscious, behind it. In spite of the appalling waste and misery of the past and the present, the future was bright with hope, though many dangers intervened. It was the essential freedom from dogma and the scientific outlook of Marxism that appealed to me...."

Pt. Nehru further explains the relevance and significance of Marxism in the contemporary world and says: "The great world crisis and slump seemed to justify the Marxist analysis. While all other systems and theories were groping about in the dark, Marxism alone explained it, more or less, satisfactorily and offered a real solution."

In conclusion we may say that, howsoever, we may disagree with Marx, his teachings and philosophy, there is no gainsaying the fact that he gave a philosophy which has revolutionized the world. Since the publication of the Communist Manifesto in 1848; the whole intellectual world has been dominated by Marxism. No other philosopher of the world has ever so much influenced the thinking of human race as Marx. In the contemporary world, Marxism is the most intellectually ambitious, systematic and influential political philosophy. It has not only affected much of modern culture and civilization, but has also provided the conceptual framework for political philosophy and the theoretical basis for the regimes of a large number of nations. It is not only a potent political philosophy, but also a call to action, a revolutionary cry to change economic and social conditions of society.

34

V.I. Lenin (1870-1924 A.D.)

Introduction

Lenin, who championed the cause of proletariat and established the dictatorship of the Communist Party, did not belong to the proletariat class. He was the son of an Inspector of Schools, a government employee. He was born in 1870 and brought up in reasonable luxury. His real name was Viladimir Iluich Ulianov. At his 17th age, he was forced to be a revolutionary when once he heard that his brother was hanged to death on a charge of plotting against the Czar. Then he was a law student in Kazan university. The university authorities, ignoring the condition which influenced Lenin to become a revolutionary, expelled him from the university. However, he took his degree as a private student from the St. Peterburg University in 1891.

His revolutionary spirit together with the ability to give an able leadership not only attracted to him a huge following but also enabled him to achieve what he had undertaken. Not minding the difficulties he experienced, he worked hard to create an atmosphere to foment a revolution as desired by Marx. The success he achieved in the revolution placed him in the position of possessing the government and the difficulties he faced were overcome by him which of course earned for him a credit to be known in history as an extraordinary theoretician and a practical politician. His works among others are: (1) Imperialism - The highest state of capitalism. (2) State and Revolution (3) Left-wing communism, and (4) Materialism and Empirico Criticism. His contributions to political thought are born of his experience while in his attempt to implement the thoughts sown by Marx.

Demonstration of Marxian Thoughts

Lenin's greatness lies in demonstrating the so far unattainable Marxian thoughts. Lenin, having full conviction in the dialectical and historical materialism as brought out by Marx, fomented a revolution in Russia and made it public that Marxism is not an empty thought but a living force. While doing so he did not follow every step shown by Marx; but as a sagacious politician he adopted and conditioned the thoughts of Marx to make them suitable to Russia. While Lenin was placed on the highest chair of the Russian government his wide and varied experiences enabled him to understand the obstruction caused to curtail the spread of communism not to speak of its continuance in power and so his pronouncement of his view on various matters in all his books.

Imperialism

Imperialism, which was not taken cognizance of by Marx, is understood by Lenin and hence his discussion on it. When Lenin was alive the English had become the highest imperial power devouring one-third of the world. It is because of this Lenin says that the mother country exploits the colonies. The mother country by virtue of its industrial advancement increases its production and as a result, the colonial territories which are virtually reduced to the position of markets and markets only are exploited. So he says that people in the exploited and exploitable colonial territories are no less than the real proletariat. The people of the exploiting country are the capitalists who foster and promote capitalism. When capitalism develops the units of industrial production becomes bigger and bigger and the units are prone to get united in trust and cartels to produce monopoly capitalism. It is because of this that Lenin is inclined to describe imperialism as the monopoly stage of capitalism. Besides, he expresses that the banks that are used by the capitalists as their tools to develop themselves at the cost of the poor section of the people too have to combine together and they wanted to control finance as masters. So he says that the monopoly of capitalism is also "finance capitalism." The thus formed "monopoly finance capitalism" becomes aggressively expansionist whose export is capital with the explicit purpose of continuing its hold over colonial countries. This policy is fraught with serious consequences of upsetting the peace of the world. This policy enables the exploiters to exploit the exploited, causes wars between nations and drives the capitalists to resort to aggressive conflicts and even wars between capitalists.

In this connection, the nature of the First war is worth remembering. It is a war fought among the capitalist nations. Lenin who snatched the opportunity to translate his dream of converting Russia into a proletariat nation, as the Czar involved in the war, induced the proletariat section. He felt that the time was ripe and entertained the thought of striking the iron when it is hot. It is also true that Russia did not reach the imperialist stage of capitalism; even then there was revolution in the line shown by Marx. Here the conception that imperialist stage of capitalism is the last stage of revolution becomes untrue. Besides, the greatest imperialistic power of his time namely Britain also did not reach stage of finance capitalism.

Revolution

Lenin feels that revolution is possible in any country — highly industrialized or highly agrarian or highly forward or highly backward. But the requisite necessities for a revolution are the existence of highly discontented and at the same time revolutionary class with clear-cut principles and objectives, the existence of a party to steer the party and to lead the class and above all the prevalence of unrest among the people.

Lenin, whose ideas and activities were influenced by Marx, appears to be careful in applying the ideas of his political master taking into account of the condition of his country. Russia was not an industrialized country like England; but it was only an underdeveloped agrarian nation like India. Marx's expectation is that revolutions will break out in a highly industrialized nation. But Russia, a highly feudalized nation, witnessed revolution and so Lenin's is the modification of Marxian theory on revolution and is born of his experience.

Lenin does not like to put a halt to world wars; on the contrary he favours and even encourages such wars for the people would be driven to the jaws of panic and poverty, a necessity for the birth of revolution to greet Communism. In fact, the world-wide economic depression on account of the First World War was a lever to activise and speed up communistic forces in Russia to make it red completely. So Lenin says that world war is "the mid-wife of world revolution."

Dictatorship of Party Instead of Class

Lenin is practical in approach. Wherever and whenever necessary he never fails to modify the theory of his master to make it applicable and practicable. So, he does not advocate the class dictatorship (Proletariat Dictatorship) as advocated by Marx; but he prefers and practises only the Party Dictatorship. Communism was his party. The dictatorship of the Communist Party is advocated and installed. He is sure that there cannot be the Proletariat Dictatorship without the rise of an organization for the proletariat viz., Communist Party. He again says that trade union consciousness is not enough; he advocated a strong party consciousness.

Lenin took a great care in maintaining the solidarity of the Party. The Party, to him, was the be-all and end-all. He wanted everyone should obey the Party. None was permitted to criticize the Party. To continue the hold of the Party in the governmental organizations, Lenin says that the Party should not accommodate the liberals for they would prove dangerous to the Party itself owing to their half-heartedness; and he wanted the Party to be a strong monolith.

State and Democracy

Lenin, like Marx, is firm to do away with the state. The state to him is "the machine for the suppression of one class by another." The state should wither away. The army that any state maintains must also go and be replaced by a popular militia. Similarly, as bureaucracy is an organization of bourgeois and intended to promote the interests of the exploiters, he says that the organ should be done away with.

He has no faith in democratic traditions as existing now. He favours the institutions run by elected representatives. However, Parliaments as he has seen in capitalist countries are denounced by him as they are the bourgeois Parliaments and so he chastises them as talking shops.

To him proletarian state is a new form of democracy. Such a state is more democratic than any other democracy existing in capitalist countries. Lenin, saluting his master in the matter of calling Communism as "the real democracy," travels a bit further and proclaims that Communism is more than democracy; Communism is the democracy of the proletariat. In such a system the rich have no place as it is the system and organization meant for the poor and the poor alone who are in majority. So the 'Proletariatic Democracy,' as he wants to call Communism, is better than the 'Bourgeoistic Democracy' existing in other parts of the world.

Religion

Religion to Marx is the opium of the people and so it is fit to be dispensed with. Lenin is in no way inferior to his master in the language used to condemn and do away with it. He, likes his master, of the view that religion helps the exploiters to exploit the poor and so he proclaims, "We, therefore, reject every attempt to impose on us any moral dogma." In the same context, he accepts they (the Communists) "have no ethics."

International Relations and National Policy

Lenin is in favour of co-existence internationally although the other nations follow a completely different political system and are wedded to different social pattern.

Internally, Lenin patronized and practiced Communism of property. He faced a worst economic crisis capable of undoing what all he had done during the time of War Communism (1917-21) in his country. He as a dynamic and practical-minded leader, unnerved by the crisis of production, faced the situation and boldly announced concessions to private property through his 'New Economic Policy.'

Conclusion

Lenin was a follower of Marx and not a mad follower because he took the concepts and ideals of Marx, imparted to them a new colour or approach wherever necessary, allowed them to undergo a change whenever necessary and adopted and applied them to Russia, his country, to convert that into a proletarian state. What remained an ideal to the critics of Marx, Lenin transformed them into a living form. Marx had unpolished and rugged dogmas; but Lenin has polished them added to them that which is needed and taken away from that which is impracticable and unwanted and made them a force to be acknowledged with sense of admiration or apprehension. Therefore, we can say that Marxs are rare and Lenins are rarer.

35
Stalin

Lenin left Soviet Russia in the anomalous situation of an industrially backward country with a revolutionary socialist regime in the midst of hostile capitalist world. The consequences of such an anomalous situation would have been serious but for Stalin to whose shoulders fill the task of solidifying the gains that Lenin had brought to the country by freeing it from the tyrannical rule of the Czar and defeating the counter-revolutionaries. Stalin, from the very beginning of his rule, established himself as a strong leader. His ideas and decisions registered deep impression on the theory and practice of Communism.

Marx had pointed out that the capitalist system would die of its own inner contradictions. But this was not what took place in Russia, where the capitalist system was yet in its infancy when Revolution came there, Marx had also anticipated that communist revolutions would occur close together in several countries. But this also did not happen which gave rise to some problems. One of them was the problem of building socialism in a single country. The other was the task of building Communism in a country which was only modestly industrialized but dominated by the peasantry. Stalin resolved with these problems and succeeded in putting Communism on a firm basis.

When Lenin succeeded in bringing about revolution in Soviet Russia and when an attempted revolution in Germany failed, the question that arose was, "should the Soviet leaders dedicate themselves to the task of defending and building the Soviet regime in Russia alone or should they stake everything in supporting revolution in other countries, even risking the power won by Soviet Russia in that process? Trotsky, one of the Soviet leaders, wanted to promote revolution in other countries even at the risk of losing Russia for it but Stalin was of the opinion that there was no chance of revolution succeeding in other countries in the near future. Stalin succeeded in ousting Trotsky from the party and established his supremacy in the party.

Stalin's reputation as a Marxist scholar was poor. In fact, theory was not the field of Stalin. Once Stalin said: "We are for the withering away of the state. And yet we also believe in the proletariat dictatorship which represents the strongest and mightiest form of the state power that has existed up to now. To keep on developing state power in order to prepare the conditions for the withering away of state power — that is the Marxist formula." Two ideas of Stalin require special mention i.e., (i) the idea of socialism in one country, and (ii) the idea of revolution.

Socialism in One Country

As said above, Stalin was opposed to the idea that of revolution in all the countries simultaneously. He wanted the Soviet people and leaders to dedicate themselves to the task of defending and building the Soviet regime in Russia alone. Stalin held that it was possible to establish socialism in one country even if the other parts of the world remained capitalistic. This was a clear departure from deposition held by Marx and Lenin.

As Dr. Wayper says, "It was a departure hastily made to serve an immediate purpose, to provide Stalin with a weapon to be used against Trotsky in the struggle for power that took place between them after Lenin's death."

The natural implication of Stalin's thesis 'socialism in one country' was the dictatorship of the leader of party. Stalin brushed aside the party and established his personal supremacy. He became the most feared man not only in Russia but also in world. Stalin did not carry very much for observing the formalities of consulting the party. "The organized vanguard of the working class and the highest form of their class associations came to be described as the voluntary association of like-minded communists which included workers, peasants and members of the intelligentsia." The doctrine of "socialism in one country" led Stalin to a virtual abandonment of Marxian theory of the state.

According to Marx, the state is bound to disappear with the establishment of socialism. While paying lip service to the theory of "wither away of the state." Stalin tried to explain the continued existence of the state in Soviet Russia. In doing so, he almost rejected the Marxian thesis.

Stalin went to the length of asserting that the state need not disappear even in the last and final stage of full Communism of capitalist encirclement of the Soviet Union is not liquidated. And this means that state shall ever remain in Soviet Russia since its encirclement will never come to an end.

According to Dr. Wayper, "what he gives with one hand, he thus at last partly takes back with the other." To Stalin, Russia was the centre of the world. It was her destiny to become the centre of a new civilization superior to that of a capitalist Europe. Isolated and backward though she was, she nevertheless possessed the truth that would save not only herself but also the whole of struggling mankind. Dr. Wayper says: "Socialism in one country was the 20th century version of Moscow — the third Rome, the dream of the 19th century Slavophil's. It was the marriage of Russian revolution with Russian history, from the marriage was born the force which carried Stalin to supreme power. And perhaps the truest view of the purges (to make clean) that followed upon it is that there were the terrible revenge taken by Russian history on the revolutionaries who had dare to deny her."

Idea of Revolution

Despite his firm adherence to the principle of socialism in one country, Stalin, did not renounce his faith in world revolution. He retained faith in it till the end of his life. In this 'socialism' he wrote that no single country should consider itself fully secure against the possibility of counter-revolution without a victory as revolution in a number of other countries. At the Seventh Congress of the Third International held in 1935 he declared as follows: "The Congress will have a great historic importance. It must open up broad revolutionary prospectives to millions of workers of the West, of the East, of America and of the colonial and semi-colonial countries; it must mark the beginning of an era of war and of revolutions."

Thus, it is clear that Stalin never deviated from the theory of world revolution. He was convinced that the change from capitalism to socialism was not possible without a revolution, and that the final victory of socialism required revolution in several countries. Where he differed from Lenin as well as from Trotsky was on the question of the ripeness of Europe for it. He did not share the belief of Trotsky that Europe was ripe for socialist revolution.

Like Marx but unlike Lenin, Stalin envisaged the possibility of a peaceful transition from capitalism to socialism. But the peaceful transition of which Stalin spoke was very much different from that of which Marx thought. The way in which socialism was introduced in countries like Poland, Hungary, Romania, Bulgaria, Yugoslavia and Czechoslovakia illustrates Stalin's idea of peaceful resolution. In each of these countries the local communist party could gain control of the government by adopting certain tactics. One common feature of these tactics was the dependence of the local communists upon the Soviet armed struggle. Thus, the world revolution as understood by Stalin was not to be the natural result of social and economic conditions as Marx has envisaged and Trotsky had expected; it was to fellow from the strengthen of Soviet Russia. In short, Stalin's world revolution was to be the Russian world revolution. Stalin wanted Russia to become the centre of the world.

Concluding, we may say that while Lenin adopted the Marxist doctrine for the purpose of creating a Communist Party in Russia, and leading the Revolution to success, Stalin had to wield the power that Lenin had owned. The task before Stalin was to preserve and strengthen the Soviet Government in a world of hostile capitalist powers and make the peasants accept a communist regime. In achieving this task, Stalin had to make some concessions in one case to the peasants and in the other to capitalist powers. But he also led a tough policy which was result of the dictatorship of a minority over a majority. He isolated the Russian people from the outside world. The dictatorship culminated in Stalin's own pre-eminence. He became God in the eyes of his followers and succeeded in strengthening the communist regime though at much cost of suffering to his people and distorting communist theory and practice.

36

Friedrich Engels (1820-1895 A.D.)

Early Life: Friedrich Engels was born on September 28, 1820 at Rhineland, the industrial town of Barmen. His father was a wealthy and prosperous cotton manufacturer. His father was a stern Protestant. Hence, he had no sympathy with the radical views of his son. At the age of 17, he was employed as a manager in one of his family's cotton mills. Then he was sent to Manchester as the agent of his father's business. When he was in England he got first hand knowledge of social conditions of that country. The pitiable plight of the slum-dwellers in England created a deep impression in his mind. Hence, his mind rapidly drifted towards the tenets of revolutionary socialism.

His Works: As Engels was acquainted with the social conditions in England, he gained for himself a European reputation by his work, "The condition of the working classes in England" which was published in 1844. In this book, he criticized capitalism. In 1844, Marx and Engels associated in the formation of the groups of working class radicals. The meeting of their groups i.e., the Congress was held in 1847 in London. It was called the Communist League. In 1848, both of them jointly produced the famous "Communist Manifesto."

In 1848, both Engels and Marx took an active part in the revolutionary activities in France and Germany. After the failure of the movement, they went to England. Dr. Engels began to look after the business of his father once again. He helped his friend Karl Marx in solving his financial difficulties. In 1869, he retired from business and gave all his time to political activity and writing.

Dr. Engels collaborated with Marx on several of his works. He himself wrote separately "Socialism Utopian and Scientific", "Anti-Duhring," "The Origin of the Family," "Private Property" and "the State". After the death of Karl Marx, Engels edited the second and third volumes of the Das Capital. He died on 5th August, 1895.

The partnership between Karl Marx and Friedrich Engels is considered as the most famous partnership in history. The quick mind and ready understanding of Engels attracted Karl Marx greatly. It led to Marx to write about him in the following manner: "You know that I am slow to grasp things and that I will always be in your footprints." But Dr. Engels never hesitated to co-operate with Marx. He played "second fiddle" to Marx's exceptional genius. Thus, he remained as the most faithful and favourite disciple of Marx.

Estimate: Dr. Engels had a great sense of fun. It is pointed out that he was more worldly than Marx. He was a tall man; he had a military bearing. No doubt he was a good linguist. His favourite thing was fox hunting. He had a relish for beer especially if it was the Viennese.

Berlin in his "Karl Marx — His life and Environment" says that "Engels was a man of solid and robust, but hardly creative mind; a man of exceptional integrity and strength of character of many varied gifts, but in particular endowed with a remarkable capacity for the rapid assimilation of knowledge. He possessed a shrewd and lucid intellect and a firm sense of reality which few if any, among his radical contemporaries could claim...."

Lightheim George says that "There is a certain ambiguity about the customary interpretation of Engels share in the development of Marxism. For the Orthodox, he is simply Marx's lifelong ally and helper in shaping the theory and practice of the movement." He was really something more than that Dr. Engels may be called as the father of Social Democratic Marxism. He was highly responsible in making socialism most scientific in a comprehensive way. His theoretical thinking is found in his Anti-Duhring. The formulation of scientific socialism is bound in the book. It is the source of almost all the theoretical thinking of the fast growing membership of the Social Democratic Movement.

If Marx was the theorist of the new proletarian movement, Engels was the propagandist and grand organizer. It is highly difficult to say which of them played the greater part. He was chiefly instrumental after the death of Marx, in giving shape to what became known as "Orthodox Marxism."

John Bowle says that both Marx and Engels were men of formidable ability. Both jointly created a social philosophy of massive range and insight. The authority of science was invoked by them for political beliefs. They were actuated by a burning sense of mission. Apart from this, they were convinced that they would succeed only when the masses were behind them. In spite of all this, history has chosen to give Marx the greater credit ascribing to Engels, the role of a junior partner.

37

Herbert Spencer (1820-1903 A.D.)

His Life: Herbert Spencer was the most ardent advocate of individualism during the 19th century. He was born in 1820 in Derby in England. He was the son of a teacher. He got very little formal education. He was a self-educated man. He was a precocious child. He was encouraged by his father in his interest in science and technology. At the age of 17, he was a trained engineer. But he did not continue in the job for long. Then he showed his interest towards political economy, sociology, biology and philosophy. He became the sub-editor of a journal called, "The Pilot" at the age of 24. He served as a sub-editor of "The Economist" from 1848 to 1853. Later on, he became a free writer.

His Works: At the age of 30, he published his famous book called, "Social Statics" in 1851. His other publications are: "The Proper Sphere of Government," "Theory of Population," "Art of Education," "Education," "The Social Organism," "Specialised Administration" "Principles of Psychology," "Descriptive Sociology," "Principles of Sociology," "Sins of Legislators," "Synthetic Philosophy," "Justice," "Principles of Ethics," "Man Versus the State," "Essays," and "Autobiography."

It goes without saying that the writings of Herbert Spencer were translated in many languages of the world. He became famous not only in Europe and America but also in China and Japan. He was one of the few philosophers whose fame spread beyond his country in his own life time.

Theory of Evolution: Spencer introduced the concept of evolution into his political and social philosophy. The scientists of the 19th century discarded their belief in God. They put forward the idea of a life force. That force was not static but dynamic. Spencer accepted the idea of perpetual evolution and applied the same to his political philosophy with a view to give more freedom of action for the individual.

Spencer held that the same basic law and evolution could be found in the physical, animal and human worlds where "transformation of the homogeneous into the heterogeneous is found there is progress."

Herbert Spencer accepted the utilitarian view that happiness was the end of life. But he also added that the end was willed by the life force. To obtain happiness, he constantly adjusted himself to his surroundings. The above kind of adjustment required a certain freedom in man. It was described by Spencer as free energy and faculty. In the universe, every man must be free. But his freedom should be regulated by a law of nature. Moral effort was needed by man to obey. Here he identified morality with physical laws. He reduced it to a system of automatic reactions.

According to Spencer, adjustments between several freedoms did not take place automatically in society. Men were always in the progress of adjustment. At this juncture, struggle was inevitable. Hence, government was very needful to help the adjustments. It should remove the obstacles of man for his free development. In the final stage, there will be no necessity of state. The individuals themselves would adjust freely. Gradually, the government would be losing its control. Again it would lessen its supervision gradually. Finally, anarchy was to be the destiny of Society.

Spencer applied the concepts of biology to social sciences. He pleaded for the "survival of the fittest." Evil is the result of the "non-adaptation of constitution to conditions." A stern discipline was seen by him in nature. Suppose if an aged and weak animal falls prey to another beast, its death creates three kinds of happiness:

(i) The old animal is spared of the suffering of slow and painful starvation.

(ii) The young ones get rid of the burden.

(iii) The beasts of prey derive happiness by killing the inferior animals.

Herbert Spencer thus emphasized the stern discipline in the society.

According to Spencer, none should interfere with suffering for sentimental reasons, for such interference prevents the operation of social laws. Unfits are to be eliminated from the society since at excreted them. As a result the whole society benefits. Spencer coined the phrase "Survival of the fittest," which was later followed by Charles Darwin to explain that stage which ensured the improvement of the quality of the human race.

Spencer expressed himself against the poor laws. He opined the state as an organism like a human being. He interpreted the state in terms of biology. The attributes of an organism and the state are similar.

(i) Both of them begin as germs, simple in structure. As they grow and develop, they become complex.

(ii) In both the organism and the society there is mutual dependence of parts.

(iii) Both of them are subject to wear and tear and there is replacement in both of them.

(iv) Both have a sustaining, distributory and regulating system.

In explaining the structure of the both he said "As the lowest type of animal is all stomach respiratory surface or limb, so primitive society is all warrior, all hunter, all builder or all tool maker. As society grows in complexity division of labour follows i.e., new organs with different functions in the animals in which fundamental trait, they become entirely alike."

Further according to him, the sustaining system of an organism is its digestive system; the sustaining system of society is its productive system including industries and agriculture. The distributory system of an organism is the circulatory system means of communication and transport serve as the distributory system of the society; the nervous system is the regulating system in an organism; the government is the regulating system in the society.

In spite of these resemblances, Spencer pointed out certain differences between animal organism and body politic. "The former was concrete in structure and its units were bound together in close contact; the latter was discrete and its units were free and more or less widely dispersed."

In the case of animal organism, consciousness was concentrated in a small part of the aggregate; there was no "sensorium" in the social body.

From the above fact, it is very clear that the state is an organ of society. Its sphere of activity therefore must be limited to the performance of its essential functions. These functions are the maintenance of peace and order and giving protection to its citizens. Government is an evil; it is a necessary evil. The scope of the government would diminish as civilization develops. As and when the human faculty's develop they became fit for social life. At that stage government will disappear. Thus, he applied the biologic analogy to uphold individualism.

Spencer explained that the modern industrial state has evolved from the military state. The latter was a primitive one. It paved the way for war. The military chief became the political leader. It expanded into an industrial state and society. The life of the state was based on voluntary co-operation. The individual is regarded as the chief end of the state. Hence, it must assure maximum liberty and happiness of its members. In this form of state people are anti-militarist, anti-imperialist, cosmopolitan and humanitarian. Finally, he contented that modern, industrialism would make men co-operate on a peaceful voluntary and non-exploiting basis. When they reach the stage, there is no necessity for government for them. It will eventually disappear to wither away.

Individualism: Herbert Spencer was a great advocate of individualism. His first major publication was "The Proper Sphere of Government." It was published in 1842. In this essay, Spencer expresses his political philosophy of extreme individualism and Laissez Faire. His individualism was the outcome of his belief in natural rights, natural economic laws and non-conformist's hostility to authority. Natural laws demanded that the government should allow nature to function freely without any artificial hindrance.

Spencer applied the law of organic evolution through natural selection to human society. After that he came to the conclusion that the state should allow nature to do its work. The first and foremost function of the state is to give maximum assistance to nature i.e., it is the duty of the state to allow every individual to fight out the struggle for existence according to his conduct and nature. There are two kinds of duties to the state. Firstly, the primary function of the state is defence against external danger. Secondly, it is the duty of the state to prevent encroachments reciprocally among the individuals within the state. In other words, it is described by him in these words, "Every man is free to do that which he wills provided, he infringes not upon the equal freedom of any other man."

Spencer eternally opposed to all organized charity, public as well as private. He also disliked all state help to education or industry. According to him, there will not be any useful purpose by giving compulsory education to the people in the state. Moreover, poor relief and social legislation seemed to serve no fruitful purpose to them in the state. The State should have no business to assist the lame, the dumb, the poor, the old and the destitute. Apart from this, the state should not undertake the construction of post offices and erecting of light houses. The above functions did not come under the category of justice which alone is the function of the State.

According to Spencer, the state is not an eternal institution. Its existence was merely incidental. In his "Social Statics" published in 1866, he maintained that the individual had the right to ignore the state. In short, the only right of the individual is equal freedom with everybody else. The only duty of the state is to protect that right against violence and fraud.

Spencer's philosophy of Laissez Faire was fully expressed in his book, "The Man Versus the State." In it he reiterated that it was harmful and horrible to interfere with the process of the survival of the fittest. Such an interference with natural selection would lower the standards of a society as a whole.

Spencer was not in favour of socialization of the means of production. For him, all socialism is slavery. Under Socialism or Communism, the individual would be a slave of the whole community. To him the divine right of parliaments, was a great political superstition just as the divine right of kings. He attacked the sovereignty of Hobbes.

In his essay entitled, "The Sins of the Legislators" he condemned the legislation passed and enforced in the past. The laws of the state were a record of "unhappy guesses." Later on some of them were repealed or amended. Thus, Spencer has given a vivid account about his individualistic philosophy.

Rights: "Rights are nothing but artificial divisions of the general claim to exercise the faculties," according to Spencer. There are two kinds of rights viz. private rights and public rights. Rights concerned with the property and family of the individual are private rights. Public rights are concerned with his relations to the State. Regarding private rights he had no belief on private property. He attacked "The subjection of women." He favoured the right of vote to women. Regarding public rights he said that government was a vicious and immoral institution. Every individual had the "right to ignore the state." In human life, each individual must receive justice and he should enjoy freedom in his life. Freedom according to him is that every man should enjoy his natural rights.

Estimate: Spencer was the most ardent advocate of individualism during the 19th century. According to Maxey, "No reputable political thinker of the present time acknowledge Spencer as his master. For the critical mind of today, he is a amateur scientist and the pseudo philosopher. Science has learned a lot about evolution since Spencer's day. Undoubtedly, Spencer had done more to the development of biology and science after Charles Darwin."

Spencer's differentiation between the military and industrial state is of lasting influence. As Ebenstein points out, "in the second half of the twentieth century Spencer's basic distinction throws a great deal of light on the political behaviour of states."

Spencer had great influence in the U.S.A, like Locke. Spencer's idea on individualism appealed to the American businessmen and industrial entrepreneurs. Due to its inherent weakness, Spencerism lost its vigour. It cannot be denied that his law played a significant role during his lifetime. However, his thought has not been abandoned fully.

38

Thomas Hill Green (1836-1882 A.D.)

Thomas Hill Green was an English historian and philosopher. He was also a theorist and a reformer. He was born in the year 1836 at Yorkshire. He was the son of a clergyman. He was educated at Rugby and the Balliod College, Oxford. He became Professor of moral philosophy in 1878 at Oxford.

He was not only a philosopher, but also was thoroughly interested in the practical politics of his country. He was elected to the Oxford Town Council by the people. For some years, he served on the governing body of a system of schools in Birmingham. According to him, the basis of sound government was the local government of the country.

T.H. Green's many lectures were published after his death in 1882. In 1879 he delivered his first lecture, "Lectures on the Principles of Political Obligation." His other publications are "Prolegomena to Ethics," "Lectures on Liberal Legislation," "Freedom of Contract" and "Lectures on the English Revolution."

Green's philosophy is taken from the writings of Plato, Aristotle, Rousseau, Kant and Hegel. Green agreed with the view of Aristotle that the supreme function of the state was to make it possible to realize their common good. Green borrowed from Rousseau the idea of moral freedom of man. In the purely metaphysical field Green was closer to Hegel. But in ethics and politics Kantian influence seems to be greater. He was Kantian in outlook.

According to Green, the State is the product of human consciousness. Human consciousness postulates liberty. Liberty involves rights and rights demand the State. It was an ethical institution which was essential for the moral development of man. The important function of the state was to enforce rights. The State might use its force since it expressed the general will of the people. To him, "will not force is the basis of the State."

From Green's "Lectures on the Principles of Political Obligation" it is seen that the people obey the State because it contributes or can contribute towards their moral life. According to him, "the function of the government is to maintain conditions of life in which morality shall be possible and morality consists in the disinterested performance of self-imposed duties." The state was neither absolute nor omnipotent. It was limited both from within and from without. He believed in the "Universal Brotherhood of man." The right of every individual to life involved a check on the authority of the state.

As an active liberal in politics, Green unlike Kant and Hegel supported a representative form of government. According to Green, the right to free life is the essence of citizenship. But it is subject to restriction by the state which has to use force in order to repel a force opposed to freedom. According to him, the object of punishment is neither to inflict pain on the criminal in proportion to his moral guilt for it is rather impossible to assess this proportion nor to bring about a moral reformation of the criminal for all true reform comes from within.

Green viewed that right to resistance was possibly justificable and not obligatory. He rejected the meaning given to the term "Natural Law" by writers like Hobbes and Locke. He also rejected the idea of the state of nature as advocated by the writers of the social contract theory.

According to Green, state was a society of societies. The rights exercised by the state over the different societies was one of adjustment. The state adjusted for each system of rights internally. It also adjusted the system of rights to the rest externally.

The part and parcel of his theory of state action was the problem of punishment. The will of the criminal was anti-social. It was a force opposed to freedom. Punishment was a force directed against the force of the criminal. The primary object of punishment is not to reform the criminal but to create terror in his mind. The future prevention of crime is the chief object of punishment. Punishment should create a terror which will prevent others from committing the crime.

Regarding property he held liberal views. He was neither a protector of private property nor as out and out critic of it. Again it is stated that he was neither a socialist nor an individualist. Every individual must have the opportunity to acquire property because everyone has the capacity to partake of common social good. That capacity is different from man to man. As a result, there was inequality in the possession of property. If a few property owner interfere in the affairs of others, it was the duty of the state to interfere. He stood for a class of small proprietors filling their own land.

There is a difference of opinion between Green and Hegel in respect of the attitude towards war. According to him, war was never absolutely right. It was a cruel necessity. It was a moral wrong, whoever may be the wrong doer, destruction of life in war is a wrong. Green refused to accept the view that wars were inevitable. Wars did not exist because states existed. Wars existed because states did not fulfil their duty of maintaining the general rights.

Green was an individualist. State was the embodiment of the Divine Spirit. He never regarded the state as an end in itself. It was a means to end and that end was the full moral development of the individuals living within the state. It is the duty of the state to do everything for the free development of moral personality; but it should not do those things which are against such development. He described the General Will as "the common consciousness of a common good." He differed from Hegel in his idea of freedom.

Many criticisms have been levelled against the theory of Green. His theory of sovereignty is not satisfactory since it is based on General Will. Further he failed to note the sub-conscious factors that influence the actions of men in the states. Again in his theory of punishment he appears to forget totally the emotions of the people. His economic ideas regarding property is unsatisfactory since it leads to danger. Barker says that "Green was both a soaring idealist and a sober realist." Thus, the ideas of Green have been criticized by many modern writers.

Theory of State: Thomas Hill Green was an English historian and philosopher. He was also a theorist and a reformer. Sources of Green's philosophy are to be found in Plato, Aristotle, Rousseau, Kant and Hegel. Green agreed with the view of Aristotle that the supreme function of the state was to make it possible to realize their common good. Green borrowed from Rousseau the idea of moral freedom of man. In the purely metaphysical field, Green was closer to Hegel. But in ethics and politics Kantian influence seems to be greater. He was Kantian in outlook.

Green was the first man in the 19th century to construct a comprehensive philosophy of state. There is a direct affinity between his metaphysics and politics between his ethics serves as a necessary interlude.

According to Green, the state is the product of human consciousness. Human consciousness postulates liberty. Liberty involves rights and rights demand the state. C.L. Wayper points out that for all his belief "that the state was the embodiment of the Divine Spirit, he never regarded the state as an end in itself. It was a means to an end and that end was the full moral development of the individuals who compose it." His ethics made him to believe passionately with Kant that everyman has a worth and dignity which forbids his exploitation for any purpose whatever. According to Green, the life of the nation has no real existence except as the life of the individual composing it. It was the duty of the state to release men so that they may be able to fulfil their personalities. The functions of the state was a negative one. According to him, the state cannot teach morality to men, nor can it make men moral since morality consists in "the disinterested performance of self-imposed duties." It is to remove obstacles which prevent man becoming moral. The state may have to use force to control the outward acts of men, whose ultimate freedom was the end to be aimed at. According to Barker, "Green, uses force to create freedom."

It is pointed out that the extent of state interference was very great. The state was constantly to adjust one group with another group. The duty of the state was to regulate the rights of its citizens. It was the duty of the state to provide compulsory education for the people. Parents could be forced to abide by the state.

To Green, the state was both natural and necessary. The state was an ethical institution. It was very essential for the moral development of man. The first and foremost function of the state was to enforce rights. If necessary it could be done through compulsion. The state was justified in using force because it expressed the general will of the people.

Green, in his "Principles of Political Obligation", has allotted a chapter for General Will. According to him, Will not force is the basis of the state. He believed in the existence of the General Will. The real basis of the state was the General Will according to him. So far as legal sovereignty is concerned he agreed with the view of John Austin. Accordingly, legal sovereignty must reside in the supreme authority within the state. There is no power above itself. But behind this legal sovereign is the General Will. This General Will determines the habitual obedience of the people. From this we know that the General Will meant the Will for the state not the Will of the state.

Although Green held that Will not force was the true basis of the state he was fully aware that there were states in which force was predominant. He did not have any faith in those states since they could not fulfil their ideal function. Green also differed from Hegel in his conception of freedom. In the opinion of Hegel, freedom is the voluntary identification of self with the laws of the state. For Green freedom is the right of a man to make the best of himself.

According to Green, people obey the state because it contributes or can contribute towards their moral life. The state was neither absolute nor omnipotent. It was limited from both within and without. The law could control the external actions of the individuals and not the eternal motives. Thus, from within the state was limited. As a result, the state was not able to promote the good life of the people indirectly. It could make its contribution by eliminating the obstacles in the way of the development of the personalities of the individuals. In some cases, it is obviously seen that the individual was also given the right and duty of resisting the authority of the state. Further Green's view was that as the state had the power of adjustment over other groups it possessed the ultimate authority.

According to Green, state was a society of societies. He advocated international court of law. He believed in "the Universal Brotherhood of man." The right of every individual to life involved a check on the authority of the state. He was opposed to a paternal form of government. As an active liberal in politics Green unlike Kant and Hegel supported a representative form of Government and advocated the extension of franchise. Green's concept of liberty is closely connected to the Kantian concept of moral will and freedom. According to Kant, "A person who is really free is one who is morally free." The state should promote morality.

Green's treatment of the problem of punishment was the part and parcel of his theory of state action. The will of the criminal was anti-social. It constituted a force opposed to freedom. Punishment was a force directed against the will of the criminal. It was not possible for the state to measure the pain of punishment. Even if it was possible, the task of the judges will become very difficult. They will be required to give a different punishment in every case. At the same time, it will not be possible to have common rules of punishment as they exist today.

The foremost aim of giving punishment is not to reform the criminal. It is neither to inflict pain on the criminal or in proportion to his moral guilt for it is rather impossible to assess this proportion nor to bring about a moral reformation of the criminal for all true reforms comes from within. The future prevention of crime is the chief object of punishment. Punishment should create a terror which will prevent others from committing the crime. The state looks not to virtue and vice but to rights and wrongs not however in order to avenge it, but in order to the consideration of the sort of terror which needs to be associated with such wrong doing in order to the future maintenance of rights. Thus, he has clearly indicated above the primary object of punishment.

Green viewed that punishment was a force used as preventive to force, opposed to freedom. Punishment had a moral purpose and a positive quality. To secure freedom of action was its ultimate aim hence it was called moral. That freedom of action was for the free will of every member of the community.

According to Green, punishment had both direct and indirect effects or consequences. As regards direct effect or consequence, it was a force preventive of a force opposed to rights. So far as indirect effect is concerned punishments was and must be a reformation of the will.

View on Rights and Liberty: Thomas Hill Green was an English historian and philosopher. He was also a theorist and a reformer. Sources of philosophy are to be found in Plato, Aristotle, Rousseau, Kant and Hegel. The purpose of Green's lectures on the 'Principles of Political Obligation' is to consider the moral function or object served by law or by the system of rights and obligations which the state enforces and in so doing to discover the ground or justification for obedience to law.

According to Green, a right is the claim of an individual to will his own ideal objects. The right arises from the self-consciousness of an individual. Rights are inherent in an individual living in society. There are ideal rights in a society. It is organized on the basis of goodwill. To him rights should be regulated by mutual recognition. Rights are essentially a social product hence they cannot be attributed to isolated individuals. He criticized Locke's idea of natural rights. "Natural Right as right in a State of Nature which is not a State or society is a contradiction. There can be no right without a consciousness of common interest on the part of members of a society. Without this there might be certain powers on the part of individuals but no recognition of these powers by others as powers of which they allow the exercise, nor any claim to such recognition and without this recognition or claim to recognition there can be no right."

Rights can be called natural rights if we regard them as rights inherent in the moral nature of man living in society. Ideal rights are broader and deeper than actual or legal rights which are recognised at any time by a state. Rights are related to morality in the sense that they are the conditions for the attainment of the moral end and recognition is given to them by the moral consciousness of individuals.

According to Green, rights are distinct from law because actual rights embodied in the laws of a country do not come up to the level of the ideal system. Rights are distinct from morality because while they can be enforced by external sanctions, morality cannot be so enforced. Right of resistance can be given to the people. He criticizes the term "Natural Law". He brings clearly the difference between natural law and positive law. He denounces the idea of state of nature advocated by the writers of social contract theory. At the same time, Green has interchanged the term "natural law" with the phrase "the law of God." Natural law is very useful and also responsible for the society to reach its goal. It is different from positive law and moral duty. Morality is a condition of the inner mind and its primary characteristic is freedom. Morality can never be enforced by external pressure.

According to him, it is wrong to think that the state is sustained by the coercive power. On the other hand, it is sustained by the General Will. According to Lancaster, "A true state is one in which power is exercised according to law and for the maintenance of rights." Thus, the basis of state is the evolution in the ideals and rights which are natural to man in society. Green while stating his theory of General Will, rejected the theories of political obligation expounded Spinoza, Hobbes, Locke and Rousseau as being too abstract and illogical.

In his 'Lectures on Political Obligations' Green begins by analyzing man's relation to nature. According to him, the most conclusive fact differentiating man from other living things is self-consciousness. "Human consciousness postulates liberty. Liberty involves rights and rights demand the state." To attain an eternal or common consciousness of a common end freedom is essential for them. Thus, the state itself becomes the product of this consciousness to promote the good of all.

The concept of liberty advocated by Green is closely connected to the Kantian idea of moral will and freedom. According to Kant, "A person who is really free is one morally free." The state should not check its self-determination but must promote those conditions under which morality can be possible. The morality which consists in the disinterested performance of self-imposed duty. Moreover, it is the duty of the state to remove all hindrances that prevent the realization of moral will. He does not accept the view of Hegel that the state is the realization of freedom. Man needs positive freedom. That positive freedom is for social good. It implies both legal and actual possibility.

Green discusses the question why people obey the state. People obey the state because it contributes or can contribute their moral life. State was a society of societies. There state supremacy over the associations is limited. According to Green, the right to free life is the essence of citizenship. Rights are possessed by individuals from the state and enjoyed by them as citizens of the state. As the state is the source of those adjustments it must possess the ultimate power. To him the object of punishment is to create terror which will prevent others from committing the crime. Thus, Green with his practical knowledge of the problems of the state and his faith in political liberalism tried to make individualism moral and social and idealism civilised and safe. Indeed his unshakable faith in man as a self-conscious and self-moralizing entity has a sound metaphysical basis.

Contributions

Thomas Hill Green was the son of an Anglican parents of pronounced evangelical views and his attempt to reconcile Hegelian idealism with Bentham's individualism is to be explained largely by his environment. The measures which the Parliament of his days was taking such as prescribing hours of labour laws, factory inspection, education grants, sanitary regulations and land-tenure reform involved a changed view of the nature of the state and of the individual than what was presented to by Benthamite radicals. These practical measures being taken by the British Parliament were not fully consistent with theory of Benthamism. Green attempted to bring about a reconciliation between the theory of Benthamism and the practice of the English Parliament and he adopted to the England of his day certain ideas of the state, the individual personality and their reciprocal relations, borrowed in some cases from the continental idealism and in others from native sources. Most of these ideas had been implicit in Mill's thought but he never worked them not fully, therefore, in a sense it may be said that "Green made explicit the doubts of the mature Mill."

Green was greatly impressed by the vital truth that Hegel had to teach the reality of the divine reason or spirit which seeks to realize itself in this world produces higher and higher forms of social organization in the process of its unfoldment. But he had a deep sense of the liberty of the subject and refused to believe in the 'reason of the state.' Green's common sense told him that freedom is something to be enjoyed not by an abstraction called the state but by flesh-and-blood individuals, and he unlike Hegel concludes that to speak of the state as the "realization of freedom" is at odds with what is possible or sensible in concrete human affairs.

As an idealist Green rejects the mechanistic view of the state and accepts organic theory of the state. Though he does not make the state an end in itself yet he gives to it the majesty that its nature demands and regards it the final authority in the society. State, according to him, is not a mere collection of individuals formed by the individuals to satisfy their selfish interest and secure material pleasures. On the other hand, it is a natural institution directed to the moral development of its members. He did not glorify the state or raised it to the level of defication yet maintained its supremacy and final authority. According to him, a true state exemplifies to the heightened degree that will for the common good which determines individual action. In such a state, there is constant harmony between individual aspiration and the demands of society. This view of Green comes very near to that of Hegelian conception of the state as the 'realization of freedom.'

But unlike Hegel, Green never regarded the state as an end in itself. It was merely a means to the end of full moral development of the individuals living within the state. Like Kant, Green believed that every man had worth and dignity which forbade his exploitation for any purpose whatsoever. In the words of Green, "the life of the nation has no real existence except as the life of the individuals composing it." Again, "so speak of any progress or improvement or development of a nation, or society of mankind except as relative to some greater worth of person is to use words without meaning." He defined strictly the functions of the state and by describing these functions in a negative way he showed that what mattered most must remain within the province of the individual. Green was never tired of telling that institutions exist for men. To quote him, "The value of the institution of civil life has in their operation as giving reality to the capacities of will and reason and enabling them to be really exercised.

Green never vested sovereignty in the state. According to him, it rested in the General Will. He described General Will as "the common consciousness of a common good." For him, the General Will was not the will of the state but it was a will for the state. He rejected Hegel's view that the laws of the state were synonymous with the General Will. The existing states were not necessarily the embodiment of the General Will. That is why Green recognised the right of the individuals to disobey the state in certain circumstances. Hegel could never recognize such a right of disobeying the state. Green's main interest was in protecting the individuals against the power of a Leviathan state. He traced individuals right not to the will of the state but to life in smaller associations and looked upon the state as only the reconciler of rights which it had not itself developed.

Green thus had a faith in the dignity of the individual and it was his faith in liberalism that made him a sober individualist. He injected a dose of morality into Bentham's individualism and rested state functions on a moral foundation. He viewed the man not as a pleasure seeking individual but as pursuing the moral ideal — the development of the free moral will. Liberalism thus became moral in his hands. It also became social inasmuch as the individual sought the development of his moral will in relation to the development of like will by others. He defenced private property on the ground that it is necessary for realizing a will that is possibly a will directed to social good. Resistance to the state is justified only when it is in the name of the common good. Then he made the idealism civilized by pruning away its absurdities and making the state a means rather than end in itself. He insisted that the state can have no end of its own but the development of the free moral will of its members. Green, as Barker points out, was not trammelled by any idealization of the majesty of the state. The individual remains the basis of his thought, Green restored liberalism to a respectable place by putting a faith in the dignity and worth of man as a moral agent. According to Barker, "Green was both a soaring idealist and a sober realist. We may differ from him with regard to certain details; but the general principles laid down by him are as sound today as they were when they were laid down by him. His firm hold on the worth of persons, his deep sense of liberty of individuals, his conviction that individual good is an intrinsic part of social good, his refusal to raise the state to mystical heights, his recognisation of a universal brotherhood and international law, his eagerness to place limits on the power of the state so that spontaneity in the performance of moral acts may not be deadened, his emphasis on rights, his view that property is a means for the expression of personality, and his admission that in extreme cases the individual has duty of resistance — all these are as sound today as they were when Green delivered his lectures in 1879-80." According to Sabine, Green's revision of liberalism closed up the gap which Laissez Faire has placed between politics and economics and put on government the duty of regulating the economic system when it fails to produce humanity satisfying results. According to MacCunn, "If it be individualism to see in every political movement the fate of human beings and in every controversy over institutions the weal or woe of fellow citizens, then there are few more declared individualists in political philosophy than Green." According to Maxey, "confronted by the advancing ranks of Hegelian state totalism, utilitarian hedonism, Marxian socialism and Spencerian individualism, liberalism stood helpless and confused. Green restored liberalism to respectable standing in the categories of political faith and gave it a working theory that enabled it to function enact as a positive political principle." To conclude with the words of Wayper, Green gave Englishmen something more satisfying than Benthamism at a price they were prepared to pay, that he left liberalism a faith instead of an interest, that he made individualism moral social and idealism and civilized and safe.

Summary of Green's Political Ideas

(1) Green accepts the organic concept of the state though he refuses to regard it an end in itself. To him it always remains a means to the moral development of its members.

(2) Freedom is not more absence of restraints but it very much a positive power of doing or enjoying things worth doing or worth enjoying. Freedom consists in the process of self-development.

(3) The state cannot promote morality directly as it cannot enter into the inwardness of our actions. It can only help in an indirect way in the process of self-realisation.

(4) Will, not force is the basis of the state.

(5) The basis of political obligation is not the power of coercion possessed by the state but because it contributes towards the moral life of the individuals.

(6) Green's purpose is not to form the machanism of the government but to discover the true basis of political obligation.

(7) Green limits the functions of the state to hindering the hindrances to good moral life.

(8) Rights are not merely personal but also social and moral.

(9) Green condemns war and regards it an attribute of an imperfect state.

(10) Green favours the idea of international brotherhood and visualizes the possibility of eradicating the war altogether.

(11) Green regards property as essential for the free play of man's moral faculties but would like to resistant it in a way that its possession by anyone does not interfere in the way of moral development of another. He would limit the property in land though not in capital.

(12) Green injected the dose of morality into individualism and removed the absurdities of idealism.

(13) The individual remains throughout the basis of his state. He made idealism safe and civilised.

39

Francis Herbert Bradley (1846-1924 A.D.)

Early Life: Francis Herbert Bradley was born in 1846 at Glasbury in South Wales. He was the son of the Dean of Westminster. He studied in the University College, Oxford. In 1870, he was awarded a fellowship at Merton College there. He devoted his full time in writing after his studies.

His Works: Bradley's philosophy is to be found in his book called, "Ethical Studies". It was published in 1876. It was his first major work. This book contained a large number of extracts from Hegel. Further he exposed the confusions of the doctrine of utilitarianism as held by J.S. Mill. His other works are: "The Principles of Logic" and "My Station and its Duties." Shortly before his death, at Oxford in 1924, he was awarded the Order of Merit. He was the first philosopher to receive this honour in spite of the opposition of Lloyd George, the Prime Minister of England and King George V.

His Views: Bradley's major work is very critical and constructive. He thought that it was his bounden duty to free English thought from the dominance of individualism and empiricism. His criticism rests on the Hegelian theory that nothing is completely real except the absolute and that the common sense, beliefs, scientific theories, religious dogmas and moral principles although justifiable within limits, do not contain anything wholly true. It is pointed out that if T.H. Green was more Kantian than Hegelian Bradley was more Hegelian than Kantian.

Bradley expounds his theory of the state in his major work, "My Station and its Duties." He gives a definition and a doctrine of state which is more Hegelian than that of Green. In other words, he out and out follows the footsteps of Hegel. He conceives of the society as well as the state as a moral organism. An individual is an integral, organic member of this moral organism and a man is what he is because of his being a member of that moral organism.

According to Bradley, to be moral is to live in accordance with the moral tradition of one's country. It is the duty of every individual to perform those duties which his station in life expects him to perform. If he does so he obeys the law of his being. Man is a social being and it is out of the question for any individual to live alone. Since a man is a member of a community the latter exerts its influence on him from every directions. The very atmosphere which he breathes is social so that the conduct of his being implies in its very fibre relations of community, on whose welfare depends the welfare of the individual. In other words the family, the national and the civilised characters come to a child because of community. One is born as a member of a community which exerts its influence upon him at every stage. Thus, the individual's consciousness of himself is inseparable from his knowing himself as a member of the community.

According to Bradley, an individual is a moral being. He is having definite social relationship in the society. At the same time, he is a member of that society. These relationships represent his station in society. It is already mentioned that he is an organic member of society. Hence, he must find his moral development in the context of these relationships or his station in society. Morality and moral development of a man gradually grow on the basis of his duties done by him.

To Bradley, the state is a system of wholes. It includes all communities which affect man. It is a systematic whole, informed by a common purpose or function. As such it has an outside a body of institutions; it has also an inner side a soul or spirit which sustains that body. Each and every part of this organism has a spirit and consciousness of its own. The parts are part and parcel of the organism. They know their position in the organism. Here Bradley agrees with Hegel in viewing the state as a "self-knowing and self-actualising individual." The right of regulation and control of individuals and associations are given to such states by Bradley.

Like Hegel Bradley conceives of the various social groups as being co-ordinated in and subordinated to the state. It is hence considered as one of the most important ideas of Bradley regarding the state.

Bradley admitted that no state in actual practice was a perfect embodiment of his ideal. The morality of the state was always on a lower state than the conscience of the people or ideal morality. Further an individual may seek to transcend the function allotted to his station in a particular community and may conceive of a higher organism than that of the state. This may lead to the realisation of all humanity as a divine organic whole.

In his both works, "Ethical Studies" and "The Principles of Logic," he acknowledged his debt to German writers. Further, he disclaimed originality. But he was never the simple "Hegelian" that some critics took him to be. In his essay on "My Station and its Duties", he expresses this exposition of the Hegelian conception of social ethics. But Bradley did not hesitate to point out the drawbacks of this doctrine if taken as a complete account of the moral life. In "The Principles of Logic" he does not accept formalism; he tried to treat logic as a special science distinct from psychology on the one hand, and from metaphysics on the other.

The philosophy of Bradley has been severely criticised on many grounds. Firstly, it is said that he had failed to make a distinction between a state and society. There is a danger that this may lead to unlimited state regulation of life. It cannot be denied that such a view gives too much of power into the hands of the state. Secondly, the phrase, "my station and its duties" as it occurs in "Ethical Studies" is difficult to interpret. It means that one should be satisfied with whatever falls to his lot. He has no business to grumble. His only duty is to carry out the duties of his station without complaining. However, such a view is not only conservative but also reactionary. It is detrimental to the growth of humanity. Thirdly, he has been called a wicked man, because there was nothing original or great in his philosophy. Most of his ideas have been found in the philosophy of Greeks. Thus, the philosophy of Bradley has been criticised on many grounds.

40

Bernard Bosanquet (1848-1923 A.D.)

Early Life: Bernard Bosanquet was an English philosopher. He was a great thinker and writer. He was born in the year 1848. During this time of his birth Europe was rocked by revolutions of France. He was the youngest son of a well-to-do clergyman of Northumberland in England. He was educated at Sherburn, Yorkshire and at Harrow. While at Oxford he came under the influence of Green and Jowett. Bosanquet spent ten years as a fellow at the University College, Oxford. In 1881, he went to London. Later on he held the Chair of Moral Philosophy at St. Andrews University of Scotland. He devoted most of his time in independent study. He was very interested in reading novels. Hence, he gave many illustrations from the novels to explain his points. He died in London in 1923.

His Works: Bosanquet was a prominent writer. He wrote many books. His important works are: "Philosophical Theory of the State", "Social and International Ideals", "Logic", "History of Aesthetic", "The Value and Destiny of the Individual" and "Knowledge and Reality."

His Views: Professor Hobhouse describes Dr. Bosanquet as the most modern and most faithful exponent of Hegel. As an idealist, he adopts T.H. Green's principles but drops some of the limitations imposed on the state by Green and thus comes very near the Hegelian conception of the state. In other words, Bosanquet begins his philosophy with Rousseau and Green and ends almost in Hegel. Bosanquet was an idealist that too an Absolute Idealist. Like that of Bradley, Bosanquet was led to formulate his own theory of aesthetics and statecraft in his works.

Will: Like all idealists, Bosanquet also believed in idealism. The starting point of the theory of Bosanquet was a conception of a free moral will as advocated by Rousseau. According to him, true freedom lay in willing rational and universal objects. There are three stages in his doctrine of will viz., distinction between the actual will of the individual and his real will, distinction between the real will of the individual and the general will of society, and the state as the supreme expression of the general will.

(i) Bosanquet used the terms actual and real will in a technical sense. He used the term actual to describe the irrational impulsive and recalcitrant will of man. Bradley pointed out that a man exerted his actual will when he acted from moment to moments as a conscious individual. As that will was corrected and amended by what he wanted at all other moments and was adjusted to the wills of others. It became the real will.

(ii) It is again pointed out by him that the real will of the individual did not stand alone. It was bound with the real wills of other individuals in society and became the general will. It goes without saying that an individual can grow only in society. So the terms general will and the common life of society, were convertible terms. From this, it is seen that full satisfaction of man could not be achieved apart from the satisfaction of the general will.

(iii) Bosanquet further pointed out that the state was the perfect embodiment of the general will. The common life of society depended upon the law and order maintained by the state. Man's life was social. Hence, his individual relations were influenced by the common social life. Society was a group of individuals who were united by common general purpose or interest i.e., the ideal of common mind or general will was not a mere fancy. But it was a living reality.

The State: According to Bosanquet, institutions were the embodiment of ethical ideas. Every social institution or group was a complicated inter-working of the minds of individuals. The totality of the group was reflected in the mind of the individuals. Examples of ethical institutions given by him are the family, the group and the state.

In the formation of his theory of state, Bosanquet was influenced by Rousseau's conception of the liberty of the individual, the general will of the community and their correlation with each other. The state was the source of all pervading adjustments. In a narrow sense, the state was a political organisation using force. It put its seal of approval on all social efforts which were beneficial to society. In a broader sense, the state stood for the general organisation and synthesis of life. It is pointed out here that the state was a necessary factor in a civilised life. It was practically synonymous with society; not an opposing force.

It is known to all that the state is not mere coercive political organisation as it includes the entire hierarchy of institutions by which life is determined. Thus, the state includes the society in it. It is the common substance of the minds of all citizens. The state exists to promote good life. The actions of the state are morally wrong.

According to Bosanquet, "The state is an ethical idea since it is the final working conception of life as a whole". Of all the institutions, it is the supreme institution having a life, mind and will of its own. Its will is the general will. The end of the state is the realisation of the best life as determined by the fundamental logic of the will. Thus, the moral purpose is the end of the state. The state promotes good life by maintaining a general system of rights. Rights are claims recognised by the state to the maintenance of conditions to favorable to the best life.

Public and Private Acts: Bosanquet distinguishes the Public Acts from Private Acts. According to him to steal or murder, to lie or to commit personal immorality cannot be public act. A public act which inflicts loss such as war confiscation or repudiation of a debt is wholly different from murder or theft. It is not the act of a private individual. It can be motivated by private malice. It is the act of supreme power. It has ultimate responsibility of protecting the lives of the individuals. This act of the state is subject to criticism.

Punishment: Bosanquet differs from Green with regard to his view on punishment. He agrees with Green that the reformation of the criminal must be the aim of punishment. At the same time, he differs from Green in assigning to punishment a positive quality. According to him, there are two regions in the mind of every man viz., conscious and sub-conscious. If his sub-conscious region is affected by an incident or by an accident sooner or later it affects his self also. Hence, punishment may affect the conscious will as to bring about a lasting reform in the character of the person punished. Thus, it is obvious that the object of punishment is not merely deterrent but also reformatory.

Bosanquet and Green: We have seen already that Bosanquet started with Green and ended in Hegel. There are some differences between the two English political thinkers — Bosanquet and Green, (i) Both stood for the necessity of the state for the realisation of the higher life of man. However, Green was not ready to sacrifice the individual for the sake of state. Bosanquet gave a high place to the state. Further he was prepared to subordinate the individual to the state, (ii) Regarding the nature of the state and the proper sphere of state action there is not so much of difference between them, (iii) Both believed that the state was an ethical institution. It could not be used directly for promoting morality, (iv) Both of them never favoured absolute monarchy. They were true to the English Parliamentary Government and considered it as the very best form of government, (v) Bosanquet and Green differed on the question of resistance to the state. According to Green, the individuals had the right of rebellion may be regarded as unnecessary and unwarranted, (vi) Regarding punishment they differed very much. Both of them believed in the deterrent nature of punishment. Bosanquet had positive views than Green in this respect. The former put stress on the psychological aspects of the problem. In other words, the object of punishment is not only deterrent but also reformatory, (vii) Both of them hold different views on the question of war and international morality. Green severely condemned was since it violated the right of every rational being to free life. But in the case of Bosanquet, the acts of the state and the personal acts of individual statesman were different from one another.

Criticism: Many criticisms have been levelled against the philosophy of Dr. Bosanquet:

(1) Critics point out that he put too much importance to the institution of state. According to him, the state is the supreme community. Hence, it will make the state irresponsible and tyrannical.

(2) The identification of the state with society by Bosanquet is wrong. Because the individual was practically merged into the state. It is not conducive to human freedom and progress. Consequently, it cannot be defended.

(3) The conception of social mind or social will and social organism of Bosanquet has been attacked by many writers. It is very difficult to separate the mind from the body.

(4) In the philosophy of Bosanquet there is no scope for an international organisation or international law.

(5) The Social will of Bosanquet has been clearly explained. According to Hobhouse, his (Bosanquet's) distinction between the actual and real will is false. Since Bosanquet used the two terms actual and real in the technical sense, his criticism is not proper.

41
Graham Wallas

The main contribution of Graham Wallas to Political Theory lies in the attention that he gave to the role of psychology in determining man's behaviour in society. According to him, most political writers have an inadequate or even an inaccurate knowledge of human nature. They do not know how men actually think and act. The old political thinkers had drawn an ideal picture of man's actions and thought him to be man of pure reason. This led to an unsatisfactory state of affairs. "For the moment, therefore, nearly all students of politics analyse institutions and avoid the analysis of men. The study of human nature by the psychologist has, it is true advanced enormously since the discovery of human evolution, but it has advanced without affecting or being affected by the study of politics." The major achievement of Graham Wallas lies in enriching the study of politics with the facts of psychology and in enriching psychology with the facts of political problems and theories.

Graham Wallas drew from the laboratory or his life. As he himself says: "my main material has been derived from any experience during more than 40 years, as a teacher and administrator, and from the accounts of their thought processes given by poets and others who were not progressed psychologists, by some of my students and by friends in England and America."

The problem before Wallas was as to how far the knowledge accumulated by psychology could be made useful for the improvement of thought to processes for a working thinker. The most important point made out by Wallas is that human conduct is governed got so much by reason as for sub-conscious process and instincts. He opens his book 'Human Nature in Politics' with the assertion: "The study of politics is just now in a curiously unsatisfactory position." The position was unsatisfactory because the expectations aroused in the minds of thinking people have not been fulfilled. The working of democracy has left people disappointed. The common view was that failure of democracy was due to lack of equality of education or due to limited franchise. But Graham Wallas held this view to be wrong.

In his opinion, failure of democracy and other political institution was because enough attention had not been paid to the facts of human nature. Man is not a man of pure reason but is "a creature compact of emotions, impulses and instincts as well as conscious reason". The political doctrines based on the view of man as purely a rational be adequate. Such doctrines bear no relation to reality. Therefore, Graham Wallas asked his readers to do away with the intellectuality of mankind. He says that "if a faithful record of all that an individual does and says in the course of a day were to be kept, we would find that a very small number of activities are the result of a deliberate search for the means of attaining ends. Most of them would be found to be either half-conscious repetitions under the influence of habit of movements which were originally more fully conscious or to have their basis in the impulsive and instinctive endowment of human nature."

To quote him, "politics is largely a matter of sub-conscious processes of habit and instinct, suggestion and limitation, and only in a slight degree the product of conscious reason." In other words, according to Wallas, reason has very little to do with man's actions and consequently with political process. The secret of a successful politician lies in his appeal not to a man's reason but to his emotions, instincts and suggestion. The appeal to emotions, as he says is the stock-in-trade of all skilled political leaders.

In short, the contention of Graham Wallas is that a student of politics must not deal with abstract men. He should deal with a full man-a-man, "creature compact of emotions, impulses and instincts as well as conscious reason." He wanted the people to overcome the tendency to exaggerate the intellectuality of mankind. Graham Wallas refers to the important impulses and instincts which influence human actions. The most important of them are affection of love, fear, desire for property, the desire to excel and the instincts of suspicion, curiosity and fighting. As a result of the impulses and instincts, the mind of men act like a harp all of whose strings throb together. Emotion, impulses and inference are often simultaneous and intermingled aspects of a single mental experience, action built on unconscious motivations is likely to prevail over rational appeals. The non-rational conduct of a man is strengthened when he believes as a member of the crowd. In a group the primitive instinct of the herd makes itself felt.

According to Wallas, "The empirical art of politics consists largely in the creation of opinion by the deliberate expectations of sub-conscious non-rational inference." The appeal to emotions is the stock-in-trade of all the political leaders. This is clearly manifest during elections. The party flag, the party election-symbols, the party slogans all tend to create public opinion by a deliberate appeal to the emotional suggestibility of the people. "The party names and symbols, the party colours, placards and songs are all lose on the suggestibility of the electorate." Graham Wallas thus refuses that in political life men act on some kind of inference as to the best means of achieving a pre-conceived end. He maintains that in politics men act under "the immediate stimulus of affection and instinct, and the affection and interest may be directed towards political entities which are very different from those facts in the world around us which we can discover by deliberate observation and analysis." Wallas asserts that a great majority of people live, as far as their mental and intellectual life is concerned, under the conditions of crowd: they substitute non-rational for rational inference. It is no longer even necessary to be gathered together in one place for suggestion to have its effect. The radio, the press and the cinema do their work too well. This is very well-illustrated by the excitement caused during the Second World War.

It may not, however, be concluded that Graham Wallas was an irrationalist. He did not exclude reason completely from politics. All that he intends to do was to point out that we must not ignore the important part played by impulses and instructs in political life. He merely emphasised on that aspect of human nature which was not given due prominence by other writers. He believed that the realization of the important part played by impulses and instincts would help to find out ways and means of remedying the disease and thereby making the politic a better one.

It is wrong to say that Wallas had no faith in education. He said that latest developments in psychology should be applied to the study of political institutions. Statistical method should be applied to the study of political occurrences. A systematic study of human nature combined with a statistical study of political institutions will provide better solution to the political and social problems humanity is faced with. We must recognize the complexity of human nature and forget the half-truths about uniformilites. We must take into consideration the group of individual differences. It is only then that we can arrive the scientific data by a quantitative classification of facts.

In his other words, particularly, "The Great Society", Wallas discussed the impact of the industrial revolution on man's social and political life. In this work, he refers to the contradiction between the progress of technology and the backwardness of social sciences.

Although advanced knowledge has been gained in the fields of psychology, sociology and political science, yet this knowledge has not come to inform the life of the people. While the social environment has changed radically due to impact of technology on society, the instinctual and impulsive life of man has changed very little. The result is a disharmony between the inner life of the individual and his social environment, because the latter frustrates man's instincts and intuitions.

In short, Graham Wallas wanted to reform the political institutions by leavening them with the fresh ideas that had developed in the field of psychology. It is certainly a great advantage to be told that there is a whole sub-conscious side human nature on which suggestion plays and where habits are formed and imitation works. We must study and analysis it, if we are to arrive at a true political theory.

Though the views of Graham Wallas have been criticised from various points of view, yet he made a great contribution to politics and wielded great influence. His writing won for him a high place in the literature of politics.

According to Rockow, "It is true that Wallas was not the first or the only writer who exposed the fallacies of the past political psychology, but it cannot be denied that in the detailed application of contemporary psychological knowledge to the concrete institutions of the democratic "state, Wallas was a pioneer."

Wallas brought to bear on politics an inductive method, the wider social experience of democracy and a truer psychology than that of the Benthamites.

He found that there was a lot of difference between the practical politics and politics taught in academic institutions.

He emphasized the discrepancy between fact and theory and wanted others to keep the same always in mind.

Although he found defects in democracy and stood for certain reforms, he did not distract the same.

His view was that the institutions could be reformed by a critical examination of the problem based on actual facts was opposed to hasty generalisations.

Our conclusions should be based on solid facts. To conclude, Graham Wallas made a great contribution to politics. There are very few books on politics which do not make a reference to his works. His quantitative method is followed all over the world.

42
McDougall

McDougall's contribution to political thought cannot be minimised or underestimated. He enriched politics by his psychological contribution. He was a contemporary of Graham Wallas. His approach to social phenomena is like that of Wallas anti-intellectual. He also views conduct as the resultant of social forces working upon the inherited instincts and tendencies of the individuals, and rejects the view that man is intelligently determined in his actions. His views compete those of Graham Wallas.

In his most important work 'Introduction to Social Psychology', McDougall substitutes the dynamic conception of psychology to the traditional view which regarded it as the state study of the state of consciousness. Like Wallas, McDougall emphasis that political theory in order to be true must take the help of psychology and thoughts of man. He regards man as a bundle of instincts, with reason as their humble servant always alert to satisfy their demands for gratification. He writes, "Take away these instinctive dispositions with their powerful impulses, and the organism would become incapable of activity of any kind; it would be inner and motionless, like a wonderful clockwork whose fire mainsprings have been removed, or a steam engine whose fire has been drawn. These impulses are the mental forces that maintain and shape all the life of individuals and societies, and in them we are confronted with the central mystery of life, and mind and will."

Thus, McDougall assigns high soul to instincts in determining man's conduct. He regards them the prime movers of all human activities and the bases of all social relationships. According to him, man is reasonable only to a slight degree; he is to a very great extent unintelligently moved in quite unreasonable ways, instinct is the primary motive and the native spring of action. Man's actions were not wholly or mainly governed by reasoned classifications regarding their consequences. As matter of fact, these actions can be understood only by tracing them back to certain natural instincts. Without instincts, action would be impossible because the last calculated deliberations were merely a means to ends which were determined by instincts.

McDougall has taken a detailed study of instincts. He has enumerated in his 'Outlines of Psychology' fourteen instincts like the instincts to escape from danger, the instincts of combat, repugnance and disgust, parental instinct, instinctive cry of distress, mating or sex instinct, curiosity, submission, self-assertion, seeking company, food seeking, hoarding instinct, constructive instinct and laughter. In addition to these fourteen primary instincts, there were some minor instincts like those of sneezing, coughing, defection and urination which did not play any great role in social life. However, the major instincts played a very important role and provided all the primary motives necessary for social institutions like family, war, religion, etc.

According to McDougall, the instincts are not acquired by the individual, but are handled down to him by heredity. They were the original of all his activities. Without them the intellectual machinery would be like a factory with the power cut off.

Unlike Graham Wallas, McDougall's method was deductive. That is why Prof. Rockow called him a Platonist. McDougall also rejected the Benthamite view that all human action can be interpreted in terms of self-interest. According to him, the human constitution embodied certain tendencies whose chief characteristic was their disinterestedness of those tendencies. The most important was the love of the mother and that was the most benevolence and altruism. He also held the view that man's nature is pluralistic and that man is moved to action not by one single factor but due to a number of factors. It was not any unitary desire but the manifold and complex tendencies of his nature which determined man's actions pleasure and pain by themselves were not springs of action. They merely modified the duration of a particular action.

McDougall has applied the above principles of human nature in explaining the behaviour of loosely organised groups like a crowd, as well as highly organised groups like army and the state in his book 'Group Mind.' According to him, a highly organised social aggregate is an organic whole. It has separate entity and a distinct individuality. A group has a mental system of its own with the individual mind as units. "Since then, the social aggregate has a collective mental life, which is not merely the sum of the mental lives of its units, it may be contended that a society not only enjoys a collective mental life, but also has collective mind or as some prefer to say, a collective soul." McDougall goes on to say, "The structure and organisation of the spirit of the community is in every respect as purely mental or physical as the structure and organisation of the individual mind." Thus, it may be said that his book "Group Mind" was a reincarnation of Plato's Republic.

The theory of McDougall has been much criticized. He puts too much emphasis on instincts. He has gone to the extremes and overlooked the role of intelligent impulses. Moreover, the behaviour of an individual is the result of both the instinctive impulses and intelligent impulses and it is different to disentangle the influence of the two. Not only our instincts but also intelligence is hereditary.

To quote Prof. Hobhouse: "We inherit not only capacities for sensation and emotion, but also capacities for distinguishing, analysing and contributing them. We have opposed intelligence as the work of the individual to instinct as the product of heredity but intelligence as a capacity is also hereditary. The propensity to inquire and the methods of analysing and comparing used in inquiry, all have a foundation in the hereditary structure."

In short, intelligence is neither separated from nor independent of instincts man both reasons and feels. He is both selfish and altruistic. Moreover, it is wrong to associate a mind to a group as independent for of the separate from the minds of the individuals who compose it. The "Group Mind" is the mind of the individuals who compose it. There is no such things as an over mind or mind over and above the individuals. If society is mental in structure it is in the sense that it exists in the minds of the individuals. By postulating a mind of the Group as independent of the minds of the individuals McDougall glorifies the group at the cost of the individual. Lastly, as Prof. Baker remarks, "McDougall while giving a full account of the genesis of instincts that act in society, hardly shows how they issue into it. He seems to do a great deal of packing in preparation for a journey on which he never starts."

However, it goes without saying that Prof. McDougall has enriched the study of political science by his psychological approach. He has emphasized certain aspects of human nature which were not well-known before.

43
Walter Bagehot

Walter Bagehot is the leader of the psychological school of thought in England. Ever since he wrote 'Physics and Politics', "political theorists have turned social psychologists". They have approached the facts of group life on the assumption that these facts are facts of group-consciousness, which it is their problem to desire and explain by the method which a natural science uses in order to describe and explain the facts of matter. His book is really the beginning of the psychological method.

According to Prof. Hearnshaw, 'Physics and Politics' is a "sociological footnote to the doctrine of evolution prevailing in the sixties."

Bagehot has been rightly called a pioneer in the field of psychological approach.

The problem which Bagehot attempted to solve was "Assuming the truth of the doctrine of natural selection, how are we to account for the momentous transition from the brute level of the struggle for existence to a human level of social organisation and co-operation?" To Bagehot this problem was the essential one and the key to all subsequent developments of the human race.

In answering his problem, Bagehot brings to light the role played by the irrational and sub-rational forces of human nature inherited from the countless ages of revolutionary process. According to him, social development is made possible by the development of the individual and the development of the individual is due to the fact that the mind "in some strange way acts on our nerves and our nerves in some equally strange way store up the consequences and some how the result, as a rule and commonly enough, goes down to our descendants."

In other words, society grows because individual grows and the individuals grow because his experience that are some how stored up in the nervous tissues of the brain are passed on to the offspring by heredity. Thus, according to Bagehot, acquired characters are transmissible. Progress is made possible because of the capacity of the individuals to acquire through conscious efforts certain qualities which they do not possess before and then transmit them to their offspring. The formula of progress is Effort, Conservation and Transmission. As regard the nature of the heritage which a generation receives from the preceding generation it is partly physical and partly psychological. The physical part consists of the reflexes which have become ingrained in the nervous tissues — out actions, impulses and instincts. The psychological part consists of the customs and traditions in the midst of which we grow and which shape our actions. He regarded tradition of the 'cake of custom', as he called it, the principal factor in the making of modern nation.

In the process of social development, Bagehot has marked out three stages — the stage of no polity, the stage of fixed polity and the state of flexible polity. These three stages may also be given the name preliminary age, military age and the age of discussion.

In the preliminary age, there was no polity or organisation. People lived the life of a brute, the life which Hobbes portrayed for the man in the stage of nature. In this age, there were no traditions of knowledge. There was a keen struggle for existence. However, soon the people came to realize that in the struggle for existence, "an aggregate of families owing even a slippery allegiance to a single head would be sure to have the better of a set of families acknowledging to obedience to anyone, but scattering loose about the world and fighting where they stood." This realization led to the development of co-operative bond. Bagehot writes: "Unless you can make a strong co-operative bone, your society will be conquered and killed out by some other society which has such a bond." In this way, the second stage in the process of social development is reached marked out by group solidarity enforced through groups customs.

These customs bring out conformity on the part of the individuals to the needs of society and tend to make it strong. During this shape, customs dominate the life of the people. Obedience to them was strictly enforced and made obligatory. There was absolutely no scope for any dissent. There was to be no freedom of thought. Imitation was the order of the day and complete obedience was demanded of every member of the group. In short, the second stage of social development was marked out by a rigid and authoritative system. In other words, it was a stage of fixed polity.

In explaining what led the people to think, act and talk alike Bagehot lays great emphasis on the role of unconscious imitation. He writes: The truth is that the propensity of man to imitate what is before him is one of the strongest parts of his nature. We must not think that this imitation is voluntary or even conscious. On the contrary, it has its seats mainly in very obscure parts of the mind, whose notions, so far from having been consciously produced, that helps in creating the 'cake of custom' and making it powerful. Bagehot's contention is that a vast majority of our sections are based upon this habit of unconscious imitation and not upon conscious reasoning.

Once the problem of achieving solidarity and coherence of the group was solved with the help of the 'cake of customs', there remained the danger that in the absence of any freedom of action and thought, the society may degenerate to stagnation and death. If the society is to make any progress, the 'cake of custom' must be broken but it is not easy to do so. Discussion gives the chance to break the cake of custom. Somehow, discussion entered into the custom-ridden society and once it entered it made its headway. It made the people question the utility of customs and made possible the spread of new ideas. The people became quiet and conscious in their notions. The stage of fixed polity gave place to the stage of flexible polity thus muging in the progress and new ideas.

According to Bagehot, only these societies can make progress which have so broken the 'cake of custom' and entered into the age of discussion. Many civilizations were arrested in their growth because they could not break the 'cake of custom'. In short, Bagehot sees in discussion several good possibilities. It is this discussion which substitutes 'government by discussion' in place of 'government by despotism' and introduces an element of liberalism in the political fabric of society. Bagehot also feels that discussion can modify human nature and teach them to think before they leap. He also sees in discussion, 'the possibility of transforming the sex instinct and diminishing its strength.' However, there can be little doubt that discussion produce new ideas, upsets old beliefs and makes for progress.

Bagehot is famous not only for his psychological approach to the study of social and political phenomena that he gave in his book 'Physics and Politics', but is also known for introducing a new approach to the interpretation of the English political institutions that is found in his another great work, "The English Constitution." Prior to Bagehot, constitutions were deemed only as legal structures. What he did was to relate constitution to life and understand it as a living thing in action. He traces the successful working of the British constitution not to the legal framework it provides but to the character of the Englishmen. According to Professor Dicey, "Bagehot has brought more knowledge of life and originality of mind to the elucidation of the theory and practice of English politics than any other man since Burke."

To conclude, Bagehot occupies a prominent place in English political thought. He was a highly suggestive writer. His emphasis on the role of unconscious imitation and discussion, let subsequent writers to carry further his approach and add more to what he said. He has exercised an abiding influence as a political psychologist and made a valuable beginning towards the psychological approach to the problem of politics. He had a versatile and prolific mind who had the capacity of presenting old subjects into a new light. His treatment of the psychological factors in political behaviour was the most penetrating of his time and may be said to have inaugurated the modern psychological school of political thought.

44
Harold Laski
(1893-1950 A.D.)

Professor Laski is considered as one of the most prominent thinkers and one of the greatest political scientists of the present century. Born in Manchester on June 30, 1893, in a Jewish family, he was educated first at the Manchester Grammar School and later on at New College, Oxford from 1911-14. He finished his education at the age of 20. Thereafter, he served the universities of MacGill, Canada and Harvard, U.S.A. In 1920, he came back to England and was appointed as a Professor at the London School of Economics and Political Science. Later on, he became the Director of that institute. He died in 1950 at the age of fifty-seven.

Laski was a great scholar, political philosopher, an author, a journalist and above all a teacher and a friend. But he was not an academic recluse. He took an active interest in politics, being a member of the British Labour Party from 1930 to 1940. He was also the Chairman of the British Labour Party Executive Committee.

Laski was not dogmatic in his views and opinions. He keenly studied the socio-economic problems of his times, analysed them and suggested practical solutions for them. In the fast changing world, Laski went on changing his own analysis and suggestions. Because of this, there appears to be an inconsistency in his views.

Laski was an ardent exponent of Pluralism, Fabianism and Marxian Socialism. He wrote: "I have never thought it consistent with honesty to be one person in the lecture room and another person outside."

Laski was a great writer. He wrote extensively on the problems of the modern state. In a period of thirty years, he published 30 books, 60 pamphlets and hundreds of articles for various periodicals and magazines. However, some of the most important of his works are:

(1) A Grammar of Politics (1925).
(2) An Introduction to Politics (1931).
(3) The State in Theory and Practice (1935).
(4) The Rise of European Liberalism (1936).

Laski's View of the State and Government

Laski took a pragmatic view of the state and government and concluded that it was only a set of persons exercising political authority without a priori claim to receive the obedience of its subjects. He defined the state in the following words:

"The essence of the state is its power to employ coercion in order to enforce the will of that group or groups which control the government, for it is by the government that the authority of the state is brought into operation. The will of the government is, in its turn, finally determined by the character of the class-relations in society.... It is the supreme consequences inherent coercive power used to protect in the postulate of any given society. That power is exercised by the government in the name of the state, of course, the latter can act only through persons."

Though Laski had become a great champion of Marxian Socialism, yet he was very apprehensive of the monistic state. In 1949, he wrote: "I confess to a frank fear of what I used to call the 'monistic' state; the fashionable phrase of the moment is 'monolithic'. The consequence is in a high degree evil. By concentrating power in a very few hands, it reduces the ordinary citizen to the position of an instrument serving one and he is decreasingly permitted to define and increasingly commanded to applaud, with the knowledge, on his part, that if he is silent, or, still more, if he is critical, he will be regarded at best as a person upon whose loyalty no reliance can be placed." Therefore, Laski demanded a wide dispersal of political and economic power in society. He pointed out that the only way to safeguard the freedom of the common people is to decentralise the bases of political and economic power in the community. Our representative institutions should be so organised as to provide greater participation of the people. And, this would only be possible when there is greater democracy in the political and industrial fields. It would also remedy the existing perversion of our political and economic institutions which is in favour of the propertied classes.

Laski's Individualism

Though Laski was a pluralist, he also consistently believed in the freedoms of the individual and the dignity of human personality. Temperamentally, he was an uncompromising individualist in thought and action. To him, the state had no right to the allegiance of the individual except in so far as his conscience allowed. He wrote: "The claim of authority on myself is legitimate proportionately to the moral urgency of its appeal. The only state to which I owe allegiance is the state in which an individual discovers moral adequacy." He added, "I shall be with my Church and against the state, with my Trade Union, if the impact of the state upon my experience seems inadequate as compared to the impact of the Church; the Trade Union. It is my activity which gives legality to law." From this statement, it is clear to what extent Laski granted to the individuals the right of allegiance to the state. He further said: "We are the more likely to press the state into the services of right, the more we fulfil that duty."

Also, even when Laski accepted the broad details of the Marxian analysis of society, he remained opposed to the theory of dictatorship of the proletariat because he put a great emphasis on the value of human personality as the creator of free society.

Functions of the State

At the same time, Laski put society above the individual and considered the good of all as something superior to the mere good of the individual. He respected the dignity of human personality: believed in liberty and equality; and upheld the right of the individual to enjoy all kinds of rights. And, to fulfil these aspirations he desired the state to create a society which would be free from the exploitation of a capitalist economy or rigours of 'totalitarian' communist economy. He wanted the state to create such healthy and congenial conditions which would promote the welfare of all.

Laski had a consistent faith in democratic state. He believed that the welfare functions of modern democratic states were inextricably mixed up with the economic functions of the state. And, since it is the duty of a welfare state to promote the economic welfare of all the people, it is imperative for the state to intervene in the spheres of production and the distribution of essential commodities. He, therefore, suggested that the state should perform the following important functions:

General Functions

(i) The state should provide sound defence and maintain police to protect the individuals from foreign aggression and internal disturbances.

(ii) While respecting the dignity of the human personality, the state should regulate the activities of the individual so that he may not become a hindrance in the way of social welfare.

(iii) The state should take measures to eliminate the evils of capitalism. It should turn free competition into co-operation and promote social amity among the employers and workers.

Economic Functions

(i) The state must act to suppress the anti-social activities of private producers, who may bring about artificial shortages or unnecessarily boost up prices to the detriment of the whole community. For this purpose, it may pass necessary legislation.

(ii) The state should intervene in the spheres of production and distribution of essential commodities. If need arises, the state should not hesitate to nationalise them. This will ensure continuity of supply, reasonable prices and a guarantee of quality. However, the motive behind nationalisation should not be profit but social service and the welfare of the society.

(iii) In the field of production of items for comforts and luxury, the state should merely be concerned with quality control.

(iv) The state should regulate the system of currency and have the power of taxation.

Social Functions

(i) The state should pass legislation to provide for healthy working conditions, to regulate working hours, and to give minimum wages to the workers.

(ii) The state should provide education, employment and insurance against sickness.

(iii) The state should encourage research and cultivate a scientific outlook and thinking.

(iv) The state should maintain a system of courts to give effect to the legal principles.

In his book, The Rise of European Liberalism, Laski traced the historical evolution of the theory and practice of liberalism. He interpreted this evolution in economic terms and concluded that the changes in the political theory and practice of liberalism were conditioned by the economic exigencies of the different phases of capitalism. In this way, he substantiated his thesis about the calls character of the modern liberal state, by examining its historical background. Finally, he concluded that the philosophy of liberalism had now entered into a phase of decline on account of the inherent contradictions and a developing crisis in the capitalist system. The only philosophy which can take its place now is the philosophy of socialism.

And, to conclude our topic we can say that the Laissez Faire individualism (also called negative liberalism) favoured the minimum functions for the state and desired the maximum freedom of the individual. The doctrine of Laissez Faire individualism was justified on economic, political, moral and scientific grounds. It was argued, on the economic basis, that a free and uncontrolled economy would necessarily lead to the development of a free society and economic prosperity of the individual as well as of the society as a whole. It is because every individual was the best judge of his self-interest and left to himself, he shall give his best and produce the best results. On the political plane, it is suggested that the more the functions of the state, the more would be its powers and proportionately less the freedom of the individual. It would neither be conducive to the individual nor the society. On moral grounds, it is pointed out that if the functions of the state are increased, the individual would lose initiative and become dependent on the state. Thereby his personality would be dwarfed and he shall become a parasite on society. On the scientific basis, the exponents of Laissez Faire individualism banked on the Darwinian theory of the "survival of the fittest." They opined that this principle should be applied to the human also and only those who have the capacity to survive should survive. The state should not give any assistance to those who are unable to survive on their own.

In brief, Professor Gilchrist summarised the main functions of the state as propounded by the Laissez Faire individualists as follows:

(1) Protection of the state and individuals from foreign aggression.
(2) Protection of individuals against each other, i.e., from physical injury, slander, etc.
(3) Protection of property from robbery or damage.
(4) Protection of individuals against false contracts or breach of contract.
(5) Protection of the unfit (Herbert Spencer did not favour it).
(6) Protection of individuals against preventable diseases as plague or malaria.

Laissez Faire individualism remained a popular doctrine till the last quarter of the nineteenth century. But after the Industrial Revolution (1760-1830), the liberal thinking regarding the state and the functions it performed underwent a change. Laissez Faire individualism (or negative liberalism) now gave way to positive liberalism. As Barker also says: "By 1880 the doctrine of Laissez Faire — the preaching of non-intervention as the supreme duty of the state, internally as well as externally — seems to have passed."

The reasons for this change, i.e., from the negative to positive liberalism, were many. The rise of capitalism resulted in massive exploitation of the working classes. Their conditions of work were horrible, the hours of work very long, wages a bare minimum for survival, and the standard of living very low and bad. This extreme exploitation, naturally, resulted in extreme reactions — idealistic, humanist, utopian socialist, Marxist and of those, who believed in positive liberalism.

The idealists did not agree with the individualists' view that the state is a necessary evil or an artificial thing. They maintained that the state is not a means but an end in itself. The humanists wanted the removal of the inhuman working conditions and demanded a positive role for the state. The Utopian socialists pointed to the injustices of capitalism and demanded a more humane consideration of the working classes and appealed to the conscience and reason of the capitalists. The Marxists challenged all the tenets and principles of capitalism. The accumulated effect of all these reactions to the Laissez Faire individualism was the growth of the theory of positive liberalism.

Positive liberalism, unlike the Laissez Faire individualism desired the state to perform social, economic, moral and cultural functions. It did not consider the state a 'necessary evil' but a positive good— an institution which could bring equilibrium, harmony and prosperity in society. Presently, the liberal states all over the world do not merely provide protection or maintain law and order but they also care and look after the general welfare of society. They create a congenial environment for the social, economic, political, moral and intellectual development of citizens. They give encouragement to art, literature, philosophy and education. The increase in the functions of the state has also increased the responsibility, power and influence of the state. And, the future of the doctrine of positive liberalism is inextricably bound up with the proper use or misuse by the state of its powers and responsibilities.

Harold Laski's Views on Liberty

Harold Laski was a consistent believer in the dignity of human personality. He was temperamentally an uncompromising individualist in thought and action. He contended that the individual must consult his conscience before deciding to obey or disobey the particular command of the sovereign. The state, he opined, which insists upon an unquestioning obedience to its orders by its citizens, reduces them to the status of moral slaves. He criticised the Hegelian conception of freedom as dialectical fraud as it equated slavery with freedom. He also criticised the modern inegalitarian society because it prevents a large majority of people from securing the material foundations of spiritually enriched life. Therefore, he revised some of the well-known dogmas, which Mill stated in his essay "On Liberty" and discussed them in the context of an international situation, when the success of fascism was posing a serious danger to the ideal of freedom in all countries. Laski always remained a consistent champion of human freedom in all its variegated aspects.

According to Laski, liberty means the eager maintenance of that atmosphere in which men have the opportunity to be their best selves. He regarded rights as an essential condition of liberty. Without rights, Laski opined, there can be no liberty because in that case men are the subjects of law unrelated to the needs of personality. Freedoms are opportunities which history has shown to be essential for the development of personality, and, freedoms are inseparable from rights. If the rights are not guaranteed, liberty becomes uncertain and illusory.

Prof. Laski has given a very comprehensive definition of liberty. He defines it in the following words:

> Liberty is the eager maintenance of that atmosphere in which men have the opportunity to be their best selves. It is a product of rights. Without rights, there can be no liberty because in that case men are the subjects of law unrelated to the meeds of personality. Liberty, therefore, is a positive thing. It does not merely mean absence of restraint.

Laski did not approve of Mill's classification of human actions into two parts, i.e., self-regarding actions and other regarding actions. According to him, all conduct was social in the sense that whatever a man did, affected the other members of society. He, therefore, lays emphasis upon the relationship of the individual's liberty with the society and is convinced that personal liberty cannot be enjoyed in isolation from society. In this context, Laski maintained that liberty also "involves restraints because the separate freedom I use are not freedoms to destroy the freedoms of those with whom I live."

An important aspect of the positive concept of liberty of Laski is the availability of opportunities for the development of the personality of the individual. Laski says: "The freedom I must possess to enjoy a general liberty are those which, in their sum, will constitute the path through which my best self is capable of attainment.... Freedoms are, therefore, opportunities which history has shown to be essential to the development of personality." This succinctly explains the positive character of liberty as visualised by Laski.

Laski refers to three different aspects of liberty. They are: (1) The Private or Individual liberty; (2) Political liberty, and (3) Economic liberty. He explains them as under:

1. Private Liberty

It means the opportunity to exercise freedom of choice in those areas of life where the results of an individual's effort mainly affect him. Laski defines it as "that aspect of which the substance is mainly personal to a man's life. It is the opportunity to be fully himself in the private relations of life." Such a thing is religion and the state should not interfere in it. Individual or private liberty also means legal protection to all alike. Private liberty is infringed if the law does not provide legal protection to the poor. Laws must be such as can be taken advantage of both by the poor and the rich. Accordingly, the demand for an excessive bail would amount, according to Laski, an invasion of private liberty.

2. Political Liberty

Political liberty, according to Laski, "means the power to be active in the affairs of the state. It means that I can let my mind play freely about the substance of public business." There should be no discrimination against an individual. Laski enumerates two essential conditions which are necessary for political liberty. They are education and a free press. According to Laski, every one has a right to receive a minimum of education. This would enable him to express his views to others. It would also help him to understand his own problems as well as those of society. Laski seems to believe in the Sophist dogma that "First of all things, I place education."

The freedom of the press is also necessary to make the political liberty of the individuals as real. He says: "A people without reliable news is, sooner or later, a people without the basis of freedom." If he press in not free and the people do not get correct news, they are not in a position to make up their own mind with regard to the problems which confront them. And, if the very basis of their judgement is wrong, the judgement itself cannot be right. Therefore, what is required is a free press so that people are guaranteed the flow of correct and unbiased news. This will ensure political liberty to the people.

3. Economic Liberty

Economic liberty means that every one has a right to earn his livelihood. It also implies that the people should be provided gainful employment by the state. According to Laski, economic liberty means "security and the opportunity to find reasonable significance in the earning of one's daily bread.... I must be safeguarded against the wants of tomorrow." Citizens should be free from the constant fear of unemployment and insufficiency. Economic liberty implies democracy in industry. This means that the workers should have a share in the administration of the productive system. The workers should not be merely cogs in the machine. They should be active participants in the management of the industry and in decision-making. If economic system is based upon fear, it is fatal to the release of creative faculties and is consequently incompatible with liberty.

Conditions for the Realisation of Liberty

According to Laski, there are three conditions which must be provided for the realisation of liberty. They are as under:

The first necessary safeguard is that there should be no special privileges in society. Freedom cannot "exist in the presence of special privileges." All persons must be considered as equal before access to power. No person should inherit any special privileges merely because he happens to be born in a rich family. The existence of a privileged class is suicidal for the freedom of the people because it hinders the growth of that atmosphere in which people enjoy their freedom. Thus, the abolition of special privileges, if they exist, is a necessary condition for the realisation of liberty. In this regard, Laski says: "Those who desire the good of all begin by the abolition of special privileges....special privilege is incompatible with freedom because the latter quality belongs to all alike in their character as human beings." Thus, the absence of special privileges is a necessary pre-requisite for the existence of liberty.

The second condition for the realisation of liberty is the presence of rights. There cannot "be liberty where the rights of some depend upon the pleasure of others." No group of persons should be strong enough to take away the rights of ordinary citizens.

The third condition for the realisation of liberty is the existence of a responsible government whose incidence of action should be unbiased. This is a very difficult ideal to achieve, but as far as possible, every effort should be made to achieve it.

Thus, we find that Laski was a great champion of positive liberty and attached great significance to human rights. But interestingly there was a shift in his attitude later on. In the preface to the second edition of his classic, A Grammar of Politics, Laski says: "In 1925, I thought that liberty could most usefully be regarded as more than a negative thing. I am now convinced that this was a mistake, and the old view of it as an absence of restraint can alone safeguard the personality of the citizen."

Laski's Rejection of Some Theories of Rights

Laski carefully distinguishes his conception of rights from certain other conceptions which have been widely accepted by political philosophers in different ages. He totally repudiates the historical theory of rights. Rights, Laski points out, do not mean the grant of some historic conditions possessed in the childhood of mankind but lost in course of time. There is no golden age to which we can return. The position of the modern state is not what it was ever before. He rather takes an evolutionary view of rights and concludes that modern democratic state provides greater scope and opportunity for the enjoyment of rights than any preceding state in history has done.

Laski considers the theory of natural rights as absurd because it conceives rights not as the products of a developing social life of the community but as those prepossessions of human beings which were inherited by the human race from its pre-civic past. He also rejects the view that rights are the reflection of natural order because such an order cannot be permanent in a world where scientific and technological developments are taking place everyday. In the Greek city-states, a free citizen possessed the right to own slaves. Aristotle defended this practice as the reflection of natural order. In modern times, none can agree with Aristotle in regarding slavery as natural. Thus, the natural order of earlier times cannot be the natural order of the present day. Therefore, there can be no permanency with regard to the rights which must be guaranteed to individuals.

Nor does Laski agree with Hobbes that rights imply the power to satisfy desire. There are desires like those of murder or homicide, which cannot be recognised by any decent society. No society will survive if such a proposition is accepted.

As regards the legal theory of rights, Laski accepts its validity only in the realm of jurisprudence. However, he considers it inadequate for the purposes of political science. He says: "It is an attractive theory; for since the courts enforce the will of the state as they discover that will, we know that claims are immediately entitled to recognition. But so purely legalistic a view has nothing to contribute to an adequate political philosophy. A legal theory of rights will tell us what in fact, the character of a state is; it will not tell us, save by the judgement we express upon some particular state, whether the rights there recognised are the rights which need recognition." Therefore, Laski does not agree to the views of the exponents of the legal theory of rights, namely, those of Hobbes and Austin, who defined rights as the expression of the will of the sovereign. Law does not create rights; it merely defines and recognises them for a particular legal community.

Laski on Rights

According to Laski, every state is known by the rights it maintains. We judge, the state according to its contribution to the happiness of man. Therefore, according to him, "Rights are the conditions of social life without which no man can seek in general to be himself at his best." He believes that rights are those powers by means of which an individual develops his personality. He, therefore, suggests that "the foremost duty of the state is to remove the hindrances that come in the way of individual rights." He makes a distinction between political and economic rights and says: "No political democracy can be real without economic democracy." Rights are rights because they are useful to citizens of a state. They may even be opposed to the social, economic and political order in a country. But their validity cannot be challenged because they are necessary for the progress of the people concerned.

Right of Allegiance to State

To Laski, the state has no right to the allegiance of the individual except in so far as his conscience allows. He writes: "The claim of authority on myself is legitimate proportionately to the moral urgency of its appeal. The only state to which I owe allegiance is the state to which I discover moral adequacy." He further observes: "I shall be with my Church and against the state, with my Trade Union, if the impact of the state upon my experience seems inadequate as compared to the impact of the Church, the Trade Union. It is my activity which gives legality to law." From the statement it is clear as to what extent Laski grants to individuals the right of allegiance to the state. He concludes by saying: "We are the more likely to press the state into the services of right, the more we fulfil that duty."

Rights of Individual against State

The question arises whether an individual has any right against the state. Laski's reply is in the affirmative. According to him, it was the duty of the state to provide individuals with those outward environments which were essential for the development of their character. The citizen had claims upon the state and the latter must maintain his rights. The state must guarantee him those conditions without which he cannot attain his best self.

Rights are Correlative with Duties and Functions

Laski believes that rights imply duties and the two are related to each other. A right is not an empty claim. It must be followed by a duty. An individual must perform his duties as it would lead to social good. He enjoys rights as a member of society. Therefore, rights are not independent of society, but are inherent in it. Also, if he has a right, the enjoyment of that right implies a corresponding duty on the part of others. Rights are real only to the extent they have been accepted by others as an obligation. The larger the number of rights enjoyed by an individual, the greater must be the duties discharged by others.

Similarly, rights are correlative with functions. An individual must make his contribution to the social good. Function is thus implicit in right. The number of rights enjoyed by an individual must correspond to the contribution which he makes in person to society. The rights which he can claim must correspond to his contribution. And, the contribution must be personal or it is no contribution at all. He does not contribute by being the child of his parents. He must do something personally which is useful to society.

Rights, therefore, depend upon the performance of the duties and functions by the individuals. They are meant for the development of personality of the individual and the promotion of the welfare of the society as a whole. Laski holds that being the members of the state we enjoy certain rights. Our rights are not against the society. He says: “I have no right to do so as I like. My rights are built always upon the relation my function has to the well-being of society.” On the contrary they could only be found within the society. Rights are meant for self-protection as well as for the protection of the other members of the society.

Particular Rights

Laski’s theory of rights can be made more explicit by a reference to particular rights which he advocates. It needs a detailed explanation of three distinct aspects. They are:

(i) Rights pertaining to the individuals;
(ii) Laski's views on Liberty and their compatibility with the notion of equality, and
(iii) Conditions for the realisation of the individual's rights.

Rights Pertaining to the Individual

Laski has referred to those rights which he considers absolutely essential for the development of the personality of individuals. He believes that the personality of the individual cannot be submerged in the corporation known as the state and so his rights are distinct claims which have validity even against the state. The foremost right of an individual is the right to legal protection. There is no validity of rights of the individuals, unless they are legally protected. Some of the important rights, discussed by Laski may be enumerated as under:

1. The Right to Work

This right is regarded by Laski as the most important right of a citizen. It is based on the idea of the performance of social function. To make life purposeful, the individual must work and contribute his share for the good of the society. Laski says: "The citizen has a right to work. He is born into a world where, it rationally organised, he can live only by the sweat of his brow. Society owes him the occasion to perform his function. To leave him without access to the means of existence is to deprive him of that which make possible the realisation of personality." But this right does not mean that the individual has a right to any particular kind of work. The right to work merely means the rights to be occupied in producing a share of those goods and commodities which are useful for society. If a citizen is not given the right to work, he is virtually denied the right to express his personality. Therefore, it is the obligation of the state and society to provide employment to its members.

Laski pleads for a system of national insurance in case the state is unable to provide work to all its citizens. He also suggests that those who are unemployed should be paid unemployment allowance by the state. He writes: "The principle of insurace against unemployment is integral to the conception of the state.... What is fundamental is the recognition that to be his best self a man must work, and that the absence of work must mean provision until employment again offers the opportunity of work." In order to provide work to all, Laski also suggests that there should be some form of economic planning for the optimum utilisation of the productive labour of the whole populace.

2. The Right to Adequate Wages

A citizen has also the right to adequate wages so that he may have a minimum "standard of living without which creative citizenship is impossible." "The contrast in the modern world," says Laski, "between men and women who have never known a decent house, a decent meal, and clothing that barely protects them against the elements, and those who have never known what it is to have unsatiated a want that the possession of property can supply is an intolerable one."

However, this right does not mean that every individual has the right to equal income. Such a proposition is impracticable. Laski says: "The right to an adequate wage does not imply equality of income; but it does...imply that there must be a sufficiency for all before there is superfluity for some." However, what this right means is that all those, who work must be given sufficient wages to maintain themselves. No person would like to die of starvation when he is giving his very best to society.

Laski believes that the realisation of the right to adequate wages is not impossible. He cites the example of Soviet Russia where goal of full employment along with the increasing standard of living of all citizens has been achieved. He says: "Either the state must control industrial power in the interest of its citizens, or industrial power will control the state in the interest of its possessors. The first need of the masses is to realise the right to adequate payment for their effort. The first principle, therefore, of industrial organisation is a system of institutions directed to that end."

3. Right to Reasonable Hours of Work

Every citizen has a right to reasonable hours of work. This means that no individual will be made to work for very long hours. What is advocated here is that every individual will be asked to put in that amount of work which does not exhaust him completely and thereby makes him unfit to fulfil his duties as a citizen. It also implies fixation of the maximum hours of work so that a worker has enough leisure for his recreational activities. The right to reasonable hours of labour is the right to discover the land of the mind. It is the key to the intellectual heritage of the race. Also the amount of work and leisure should be equitably distributed in the community. There should be no division of the society into a working class on the one hand, and a leisured class on the other.

4. Right to Education

Laski maintains that every "citizen has the right to such education as will fit him for the tasks of citizenship." Education is an indispensable condition for the development of the personality of the individual. Long ago, Antiphon the Sophist said: "First of all things, I place education." Education makes an individual a better citizen. And, a citizen cannot contribute his best self to the community in the absence of proper intellectual training. There is no more "fundamental division in the modern state," says Laski, "than that between those who have the control of knowledge and those who lack such control. In the long run, power belongs to those who can formulate and grasp ideas. Granted that such ability exists in a wide range of inequality, there is yet, once more, a minimum basis of education below which no one of average intelligence can be permitted to fall."

However, the right to education does not mean the right to an identical intellectual training for all citizens. What it means is that every individual must be given that minimum of education which is essential for the performance of duties by him. By minimum education, Laski means the attainment of such traits which enable a man to take rational decisions. To provide education is the responsibility of the state and it should make adequate arrangements for educating its citizens. And, the access to education should not be determined by the capacity of the parents to pay for the education of a child, but it should depend on the calibre of the individual.

The Right to Political Power

Laski also lays emphasis on the right to political power. This right includes three derivative rights. In the first place, it implies that every individual should have the right to vote. In this regard, Laski favours universal adult suffrage. Secondly, it implies a right to get elected as a representative of the people and hold any political office. The considerations of religion, race, caste, creed, colour or sex are irrelevant. Thirdly, it means the selection of the members of bureaucracy on the basis of comparative merit. Laski is aware of the limitations of the workers to enjoy political power in the representative democracies in capitalist countries. Yet, he does not commend the Soviet system either because he believes that this right does not exist there at all.

The Right to Freedom of Speech and Expression

Laski is an ardent and enthusiastic supporter of this right. He considers it absolutely essential for the development of human personality. It is also fundamental to the concept of democracy. Laski is vehemently opposed to the stifling of the opinion in any form or at any time. All opinions, whether in the sphere of politics, religion, morality, science, art or literature should be allowed to be expressed freely without hindrance, censorship or penalty. Even in times of emergency or war, this right cannot be abrogated. He says: "Freedom of speech is a right that war does not mitigate."

Laski explains that this right necessarily arises from the fact that man must give expression to his inner thoughts. If this right is denied, his personality will be dwarfed. It also helps the rulers to become acquainted with the opinion and desires of the people and prevents upheavals in society. He adds: "A government can always learn more from the criticism of its opponents than from the eulogy of its supporters."

However, Laski is cautious that the right to freedom of speech can be protected by full judicial safeguards. He regards preventive detention as inconsistent with the right of freedom of speech. This right also implies a complete and genuine independence of the judiciary and its complete separation from the executive.

The Right to Freedom of Association and Public Meetings

Laski considers this right to be as important as the right to freedom of speech and expression. Being a pluralist, he argues that every individual must be guaranteed freedom to form an association and hold public meetings. The denial of this right, he points out, leads to the formation of secret societies which aim at the destruction of the state. To prevent such eventualities, the democratic states recognise this right of the individual.

Right to Property

Laski grants to the individual the 'right to property', but hastens to add that this right is limited only to that extent which is necessary for the growth of the personality of the individual. He says: "If property must be possessed in order that a man may be his best self, the existence of such a right is clear." But the extent of the property rights is to be determined by the considerations of the common food of the society and the performance of functions by the individual. The individual can have this right only to the extent he contributes to the good of society. Otherwise, he cannot have an absolute right to property. Laski says: "I have the right to property if what I own can be shown to be related to the common welfare as a condition of its maintenance.... No man, in such a background, has the right to own property beyond that extent which enables the decent satisfaction of impulse." Laski's views on the right to property can be succinctly summed up as under:

> "There is nothing inherently wrong in the notion of private property. There is a sense in which it may be so held or genuinely to express personality and to contribute to enrichment. But so to be held, it must be derived from personal effort organised in such a way as to involve an addition to the common welfare. It must never be so large in amount that its owner exercises power by reason of its sheer magnitude, it must never be so small that its possessor cannot be himself at his best. The more equal its distribution, the more likely is the contribution of the citizen to be judged in terms of its social value, to become implicit with purpose as the way to recognition. Regarded as the result of function, it falls naturally into the proper place in society."

How to Safeguard the Rights?

Laski's View:

According to Laski, there are three very essential conditions which help the task of safeguarding the rights of the individuals. They are:

1. Decentralisation of authority;
2. Existence of consultative bodies, and
3. Non-interference by the state in the internal affairs of the associations.

Laski pleads for a decentralised society. In such a society, people are likely to take more interest in those problems which affect them intimately. They develop their critical faculties and cultivate the habit of questioning the authority of the state whenever it violates the laws of the country. Thus, a sense of responsibility is developed among the people and in a decentralised society they get an opportunity to exercise power. Concentration of power at one place, on the other hand, is more likely to create a sense of irresponsibility. Hence, a decentralised society is essential for safeguarding the rights.

A second safeguard for rights is the establishment of consultative bodies in the different departments of the Central government. These consultative bodies should comprise experts whose duty would be to advise the department concerned on the problems facing it and suggesting a course of action to solve those problems. It would, thus, help the government to frame right policies and implement them in the right spirit.

Finally, the state should scrupulously refrain from interfering in the internal matters of other associations. The associations should have full autonomy. They should be allowed to chalk out and implement their own programmes because these associations also help the individuals in the development of their personality. The state should not intervene so long as an association does not openly advocate the use of force for its overthrow.

However, the effectiveness of the above safeguards for the maintenance of rights ultimately depends upon the quality of the people and their organised public opinion. Therefore, in the last analysis, conditions for the maintenance of rights are created by an enlightened and organised public opinion which in turn will depend upon social, economic and political conditions of the state.

To conclude, according to Laski, any system of rights has three different aspects. They are the interests of the individual, the group and the community. Rights must aim at the enrichment of all the three.

45
Other Political Philosophers

(i) MACIVER

MacIver, an American socialist, is a great exponent of positive liberalism. In his writings, he has supported and pleaded for the positive functions of the state. He believes that the state is one of the associations among many others although it exercises functions of a unique character. In his book, The Modern State, he writes: "It [State] commands only because it serve; it owns only because it owes. It creates rights not as the lordly dispenser of gifts, but as the agent of society for the creation of rights. The servant is not greater than his master."

MacIver's Views on the Origin and Evolution of the State

MacIver examines the question of the origin and evolution of the state purely from the sociological point of view. He traces the origin of the state through the family, the institution of property, customary law and war and conquest. MacIver holds that the first of all societies in beast and bird and man is the family, but it cannot exist in mere isolation. The mating impulse leads the adolescent outside the old family to form a new one. Each new family is the union of two families. Families combined to form a gene or clan over which a chief kinsman presided. A still wider group of clans formed a tribe, composed of those who traced descent to a common ancestor, and were ruled over by a chief who possessed military, judicial and religious authority. MacIver observes, the "natural authority of the pater-families prepared the way for the tribal chief."

In this way, he argues that wherever the family exists, government already exists. In the family, the primary social unit, says MacIver, "there are always present the curbs and controls that constitute the essence of government....which is the continuation by the more inclusive society of a process of regulation that is already highly developed within the family. The same necessities that create the family create also regulation.... Here is government in miniature, and already government of quite elaborate character."

Another factor which contributed to the evolution of the state was property. First, there was a change from nomadic life, dependent mainly on pasture, to agriculture and settlement on a definite piece of territory. This led to the replacement of the bond of kinship to that of life in common in given place; it also created the need for an authority able to define and enforce the respective rights of individuals to a share of the land within the territory of the group. In other words, the state appears as bound up with the development of property — first of land, then with other forms of wealth gradually created — and with the problems which property involve. Thus, the institution of private property and its systematic development brought the nomadic herdsmen to the threshold of the state. In fact, MacIver opines, it may be said that property created the state.

Further, MacIver opines that customary law is another important factor in the evolution of the state. He says: "Custom is the king of man." In primitive society, customs regulated the lives of people from birth to death. The customs were enforced by the chief patriarch, who was both a judge and executioner. At a later date, these customs were transformed into laws. Emphasising the importance of customary law in the evolution of the state, MacIver says: "The display of leadership and exercise of authority is found, wherever society exists. It gives form and character to an urchin's club as well as to a cabinet committee; to a gang of thieves as well as to a convocation of clerics. But no one would call all such leadership and authority 'political' and neither should we say that wherever we find a headman in a savage tribe we are in the presence of state. We cannot say when or where the state begins. It is implicit in the universal tendency to leadership and subordination, but it only emerges when authority becomes government and custom is translated into law." Moreover, customary law precedes judges and courts of law. However, MacIver concludes, if custom is to have authority it "must be allowed and sanctioned by myth. If the myth is rejected, the custom collapses."

War and conquest, says MaIver, have played their role not only in the extension of the area of government but also in the consolidation of political power.

Besides the above factors, MacIver adds that the concentration of population in the cities, i.e., urbanization, the division of society into classes and the factors of common race and nationality were responsible for the evolution of the state.

Conclusion

From the above discussion of the origin of the state, it is quite evident that no definite stage in the history of civilisation can be pointed out at which the state may be said to have been born. The state is the result of a slow and gradual growth. It originated and developed through a plurality of factors among which kinship, religion, economic necessities, war and political consciousness have contributed a great deal. These factors worked together, "some more prominently than others and all aided by the forces of history and natural tendencies of mankind, enter into the process by which uncivilised people are brought out of anarchy and subjected to the authority of the state." And, moreover, the pattern of the evolution of the state and the character and circumstances of each people must have definitely varied from one part of the world to another. The transition from family to society and from society to state, as explained, did not take place in a simple, orderly of uniform pattern in the course of a year or two or even thousand years. All the same, the spirit of organisation, as Woodrow Wilson says: "is a natural twin born with man and the family." In its simple and rudimentary form, germs of governmental organisation were found in the family discipline. Religion reinforced family discipline and gradually created a wider discipline necessary for the existence of the state. Custom was the first law and there was a religious sanctions behind every custom and the magicians, who controlled religious sanctions were power for the creation of rights. The servant is not greater than his master. The state alone has the responsibility and consequently the authority to maintain the 'universal external conditions' of social order.

At the same time, MacIver opines, the state is dependent for its responsibilities, liabilities and authority on the will of the community. He does not dispute the continuing need of the state but maintains that the state has the essential character of a corporation. It has definite limits, definite powers and definite responsibilities. As a corporation, "It has the subject of rights and obligations which belong to it as a unity."

According to MacIver, the state is an order-creating organisation. It describes business to maintain order. But, order according to law — law which must have the backing and approval of the community. MacIver does not believe in order for the sake of order. There is such a thing a peace of the desert of order in a military regiment. Such a conception of imposed order does not appeal to the rational and progressive mind of MacIver. Order is for the sake of life. It is the business of the state to provide decent and healthy conditions for a progressive and cultural existence in which the personality of the individual has free scope for development.

MacIver's Concept of a Limited State

In one of the most famous chapters of his book, MacIver deals with the true sphere of the state activities and limitations thereon. He believes in the concept of a limited state, a constitutional state, i.e., a state whose business is carried on according to fundamental rules made for the state by the general will of the community. He does not believe in the concept of an authoritarian, absolutist and omnipotent state. The service rendered by the state is of a limited character. The state should not seek to do everything simply because it is not capable of doing that, being just an association. It can serve or subserve only a limited end and purpose. Many things the state simply cannot do. Many other things it should avoid doing for intruding into spheres that are not properly its own; such intrusions may do more harm than good. MacIver does not agree with the romantic view of Burke contained in the 'Reflections of the French Revolution' that "the state is a partnership in all arts, a partnership in all science, in every virtue and in all perfections." The state is not a mystical unity to MacIver as it appeared to the imaginative mind of Edmund Burke. Whereas Burke was a nomatist, MacIver is a scientist and adopts a rational attitude towards the state and its role and functions.

According to MacIver, the sphere of state action should be determined by what the state can do as an organ (but not the organ of the community). The question for him is not what the state should or should not do but what the state is permitted to do by other social organisations and by the limited nature of the state itself. The state stands for the common interests of all the individuals and associations, "but not for the whole of the common interests." The political interests of thousand associations, cultural and economic, are also parts of the common interest. The function of the state is merely to give "a form of unity to the whole system of social relationships."

Functions of the State

According to MacIver, the twin functions of the state are to respect personality and to maintain order. The former is the negative while the latter is the positive aspect of the state's function. He agrees with the view of T.H. Green that the worth of doing a thing lies in the spontaneous urge to that thing. In other words, state interference and state regulation is a clumsy intrusion in those things which are related to human personality of whose worth and quality are determined by the spontaneous urge of the personality.

MacIver recognises definite limits to political control; 'there are things which are not Caesar's.' These limits are as follows:

State not to regulate or control opinion. The first thing which the state must not seek to regulate and control is opinion, whatever that opinion may be. Opinion should be fought with opinion, not with force. Opinions are the outcome of convictions and, therefore, their forcible suppression would hamper the free growth of personality. However, MacIver admits of two limitations on the free expression of opinion. One is libel. The other is a comment on a sub-judice case. Freedom to express opinion does not mean libellous or defamatory opinion or public comments on a case which is sub-judice.

State also not to regulate morality and religion. MacIver agrees with the idealists in holding that it is necessary to separate the inner sanction of morality from political law. Law cannot prescribe morality. Thus, apart from the freedom of opinion which the state has no right to regulate and control, morality and religion are two other things that are not Caesar's. Morality is essentially personal and individual. It is a matter of conscience and conviction. He says: "The ethical appeal is always to the individual's own sense of what is right and wrong, in the last resort always to his sense of what is good and evil." The state can, through its law, control and regulate only the outward actions of the individual. It cannot reach the innermost springs of human action.

But, MacIver makes it absolutely clear that individual, on moral grounds, is in no way entitled to defy law. If he does so, he must suffer the consequences provided by law. The state cannot be expected to abdicate the discharge of its proper duty which is the maintenance of law and order. He says: "We obey the law but necessarily because we think that the law is right but because we think it is right to obey the law." Law is related to morality but law does not and cannot cover all the ground of morality. To turn all moral obligation into legal obligation would be to destroy morality. Happily, it is impossible.

The State cannot regulate customs. Another thing not Caesar's is the sphere of customs. MacIver says: "Customs grow everywhere in the soil of society, unforced natural growths which reveal the underlying conditions of belief and mode of life." The state has little power to make customs and perhaps less to destroy them, although indirectly it influences customs by changing the condition out of which they spring. The attack on customs can even prove dangerous for the state. MacIver says: "Custom, when attacked, attacks law in turn, attacks not only the particular law which opposes it, but what is more vital, the spirit of law-abidingness, the unity of the general will." However, it does not mean that the state should tolerate every archaic and rotten custom.

State has no control over fashions. Another thing which is also not Caesar's is fashion over which the state has even less control than over custom. Every fashion is rooted in personal preferences and the state cannot possibly regulate it. A king may set a mode by following it himself — but not by prescribing it. The regulation of fashion by the state would surely be regarded as a monstrous tyranny and it might lead to a revolution.

Culture is beyond the competence of the State. Another thing in which the state should not interfere is culture which is the expression of the spirit of a people or of an age. It is beyond the competence of the state. The state reflects it and does little more. Culture is the work of a community sustained by inner forces far more potent than political law. As the state cannot comprehend the intimacies of life associated with culture, it should not regulate or control it.

The State should not interfere with the working of other associations. According to MacIver, the state is one of the 'associations' among many others within the community, although it exercises functions of a unique character. He, therefore, pleads for the full autonomy of 'associations' and points out that the state is not the creator of other associations. They arise naturally and spontaneously and are "as native to the soil of the society as the state itself." The different needs of human beings are best served by different associations. Therefore, there should be due recognition by the state of the important role played by them; they should have full autonomy; and the state should not interfere with them.

Thus, MacIver sets definite limits to the sphere of state activity. The state has limited functions to perform and since there are aspects of life withdrawn from its competence, it should not exercise power which may overwhelm these other aspects of associations which fulfil other functions. Power should be relative to function.

Proper functions of the state. According to MacIver, what the state should do is what, as an organ of the community, it can do. What service it should render is that of which it is in fact capable. The state should provide those external conditions of social living which are of a universal concern in view of the acknowledged objects of human desire. The state is after all a social agent. It is a form of service and not a mystical power.

MacIver decides the proper functions of the state under three broad heads — order, protection and conservation and development. He explains them as follows:

Creation of order: (a) The primary business of the state is the creation of order. To secure universal order within its frontiers is the most obvious thing which the state can do and it has been at all times a peculiar mission of the state. Every state imposes it whether it is democratic or despotic, whether imperial or federal. But the form of order is always determined by a dominate purpose. There is one form of order in a slave state, another among a free people. One form in a class state, another in a democracy. The conception of order changes as we pass from the ideas of state as exploitative to the ideas of state as....administrative. It ceases to be an order as a condition of domination and becomes an order as a condition for the common welfare. Order is then the first business of the state. The order which the state stands for is that universal order which is so desirable and so necessary that the community empowers the state to impose it. The state must provide such conditions that people can lead their lives in a decent relation to one another, to prevent confusion and chaos, to regulate forms of commerce and communications so that life should run more smoothly for all concerned, to see that everything has and holds its appointed place and also holds itself (state) and finally to take in its own keeping and so to minimise the exercise of coercion necessary for the fulfilment of its task — such is the primary function of the state. The state is the governor of the machine of civilisation.

But order is only a part of a larger task. Order within the community is justified only as it serves the needs of the community. Order without further definition is a dangerous term; to insist on order as such is to make the state a police state. An order that is to serve the community must be in conformity with and limited by the ideals of the community, particularly the ideals of justice and of liberty. So MacIver does not believe in order for the sake of order. According to him, the conception of order extends to and includes protection, conservation and development. To protect the weak instead of the strong is a part of the state's function. Such protection is gradually taking the form of provision of minimum standards of living, so that the necessaries of health and decency shall not be denied by accident or misfortune or capacity, to any member of the community. It is being increasingly recognised that men are so bound up in families and groups that the whole suffers from the privation and degradation of any and that the state can act as the Welfare Insurance Corporation.

(b) Just as the conception of order widens into that of protection so does protection in turn finds a wider interpretation in the business of conservation and development. It is the proper business of the state, with its command of resources and its universal reach, to develop the natural resources within its territory and to enable its citizens to lead a decent standard of living. Such like subjects as agriculture, industry, forests, trades and commerce, currency and coinage come within the proper sphere of state activity and state regulation. The state represents the general interests but any other association representing partial interests cannot be permitted to take control of such activities. The state as the general representative of the community and concerned primarily with ensuring the conditions of universal welfare has to undertake the task of economic development. It has to safeguard such interests but it cannot be allowed to exploit and exhaust the natural resources to the detriment of the general interest and of posterity. The trend towards increasing state regulation of economic activities is thus unavoidable.

(c) In addition to the developing natural economic resources, it is, according to MacIver, the proper business of the state to conserve and develop human capacities though this must not be understood to entitle and qualify the state to interfere with or regulate all aspects of spirit and mind.

Twin Functions of the State

According to MacIver, the twin functions of the state are to respect personality and to maintain order. The former is the negative while the latter is the positive aspect of the state function. He agrees with the view of T.H. Green that the work of doing a thing lies in the spontaneous urge to do that thing. In other words, state interference and state regulation is a clumsy intrusion in those things which are related to human personality or whose worth and quality are determined by the spontaneous urge of the personality.

Role of the State

According to MacIver, the state stands for the common interests of all the individuals and associations, "but not for the whole of the common interests." "The political interests of a thousand associations, cultural and economic, are also parts of the common interest." The function of the state is merely to give "a form of unity to the whole system of social relationships."

MacIver, therefore, holds that society is plural, authority is neither unlimited nor independent of the will of the community and the state as well as other associations enjoy allegiance of individual citizens.

As Sociologist

MacIver, a sociologist, views everything from the angle of sociology. He analyses society, the state, human associations, human relationships, their organisations, functions and mutual relationships. After a deep analysis, he comes to the conclusion that the plurality of social life is a fact of the modern society. Like other pluralists he believes that different 'groups' or 'associations' perform very important and vital functions by providing the individual citizens with the opportunity to pursue and achieve their varied interests. These interests, because they are after highly personal, are best served through individual initiative, thus leaving the state to be concerned with general functions.

According to MacIver, the state is one of the associations among many others within the community, although it exercises functions of a unique character. The state alone has the responsibility and consequently the authority to maintain the universal external conditions of social order. At the same time, MacIver opines, the state is dependent for its responsibilities, liabilities and authority on the will of the community. He does not dispute the continuing need of the state but maintains that the state has the essential character of a corporation. It has definite limits, definite powers and definite responsibilities. As a corporation, "it has the subject of rights and obligations which belong to it as a unity."

MacIver pleads for the full autonomy of 'associations' and points out that the state is not the creator of other associations. They arise naturally and spontaneously. They are "as native to the soil of the society as the state itself." The different needs of human beings are best served by different associations. Therefore, they should have a full autonomy in order to perform their functions well and there should be a due recognition of the important role played by them. The grant of autonomy would also limit the powers, jurisdiction and sphere of activity of the state.

A fuller explanation of the 'pluralistic theory' as built up by MacIver is given in the subsequent pages.

Criticism of Monastic Theory

MacIver, like Laski, forcefully criticises the monistic theory of absolute sovereignty and does not accept it as the final power of the state. He considers it the mere exercise of limited function and an attribute akin to the attribute of any other association in society. He says: "The sovereignty of the state is no simple final power, as free and unconditioned over human life as the will of an overruling God might be supposed to be. It is the exercise rather of a function, limited by and dependent on the prevailing conception of what that function should be, and no less limited by, and dependent on, the kind and degree of organisation established for its exercise. It is the attribute of an association and is no more absolute than the association itself." MacIver further points out that the theory of state has too long been dominated by the legalistic conception of sovereignty and opines that the state is nothing but an association like any other association in society and the law of the state is only a form of social regulation. In this regard he writes: "The legalistic doctrine is formal.... Legally, the state is unlimited, but it is no more absolute on that account than, say, the Church, because it is the source of ecclesiastically law, or the royal and Ancient Club, because it alone prescribes the laws of golf.... We merely insist that political law is but one form of social regulation. The state is one of the organs of community, and we must reconcile with this cardinal fact both its great services and its greater claims."

MacIver also condemns the 'power element' inherent in the monistic view of sovereignty. He writes: "The legalistic doctrine speaks in terms of power and not of service. But power is only an instrument of service.... No one ever regards the service of the state as unlimited, and therefore, the conception of unlimited sovereignty is dangerously false. To attribute power to government beyond the limit of its capacity for service is the grave error on which all tyranny is based."

MacIver further maintains that in modern times because of the complexity of social organisation, the old concept of 'unlimited sovereignty' does not hold good. Instead, in the modern industrialised plural society, sovereignty is 'relative' as well as limited. He writes: "The great difference between the political thought of our own times and that of the past is the definite assertion of the limited and relative character of sovereignty. In other ages, men have protested against absolute power, appealing on moral grounds.... The newer doctrine arose out of the social developments of the nineteenth century. The trend towards democracy seemed to settle the question as to the residence of sovereignty, so that men turned rather to examine its nature. The complexity of social organisation which the industrial age had brought, overthrew, as we have seen, the simple anti-thesis of the individual and the state. The real powers exercised by the numerous and often vast associations of the new age confounded the idea of single all-comprehensive authority."

State and Society

Explaining the shortcomings of the 'monistic theory' and the concept of 'absolute state', MacIver points out that it is a misnomer to identify the 'State' with 'Society'. The two, according to him, are not identical. He says: "To identify the social with the political is to be guilty of the grossest of all confusions, which completely bar any understanding of either society or the state." Therefore, in order to have a better understanding of 'Society' and the 'State', it is imperative for us to understand the distinction between the two.

MacIver explains that the two are neither coextensive nor synonymous. Society is the source and matrix of all social organisation. The state is the organisation of society from the political aspect. In addition to the state, society comprises other non-political associations which render useful services to the individual. Man is creature of competing loyalties. Only a part of his life is linked to the state. The state does not exhaust the associative impulse of the individual.

Also, the state far from being identical with society is only an instrument or at the most an organ of society. It has been created for the achievement of certain specific objectives. It is not an end in itself but only a means to the achievement of ends cherished by the social consensus at a particular time.

Further, the state and society are different in their origin, scope, functions, aims and methods of operation.

Society is natural and instinctive, the state is the creation of will and reason. In origin, society is prior to the state. It is an association for the satisfaction of mutual wants. It exists even in the animal world. Wherever, there are inter-developmental and reciprocal relations, there is a society. Man has adopted society and made it more complex. State is a later development. In fact, state is a part of society, but not society itself. "The State", to quote MacIver, "exists within society."

The scope of the state is narrower than that of the society. MacIver says: "There are social forms, like the family or the Churches or the club, which owe neither their origin nor their inspiration to the State; and social forces like custom or the competition, which the state may protect or modify but certainly does not create; and social motives like friendship or jealousy, which establish a relationship too intimate and personal to be controlled by the great engine of the state."

State and Associations

MacIver, like Laski, points out that the state is nothing more than an association and pleads for the independence and autonomy of associations in the society. In addition to the state, society comprises a large number of non-political associations which come into being naturally and independently of the state. Each of these associations, including the state, belongs to the same genus and their ultimate purpose is to enable the individual to satisfy his needs and achieve his best self.

Explaining the importance of associations, MacIver says that the whole course of social development has been characterised by the growth of voluntary associations. In ancient Greece and elsewhere state and society were one but in course of time the Church became so powerful as to challenge the authority, if not threaten the existence, of the state. Similarly, other voluntary associations in the cultural and educational fields emerged to perform a useful purpose which the state either could not or would not perform. After the Industrial Revolution, numerous economic associations came into existence to render useful service to the individual in the economic sphere. Many of these associations have now been legally acknowledged as possessing each a distinct personality of its own. They are given the status of a corporation capable of enjoying rights and owing duties. In MacIver's opinion, the state is also one of the corporations of society. Every association has got a distinct life and sphere of its own. No association can hope to satisfy all the wants and needs of the individual and the service rendered by each association, including the state, is of a limited character.

To MacIver, the source of authority of all associations is inherent in their own nature and functions. Therefore, the state cannot claim absolute power over other associations.

Power, according to MacIver, must correspond to service or functions. In other words, a limited service implies a limited authority of the state. The state is no God, Omni-competence, indeed, means incompetence for though service rendered by the state is of a great value, yet certain things the state cannot and should not do. In certain spheres the state is things the state cannot and should not do. In certain spheres the state is but a clumsy instrument. We do not sharpen pencil with an axe. What the state should do depends upon what it is capable of doing. The state should be an unwelcome intruder if it tries to control the sphere which properly belongs to other associations. MacIver accepts that undoubtedly the state is a unique association. But, he opines, it does not mean that it can be permitted to poke its nose in the internal affairs of voluntary associations nor can it be allowed to determine the existence or otherwise of such associations.

The state is no Lord, commanding this association to go, or that association to come or another association to do this or that. In this way, MacIver makes a clear distinction between the 'State' and 'Associations'; defines their respective importance and roles; limits the powers of the state and draws the conclusion that the society is plural.

Force — A Function and not the Power of the State

The state can use force, and coercion to secure respect for its law. But the use of force does not make the state absolutely sovereign. The state is justified in using force in view of the universal nature of the service it performs. Its laws apply to all within its territory and all have to obey the law whether they like it or not. The membership of the state is universal. A man has to be a citizen whether or not he is a member of any other association. It is in view of its universality that the state uses force but it does not use force for the love of it or merely for the sake of force. MacIver views force as a function rather than power. It is an instrument of service rather than an engine of domination. Force is not the essence but only the criterion of the state. The exercise of force is not the basic function of the state which performs numerous non-coercive duties. Force is not an end but only a means. If we regard force as the basis of the state it would turn the means to an end and make the state authoritarian despotism. The state is based on the idea of a close social unity whereas force destroys that unity. Unity founded on force cannot be lasting, for human nature rebels against permanent repression. MacIver believes in the service conception of the state and not in the power conception. The force and power of the state come into glaring prominence during war, when the state tends to arrogate to itself the role of society as a whole, interferes in the internal life of other associations. During war, the state becomes paramount....over other associations and commands its people to forget what they are, husbands or wives or friends, or blood brothers, etc., and to remember only that they are citizens. This dominant role of the state during war is most dangerous and uncalled for. MacIver is a war-hater. He stands for the outlawing of war but so long the Modern State claims to possess absolute sovereignty so long will it be impossible to abolish war. The term absolute sovereignty must, therefore, be erased from literature of Political Science. Herein, he stands foursquare with Harold Laski.

State — An Order-creating Organisation

According to MacIver, the state is an order-creating organisation. It describes business to maintain order. But order according to law — law which must have the backing and approval of the community. MacIver does not believe in order for the sake of order. There is such a thing as peace of the desert or order in a military regiment. Such a conception of imposed order does not appeal to the rational and progressive mind of MacIver. Order is for the sake of life. It is the business of the state to provide decent and healthy conditions for a progressive and cultural existence in which the personality of the individual has a free scope for development.

MacIver's Concept of a Limited State

In one of the most famous chapters of his book, MacIver deals with the true sphere of the state activities and limitations thereon. He believes in the concept of a limited state, a constitutional state, i.e., a state whose business is carried on according to fundamental rules made for the state by the general will of the community. He does not believe in the concept of an authoritarian absolutist and omnipotent state. The service rendered by the state is of limited character. The state should not seek to do everything simply because it is not capable of doing that, being just an association. It can serve or observe only a limited end and purpose. Many things the state simply cannot do. Many other things it should avoid doing for fear of intruding into spheres that are not properly its own, such intrusions may do more harm than good. MacIver does not agree with the romantic view of Burke contained in the Reflections of the French Revolution, that the state is a partnership in all arts, a partnership in all science, in every virtue and in all perfections.

The state is not a mystical unity to MacIver as it appeared to the imaginative mind of Edmund Burke. Whereas Burke was a nomist, MacIver is a scientist and adopts a rational attitude towards the state and its role and functions.

Twin Functions of the State

According to MacIver, the twin functions of the state are to respect personality and to maintain order. The former is the negative while the latter is the positive aspect of the state function. He agrees with the view of T.H. Green that the work of doing a thing lies in the spontaneous urge to do that thing. In other words, state interference and state regulation is a clumsy intrusion in those things which are related to human personality or whose worth and quality are determined by the spontaneous urge of the personality.

Role of the State

According to MacIver, the state stands for the common interests of all the individuals and associates, "but not for the whole of the common interests". "The political interests of a thousand associations, cultural and economic, are also parts of the common interest." The function of the state is merely to give "a form of unity to the whole system of social relationship."

MacIver, therefore, holds that society is plural, authority is neither unlimited nor independent of the will of the community and the state as well as other associations enjoy allegiance of individual citizens.

(ii) DUGUIT

One of the main controversial questions in the history of political thought has been the relation of the state to law. The controversy has principally arisen from the different senses in which the term 'law' has been used by the disputants. Some apply the term law to rules of conduct which people obey independently of any pressure from outside. Some apply the term to uniformity of social behaviour. Still others consider that laws are the rules that have the stamp of some moral approval. To some laws are the dictates of one's own conscience. Others call laws the customs that have been generally followed. With other laws are the commands of the state.

Duguit and Krabbe are among those writers, who deny the claim that my action of the coercive state can establish the discrimination between lawful conduct. They hold the positivist conception of the state as a pernicious untruth. They argue that law is not really made by any organised body of men. They concede that in the society there are definite agencies to issue commands obeyed by the bulk of the community but they hold that not all of these commands deserve to be called laws. Some other quality is essential to give these rules the real characters of law.

Duguit describes his criterion as realistic and objective in contradiction to the metaphysical subjectivism of the positivist doctrines. Krabbe hold to subjective explanation and find the source of law in the conscience of man.

Law for Duguit is the name for the rules of conduct which actually control men living in society. The obligation to obey these rules arises not because the same have been commanded by any external authority but only and solely directly from the necessities of social life. If the advantages of social life are to be maintained, certain rules must be observed; otherwise society disintegrates. Men are naturally conscious of these rules and are impelled by self-interest to obey them. Man is a social animal. He knows that in order to live in society and gain by its membership he must observe certain rules of behaviour.

The basic fact of social life is social solidarity. The basis of political obligation lies in the very existence of society. The members of society should do everything that maintains social solidarity and avoid everything that diminishes it. This principle of social solidarity binds the rulers as well as members of society. Social existence requires certain kinds of behaviour and certain types of institutions. It is the inherent discipline of society which ensures that the members function in the particular array and in the proper order. The state is as much bound by the rules of social solidarity as the individuals are.

In other words, according to Duguit, there is no essential connection between the state and law. Law is independent of, and anterior to, above and more comprehensive than the state. The state may also act in an unlawful manner if it is acts against the principles of social solidarity. The authority of the state is legal only if it sustains law or guarantees co-operation towards social solidarity. What the state does in relation to law into adopt an already existing rule of law to a given act of facts. The legal validity of any act of the state depends upon the end which it serves. The authority of the state has no legal or moral justification save in so far as it serves the end of social solidarity. What given legal quality to the state is not the coercive power possessed by it but the ends which it commands of the services.

According to Duguit, the whole of law can be reduced to certain rules and those are:

(i) respect all acts determined by the end of social solidarity;
(ii) abstain from acts determined by any contrary ends, and
(iii) do everything possible to develop that solidarity.

Thus, Duguit made a full and sharp discrimination between state authority and authority of law. Both reflect facts; both apply to men living in society and give rise to commands sustained by sanctions which secure their habitual obedience. Duguit rejected the conception of the absolute and unquestionable authority of law. As a matter of fact, there is no such things as state in the political theory of Duguit. State is merely a body of men inhabiting a definite territory in which the strong impose their will on the weak. The state is not a distinct entity; it is not an abstract or corporate personality. The law cannot be the demand of sovereign power because such a power itself is subject to law. Law is a way of life derived from the necessities of social existence. The sanction of law is the necessity of maintaining the public services which are necessary for the survival of society or, more specifically, of social solidarity. The sanction of the laws comes from below, from the irresistible compulsions of social life.

According to Duguit, laws are obeyed because "we are, for good or ill, members of society and therefore, necessarily subject to its social discipline. It is clear to us that law has an obligatory nature not transcendental and abstract, but based on the facts of life."

According to Allen "Duguit is undoubtedly one of the most original and stimulating of modern jurists. He absolutely refused to be bound by any social or legal principles, or supposed principles, which he had not thought out for himself and he has been almost completely in revolt against the traditional axioms and even terminology jurisprudence. The greatest value of Duguit's work lies in his insistence on the systematic exposition of the principle of responsibility of the state."

(iii) KRABBE

Krabbe agrees with Duguit on certain points and differs from him on others. He agrees that there is no such thing as sovereignty in the modern political community. He, like Duguit admits that the institutions called sovereign are themselves subject to laws; hence they cannot be considered sovereign law-givers. Krabbe points out that the legislature is not the creator of law but rather an instrument that the legislature is not the creator of law but rather an instrument that discovers law and codifies it. Law itself emerges from society. Thus, both Duguit and Krabbe admit that law is not the command of the sovereign but something that emerges from the society.

But Krabbe differs from Duguit as he explains law according to the source from which it springs. According to him, "Law is the expression of one of the many judgements of value which we human beings make by virtue of our disposition and nature. We obey law because it appears to us just and good and not because of fear of punishment which its disobedience involves."

Law is what is just and good from our standard of value and judgement. It is not a "matter of external legal authority but an internal human matter."

Krabbe, however, does not insist on the value judgement of each individual. Law is the rule of a community and, therefore, it is upon this sense of right that all law is based, whether it is positive law, customary law or the unwritten law in general. Any statute which does not rest upon this sense of right is not law. Thus, it is must be found that many legislative enactments may lack the quality of law. What gives legal quality to a law is not the force possessed by the sovereign but it is that ethical element which is based upon the feeling or sense of right. It is evident that communal life cannot exist without this feeling or sense among the citizens. The sense of right is an original force in human life whose reality is experienced everywhere.

According to Krabbe, it does not lie in the power of any man to decide as to what shall have the force of law and what not. Nothing is really law except what proceeds from the single source which alone can give a rule the quality of law, the ultimate sense of right. What does not come from the sense of right may be enforced by the power of the state, but that does not and can never be law. The law requires a common conviction as to what is right. It may be true that the unanimity of conviction as to what is right, seldom occurs. Yet the purpose of a community can be realised only if there is such a unanimity. The value of having a unanimity of conviction is fundamental. It is an indispensable condition for attaining the end of the community. This end can be attained in a variety of ways but it cannot be attained without having a single rule. Our sense of right attaches the highest value of having a single rule and thereby arises the law. In short, according to Krabbe, since a community exists for some social i.e. common good, it postulates unity of legal rule; and this unity is achieved only when members have a common conviction as to what is right. Law is independent of the state. Krabbe accepts no authority as valid except that of law. In his political theory, the state disappears as source of law.

Thus, both Duguit and Krabbe — regard law not as an artificial product but as something natural, something inherent in the social process, a result of social evolution. But whereas for Duguit society is the basic fact, for Krabbe it is the individual. Duguit lays emphasis on social needs, especially, the need of social solidarity. For him, social needs come prior to individual needs. But Krabbe lays emphasis on human deeds which determine social structure. Or it may be said that whereas Duguit is collectivist. Krabbe is humanitarian and democratic. In Duguit's political philosophy, social structure determines human needs, whereas in Krabbe human needs determine the social structure. Moreover, Duguit takes it for granted that the main purpose of social organisation is the maintenance of social solidarity and the running of public services. In Krabbe's political philosophy the ends is not predetermined. It depends upon the social evolutions. It results from the consensus arrived at by the members of society. They may determine the social values in anyway. In other words, Krabbe gives the freedom of self-determination to the members of society; but no such freedom is given by Duguit since the end is predetermined, i.e., the maintenance of social solidarity. Duguit, the private interests of the individuals are totally subordinated to the interests of society. The emphasis laid on social solidarity and running of public services is missing in the political theory of Krabbe. Duguit in a sense may be called a totalitarian since in social good he sees private good. Duguit has given no importance to the nation of right in his concept of law. He has rather banished it altogether the emphasizes social needs and especially the need of social solidarity. His concept of law may be called 'ultra-materialistic'. Krabbe, on the other hand, makes the sense of right the basis of law. The duty to obey the law arises from this sense of right and not any needs of society. Krabbe relates law to the sense of right whereas Duguit relates it to social needs. Duguit's approach to law is objective, whereas the approach of Krabbe is subjective. The basic fact for Duguit is social solidarity; for Krabbe it is human needs. For Duguit, law is array of life derived from the necessities of social existence; for Krabbe it is the expression of value-judgement. Both, however, deny the command of the sovereign as the source of law and hold that law emerges from society rather than being enacted by sovereign authority.

(iv) NORMAN ANGELL

Norman Angell was a great thinker of the twentieth century. He was an apostle of world peace and internationalism.

His two books, 'The Great Illusion' and 'The Fruits of Victory' won for him wide popularity.

The book 'Great Illusion' was universally acclaimed and translated into many foreign languages. Through this book, he was called Grotius of the twentieth century.

Norman Angell put his attention mostly to the problem of world peace. According to him, the existing international lawlessness is due to the fact that men are swayed by their primitive impulses. Nationalism is a destructive force. Under it the foreigner is despised. But this does not mean that Norman Angell finds no virtue in nationalism. He writes, "Nationality is a very precious manifestation of the instincts by which alone man can become socially conscious and act in some corporate capacity. The identification of 'self' with society, which patriotism accomplishes within certain limits, the sacrifice of 'self' for the community which it inspires — even though only when fighting other patriotisms are moral achievements of infinite hope."

Nationalism often makes appeal to service, self-sacrifice and loyalty, that in spite of these virtues, nationalism in its exclusive capacity is full of dangers. Nationalism is to be subordinated to internationalism. The allegiance of the people is to transcend the natural borders and cover the world community. In the view of Norman Angell, federalism is the best solution to the conflict of loyalties.

Norman Angell put his plea for internationalism and world peace on a new basis. He started his argument with "a synchronised bank rate the world over and reacting boweses." A single system of credit has been created all over the world as a result of the improved means of communication.

He put his view in these words: "The telegraph involves a single system of credit for the civilized world, that system of credit involves the financial interdependence of all states: that financial interdependence involves peace." Thus, Angell put his whole case on the system of banking in the world. "In banking and for that matter in other economic things also, the world is one society. Politically, it is several distinct societies tending to compete with one another. Of these two facts, the former is the more important and determines action to a great extent. It pays men better to think and feel as members of a universal economic society, whose attribute is peace, than to think and feel as members of limited political societies whose attribute is war. The protect is the rudder of human nature; and therefore, as soon as they realise this fact men will cease from war." It may, however, he said that an international credit system can hardly avoid war.

Norman Angell did not attach any great value to the institution of the state. To him it was merely "a political mechanism" and not a "homogeneous personality". It was according to him, delusion to ascribe any personality to the state. It was not a unit with a single life or a single conception of life. Within it were contained many conceptions of life, some of which were mutually exclusive and some of them "Agreeing absolutely with conception in foreign states."

The state was merely a loose federation of groups. It could not claim sovereignty over the other groups. There was not any real national feeling in a state. To quote his words, "The formation of states has disregarded national divisions altogether."

Men were combined together by a common feeling of economic interests, profession or class which were non-geographical and non-political. The real divisions were not between nations but between the opposing conceptions of life.

According to Norman Angell, parties were the fundamental groupings or conceptions of life which constituted the real psychic communities. The parties were primarily representative of different conceptions of life in the field of social conflict. The problems of social conflict "were much more profound and fundamental than any conception which coincides or can be identified with state divisions." Angell substituted the conflict between international parties in place of a conflict between states.

Angell preached the futility of war. War involves destruction and not any good of society. He emphasized the economic interdependence of the states and the need to banish force in human relations. He writes: "The victor on the Egyptian vase has his captured enemy on the end of rope. We say that one is free, the other is bound. But as Spencer has shown us both are bound. The victor is tied to the vanquished; if he should let go; the prisoner would escape. The victor spends his time seeing that the prisoner does not escape; the prisoner his time and energy trying to escape.... Only if they strike of bargain and co-operate will they be in the position each to turn his energy to the best economic account." This points out to the necessity of international co-operation and not the imposing of decisions of others. The states should be organised into an international community on the basis of consent.

To conclude, Norman Angell was the most outstanding advocate of the noblest of causes — the cause of world-peace. He warned the people of the world that unless they curbed their emotions, peace rather human existence would become impossible. Continuous wars fought from time to time would destroy all civilization. On account of his pacific views and ardent appeal for the cause of world peace, Norman Angell occupies an honoured place in the history of political philosophy of the 20th century.

(v) MISS FOLLETT

Miss M.P. Follett was a great social worker, who was reorganised as an expert on personnel problems and industrial management in her country, the United States. She wrote a large number of books; chief among which are, "The New State", "The Creative Experience" and "The Speaker of the House of Representatives." Miss Follett used terminology which make her books almost unintelligible to the uninitiated. She was primarily interested in the significance of motor-level in political experience.

Miss Follett gave chief attention to group psychology and attempted to discover the proper group basis for political organisation. She endorsed many of the criticisms and proposals given by the pluralists in England and gave the most discriminating and extended discussion of the pluralistic concept of state sovereignty. But she can hardly be called a pluralist because she recognized the unifying functions of the state.

According to Miss Follett, "The state cannot be composed of groups because no group nor any number of groups can contain the whole of me, an ideal state demands whole of me.... My citizenship is smoothing bigger than any membership in the vocational group. We want whole man in politics. The ideal unified state is not all abortive. It is all-inclusive. The true state gathers up every interest within itself, it must take our many labours and find how it can make them alone. The home of my soul is in the state." According to her, we cannot stop with the groups and we have to go beyond that to the state. Groups, no doubt, are necessary for man's life as there are divergent needs. But the groups even a number of them do not exhaust the full capacity of the modern man. The range of his activities is much wider than that of any group or groups. It is for this reason that there arises the need of the state. It is only as a member of the state that the individual can realize himself. The state is not a mere aggregate of groups. It is their unity. It has to incorporate all the groups and has to be a unifying and unified state. The sovereignty of the state does not destroy the sovereignty of the groups.

Thus, the state of Miss Follett is an ideal state which unites all the individuals and groups. While being loyal to such a state one is loyal to the whole. The unifying state acquires authority through the liberty of all by means of the functions of each. Thus, while Miss Follett recognizes the value of the groups in realizing the diverse needs of the people, she makes the state sovereign. It is sovereign to the extent it unifies all the groups into a common life. A group is sovereign to the extent it is able to unite its members into a whole and an individual is sovereign to the extent he is able to unite the heterogeneous elements of his nature into a whole. According to Follett, sovereignty is "the power engendered by a complete interdependence becoming conscious of itself."

According to Miss Follett, public opinion should be created. The will of the people arises on a motor-level. It is a part of the whole social process. It is a stimulus from total environment and response to total environment. In this way, energy is released. We have the will of the people ideally when all desires are satisfied. In a poor society, people can have no will because their desires remain unsatisfied. The aim of democracy should be integration of desires. Differences must not be crushed. Truth emerges out of differences. Self-government is a creative process and nothing else. Democracy is merely an attempt to create unity.

According to Miss Follett, the problem of democracy is to find an outlet for our motor impulses within the conditions which produce them. As progress is through the releases and integration of the action tendencies of each and every individual in society, we should so provide that such activity takes place normally. Miss Follett laid great emphasis on this point. Thinkers after thinkers are trying to find out some way to get rid of conflict. The economists find this way in the removal of the struggle between the capital and labour. The internationalists would rid us of the conflict between the nations. The biologists give us the tooth and claw theory. There are sociologists who say that conflict is built into the structure of the world. According to Miss Follett, there is confusion on the point, both among those who wish to abolish it and those who wish to retain it. What people often means by getting rid of conflict is getting rid of diversity. But this is not possible. We may abolish conflict but cannot get rid of diversity. Diversity is the most essential feature of life and we must face life as it is.

(vi) DEWEY

John Dewey was born on October 20, 1859 in Burlington, Vermont. He belonged to a middle class family. He was the third of the four sons in the family. He received his early education in his native place.

This child of rural Vermont became the voice of scientific method of disciplined inquiry and instrument of freedom. Dewey is recognised as a peculiarly American philosopher.

Dewey's primary interest, as a social and political philosopher, was in helping to resolve the problems that have perplexed mankind. These problems are the common ones such as bad sanitation, poor working conditions, unequal distribution of wealth and the exclusion of the mass of people from the material and cultural values produced by the Industrial Revolution. He gave to his philosophy the name of instrumentalism as he regarded it as an instrument for dealing with concrete problems.

The object of his philosophy was to solve problems. It was no use of having a philosophy devoid of realism and serving no useful purpose. Therefore, the purpose of Dewey's philosophy is to solve problems, to make confused situations clear and manageable, to rescue men from the difficulties in which they find themselves. An effective philosophy must recognise the 'real' situations and provide a practicable solution to them. The old philosophies could not be employed to clarify the concrete social problems. They provided readymade principles to be imposed without any reference to reality. They dealt with the ideal states and not with the states as they are in actuality. Knowledge must be used to solve the problems here and now.

Holding the views, he did as to the practical nature of philosophy, Dewey's approach to politics was quite different from that of the traditional political thinkers. His approach was pragmatic. He considered as irrelevant all the discussion about the origin of the state, its growth, its nature or its end — with which most of the philosophers have concerned themselves. What he was interested in was the actual problems that exist in actual states. He did not believe that we can succeed in solving these problems if we begin to look for the origin, nature or essence of the state. He condemned what he called the "logic of general notions." The philosophies of the old philosophers simply obscured the real issues which can be dealt with by the method of intelligence, by scientific enquiry and by experimentation. He said: "It is not the business of political philosophy and science to determine what the state in general should or must be. What they may do is to aid in creation of method such that experimentation may go on less blindly, less at the mercy of accident more intelligently, so that men may learn from their errors and profit by their success. The belief in the political fixity, of the sanctity of some form of state consecrated by the efforts of our fathers and hollowed by tradition is one of the stumbling blocks in the way of orderly and directed change. It is an invitation to revolt and revolution."

To John Dewey then there is nothing mysterious about states. As a pragmatist stated: "The state is the organization of the public effected through officials for the protection of the interests shared by its members." This is a common-sense view of the state. Dewey believed that had philosopher taken this common-sense view of what goes on in the governing of man they would not have spent their time explaining the 'nature of the state' in terms of divine institution a social contract, the embodiment of reason, and so on states, according to Dewey, are the consequences at specific needs; they come into existence as they are required; they group and develop as they face new and more complicated problems. They are the consequences of specific needs. Thus, in Dewey's concept of state there is nothing of some prepotent force which by fiat or nisius might have generated a mystical state. The state results from certain needs of individuals which it is beyond their capacity to satisfy. Therefore, as Dewey said, the formation of states becomes a series of experiments.

Dewey also cut short the old question of the best form of state. The controversy about the best form of the state is meaningless; the goodness of state depends upon the efficiency of the officials through whom it works. This can be revealed only by a state's history; the absolutely best state cannot be identified until history is ended and it is possible to survey all forms of the state.

Similarly, Dewey dealt in a summary fashion the question of the proper functions of the state. His view of society was pluralistic. He regarded the state only as one of the many associations in which men are grouped.

According to him, "state has no precedence over these associations. He likened the state to the conductor of an orchestra, who himself make no music but harmonize that made by the performers. What a state should do is relative to the needs of the given society. All the states cannot perform identical functions. The role of the state is to be determined by a consideration of the consequences of action in particular situations. Therefore, the state should not be prelabelled as collectivistic or Laissez Faire. Rather it must be regarded 'neutral' in determining the extension of power. But word 'neutral' must not be misunderstood. It does not mean indifferent. The purpose of the state is the creation of methods such that experimentation may go no less blindly, less at the mercy of accident, more intelligently, so that man may learn from their errors and profit by their successes."

According to Dewey, the proper business of government is to provide for the development of what he called individuality. Individuality is not individualism. By individuality, he meant the complete and harmonious development of the capacities of man.

To insist on individualism in a society increasingly corporate amounts to denying men the opportunity to develop the non-pecuniary, human attributes of personality.

According to Dewey, until historic individualism is abandoned as the organising principle of society, the individual will be alienated from that society, his ambitions permanently thwarted. Individuals will liberate imagination and endeavour for the task of making corporate society contribute to the free culture of its members. Only be economic revision can the sound element in the older individualism equality of opportunity be made a reality. Dewey believed that his "economic revision", could be accomplished only if government consciously adopted the method of experimentation. The hampering influence of traditional individualism could be ended only "by organised social reconstruction". We should either surrender our professed beliefs to the predominant material orientation, or we should through organized endeavour institute the socialized economy of material security and plenty that will release human energy for pursuit of higher values.

John Dewey stood for a democratic form of government. In his view, the only society in which 'individuality' can be substituted for individualism is a democratic one. Only in such a society will it be possible to use the experimental method successfully. Dewey conceded that the political apparatus of democracy was of great value potentially, but he held that we must go beyond the elaboration of political devices for choosing officials and enforcing responsibility. We must introduce into social problems the method of experimentation.

Democracy is based on the faith in the capacities of human nature. Faith in human intelligence and in the power of pooled and co-operative experience. Dewey did not believe that these qualities are present in the individuals but he felt that if given a show they will grow and be able to generate progressively the knowledge and wisdom needed to guide collective action. Dewey, while elaborating his stand-point regarding the functioning of democracy said that "to get rid of the habit of thinking of democracy as something institutional and external and to acquire the habit of treating it as a way of personal life is to realize that democracy is a moral ideal and so far as it becomes a fact is a moral fact. It is to realise that democracy is a reality only as it is needed a common-place of living." Thus, according to Dewey, democracy as compared with other ways of life is the sole way of living which believes whole-heartedly in the process of experience as end and as means.

Dewey's belief in the feasibility of the reforms which he regarded as essential to the realization of 'Individuality' rested upon his faith in the possibilities of education. He laid great emphasis on education. He regarded traditional schooling too formal and too authoritarian. He regarded school as simply one of the instruments manipulated by the ruling few so as to justify their own privileges. This contention of Dewey was that the purpose of learning was not merely to understand the past but also to change the existing world. Properly understood, education consists of every contact with nature and society of experience in general.

To conclude, John Dewey has been called the "philosopher of the common man". It only indicates to his humane approach to the problems of politics. For Dewey whatever is practically useful is true. If ideas, meanings, conceptions, notions, theories, systems are instrumental to an active recognisation of a given environment, to a removal of some specific trouble and perplexity, they are valid, sound, good and true. But if they fail to clear up the confusion and eliminate the defects rather increase confusion, uncertainty and evil when they are acted upon, they are false. This is all what appeals to common-sense.

Dewey spoke for those who were tough-minded enough to give up the quest for certainty. He looked upon knowledge a short of power rather than as an understanding of ultimates. It is the consequences that determine the truth of an idea. Truth is not something unalterably fixed. Truth is whatever works in a given situation.

Dewey was a thinker, who was immersed in a practical concerns and applied instrumentalism to social and political questions. He was not, of course, the first person to urge that empirical and quantitative methods be applied to the study of politics and government. But he, of course, the first person to urge that empirical and quantitative methods be applied to the study of politics and government. But he, of course, put forth a method of inquiry that has now been adopted in contemporary investigation and interpretation. The 'realistic' view of politics, has greatly influenced the American politics during the last generation.

George Raymond Geiger is right when he remarks that "it would be more hopeful to suggest that when men are finally ready to apply the recognized techniques of inquiry to the solution of social riddles, the thought of John Dewey will be there, waiting to give them inspiration and guidance."

(vii) RUSSELL

Bertrand Russell is considered as one of the greatest thinkers of the 20th century. He belonged to a very famous family of England and he was both a practical and theoretical philosopher. He is considered as a master thinker in mathematics, science and politics. In his book, "Mysticism and Logic" which is the most characteristic title among his works, he made a merciless attack on the illogical of mysticism. He glorified the scientific method. He puts emphasis on logic and regards mathematics as divine. He usually thinks of philosophy as an inferior pursuit compared with mathematics and science. He has a passion for a clarity, and that is why that he was impressed by the exactness of mathematics.

To quote him: "Mathematics, rightly viewed, possesses not only truth but supreme beauty — a beauty cold and austere, like that of sculpture, without appeal to any part of our weaker nature, without the gorgeous trappings, of painting or music, yet sublimely pure and capable of a stern perfection such as only the greatest art can show." According to him, the aim of philosophy should be to equal the perfection of mathematics by confining itself to statements similarly exact and similarly true before all experience.

From such a starting point, Bertrand Russell was almost destined to pass into agnosticism. He found so much in Christianity that could not be phrased in mathematics, that he abandoned it all except its moral code. He is scornful of civilization that persecutes men who deny Christianity, and impressions those who take it seriously. He can find no God in such a contradictory world. We talk of evolution and progress but progress is an egotistical phrase and evolution is but one half of an unmoral cycle of events terminating in dissolution and death. To quote him, "Organic life, we are told, has developed gradually from the protozoan to the philosopher; and this development, we are assured, is indubitably an advance. Unfortunately, it is philosopher, not the protozoans, who gives us this assurance."

Russell could not achieve popularity early in life. His popularity as a lover of humanity came suddenly after the First World War. His passion for humanity brought him into conflict with the orthodox conservatives. He was even outlawed and denounced as a traitor to his motherland. But unmindful of the consequences he continued his philosophy of pacificism. He was horrified by the war. Even the interests of the empire did not weigh him much. He was in search of the causes of war. His conclusion was that private property was the cause of war and Communism was the only cure.

According to Bertrand Russell, all property has its origin in violence and theft. He wrote that in the Kimberley diamond mines and the Rand gold mines the transition of robbery into property was going under the nose of the world. "No good to the humanity, of any sort or kind, results from the private ownership of law. If men were reasonable, they would decree that it should cease tomorrow, with no compensation beyond a moderate life-income to the present holders." Since the private property is protected by the state, and the robberies that make property sanctioned by legislation and enforced by arms and war, the state of great evil. Russell wanted the co-operative and producers' syndicates take the functions of the state.

Russell is a great champion of individual liberty. Liberty to him is the supreme good. Without it development of personality is impossible. Only by free discussion we can pick our way through errors and prejudices to the total perspective which is truth. Freedom of thought and speech would go like cleansing draught through the neuroses and superstitions of the modern mind. Hatred and war come largely of fixed ideas or dogmatic faith. People should be allowed to differ and discuss their differences.

According to Russell, we are not so educated as we think; we are but beginning the great experiment of universal schooling; and it has not had time to affect profoundly our ways of thinking and our public life. We think of education as the transmission of certain body of settled knowledge. When it should be rather the development of scientific habit of mind. He advocated greater use of science and of scientific method in education. With use of these methods, it was the belief of Russell, that education may prove the great solvent of our ills. There is nothing that man might not do if our splendid organization of schools and universities were properly manned, and directed intelligently to the reconstruction of human character.

Russell stands for the complete outlawry of war. He does not approve the use of force by the state in its external relations. He has condemned conscription. He suggests a single government of the world with a monopoly of political power. There must be an equitable distribution of wealth among the various nations and no nation should be kept low throughout the world. The use of force by the state creates the spirit of exclusiveness among nations. As the functions of the state are increasing, there is a rise in the size of bureaucracy which regiments the lives of the people in various ways. But Russell does not want to abolish the state. He gives certain functions of the state are increasing, there is a rise in the size of bureaucracy which regiments the lives of the people in various ways. But Russell does not want to abolish the state. He gives certain function to the state. What cannot be done by the individual but has to be done in his interests, should be given to the state. The state must encourage scientific research and remove economic injustice.

Russell approaches a theory of politics from the psychological point of view. Politics to him is the study of power. He admits the need for a coercive power against crime. He wants that the best for power which is natural in human beings should be controlled. But the state which bases most of its authority on force does not find favour with him. According to him, impulses, not conscious purpose, determine man's conduct. There are two kinds of impulses — the creative and the possessive. Impulses should not be crushed. It is the task of the total institutions to direct them to healthy channels. Russell writes that "The supreme principles, both in politics and in private life, should be to promote all that is creative, and so to distinguish the impulses and desires that centre round possession."

Russell feels that the world has become the victim of dogmatic political creeds, of which, in our day the most powerful are Capitalism and Communism. He writes: "Capitalism gives opportunity of initiative to a view; Communism could (though it does not in fact) provide a servile kind of security for all. Unfortunately, our political theories are less intelligent than our science, and we have not yet learnt how to make use of our knowledge and our skill in the ways that will do most to make life happy and even glorious."

It may also be said that Russell stands for a simple and unsophisticated life. Once he praised China for its simple life, open-mindedness and realism. But now he regard it as the great threat to world peace and humanity. Russell had also praised Communism but when he visited Soviet Russia he was disappointed to find that Russian Government could not risk such a measure of democracy as was necessary for a liberal philosophy. He was annoyed at the suppression of freedom of speech, expression and thought and by the monopoly and systematic use of every avenue of propaganda by the state. Russell stands for freedom and is opposed to dogmatic authoritarianism. He has condemned both the ideals and methods of fascism.

As regards the philosophy of his history he does not approve the theories of Marx, Hegel, St. Augustine and Plato. According to him, it is not possible to discover a comprehensive law of historical development which will apply in all cases. There are bound to be variations and the views are bound to differ according to the point of every individual thinker. Economic factor alone does not determine the course of events. While Russell gives adequate weight to the economic factor, he does not overlook the other factors like vanity, rivalry, love of power and love of money. Man also as a thinking animal has the capacity to change his environments by the force of his ideas.

Bertrand Russell is not only an arm-chair philosopher. His method is inductive and empirical. He is an empiricist. He thinks that in order to serve the purpose of individual good, a reconstruction is fundamental. The capitalist autocracy in industry must be abolished. Socialism is not only inevitable, but also care must be taken not to substitute for the dictatorship of the capitalist, the dictatorship of the bureaucrat. The reconstructed society must beware itself not only of the evils of property but also of the evils of power. Equalization of power must follow equalization of property. A vast disposal of power by functional and territorial federalism is necessary. Russell sports the principle of self-government in industry.

To conclude, the world has convinced Bertrand Russell that it is too big for formula, and perhaps too large and heavy to move very rapidly towards his heart's desire. And there are so many hearts and so many desires. One finds him now "can older and wiser man", swallowed by time and a varied life; as wide awake as ever to all the ills that flesh is heir to any yet matured into the moderation that knows the difficulties of social change. Today, he is a champion of world peace and an active supporter of the policy of nuclear disarmament. He believes that nations should renounce war as an instrument of their policy. Indeed, he is today a great humanitarian, a champion of human rights, envyıng everythıng that destroys or hinders the development of human personality. The world honoured his scholarly abilities by awarding him the Nobel Prize for literature in 1950.

Index